Palgrave Dictionary of Public Order Policing, Protest and Political Violence

Palgrave Dictionary of Public Order Policing, Protest and Political Violence

Peter Joyce
Manchester Metropolitan University, UK

and

Neil Wain
University of Cambridge, UK

© Peter Joyce and Neil Wain 2014

All rights reserved. No reproduction, copy or transmission of this publication may be made without written permission.

No portion of this publication may be reproduced, copied or transmitted save with written permission or in accordance with the provisions of the Copyright, Designs and Patents Act 1988, or under the terms of any licence permitting limited copying issued by the Copyright Licensing Agency, Saffron House, 6–10 Kirby Street, London EC1N 8TS.

Any person who does any unauthorized act in relation to this publication may be liable to criminal prosecution and civil claims for damages.

The authors have asserted their rights to be identified as the authors of this work in accordance with the Copyright, Designs and Patents Act 1988.

First published 2014 by
PALGRAVE MACMILLAN

Palgrave Macmillan in the UK is an imprint of Macmillan Publishers Limited, registered in England, company number 785998, of Houndmills, Basingstoke, Hampshire RG21 6XS.

Palgrave Macmillan in the US is a division of St Martin's Press LLC, 175 Fifth Avenue, New York, NY 10010.

Palgrave Macmillan is the global academic imprint of the above companies and has companies and representatives throughout the world.

Palgrave® and Macmillan® are registered trademarks in the United States, the United Kingdom, Europe and other countries.

ISBN 978–1–137–27007–8   hardback
ISBN 978–1–137–26975–1   paperback

This book is printed on paper suitable for recycling and made from fully managed and sustained forest sources. Logging, pulping and manufacturing processes are expected to conform to the environmental regulations of the country of origin.

A catalogue record for this book is available from the British Library.

Library of Congress Cataloging-in-Publication Data

Joyce, Peter.

Palgrave dictionary of public order policing, protest and political violence / Peter Joyce, Manchester Metropolitan University, UK, Neil Wain, University of Cambridge, UK.

  pages cm

Summary: "Events of protest and dissent have been the subject of much global debate and media attention. However, no one book has dealt with the wide range of protests nor with the terminology associated with the state and police response to it. This dictionary explores a variety of issues related to the policing of public order, protest and political violence providing a comprehensive overview of international protest since 1945. It defines the key terms associated with these activities and, through the use of a number of international case studies, it includes numerous examples of protest and dissent that have taken place across the world, and the groups and organisations which have utilized these forms of political expression. Written in an accessible style, each entry is accompanied by a list of sources and suggestions for further reading through which readers can extend their knowledge of each of the topics. This unique and in-depth resource will be an essential guide for scholars across Criminology, Criminal Justice, Policing, Political History and International Relations."—Provided by publisher.
  ISBN 978–1–137–26975–1 (paperback)
  1. Riot control—Dictionaries. 2. Crowd control—Dicitionaries. 3. Protest movements—Dictionaries. 4. Demonstrations—Dictionaries. 5. Police—Dictionaries. I. Wain, Neil.
  II. Title.
  HV8055.J69 2014
  363.32'303—dc23   2014022917

Typeset by MPS Limited, Chennai, India.

*To our respective families
Julie, Emmeline and Eleanor Joyce
and
Jane, Jessica, Hannah, Esther and Samuel Wain*

Contents

List of Entries viii

Preface xi

About the Authors xiii

Dictionary 1

Index 358

List of Entries

Animal rights protest groups	1
Anti-globalisation	5
Anti-globalisation movement	8
Anti-globalisation/anti-capitalist protests (UK)	9
Anti-globalisation/anti-capitalist protests (worldwide)	12
Anti-National Security Agency protests (Germany) 2013	16
Arab Spring (Arab world) 2010 onwards	17
August riots (England) 2011	28
Austerity protests (worldwide) 2010–13	33
Banlieue riots (Paris) 2005	41
Battle of the Beanfield (Wiltshire, England) 1985	49
Battle of the Bogside (Derry, Northern Ireland) 1969	50
Bloody Sunday (or the Bogside Massacre) (Derry, Northern Ireland) 1972	56
Bradford riots (Manningham, Bradford) 1995	58
Broadwater Farm Estate riots (Haringey, London) 1985	64
Building workers' strike (England and Wales) 1972	66
Burntollet Bridge (Derry, Northern Ireland) 1969	70
Chicago Democratic National Convention riot (Chicago) 1968	72
Civil disobedience	76
Copycat riots (England) 1981	80
Counterculture protest	84
Counter-terrorism	86
Dale Farm evictions (Essex, England) 2011	95
Demonstrations	98
Direct action	102
'Dirty protest' (Northern Ireland) 1978–81	106
English Defence League	110
Environmental protest groups	112
Fracking protests	118

Fuel crisis (Britain) 2000	121
G20 protests (London) 2009	126
Gdańsk Shipyard protests (Gdańsk, Poland) 1980–9	129
Greenham Common (Berkshire, England) 1981–2000	135
Grosvenor Square (London) 1968	137
Hactivism	140
Housing estate riots (England) 1991–2	142
Islamic terrorist groups	146
Kettling (containment)	154
Lewisham disorders (Lewisham, London) 1977	157
Live animal exports protests (England) 1994–5	160
Los Angeles riots (Los Angeles, California) 1992	163
Miners' dispute (Britain) 1972	166
Miners' dispute (Britain) 1973–4	168
Miners' dispute (Britain) 1984–5	172
Monsanto protests (worldwide) 2013	177
Nationalist terrorist groups	180
News International dispute (Wapping, London) 1986	185
Northern Ireland: security policy during the 'Troubles'	187
Notting Hill carnival riot (Notting Hill, London) 1976	197
Northern England town riots (Bradford, Oldham and Burnley) 2001	199
Occupy movement	204
Paramilitary policing (England and Wales)	210
Peace movement	211
Political policing	216
Post-Arab Spring	225
Protest Liaison Officers (England and Wales)	237
Protest songs	239
Provisional IRA	242
Public disorder theories and models	250
Public order legislation (England and Wales)	256
Public order policing (England and Wales)	266
Public order policing (France)	276

Pussy Riot protest (Moscow) 2012	279
Red Lion Square (London) 1974	281
Riot police	284
Riots	287
Self-immolation	291
Social media and the policing of protest and disorder (worldwide)	292
Southall disorders (Southall, London) 1979	295
States of emergency	301
Stockholm riots (Sweden) 2013	307
Student protests (England) 2010	309
Student riots (Paris) 1968	312
Subversion	317
Tea Party movement	320
Terrorism	321
Third force	327
Tiananmen Square protest (Beijing) 1976 and 1989	328
Trafalgar Square anti-Poll Tax rally (London) 1990	330
UK Uncut	335
Urban guerrilla groups	338
Walking (with a political purpose) (England) 1977 onwards	345
Whistleblowing (worldwide)	347
Workplace protest	353

Preface

This book discusses public order policing, protest and political violence. It considers the nature of protest and political violence, the groups and organisations that are engaged in activities of this nature, and discusses the response of the state and the police to such events. It is presented in dictionary format with the aim of drawing together in one work a wide range of topics that are related to this broad subject area.

The activities associated with protest and political violence are varied. These include demonstrations and various forms of direct action, including civil disobedience and industrial disputes. Countercultural forms of protest are also considered, including protest conducted through music and also by styles of living that are different from those adopted by mainstream society. Political violence is considered in relation to riots and terrorism, accepting the view that some participants to such events regard their actions as purposeful, designed to bring about political changes (even if other participants are involved for other reasons, such as the presence of looters at riots). This book defines these activities and also considers the role performed by contemporary technology (such as social media) in facilitating protest and other forms of political violence.

The book includes detailed case studies of a number of protests, commencing in 1968. This year has been chosen because it witnessed a number of protests across the world that were especially associated with students and young people. Accordingly, events that took place in Paris, Chicago and London are examined.

It would clearly be impossible to include every protest that has occurred since 1968 and thus it has been necessary to present a highly selective number of case studies of events that have taken place to provide specific illustrations of protest and political violence. This selection has been governed by a number of factors, the most important of which is to provide specific examples of the wide array of activities that are embraced by the terms 'protest' and 'political violence' (including protests that are designed to affect the commercial practices of private sector bodies as well as to effect changes in the direction of public policy).

The case studies that have been selected to illustrate these objectives are drawn from across the world, reflecting the historical and contemporary importance of protest and violence in the political affairs of nations which possess different political systems. They have also been chosen to illustrate the range of outcomes that may be achieved through the use of protest and political violence, ranging from attaining relatively minor changes in the direction of public or commercial policy to achieving the overthrow of a government and the initiation of regime change.

In addition to the inclusion of case studies, the book also seeks to examine policing methods and practices that are adopted in connection with protest. This aspect of the discussion includes entries that examine specific police units whose role is to respond to anticipated (or actual) public disorder and the tactics they may deploy. Other entries consider police powers and the legislation from which these are derived in connection with specific forms of protest that include demonstrations, industrial disputes and terrorism.

The book also considers some of the main groups that use protest as their chief form of activity to secure changes to public policy or to commercial practices. The entries associated with this aspect of protest place a number of organisations under a number of umbrellas, such as environmental protest groups, the peace movement, groups in opposition to capitalism and globalisation, Islamic terrorist organisations and urban guerrilla groups. As with other areas embraced by this book, the account is selective and primarily focuses on groups associated with causes of global concern.

This book assumes no prior knowledge of the subject areas that are considered and is especially designed to whet the appetite of the reader to undertake further investigation into them. To aid this objective, each entry provides suggestions for further reading that will further enhance knowledge and understanding of public order policing, protest and political violence.

About the Authors

Peter Joyce is Principal Lecturer in the Department of Sociology at Manchester Metropolitan University, UK. He has published widely in the areas of criminal justice policy, policing and British politics.

Neil Wain is Resident Scholar at the Jerry Lee Centre of Criminology at the University of Cambridge, UK. He was an Assistant Chief Constable with Greater Manchester Police and was responsible for specialist operations and major events. He has delivered police training programmes in the UK, the USA, India and the Caribbean. He is the Vice President of the British Society of Evidence Based Policing (www.sebp.police.uk).

A

ANIMAL RIGHTS PROTEST GROUPS

The philosophy of animal rights views all creatures that inhabit the planet as animals and insists that non-human animals should be treated in the same way as human animals. In particular, animal rights insists that non-human animals should not be regarded as property (and/or 'things'), since this accords them an inferior status within society and justifies them being exploited and used as food, for clothing, entertainment and research, or being forced to perform heavy work, which is epitomised by the image of donkeys being forced to carry heavy loads on their backs.

The treatment of non-human animals in a manner that is inferior to the treatment accorded to human animals is referred to as speciesism (Ryder, 1971), which rejects as a form of discrimination the allocation of different values, rights or considerations to individuals based on their species membership. It has been argued that 'there can be no reasons – except the selfish desire to preserve the privileges of the exploiting group – for refusing to extend the basic principle of equality to members of other species ... attitudes to other species are a form of prejudice no less objectionable than prejudice about a person's race or sex' (Singer, 1995: xiii).

Groups that seek to place issues affecting animals on the policy-making agenda are inspired by a wide range of philosophic positions regarding how non-human animals should be viewed and what measures should be adopted to enhance their treatment within society. However, a broad distinction exists between animal welfare groups (that seek to promote the better treatment of animals to avoid unnecessary suffering, but without challenging their status as being inferior to that of humans) and organisations that embrace the doctrine of animal rights that contends that animals have interests (especially an interest to avoid suffering) that should be accorded equality with measures that defend fundamental human interests. For the former, concern for animals is based upon moral considerations, whereas for the latter, it is underpinned by a political perspective regarding the status that animals should occupy within society.

In the UK, an example of an animal welfare group is the Royal Society for the Prevention of Cruelty to Animals (RSPCA). This organisation investigates allegations of animal cruelty and may (as a prosecuting authority) initiate legal action against those whose actions have caused unnecessary suffering to animals. The League Against Cruel Sports is also a UK-based animal welfare organisation that seeks to prevent cruelty to animals associated with 'sports' that include fox hunting, cock fighting, game-bird shooting and other forms of wildlife crime. It is at the forefront of current attempts to ensure that the legislation outlawing fox hunting with dogs is not repealed. Many of these concerns are also shared by Hunt Watch, which was set up in 2005 to coordinate the work of all hunt monitoring groups in the UK.

An international organisation that seeks to combat the cruelty, abuse neglect and suffering experienced by animals around the world at the hands of humans is the World Society for the Protection of Animals (WSPA). This has the status of a charity that raises money from individual donors (termed 'animal protectors'), which is used to promote campaigns against animal cruelty. These have included opposition to factory farming, the trade in wildlife and sea turtle farming. Since 2011, the WSPA has campaigned against the mass culling of dogs to prevent the spread of rabies and instead advocates programmes of mass vaccinations in countries where rabies exists.

One group whose agenda goes beyond that of animal welfare is People for the Ethical Treatment of Animals (PETA). This is 'an animal rights organization founded on the premise that animals are not ours to use for food, clothing, experimentation, or entertainment. Since 1980, PETA has grown from a handful of volunteers to an international organization with more than 3 million members and supporters' (PETA, 2013). Its activities include mobilising public opinion against organisations that are responsible for animal cruelty, one recent example of this being the campaign seeking to persuade the American Southwest Airlines to end its commercial relationship with Seaworld on the grounds of animal cruelty, especially that experienced by orcas. PETA frequently uses celebrities in connection with its campaigns: the support given to local activists to end bullfighting in the Catalonia region in Spain in 2012, for example, secured support from Ricky Gervais. However, more militant animal rights activists dismiss its activities as constituting 'new welfarism' (Francione, 1996).

An international organisation that promotes animal rights is the Animal Liberation Front (ALF). It originated in the UK as the Band of Mercy in 1971, whose diverse agenda was directed at targets that included hunting, research and animal testing laboratories and a seal cull of the Norfolk Coast. A wide range of direct action tactics were used that included arson (committed against a research laboratory in Milton Keynes in 1973 and boats involved in a seal cull in 1974), causing damage to premises and property associated with animal testing and other forms of animal abuse, and freeing ('liberating') animals from a farm in Wiltshire in 1974. The perceived violent nature of these tactics brought the Band of Mercy criticism from other bodies (including the Hunt Saboteurs Association) whose concerns were of a similar nature.

The Band of Mercy adopted the name of the Animal Liberation Front in 1976 and spread beyond the UK, now being active in over 40 countries. It is leaderless, has no formal hierarchy and constitutes an underground movement. It utilises a cell structure, which makes it difficult for law enforcement agencies to penetrate, and also provides activists with a considerable degree of autonomy in connection with the operations that they mount. Some activists also operate in isolation and are known as 'Lone Wolves'. The highly decentralised structure of the ALF also means that leading activists who operate above ground and act as spokespersons for it cannot be held responsible for actions carried out in its name. The underground activities performed by the ALF are also supported by more formal, aboveground organisations, including the Animal Liberation Front Supporters Group (ALFSG), which supports ALF activists in prison across the world and to promote an understanding 'of the reasons why decent, caring people feel forced to break the law' (ALFSG, 2012).

The tactics of the ALF embrace various forms of direct action, for example, mounting raids to remove animals from laboratories and farms, and destroying facilities and equipment that are related to animal abuse. It has been claimed that in the first year of its operations, ALF actions 'accounted for £250,000 worth of damage, targeting butchers shops, furriers, circuses, slaughterhouses' (Monaghan, 2000: 160). The ALF claims to be non-violent (at least in connection with violence against people), but some of its actions (sometimes performed by ALF activists using the name of a different body, including that of the Animal Rights Militia [ARM]) have been identified with violence and have led to its members being labelled as 'terrorists' in both the UK and the USA. The term 'extensional self-defence' has been coined with reference to the justification of violence as a necessary measure to defend animals who have no means of defending themselves (Best, 2004).

A number of campaigns have been conducted by animal rights organisations. In 1982, an attempt to force the company manufacturing Mars Bars to cease using monkeys for tooth decay tests took the form of a claim by the ALF (sent to the *Sunday Mirror* newspaper) that Mars Bars in stores located in a number of cities across England had been injected with rat poison. Although the contamination claim was a hoax, it resulted in the company temporarily ceasing production of the product and caused the removal of Mars Bars from the shelves of retail outlets. This tactic was later used in other campaigns. In 2007, for example, the ARM claimed to have contaminated tubes of the ointment Savlon, which was manufactured by Novartis, a company that made use of the services provided by Huntingdon Life Sciences (HLS). This led to a number of retail outlets withdrawing this product from their shelves.

In 1999, a major protest was mounted against HLS, which used animals to test the safety of new drugs. It was Europe's largest animal testing laboratory. The protest (termed Stop Huntingdon Animal Cruelty or SHAC) involved mounting a permanent presence outside the firm based in Cambridge to lobby staff who were employed there, which was coupled with more violent tactics that included physical attacks on staff, their homes and property, such as cars, and planting fake and real home-made bombs at the homes of employees of the company. The campaign of violence extended to directors of companies which had links with HLS, who were also subject to libellous accusations that included letters being sent to their neighbours claiming that they were paedophiles. Many of these tactics were associated with the campaign mounted in connection with the breeding of guinea pigs for medical research at Darley Oaks Farm, Newchurch, Staffordshire between 1999 and 2005 that was attributed to the ARM.

Economic pressure was also exerted against HLS. One innovation was pressurising corporate shareholders to sell their shares in HLS, using tactics that included activists turning up at the homes of those they consider to be collaborators of the company in a bid to persuade them to sever their links with it (a practice known as 'doorstepping') and sending letters and flooding the switchboards of city backers with telephone calls. These actions led to HLS being dropped from the London and New York Stock Exchanges in December 2000 and March 2001. In 2003, HLS obtained a permanent injunction against SHAC which led to the reduction of violent actions against the company and those it employed.

These forms of economic pressure are conducted worldwide and have made considerable use of the Internet to mobilise supports to undertake actions and to enable activists to discover personal information about those they target (such as addresses and telephone numbers) (Cohen, 2007).

In the UK, the Criminal Justice and Police Act 2001 outlawed practices associated with animal rights organisations that included 'doorstepping' and sending intimidatory mail and email to staff engaged in research involving animals and to shareholders in companies that were involved in such activities. In 2004, the National Extremism Tactical Coordination Unit was set up to monitor illegal animal rights activities performed by the ALF and similar bodies.

In America, the 1992 Animal Enterprise Protection Act (amended in 2006 by the Animal Enterprise Terrorism Act) was enacted in response to animal rights activities. This legislation created the federal crime of 'animal enterprise terrorism' to penalise those who intentionally damaged or caused the loss of any property (including animals or records) used by the animal enterprise or who conspired to do so. The first prosecution conducted under the 1992 legislation took place in 2006 when the US government successfully prosecuted six members of SHAC.

See also: direct action, terrorism

Sources and further reading

ALFSG (2012) 'The Animal Liberation Front Supporters Group', www.alfsg.org.uk/index.html (date accessed 19 April 2014).
Best, S. (2004) 'Gaps in Logic, Lapses in Politics: Rights and Abolitionism' in J. Dunayer, *Speciesism*. Derwood, MD: Ryce Publishing.
Cohen, N. (2007) 'Doorstep Protest: Very Real, Very Virtual', *New York Times*, 26 November.
Francione, G. (1996) *Rain without Thunder: The Ideology of the Animal Rights Movement*. Philadelphia: Temple University Press.
Mann, K. (2007) *From Dusk 'til Dawn: An Insider's View of the Growth of the Animal Liberation Movement*. London: Puppy Pincher Press.
Monaghan, R. (2000) 'Terrorism in the Name of Animal Rights' in M. Taylor and J. Horgan (eds), *The Future of Terrorism*. London: Routledge.
PETA (2013) 'PETA's Guide to Becoming An Activist', www.peta.org/action/activism-guide (date accessed 19 April 2014).
Ryder, R. (1971) 'Experiments on Animals' in S. Godlovitch, R. Godlovitch and J. Harris (eds), *Animals, Men and Morals*. New York: Grove Press.
Singer, P. (1995) *Animal Liberation*, 2nd edn. London: Pimlico.

ANTI-GLOBALISATION

Anti-globalisation has been associated with protests conducted across the world since the 1980s.

Opposition to capitalism is associated with two social movements – the anti-capitalist movement and the anti-globalisation movement. Anti-capitalism seeks to replace capitalism with an alternative economic system and embraces a wide array of political ideologies that includes socialism, anarchism and communism. The anti-globalisation movement is opposed to the globalisation of capitalism, especially the undemocratic nature of this development. This movement may, however, embrace those opposed to all aspects of capitalism. Anarchists, for example, commonly participate in anti-globalisation protests.

Globalisation is not a new phenomenon and arose towards the end of the nineteenth century. However, its pace slowed down for much of the twentieth century, but picked up in the later decades of the century in response to neoliberalism: 'Neoliberal policies include privatizing public industries, opening markets to foreign investment and competition, creating fiscal austerity programs to curtail government spending, removing controls on capital flows, reducing tariffs and other trade barriers, and ending government protections for local industry' (Engler, 2007: 151).

These policies were promoted by international institutions such as the Organisation for Economic Co-operation and Development (OECD), the World Bank (WB), the International Monetary Fund (IMF) and the World Trade Organization (WTO), and gave rise to opposition since the 1990s in the form of the anti-globalisation movement, which has particularly criticised the operations of the world's trading system. Movement participants argue that neoliberal policies 'have created sweatshop working conditions in the developing world, threatened unionized jobs and environmental protections in the global North, benefited the wealthy at the expense of the poor, and endangered indigenous cultures' (Engler, 2007: 151).

The anti-globalisation movement (which is sometimes referred to as the counter-globalisation movement or the global justice movement) is especially critical of the power wielded by multinational corporations whereby politicians 'jump to the commands of corporations rather than of their own citizens' (Hertz, 2001d: 5). This power has been enhanced by privatisation (a policy that is viewed as being driven by large corporations) (Hertz, 2001b), the deregulation of financial markets and through trade agreements promoted by international institutions, especially the WTO. Anti-globalisation protesters view the WTO and the IMF as key agents of the global economy which seek to manage it in a manner that is beneficial to the USA and to American-owned multinational corporations, but which act to the detriment of developing nations where wealth has not trickled down as had been predicted (Hertz, 2001d: 202) and where what has been described as a 'race to the bottom' exists – 'multinationals pitting developing countries against each other to provide the most advantageous conditions for investment, with no regulation, no red tape, no unions, a blind eye turned to environmental degradation. It's good for profits, but bad for workers and local communities' (Hertz, 2001b).

However, protesters are not opposed to all forms of globalisation (thus suggesting that the term *anti-globalisation* is a misnomer) since 'the left and the workers movements ... were founded on the principle of international solidarity – that is, globalization in a form that attends to the rights of people', but is opposed to those aspects of it that promote 'private power systems' (Chomsky, 2002).

The chief criticisms of this movement are directed against the exploitation of labour and natural resources (and the consequent environmental damage caused by the latter) in developing nations and the undermining of national sovereignty by global institutions and institutions. The WTO trade agreements, for example, are binding on all member states and have been criticised for limiting the ability of national governments to safeguard the interests of their citizens (Hertz, 2001a). Free trade is depicted as benefiting the northern hemisphere to the disbenefit of the southern hemisphere, thus increasing the disparity between the world's 'haves' and 'have-nots'.

Critiques of globalisation have also been associated with positive reforms that include fair trade, the advancement of human rights and sustainable development. In particular, the 'anti-globalization movement advocates participatory democracy, seeking to increase popular control of political and economic life in the face of increasingly powerful corporations, unaccountable global financial institutions, and U.S. hegemony' (Engler, 2007: 150–1).

Anti-globalisation protests are not confined to international financial institutions that promote global capitalism and have also been directed at multinational companies such as Nike and Monsanto that have benefited from its operations. Protests have also assumed a localised form, examples being strikes by unions in South Korea, fights against water privatisation in Bolivia and South Africa, and the struggle against development of hydroelectric dams in rural India (Engler, 2007: 152).

Other issues promoted by the anti-globalisation movement included mounting protests to the invasions of Afghanistan in 2001 and Iraq in 2003, and on the grounds that national leaders who acquiesced to these American-driven initiatives were riding roughshod over the objections to such a course of action by the majority of their citizens. The 'No Borders' campaign to combat the international regime of migration control has advocated the elimination of national boundaries and has targeted the International Organization for Migration (IOM), which is accused of implementing 'the dominant and repressive migration politics' (Noborder network, 2013).

See also: anti-globalisation movement, anti-globalisation/anti-capitalist protests (UK), anti-globalisation/anti-capitalist protests (worldwide), Monsanto protests (worldwide) 2013

Sources and further reading

Chomsky, N. (2002) *Znet*, 7 May, quoted in 'Globalisation', http://fileserver.nettexts.com/asset.aspx?dl=no&id=14347 (date accessed 19 April 2014).

Engler, M. (2007) 'Defining the Anti-globalisation Movement' in G. Anderson and K. Herr (eds), *Encyclopaedia of Activism and Social Justice*. London: Sage.

Hertz, N. (2001a) 'A Bad Day for Democracy', *The Observer*, 6 May.

Hertz, N. (2001b) 'Why We Must Stay Silent No Longer', *The Observer*, 8 April.

Hertz, N. (2001c) Why We Stayed Away', *The Observer*, 10 June.

Hertz, N. (2001d) *The Silent Takeover: Global Capitalism and the Death of Democracy*. London: Heinemann.

Noborder network (2013) 'The IOM, Spies and Migrant Hunters' www.noborder.org/iom (date accessed 19 April 2014).

ANTI-GLOBALISATION MOVEMENT

Opponents of the globalisation of capitalism have staged a number of large-scale protests to articulate their views. Allegations of the political impotence of governments in their dealings with international agencies and multinational corporations are used to justify this form of political activity, since it is the only method through which citizens can voice their objections to the policies that these bodies promote.

The anti-globalisation movement embraces a wide array of movements with diverse agendas and tactics. Its constituents 'include trade unionists, environmentalists, anarchists, land rights and indigenous rights activists, organizations promoting human rights and sustainable development, opponents of privatization, and anti-sweatshop campaigners. These groups charge that the policies of corporate globalization have exacerbated global poverty and increased inequality' (Engler, 2007: 150).

This situation often means that a protest associated with the anti-globalisation movement consists of several groups of participants, differentiated in terms of their specific objectives and the tactics of protest that they utilise to further their cause, especially their willingness to break the law. The movement lacks any formal structure (although the International Council of the World Social Forum meets annually and acts as a site for anti-globalisation activist networking and transnational strategising; Engler, 2007: 150), but does, through the use of the social media, also manage to organise large-scale protests on a global basis.

The tactics associated with the anti-globalisation movement include direct action and civil disobedience, typically designed to disrupt meetings of international financial institutions such as the World Trade Organization (WTO), the International Monetary Fund (IMF), the World Bank (WB), the World Economic Forum and the summit meetings of the richest industrialised countries (the G7, G8 and G20). Violence (frequently dubbed 'riots') has often occurred at protests directed at these events, especially associated with Black Bloc tactics.

The violence that arises at anti-globalisation protests is frequently directed at local outlets of multinational corporations such as McDonald's and Starbucks as well as law enforcement agencies. These symbols of global capitalism are attacked as protesters believe that 'these international chains are responsible for damage to the environment and prevent the development of local industries, forcing businesses to close and thus being responsible for creating poverty and debt in the developing world. These companies are also perceived as being responsible for the creation of a new global culture which is rejected by emerging groups of cultural activists who wish to preserve local identities' (Joyce, 2002: 33).

Although many anti-globalisation protesters do not advocate violence to further their aims, the policing of protests with which they are associated generally fails to draw any distinction between the tactics of the diverse groups that attend and treats all participants as potentially violent demonstrators. This situation (which is partly explained by deficient police intelligence relating to the composition of anti-globalisation protests and the tactics used by the key participating groups) has led to injustices, which included the kettling of the Climate Camp participants at the 2009 G20 protests in London. This action was declared unlawful by the High Court in 2011.

See also: anti-capitalism protests (UK), anti-globalisation protests (worldwide), kettling (containment), public order policing (England and Wales)

Sources and further reading

Engler, M. (2007) 'Defining the Anti-globalisation Movement' in G. Anderson and K. Herr (eds), *Encyclopaedia of Activism and Social Justice*. London: Sage.

Joyce, P. (2002) *The Politics of Protest: Extra-parliamentary Politics in Britain since 1970*. Basingstoke: Palgrave.

ANTI-GLOBALISATION/ ANTI-CAPITALIST PROTESTS (UK)

Anti-globalisation protests have regularly occurred in the UK since the 1980s. These have often been referred to by the media as 'anti-capitalist' protests and the following account briefly refers to a small number of these events.

The first major protests associated with opposition to capitalism were the Stop the City demonstrations in September 1983 and March and September 1984. These were described as a carnival against war, oppression and destruction. Although these were termed 'demonstrations', they were primarily examples of direct action which sought to blockade the City of London and thereby cause losses to the financial institutions that were located there. The aim was 'to put enough bodies in the way to effectively cut off the routes whereby the bankers and stockbrokers would get to work, block the entrances to the office buildings themselves and stop business activity in "The City" ... for a day' (Dangerous Minds, 2011).

The Stop the City protests attracted participants with a diverse range of interests. In March 1984 these included anarchists associated with London Greenpeace, activists from the peace and animal rights movements, and from protesters drawn from various strands of counter-culture, including anarcho-punk (History is Made at Night, 2011). There was no single organisation behind the protests and the diverse range of tactics that were deployed made the March 1984 event difficult for the City of London police to manage: 'Rather than get caught up in ritual set piece confrontations with the police, there was endless movement with groups heading off in all directions and no direction, blocking traffic and forcing the police to spread themselves thinly' (History is Made at Night, 2011).

The events in 1983 and 1984 were the forerunners for later anti-capitalism demonstrations in London in 1999 that included the Carnival Against Capitalism in 1999 and a number of demonstrations that have taken place on May Day. The Occupy London protest against economic inequality (which sought to camp outside the London Stock Exchange, but which instead camped outside St Paul's Cathedral between October 2011 and June 2012) is a further example of an action that occurred in the financial centre of London.

Actions of this nature have drawn participants from diverse backgrounds who have utilised a wide range of tactics, including demonstrations, civil disobedience and more violent manifestations of direct action. Counterculture protest has also been associated with opposition to capitalism. The police operation to prevent the holding of the Avon Free Festival in 1992 (which resulted in an alternative event being staged at Castlemorton) was an episode of counterculture protest directed at the morals and standards of behaviour derived from capitalism, in particular its emphasis on materialism and private property ownership. Those involved saw the countryside 'as a leisure facility and not the site of agri-business' (Baxter, 1992: 222). What has been described as the '"uneasy combination" of New Age Traveller and the raver' (Baxter, 1992: 222) was further cemented when the Criminal Justice and Public Order Act 1994 placed legislative restrictions on events that were associated with both New Age travellers and ravers.

The Carnival Against Capital (sometimes referred to as J18) took place on 18 June 1999 and was part of the Global Carnival Against Capitalism that was organised to coincide with the twenty-fifth G8 Summit, which took place in Cologne, Germany. The day involved a number of actions. These included a Critical Mass bicycle ride that brought rush-hour traffic in the City of London to a standstill, the occupation of Southwark Bridge, which was transformed into a street party, and a 'die-in' carried out by the Campaign Against Arms Trade that closed a branch of Lloyds Bank. A number of marches started at around noon, which came together and converged on the London International Financial Futures Exchange, which a small number of the protesters managed to storm.

The protesters totalled around 4,000 and £2 million of damage was caused, which included attacks on a McDonald's restaurant and a Mercedes car showroom. Forty-two people were injured and there were 71 arrests (Mansley, 2014: 86). Police used horses and CS spray to disperse the demonstrators, who were eventually forced out of the City of London. A subsequent event, the anti-WTO protest in London on 30 November 1999 (known as N30), witnessed the first use by the police of the tactic of kettling to control demonstrators (Mansley, 2014: 86–7), although variants of this tactic had first been used at the March 1984 Stop the City Protest, entailing the use of police lines to curb in demonstrators and at the 1995 Disability Rights Demonstration in Parliament Square.

The 1 May 2000 protests witnessed guerrilla gardening in Parliament Square, an attack on the McDonald's restaurant in the Strand and vandalism in which the Cenotaph and a statue of Winston Churchill in Parliament Square were defaced. Running battles took place between the police and demonstrators and around 96 protesters were arrested. The event was policed by around 5,000 officers drawn from the Metropolitan Police, the City of London Police and the British Transport Police (BBC, 2000).

Further protests took place in London on May Day 2001. This anti-globalisation protest was initiated by a mass cycle ride by Critical Mass through the City of London. This was followed by a demonstration which spilled over into violence in several locations. This was attributed to 'violent anarchists' who were said to have caused a 'trail of destruction' – more than 20 shopfront windows in the area of Tottenham Court Road 'were smashed with rocks and other missiles, including those of Bank of Scotland, Abbey National, Royal Bank of Scotland, Barclays Bank, Coffee Republic and Habitat. The rioters also attempted to set fire to a Tesco store on nearby Goodge Street' (Left, Jeffery and Perrone, 2001).

In order to contain the violence and avoid a repetition of events that took place the previous year, 6,000 police officers were deployed (Left, Jeffery and Perrone, 2001). The police again used the tactic of kettling in Oxford Circus, which they perceived to be the flashpoint for violence. However, the use of this approach also resulted in bystanders and peaceful protesters being contained in this manner.

See also: counterculture protest, demonstrations, G20 protests (London) 2009, kettling (containment), Occupy movement, public order policing (England and Wales)

Sources and further reading

Baxter, J. (1992) 'Castlemorton and Beyond'. *Policing* 8(3): 222–31.

BBC (2000) '2000: May Day Violence on London Streets', 1 May, http://news.bbc.co.uk/onthisday/hi/dates/stories/may/1/newsid_2480000/2480215.stm (date accessed 10 April 2014).

Dangerous Minds (2011) 'The Original Occupy Wall Street: Stop the City, 1984', 16 October, http://dangerousminds.net/comments/the_original_occupy_wall_street_stop_the_city_1984 (date accessed 10 April 2014).

Engler, M. (2007) "Defining the Anti-globalisation Movement" in G. Anderson and K. Herr (eds), *Encyclopaedia of Activism and Social Justice*. London: Sage.

History is Made at Night (2011) 'Stop the City 1984', http://history-is-made-at-night.blogspot.co.uk/2011/10/stop-city-1984.html (date accessed 10 April 2014).

Joyce, P. (2002) *The Politics of Protest: Extra-parliamentary Politics in Britain since 1970*. Basingstoke: Palgrave.

Left, S., Jeffery, S. and Perrone, J. (2001) 'Violence Erupts in Central London', *The Guardian*, 1 May, www.theguardian.com/world/2001/may/01/mayday.immigrationpolicy1 (date accessed 10 April 2014).

Mansley, D. (2014) *Collective Violence, Democracy and Protest Policing.* Abingdon: Routledge.

ANTI-GLOBALISATION/ ANTI-CAPITALIST PROTESTS (WORLDWIDE)

A number of major anti-globalisation events have taken place throughout the world since the latter decades of the twentieth century. These usually took the form of protests held in conjunction with the meetings of international bodies and included protests held in West Berlin in 1988 (at the annual meetings of the World Bank and the International Monetary Fund), in Paris in 1989 (at the G7 Summit) and in Madrid in 1994 (to coincide with the fiftieth anniversary of the the International Monetary Fund (IMF) and the World Bank). On 18 June 1999 anti-globalisation protests took place in a number of cities across the world (which included London's Carnival Against Capital) to coincide with the twenty-fifth G8 Summit that was being held in Cologne, Germany.

This entry briefly discusses some of the major anti-globalisation protests that have taken place since the late 1990s.

Seattle (1999)

A World Trade Organization (WTO) Ministerial Conference took place at Seattle, Washington on 30 November 1999. Large-scale protests (called N30) took place in the streets surrounding the hotels and the Washington State Convention and Trade Center where the conference was taking place. It was estimated that around 75,000 people were involved in these protests, which lasted for a week (Engler, 2007).

Numerous forms of activity were associated with the protests: 'Groups like Art and Revolution created giant puppets to carry in the demonstrations, activists inspired by British Reclaim the Streets actions held parties in intersections blocked by protesters, and musicians formed activist marching bands' (Engler, 2007). A large permitted march by the American Federation of Labor-Congress of Industrial Organizations (AFL-CIO) took place in the vicinity of the Convention Centre, which was supplemented by protests mounted by 'student, anarchist, and militant environmentalist "affinity groups"' who 'formed a nonviolent human blockade around the convention center, preventing trade ministers from holding the opening session of the meeting' (Engler, 2007), thus prolonging its duration until 3 December. The police responded to the blockades with tear gas and rubber bullets in an attempt to disperse the demonstrators, following which the windows of bank and premises owned or franchised by corporations such as Nike and Starbucks were smashed, activities that were associated with anarchists using Black Bloc tactics (Engler, 2007).

A municipal form of a state of emergency was temporarily enacted and a curfew was imposed. The damage caused amounted to $3 million and 600 arrests were made (Narr et al., 2006: 49). Many more individuals were injured.

The 1999 WTO protest in Seattle 'was a defining moment in how local law enforcement manages mass demonstrations' (Narr et al., 2006: 1). It was observed that 'clearly-organized anti-globalization and anarchist protesters conducted a determined programme of property destruction and violence against law enforcement officers'. In turn, the Seattle Police Department was 'heavily criticised for its management of the demonstration', whose actions included 'the implementation of curfews, and the use of pepper spray and tear gas on protesters and residents alike' (Narr et al., 2006: 1).

The violent nature of these protests led to them being dubbed the 'Battle of Seattle'. It has been observed that this event, 'while not the first appearance of the global movement, dramatically altered the debate about trade and development taking place within international institutions. It served as a prototype for many future protests and also marked the moment when "anti-globalization" as a term gained widespread usage' (Engler, 2007: 152). The scale of the protests may have stiffened the resolve of developing nations not to concede to American and European demands relating to the promotion of the neoliberal free trade agenda. This opposition led to the talks resulting in deadlock.

A further series of protests directed against the IMF and the World Bank occurred in Washington DC in April 2000. Police tactics in response to the protests included that of mass arrests. Almost 700 people were arrested, many of them non-violent demonstrators and bystanders (Narr et al., 2006: 2). Those detained included the eminent *Washington Post* press photographer Carol Guzy, then a three-times Pulitzer Prize winner. Robust actions of this nature were also pursued against anti-globalisation protesters at the annual meetings of the IMF and the World Bank in Washington DC in September 2002. Around 650 people were arrested, including a number of reporters.

Prague (2000)

A summit of the IMF and the World Bank took place in Prague (capital of the Czech Republic) on 26 September 2000. This event had been preceded by a meeting of the World Economic Forum in Melbourne, Australia, in which around 2,000 anti-globalisation protesters (organised by the S11 Alliance) had sought to prevent delegates from attending through the use of peaceful and violent tactics.

The event in Prague also witnessed anti-globalisation protests, with around 12,000 participants coming from all over the world: 'Black-clad anarchists from Bristol could be seen rubbing shoulders with Slovak environmentalists. Members of the

Italian group Ya Basta! ... could be found marching in matching white fire suits, followed by Greek workers in red bandanas carrying flags with the hammer and sickle, There were Canadians and Americans, Swedes and Poles' (Straus, 2000). INPEG (the Iniciativa Proti Ekonomicke Globalizaci or Initiative Against Economic Globalisation) acted as an umbrella organisation to coordinate the activities of some of the groups that attended the protest.

The main demonstration occurred on 26 September. Protesters approached the conference centre where the summit was being held from three directions, reflecting three different groups who were participants to this protest: 'one engaging in various forms of civil disobedience (the Yellow march), one (the Pink/Silver march) advancing through "tactical frivolity" (costume, dance, theatre, music, and artwork), and one (the Blue march) engaging in violent conflicts with the baton-armed police, with the protesters throwing cobblestones lifted from the street' (Vidal and Connolly, 2000). The latter march sought to reach the summit venue in order to bring the meeting to a close. The police responded with the use of tear gas and water cannons to force them back, following which shopfront windows in Wenceslas Square were smashed. The restraint shown by the police on the first day of the protest was abandoned the following day (27 September), when around 850 protesters were rounded up and placed in prison. However, the protests did succeed in ending the summit on 27 September, a day earlier than had been planned. The protests caused damage to property amounting to around $2.5 million (Straus, 2000).

Genoa (2001)

The G8 Summit that was held in Genoa, Italy, between 18 and 22 July 2001 was faced by a large number of anti-globalisation protesters, numbering around 200,000 and drawn from around 700 groups from across the European Union (EU). The main protest organiser was the Genoa Social Forum, which sought to avoid violence but more radical groups including the Italian *Ya Basta!* and the German *Freie Arbeiterinnen Union* (FAU) were willing to endorse such a tactic.

Police actions sought to prevent protesters from disrupting the meeting. Suspected activists were denied the freedom of movement to which they were entitled under the Schengen Treaty and were prevented from entering the country – actions that led to border riots. In addition, an exclusion zone was declared around the city, which was justified by the fear of a terrorist attack. The meeting itself was held inside what was declared to be a 'Red Zone' that was barricaded to stop protesters from reaching the delegates.

These measures were viewed by the protesters as a denial of their right to exercise non-violent protest. The main events at which violence occurred were the 20 July Day of

Action and the 21 July International March. These events were met with robust police actions both on the streets and away from the protests. The former included the death of a Genoese anarchist, Carlo Giuliani, who was killed on 20 July as the result of being shot in the face by a member of the Carabinieri whilst attempting to throw a fire extinguisher at a police vehicle, which then ran over him. The latter included night-time raids on the Diaz-Pascoli and Diaz-Pertini schools, which were occupied by housing activists and journalists, on 21 July.

Several hundred peaceful demonstrators, rioters and police were injured, and hundreds were arrested during the days of the G8 meeting. Most of those arrested were charged with 'criminal association' under the country's anti-Mafia and anti-terrorist laws. Legal proceedings were initiated against a number of police officers for their part in these events and charges that included conspiracy to pervert the course of justice, the use of excessive force and planting evidence were brought. Police actions against the protesters sparked a wave of demonstrations across Italy on 24 July.

Other state officials, including prison officers, were accused of abusing detainees in their custody. Over 200 people were detained at Bolzaneto temporary detention centre, where they were 'made to stand for hours in painful positions, beaten, threatened, including with rape, subjected to body searches carried out in a deliberately degrading manner and other humiliations' (Amnesty International, 2010). It was argued that actions of this nature constituted torture, but the absence of a crime of torture in the Italian criminal code prevented proportionate action being taken against these officials. Amnesty International thus 'reiterated its call on the authorities to introduce a crime of torture consistent with the requirements of the Convention against Torture' (Amnesty International, 2010).

A number of senior police officers were acquitted at a trial held in 2008, but this verdict was reversed in 2010 and 25 were convicted of grievous bodily harm, libel and falsifying evidence. The first two of these offences were timed out by the Italian statute of limitations by the time the case went to the Court of Cassation in 2011. However, the guilty verdicts passed on 15 officers in 2010 for falsifying evidence were upheld and sentences of five years' imprisonment were imposed. The automatic deduction of three years from this sentence meant that none of these officers went to prison, but all were suspended from duty for five years (Kington, 2012),

See also: anti-globalisation, anti-globalisation movement, anti-globalisation/anti-capitalist protests (UK), counterculture protest, states of emergency

Sources and further reading
Amnesty International (2010) 'Convictions of Abuse During Genoa G8 Protests

Upheld', *Amnesty International News*, www.amnesty.org/en/news-and-updates/convictions-abuse-during-genoa-g8-protests-upheld-2010-03-08 (date accessed 19 April 2014).

Engler, M. (2007) 'Defining the Anti-globalisation Movement' in G. Anderson and K. Herr (eds), *Encyclopaedia of Activism and Social Justice*. London: Sage.

Kington, T. (2012) 'Court Upholds Convictions of Italian G8 Police', *The Guardian*, 6 July.

Narr, T., Toliver, J., Murphy, J., McFarland, M. and Ederheimer, J. (2006) 'Police Management of Mass Demonstrations: Identifying Issues and Successful Approaches', Policy Executive Research Forum. Available at: www.policeforum.org/assets/docs/Critical_Issues_Series/police%20management%20of%20mass%20demonstrations%20-%20identifying%20issues%20and%20successful%20approaches%202006.pdf (date accessed 19 April 2014).

Straus, T. (2000) 'Prague Protests: The Anti-globalisation Movement Gets Global', *Organic Consumers Association*, www.organicconsumers.org/corp/praguesuccess.cfm (date accessed 19 April 2014).

Vidal, J. and Connolly, K. (2000). 'Barricades Burn in Battle of Prague', *The Guardian*, 27 September, www.theguardian.com/business/2000/sep/27/imf.economics1 (date accessed 19 April 2014).

ANTI-NATIONAL SECURITY AGENCY PROTESTS (GERMANY) 2013

Protest is frequently directed at public policy pursued within the country where the protest occurs. However, this is not always the case and protests can be directed at activities conducted by other countries that affect the citizens of the country where the protest occurs. One example of this was the protests in Germany on 2013 against the American spy programme.

These protests stemmed from allegations made by a former National Security Agency (NSA) contractor, Edward Snowden, regarding the existence of a wide-ranging American spying programme that targeted Internet and telephone communications worldwide. This was alleged to have included communications involving a number of world leaders, including the mobile phone of Angela Merkel, the German Chancellor. Germans are especially sensitive concerning domestic surveillance because of the activities that were carried out by the German Gestapo and the East German STASI secret police between 1945 and the fall of the Berlin Wall in 1989 (Khazan, 2013).

Of particular concern to Germans was his allegation that German citizens were more scrutinised than any other nationality (Collier, 2013). President Barack Obama was met by a small number of protesters on the occasion of his visit to Berlin on 18 June 2013. Subsequent activities included marches on the US Army's 'Dagger Complex' situated in Griesheim (near Frankfurt) in Germany on 13 and 20 July 2013, which was alleged to be an NSA listening post. The organiser of these protests was Daniel Bangert, who used Facebook to publicise them.

A far larger event was planned for 27 July 2013. This protest was coordinated by 'The Stop Watching Us' campaign, which attracted support from a number of private and political organisations whose demands included an investigation by the European Parliament. Although it was anticipated that this protest would attract thousands of Germans, the actual numbers involved were more modest, numbering hundreds in most cities, apart from Berlin, Frankfurt and Hamburg, where they were more significant. However, other forms of protest against related activities have demonstrated a wider degree of support – an online petition against the criminal prosecution of whistleblowers (such as Snowden and Bradley Manning) and the PRISM Internet monitoring programme (which is the NSA's digital anti-terrorist surveillance programme). This petition attracted 40,000 supporters by July 2013 (Strange, 2013).

See also: political policing, subversion, whistleblowing

Sources and further reading

Collier, K. (2013) 'Massive Anti-NSA Protests Planned for 39 German Cities', *The Daily Dot*, 26 July, www.dailydot.com/news/germany-anti-nsa-surveillance-program-protests (date accessed 19 April 2014).

Khazan, O. (2013) '"Yes We Can": Germans Protest at Checkpoint Charlie as Obama Arrives in Berlin, *The Atlantic*, www.theatlantic.com/international/archive/2013/06/yes-we-scan-germans-protest-at-checkpoint-charlie-as-obama-arrives-in-berlin/277008 (date accessed 19 April 2014).

Strange, J. (2013) 'German Anti-NSA Protests Attract Small Crowds', *Deutsche Welle*, 28 July, www.dw.de/german-anti-nsa-protests-attract-small-crowds/a-16981027 (date accessed 19 April 2014).

ARAB SPRING (ARAB WORLD) 2010 ONWARDS

The term 'Arab Spring' refers to a wave of protests that occurred in the Arab world. The first action occurred in Tunisia on 17 December 2010 when a young university graduate named Mohamed Bouazizi burned himself to death in the town of Sidi Bouzid when the authorities confiscated his only means of subsistence, a vegetable barrow, for not having a licence.

This event set in motion a range of protests that had significant political repercussions across the Arab world, some of which are ongoing. These initially took the form of attempts to oust dictatorships, an aim that united a disparate range of opposition groups. However, the absence of any clear vision as to the future direction of society once the incumbent rulers had been ousted made for a turbulent future in the region.

This entry focuses on protests that led to regime changes in a number of countries that were affected by Arab Spring or, where Arab Spring protests failed to trigger regime changes, on protests that continued subsequently. The cut-off dates for this entry is 2011 or 2012, depending on the way in which events have unfolded in the countries that are referred to. A subsequent entry on the post-Arab Spring period will consider protests that have continued in countries that experienced regime changes or, where these have failed to occur, from 2012 to the beginning of 2014.

Tunisia

In Tunisia, the self-immolation of Bouazizi resulted in demonstrations that were initiated in Sidi Bouzid, but then spread across Tunisia. These were spearheaded by students and intensified following Bouazizi's death on 4 January 2011. Facebook played an important role in mobilising the protesters. These events occurred against the background of adverse economic circumstances affecting large numbers of the population, which included inflation, high levels of unemployment, low wages, poverty and poor living conditions. These conditions were acutely felt outside of the country's capital, Tunis, where the high cost of basic foodstuffs was a particularly significant issue.

Protesters also complained of corruption and the absence of fundamental political liberties under the rule of the existing political elite headed by President Zine El Abidine Ben Ali, who had been in power for 23 years. His actions had included censorship of the Internet to prevent access to cables from the American Embassy in Tunis in 2009, which were leaked by WikiLeaks. The regime was accused of having lost touch with its people in these cables.

Although Tunisia was regarded as politically stable, having had just two presidents since gaining independence from France in 1956, this situation masked the extent of opposition to the state within the country. Labour unrest had occurred since the late 1970s (which led to the suppression of the General Union of Tunisian Workers (UGTT)), a number of clashes had occurred between the state and the Islamic movement Al-Hahda (Ennahda) since the 1990s and concerns by younger people (especially graduates) relating to the lack of employment and prospects in society made student protests, associated with organisations that included the General Union of Tunisian Students (UGET), a potent threat to political stability (Marshall, 2013).

The government responded to protests in January by closing schools and universities indefinitely and imposing a curfew. Violence was meted out against demonstrators by the state's security forces, whose actions included using water cannons, tear gas and shooting live ammunition into crowds to disperse them. Demonstrators retaliated with stones and petrol bombs, and the situation descended into lawlessness characterised by gangs of Tunisians attacking commercial property and government buildings, and engaging in looting, while armed gangs loyal to the President resorted to random shooting of those they regarded as protesters. The key demand of the demonstrators became that of calling on the President to resign.

The inability of the police and security forces to contain the unrest resulted in the ousting of President

Zine El Abidine Ben Ali on 14 January 2011, who fled to Saudi Arabia. He was the first Arab leader to be driven from power by a popular uprising. In June 2011, he was tried in his absence and sentenced to 35 years' imprisonment.

Egypt

Events in Tunisia inspired similar protests in Egypt, where power was monopolised by President Hosni Mubarak, who had been in power since the assassination of President Anwar Sadat in 1981. Political dissent was not tolerated under the country's Emergency Law, which limited public gatherings and permitted the state to arrest and detain suspects without charge. Those detained were subjected to harsh treatment, including torture, by the security police. Corruption (in the form of tax evasion, bribery and theft) was rife and the wealth of the ruling elite was contrasted with the poverty of the masses, half of whom were estimated to live on $2 a day or less.

Protests commenced on 25 January 2011 (the 'Day of Anger'), when tens of thousands of Egyptians took to the streets of Cairo and other cities to demand an end to the rule of President Mubarak. The social media played an important role in orchestrating these events. Cairo's Tahrir Square became the focus of this and subsequent demonstrations. Attempts to stifle the scale of the protests by the use of security forces and of gangs of the President's supporters to physically assault demonstrators, and by seeking to prevent Internet access within the country in order to hinder their organisation failed. Mubarak made various attempts to alter the nature of his government by appointing a new cabinet and installing a vice president, but his insistence on remaining in office until the end of his term (even though he promised he would not run for a further term of office in September 2011) ensured the continuance of protests.

A statement by the military on 31 January that it recognised the legitimate demands of the protesters and would not use force against them made Mubarak's position untenable. He resigned on 11 February and transferred power to the Armed Forces of Egypt, which ruled the country through an 18-member council. This dissolved Parliament, suspended the constitution, lifted the emergency laws that had operated for 30 years and on 4 March 2011 appointed a civilian, Essam Sharaf, as Prime Minister.

Libya

Muammar Gaddafi took power in Libya in 1969. He sought to establish a 'new form of government whereby an Islamic state was ruled on socialist principles' (Coughlin, 2011), but this was characterised by authoritarian rule and the suppression of all dissent.

Protests in Libya began on 15 February 2011 outside the police headquarters in Benghazi following the arrest of the human rights lawyer

Fethi Tarbel, who represented the relatives of prisoners who had allegedly been massacred by security forces in Tripoli's Abu Salim jail in 1996. These protests (whose organisation was aided by social media sites) continued on subsequent days (including the 'Day of Rage' on 17 February) and the harsh reaction of the government towards them led to clashes between the security forces and demonstrators. The violence became escalated, transforming the protests into a civil war.

By 18 February, this city and other neighbouring towns in the east of the country were under the control of the opposition and attempts by the government to recapture the area (including the use of African mercenaries) proved unsuccessful. The remaining government pocket of resistance at the Katiba compound in Benghazi was overwhelmed on 20 February. The fighting spread to Misrata, which fell to the opposition forces on 23 February, and by the end of that month, significant parts of Libya were controlled by the opposition. A fierce battle for the control of Zawiya took place in February and March in which the government used air strikes and artillery barrages in an attempt to regain control of it.

The government launched a major counter-offensive operation in early March that involved the use of air strikes, artillery, tanks and amphibious landings against opposition-controlled areas. These assaults succeeded in recapturing a number of cities that had fallen into opposition hands, including Brega, Ajdabiya and Zuwetina. Benghazi was surrounded by government forces by the end of the month.

Although the Gaddafi regime may have ultimately been able to overcome opposition forces, the level of violence that was deployed prompted outside intervention. This proved crucial to the downfall of the regime. On 26 February, the United Nations Security Council passed a resolution that froze Gaddafi's assets, restricted the travel of Gaddafi and other key members of his regime, and referred the government's treatment of protesters to the International Criminal Court (ICC). On 27 June the ICC issued arrest warrants for Gaddafi, his son Saif al-Islam and his intelligence chief Abdullah al-Senussi on charges of crimes against humanity.

These international measures prompted the formation of the Libyan National Council (usually referred to as the Transitional National Council of Libya or the Transitional National Council). This was formed in Benghazi on 27 February 2011 to act as the political face of the revolution. It issued a statement on 5 March that it declared itself to be the legitimate government of Libya and was recognised on 10 March by France as the legitimate representative of Libya's people. The USA and the UK followed suit and recognised this body in July.

On 17 March, the United Nations Security Council adopted a resolution (1973) that imposed a 'no-fly zone over Libya' and authorised the use of 'all necessary measures' (United

Nations Security Council, 2011) to protect civilians. This prompted the government to declare an immediate ceasefire, although fighting continued and government forces entered Benghazi with tanks on 19 March. The government was also reported to have cut off water, electricity and communications in rebel-held Misrata, claims that were denied by the government.

On 19 March, a number of planes belonging to the French Air Force entered Libyan airspace and this formed the prelude to military intervention by a coalition of North Atlantic Treaty Organization (NATO) countries in which France, the UK and the USA played a prominent role. Initially, the USA controlled the no-fly-zone operations until these were taken over by NATO on 31 March. Libyan ground forces and military targets were attacked and NATO ships enforced a blockade of the country. By the end of the month, Libyan air defence systems and the Libyan Air Force had mostly been destroyed as a result of these attacks. The Libyan opposition also secured other forms of assistance from outside the country that included financial aid for humanitarian assistance and equipment that included fuel trucks, ambulances and medical equipment. Some weaponry and military advisors were also provided.

The military operations conducted by NATO forces enabled the opposition to commence ground operations against the Gaddafi regime, aided by air support provided by Coalition forces. Ajdabiya was captured on 26 March and the opposition subsequently took control of Brega, Ra's Lanuf and Bin Jawad. However, government counter-attacks regained control of much of this territory by the end of March and fierce fighting also occurred for the control of Misrata and Brega, which lasted into April. Claims were made of the government's use of cluster bombs. On 30 April, a NATO air strike hit the home of Gaddafi's youngest son and it was reported that he and three of Gaddafi's grandchildren were killed as a result. This event prompted Russia and China to express concerns that NATO had gone beyond the United Nations (UN) resolution's authorisation to take 'all necessary measures' to protect civilians. Following the attacks, mobs of Gaddafi supporters burned British and Italian embassies, a US consulate and a UN office, which led to the UN pulling its staff out of Tripoli.

A large number of air strikes were carried out by the Coalition forces in May, which included attacks mounted at targets in Tripoli, including one on Gaddafi's compound. These continued into June. Both sides to the conflict mounted offensive and counter-offensive actions, and for a time it seemed that a state of stalemate existed. However, aided by NATO air strikes, opposition forces made significant gains in August and advanced on Tripoli, forcing the Gaddafi family to leave their fortified compound. Tripoli was entered by opposition forces on 21

August. A number of other cities that included Tarhuna, Sirte (Gaddafi's home town) and Sabha remained under the control of government forces, but these were captured. Sirte fell on 20 October 2011 and Gaddafi and several other leading members of his regime were killed. The fall of Sirte marked the end of the war.

Yemen

Protests began in Yemen in January 2011. Although these were inspired by similar events elsewhere in the region, they were fuelled by a number of internal issues that included the desire for political reform, high levels of poverty and unemployment: 'Yemen is among the poorest countries in the world, with more than 40 percent of its 24 million people living below the poverty line. The country is beset by widespread unemployment, illiteracy, and a burgeoning youth population. It is running out of water as well as oil, one of its few sources of foreign exchange and state revenue' (Human Rights Watch, 2012: 13). The internal political situation was further complicated by the presence of Al-Qaeda (who had moved into the country following the closure of their training camps in Afghanistan and Pakistan) and the existence of a secessionist movement in the south of the country.

The trigger for protests occurred on 1 January 2011 when Parliament (which was dominated by the ruling party, the General People's Congress) supported an amendment to the constitution that would enable the President, Ali Abdullah Saleh, who had been in power since 1978) to stand for re-election following the end of his seventh term in office. This prompted concerns that he was proposing to remain in office indefinitely.

Major demonstrations in the capital city of Sana'a occurred in late January and early February, which called for the resignation of the President. One of these (held in Sana'a and Aden on 3 February) was termed the 'Day of Rage'. These street protests were joined by the parliamentary opposition and were repressed by the police. Initially, Saleh offered concessions that included a promise that he would not seek re-election in 2013 and reforms affecting welfare and taxation.

The resignation of Egypt's President Mubarak on 11 February prompted further protests against President Saleh, including events dubbed the 'Friday of Anger' on 18 February, the 'Friday of Rage' on 25 February and the 'Friday of No Return' on 11 March. These events involved tens of thousands of protesters in the major cities of Sana'a, Ta'izz and Aden, who clashed with supporters of the President and his party. Sit-ins took place in a number of cities in what were referred to as 'Change Square' protest camps.

These episodes were responded to by the security forces, the military (and pro-government gangs), resulting in the deaths of many protesters. In one event in Ta'izz on 29 May 2011, it was reported that 'state security forces and armed gangs converged on Freedom Square ... The attackers shot protesters with assault rifles. They set fire to protesters' tents. They stormed nearby hospitals and a medical tent filled with wounded protesters. Then they bulldozed the camp to the ground. By dawn, the forces had killed 15 protesters and wounded more than 260 others' (Human Rights Watch, 2012: 1). In total, 270 protesters and bystanders were killed from February to December in attacks by Yemeni security forces and pro-government assailants on demonstrations against Saleh and thousands more were injured (Human Rights Watch, 2012: 16).

These protests continued and became transformed into a civil war towards the end of May in which the opposition to the President was joined by army deserters and Hashid tribesmen (led by Sheikh Sadiq al-Ahmar) who confronted the President's security forces and militias that were loyal to him. Gunmen believed to be linked to Al-Qaeda seized the city of Zinjibar (the capital of Abyan Province) on 29 May following a battle with security forces. The civil war was characterised by the indiscriminate use of force by government forces against areas of the country that were controlled by the opposition.

Attempts from outside the country under the auspices of the Gulf Cooperation Council for Saleh to cede power were initially unsuccessful and on 3 June he and other officials were injured in an assassination attempt which forced him to go to Saudi Arabia for treatment. His Vice President, Abd Rabbuh Al-Hadi, governed in his place. In August the political opposition established a Transition Council.

Further demonstrations seeking the ousting of the President took place that included 'Mansouron Friday'. This involved tens of thousands of people. Clashes between rival military units and tribes loyal and hostile to Saleh occurred in Sana'a in September 2011.

On 12 September (whilst still in Saudi Arabia) Saleh signed a decree that authorised the Vice President to negotiate with the opposition and sign the Gulf Cooperation Council proposal. Following a call by the UN Security Council on 21 October for him to stand down, Saleh (who briefly returned to Yemen towards the end of September) signed a deal on 23 November with the parliamentary opposition whereby he would hand over his powers to the Vice President in return for immunity from prosecution for him and his family. In January 2012 Parliament adopted a law that gave Saleh immunity and also approved Vice President Abd Rabbuh Al-Hadi as the consensus candidate in the subsequent presidential election. This was held on 21 February 2012 and was won by the only candidate, the Vice President. Saleh resigned from office on 27 February, but remained Chairman of the General People's Congress, a position which enabled him to retain influence in the country. One example of this is that he will nominate members of his party who will take place in the National Dialogue, an assembly that will prepare a draft constitution and prepare the 2014 general elections (Alsarras, 2013).

Syria

Syria had been ruled by the Baathist regime since 1964, which was now headed by President Bashar al-Assad. The family derived from the Alawites, a branch of Islam that self-identifies with Shi'a Muslims in a country where around three-quarters of the population are Sunni Muslims. The latter population experienced high levels of poverty, with rises in the price of commodities and unemployment (especially among young people) being significant problems. The country had been governed by emergency rule from 1963 to 2011, enabling human rights to be sacrificed to the considerable powers exercised by the security forces. The Ba'ath Party was the only political organisation allowed to exist and although elections were held, they were not free.

Social and political conditions provided the background to the protests that began in January 2011. Local Coordinating Committees were formed to organise the protests against the regime. An opposition government in exile, termed the Syrian National Council, was organised in Istanbul in August 2011, although its influence both within and outside the country has been limited. This body merged with other opposition forces in November 2012 to form the National Coalition for Syrian Revolutionary and Opposition Forces. However, this failed to unite all aspects of the opposition, Islamic factions, for example, viewing it as Western-sponsored (Glass, 2012).

The assault and arrest by a police officer of a man in Old Damascus on 26 January 2011 triggered a relatively small-scale protest which called for the man's release. This action was followed by the arrest of 15 children in Daraa on 6 March for writing slogans that were critical of the government. This event also triggered protests against the arrest and abuse of the children. It has been observed that 'the movement started as protests calling for more freedom and dignity. The way the government handled the events since those first days drove more and more people to oppose President Bashar al-Assad'. However, 'at first, no-one was calling for the regime to fall' (Sinjab, 2013).

On 15 March, thousands of protesters took to the streets in a number of cities, with Suhair Atassi becoming the spokesperson for what became termed the 'Syrian Revolution'. Further demonstrations occurred in Damascus and other cities, calling for the release of political prisoners. These protests prompted Assad to dismiss his government, release political prisoners and lift the state of emergency. However, he also ordered the security forces to crack down on demonstrators, who he blamed on foreign influences.

On 18 April, 2011, around 100,000 demonstrated in Homs, calling for the President to resign. Protests continued, to which the government responded with coercive tactics that included arrests and the use of the military. Demonstrators had tear gas fired at them and some were shot. Although Assad made conciliatory gestures (which included the possibility of changing the constitution and ending the control wielded by the Ba'ath Party), this failed to halt protests and an armed opposition under the name of the Free Syrian Army (FSA) was formed by defecting Syrian Army officers in July 2011.

On 31 July 2011, Syrian Army tanks were used to quell disorder in a number of cities and more than 100 people were killed. This, however, failed to halt the protests, with an anti-government demonstration called 'God is with us' taking place on 5 August 2011. This resulted in a number of protesters being shot by the security forces. By the end of 2011, the violence reached the country's main cities of Damascus and Aleppo and escalated into a civil war in which areas of the country fell under the control of the FSA.

The violent response by the government to the protests prompted international concerns. Sanctions were imposed against the regime by the USA and the EU in April and August 2011, with the Obama administration calling on Assad to step down. An embargo on oil imports from Syria was imposed by the EU in September, and in November the Arab League imposed economic sanctions on the regime and voted to remove it from the League. Observers from the Arab League were allowed into the country in December, but they left after a month as a result of security concerns. A UN resolution that condemned the actions of the government was, however, vetoed by Russia and China in October 2011, and in January 2012, the same two countries vetoed a proposal by the Arab League for a diplomatic resolution to the conflict.

Early 2012 witnessed opposition attacks and government counterattacks. Government operations (which included bombarding opposition strongholds and massacring inhabitants when an area had been recaptured) resulted in large-scale loss of life – around 500 civilians were killed in one night (4 February) in the Homs province. In February, a peace plan supported by the former UN Secretary General Kofi Annan (who was acting as the UN's special envoy to Syria) was put forward, which was supported by both Russia and China. This, however, failed to halt the violence and Annan's visit to Damascus in March 2012 proved to be similarly unsuccessful in ending the fighting.

Although government forces continued to make progress against rebel-controlled areas during March 2012, they were not defeated and mounted hit-and-run operations of their own. This situation resulted in a ceasefire being declared in April 2012, although this was not rigidly adhered to and violence continued. Rumours that massacres were taking place began to surface in the middle of 2012, and in June the UN suspended its observer mission in the country.

In August 2012 large battles commenced in Aleppo in which government forces used air and artillery strikes in an attempt to drive the opposition from the city. The use of these tactics in densely populated urban areas created a major refugee problem. Also in August, Kofi Annan stepped down as the UN's special envoy to Syria and reports emerged that the USA was willing to offer various forms of support to the Syrian opposition. However, initiatives associated with the UN, including a General Assembly resolution in August calling on Assad to resign and other outside pressures (such as the Arab League giving Syria's seat to the opposition Syrian National Coalition in March 2013), did not resolve the conflict.

By early 2013, it was estimated that the death toll had reached 80,000, with many more people missing. Those fleeing the fighting were considerably in excess of one million. Additional accusations were made that protesters were subjected to imprisonment and torture by the government, although claims were also made of human rights abuses by the opposition. The regime's use of warplanes in rebel-occupied areas worsened the extent of suffering and in 2013, the government was accused of using chemical weapons such as sarin nerve gas against opposition-held areas (Lister, 2013), although this claim was not substantiated.

By mid-2013, there seemed to be little hope of the stalemate resolving itself. It appeared that the Assad regime would not be toppled by the weight of people power and events that included a demonstration in a rebel-occupied area of Damascus in May 2013 (at which protesters were shot at by FSA fighters) illustrated that the regime possessed some degree of popular support. However, it was also apparent that it was not able to totally extinguish the opposition forces. Outside military intervention was an unlikely occurrence and concerns regarding the nature (especially the sectarian orientation) and long-term aims of the groups opposing the regime limit the scope for associated measures such as providing arms to the rebels. However, the violence had considerable potential to destablilise the region.

The outbreak of violence in Syria soured its relationship with the neighbouring state of Turkey, which offered refuge to hundreds of thousands of civilians fleeing the violence and from where the Syrian National Council was created and out of which the FSA operates. Sanctions were imposed by Turkey against Syria and trade relations were broken off towards the end of 2011. In April 2012, shots were exchanged between Syria and refugee camps in Turkey, and a Turkish warplane was shot down by the Syrians in June. Artillery fire across the Turkish–Syrian border was exchanged in October, which prompted the Turkish Parliament to authorise military actions against

Syrian targets. Tensions between the two countries continued and in May 2013 two car bombs exploded in the border town of Reyhanli, killing 40 and leaving around 100 wounded. Turkey blamed this event on Syria.

Algeria

The stance adopted by the government towards other countries in the region facing popular dissent was to support the established governments in Libya and Syria. Although protests occurred in Algeria (for example, between young people and the police in December 2012 who were protesting against unemployment and the high price of food), these 'withered away when the regime made it clear it was not about to cave in to protester demands and the Algerian public had no appetite for confrontation since they were still convalescing from years of brutal civil war' (Hussain, 2013). Following the cancellation of the 1991 legislative elections, violence broke out between the Islamists and the government, in which 200,000 people were estimated to have been killed.

Political changes have taken place in the country in the wake of events elsewhere in the region, but have 'been internally driven, whether through outright and publicised challenges by reformist factions or internecine secret manoeuvring' (Abderrahmane, 2013). These changes included the removal of the Secretary General of the ruling National Liberation Front, Abdelaziz Belkhadem, by an internal party vote and the resignation of former Prime Minister Ahmed Ouyahia as Secretary General of the National Rally for Democracy, the country's second-largest political party, in 2013.

However, the extent to which Algeria is immune from the Arab Spring in the future is contestable. Although the country's governing party, the National Liberation Front, secured 48 per cent of the seats, it received only 17 per cent of the vote in the 2012 legislative elections. The main Islamic party, the Islamic Salvation Front, has been banned since 1992 and called upon its supporters to boycott the elections, the turnout for which was 43 per cent (Archy, 2012).

See also: post-Arab Spring, public disorder theories and models, whistleblowing

Sources and further reading

Abderrahmane, A. (2013) 'Algeria: Arab Spring or a Political Summer?', *AllAfrica*, http://allafrica.com/stories/201303050297.html?viewall=1 (date accessed 19 April 2014).

Alsarras, N. (2013) 'Yemen and the Arab Spring: Revolution on Hold', 26 February, http://en.qantara.de/Revolution-on-Hold/20726c502/index.html (date accessed 29 May 2014).

Archy, L. (2012) 'Algeria Avois the Arab Spring?', http://carnegieendowment.org/2012/05/31/algeria-avoids-arab-spring/b0xu (date accessed 29 May 2014).

Coughlin, C. (2011) 'Libya: Overthrowing Gaddafi Will Be Just the Beginning', *Daily Telegraph*, www.telegraph.co.uk/news/worldnews/africaandindianocean/libya/8716386/Libya-Overthrowing-Gaddafi-will-be-just-the-beginning.html (date accessed 19 April 2014).

Glass, C. (2012) 'Aleppo: How Syria is Being Destroyed', *New York Review of Books*, www.nybooks.com/articles/archives/2012/dec/20/aleppo-how-syria-being-destroyed/?pagination=false (date accessed 19 April 2014).

Human Rights Watch (2012) '"No Safe Places". Yemen's Crackdown on Protests in Taizz', www.hrw.org/sites/default/files/reports/yemen0212webwcover.pdf (date accessed 19 April 2014).

Hussain, G. (2013) 'After the Arab Spring: Algeria's Standing in the New World', *The Commentator*, www.thecommentator.com/article/3030/after_the_arab_spring_algeria_s_standing_in_a_new_world (date accessed 19 April 2014).

Lister, S. (2013) 'David Cameron: Proof Grows that President Assad Used Sarin in Syria's Civil War', *The Independent*, 8 May.

Marshall, A. (2013) 'Tunisia's Unfinished Revolution: From Dictatorship to Democracy?', *Truthout*, http://truth-out.org/news/item/14632-tunisias-unfinished-revolution-from-dictatorship-to-democracy (date accessed 19 April 2014).

Sinjab, L. (2013) 'Syria Conflict: From Peaceful Protest to Civil War', *BBC News, Middle East*, www.bbc.co.uk/news/world-middle-east-21797661 (date accessed 19 April 2014).

United Nations Security Council (2011) Security Council Resolution 1973 (on deploring the failure of the Libyan authorities to comply with resolution 1970 (2011)), 17 March, S/RES/1973, www.un.org/en/ga/search/view_doc.asp?symbol=S/RES/1973(2011) (date accessed 19 April 2014).

AUGUST RIOTS (ENGLAND) 2011

The shooting by the police in Haringey, London of Mark Duggan on 4 August 2011 and the police handling of this incident (especially communication with his family) triggered a disturbance in that locality. This set off a wave of riots across England between 6 and 10 August.

It was estimated that around 13,000–15,000 people were involved: 'in total more than 5,000 crimes were committed ... 1,860 incidents of arson and damage, 1,649 burglaries, 141 incidents of disorder and 366 incidents of violence against the person'. Five people lost their lives in the disturbances (Riots, Communities and Victims Panel, 2011: 11 and 24) and the cost of policing them amounted to £89.827 million (Home Affairs Committee, 2011: para. 57). Outside of Haringey, there was no one obvious incident that triggered these events, leading to suggestions that these episodes were 'copycat' events in which local people emulated activities taking place elsewhere in England.

The disorders took place against a background of recession and economic and social disadvantage that particularly affected young people. In England and Wales, 70 per cent of those brought before the courts were living in the 30 per cent most deprived areas of the country and of the children brought before the courts, two-thirds had special educational needs and the majority came from the 10 per cent lowest income areas (Riots, Communities and Victims Panel, 2011: 11 and 12): 'the median local authority where rioters came from was ranked 69th most deprived by employment, and 60th by income. Some 23 per cent of families in these areas suffer from three or more disadvantages, compared to nine per cent in the median authority area' (Riots, Communities and Victims Panel, 2012: 30).

It would thus appear that there was a link between deprivation and rioting (Riots, Communities and Victims Panel, 2011: 60) and that those who rioted were dissatisfied with their situation in a period of recession and the ever-growing gap between rich and poor. This problem was more acutely felt by younger people 'who had no hopes or dreams for the future' (Riots, Communities and Victims Panel, 2011: 14). However, ethnicity was not an underpinning of this sense of exclusion. Nationally the figure of those charged with offences during these events showed an almost even split of 46 per cent black and 42 per cent white (Ministry of Justice, 2011: 4).

Although deprivation was an important explanation of the disorders, many of those involved in them defined this in terms of exclusion from full participation in the consumerist society based upon 'a culture that has increasingly defined status through material possessions and the accumulation of possessions as worthy in its own right' (Unwin, 2011: 1). This was especially evident in the goods that were the targets of looters, whose actions suggested that they viewed the riots as an opportunity to acquire by looting and stealing the designer items ('Brands') that they could not otherwise afford. The prominent role played by looting in the 2011 disturbances led the Coalition government to argue that greed and criminality were again the root causes of these riots – the disaffected were judged to be those who either instigated or who took advantage of the disorders to further their existing criminal careers. This view might be justified by the arrest figures.

More than 4,000 suspected rioters were arrested by the police across England and Wales and most of those brought before the courts were males with previous convictions (the 'usual suspects'), three-quarters of whom were aged 24 or under. Initial figures by the Ministry of Justice relating to around 2,000 defendants brought before the courts in England and Wales by 12 October 2011 indicated that 76 per cent of defendants had a previous caution or conviction (80 per cent for adults and 62 per cent for juveniles). In total, these 2,000 offenders had committed almost 20,000 previous offences (Ministry of Justice, 2011). The remedy derived from this explanation was moral rather than structural – to seek to reconstruct the basis of the ideal society founded on the family, schools and work.

The government regarded gangs as a key contributor to the disorders – one in five of those arrested in connection with the riots were said to be known gang members (May, 2011: 3) who exerted 'a disproportionate and devastating impact' on some of the most deprived communities (I. Smith, 2011: 4). This prompted the government to put forward a cross-government approach to tackling gang and youth violence based upon providing support, prevention, pathways out, punishment and enforcement and partnership work (Home Office, 2011: 8–9).

However, the importance attached to gangs as an explanation for the disorders was disputed. The term lacks precise meaning (Home Affairs Committee, 2011: para. 20) and it was argued that most convicted rioters were not gang members (Riots, Communities and Victims Panel, 2011: 55). One expert pointed out that as the main purpose of gangs is to make money from selling drugs, the riots detracted from their core business since the police presence made it impossible to operate. It was concluded that rioters and gangs were not the same thing (Pitts, quoted in Castella, 2011).

A further explanation relating to organisation argued that this was provided by hardened criminals who used disorders as an opportunity to orchestrate looting and provide a means through which stolen goods could enter the black market economy.

Social media (which includes Facebook, Twitter and BlackBerry Messenger) was also stated to have played a part in encouraging the spread of disorder. This form of communication was used to mobilise peer groups and facilitate the rapid congregation of crowds. It was also used as a mechanism to disseminate information regarding police activities, warning youths to move away from areas that were well-protected by the police and go to others that were unguarded. The perceived contribution made by the social media to events in 2011 led to it being dubbed 'a game changer' for the police service (O'Connor, 2011).

The relationship between the police and young people was also put forward as a factor accounting for the disorders. In a study that involved interviews with 270 rioters, most respondents (85 per cent) stated that policing was either an 'important' or 'very important' factor to explain the riots: 'they repeatedly expressed frustrations about their daily interactions with the police, saying they felt hassled, bullied and complaining they were not treated as equals'. The focus of much of this resentment was the manner in which stop and search powers were used and the riots were seen as a chance to get back at the police (M. Smith, 2011: 2).

A final observation in connection with events in 2011 was that participants lacked common objectives, which also led to the conclusion that there was no single cause of these disorders (Riots, Communities and Victims Panel, 2011: 7 and 11). A report prepared for the Cabinet Office presented a typology of involvement in the events. It argued that the crowds involved contained diverse groupings that included watchers, rioters, looters, bystanders, protesters, retaliators, thrill-seekers, opportunists and sellers. It also pointed out that there was some movement between these categories – for example, a person who turned up simply to watch might opportunistically become a looter (Morrell *et al.*, 2011: para. 3).

The August 2011 riots highlighted two important issues for policing – how to prevent the loss of control of the streets and how to regain it once it is lost.

The most effective police tactic is to ensure that riots do not occur in the first place. Improved engagement with potentially disaffected communities is thus the pre-requisite to preventing episodes of this nature, using a partnership approach and involving community leaders. The use of stop and search powers remains an issue on which latent hostility between police and public can be based, and led to suggestions that police and communities should work together to improve the way in which these powers were used (Riots, Communities and Victims Panel, 2011: 71).

Rumour management also plays an important role in preventing rioting or limiting the extent of its spread if it breaks out. This was defective in the event that triggered the riots in Tottenham, where an 'information vacuum' was discerned in which 'unfounded reports by social media could gain currency' (Riots, Communities and Victims Panel, 2011: 11). One example of good practice was provided by the Greater Manchester Police, which used its Twitter account to provide authoritative reports regarding rumours that were circulating and to mobilise support for police actions.

Police tactics when disorder has broken out provide the potential for defusing or accelerating acts of violence. It was observed that 'a perception that the police could not contain the scale of rioting in Tottenham and then across London' was the key trigger to the spread of disturbances. 'Rioters believed that they would be able to loot and damage without being challenged by the police' (Riots, Communities and Victims Panel: 2011: 12). The Home Affairs Committee believed that the loss of control by the police of the streets was the 'single most important reason' in explaining the spread of the disorders (Home Affairs Committee, 2011: para. 47).

Regaining control of the streets once it has been lost is an issue high on the contemporary police agenda. In his evidence to the Home Affairs Committee on 29 November, Her Majesty's Chief Inspector of Constabulary, Denis O'Connor, suggested that tactics used to police demonstrations ('stand, hold and protect') needed to be augmented in riots that were characterised by mobile crowds ('flash-mobbing') by tactics that sought to 'disrupt and intercept'. One way to achieve this would be to utilise vehicles in an offensive manner. He also argued that devolved command might be a consideration to cope with mobile crowds (O'Connor, 2011).

The weaponry available to police disorderly crowds became an important aspect of future thinking. It was reported that the Metropolitan Police Service considered spending money on weaponry such as water cannons and training more officers in the use of baton rounds (now referred to as 'Attenuating Energy Projectiles') (Laville, 2011). There are, however, practical problems with the adoption of a more coercive approach to events of this nature. Water cannons would have been more or less useless against mobile crowds of the sort that appeared in many of the riot-affected areas, while the history of the use of baton rounds in Northern Ireland during the 'Troubles' indicated dangers arising from the use of such weaponry. This is a particular difficulty given the diverse make-up of crowds in August 2011, where bystanders rather than looters may have ended up severely injured by a ricochet from a weapon of this nature. The Home Affairs Committee concluded that water cannons and plastic bullets would have been an inappropriate as well as a dangerous response to events in 2011 (Home Affairs Committee, 2011: para. 32), although a report by Her Majesty's Inspectorate of Constabulary (HMIC) proposed that a new framework for resolving public disorder should include the rules of engagement for weaponry of this nature (HMIC, 2011: 5).

See also: Banlieue riots, Bradford riots (Manningham, Bradford) 1995, Broadwater Farm Estate riots (Haringey, London), 1985, copycat riots (England) 1981, G20 protests (London) 2009, public order policing (England and Wales)

Sources and further reading

Castella, T. (2011) 'England Riots: What's Behind the Evidence Gangs were Behind the Riots?', *BBC News Magazine*, 16 August, www.bbc.co.uk/news/magazine-14540796 (date accessed 22 April 2014).

Her Majesty's Inspectorate of Constabulary (2011) *The Rules of Engagement: A Review of the August 2011 Disorders*. London: HMIC.

Home Office (2011) *Ending Gang and Youth Violence: A Cross-Government Report including Further Evidence and Good Practice Case Studies*. London: TSO, Cm. 8211.

Home Affairs Committee (2011) *Policing Large Scale Disorder: Lessons from the Disturbances of August 2011*. Sixteenth Report of Session 2010–12. London: TSO, HC 1456-I.

Laville, S. (2011) 'Met Considers Buying Water Cannon', *The Guardian*, 30 November.

May, T. (2011) 'Ministerial Foreword' in Home Office' *Ending Gang and Youth Violence: A Cross-Government Report including Further Evidence and Good Practice Case Studies*. London: TSO, Cm. 8211.

Ministry of Justice (2011) *Statistical Bulletin on the Public Disorder 6th to 9th August 2011*, www.justice.gov.uk/publications/statistics-and-data/criminal-justice/public-disorder-august-11.htm (date accessed 22 April 2014).

Morrell, G., Scott, S., McNeish, D. and Webster, S. (2011) *The August Riots in England: Understanding the Involvement of Young People*. London: National Centre for Social Research, prepared for the Cabinet Office.

O'Connor, D. (2011) Evidence before the Home Affairs Committee, 29 November, www.publications.parliament.uk/pa/cm201012/cmselect/cmhaff/uc1456-viii/

uc145601.htm (date accessed 22 April 2014). This evidence was in the format of uncorrected evidence which was not a formal record of the proceedings of this Committee.

Riots, Communities and Victims Panel (2011) *5 Days in August: An Interim Report on the 2011 English Riots.* London: Riots, Communities and Victims Panel.

——. (2012) *After the Riots: The Final Report of the Riots, Communities and Victims Panel.* London: Riots, Communities and Victims Panel.

Smith, I. (2011) 'Ministerial Foreword' in Home Office, *Ending Gang and Youth Violence: A Cross-Government Report including Further Evidence and Good Practice Case Studies.* London: TSO, Cm. 8211.

Smith, M. (2011) 'Young People and the 2011 "Riots" in England – Experiences, Explanation and Implications for Youth Work', *Infed*, www.infed.org/archives/jeffs_and_smith/young_people_youth_work_and_the_2011_riots_in_england.html (date accessed 22 April 2014).

Unwin, J. (2011) *The Riots: What are the Lessons from JRF's Work in Communities?* York: Joseph Rowntree Foundation.

AUSTERITY PROTESTS (WORLDWIDE) 2010–13

Austerity measures are designed to reduce a country's budget deficit and are triggered when a government is unable to honour its debts. These have been put forward in the wake of the international debt crisis that has affected a number of nations since 2008.

Austerity measures are typically imposed by bodies external to the country that is seeking financial aid (in the form of 'bail-out loans') to stave off a nation's bankruptcy. These loans are administered by the International Monetary Fund (IMF), the European Central Bank (ECB) and the European Union (EU) (collectively termed the *troika*).

There are typically two aspects to austerity measures. They entail cuts in public spending through policies that include the reduced provision of public services and welfare benefits, wage cuts, pay freezes, redundancy and reforms to labour laws to make it easier to hire and fire workers. Austerity measures are also associated with rises in taxation through which governments seek to boost their income in order to reduce their level of indebtedness. These rises may embrace a wide range of taxes that include income tax, property tax, fuel duties and sales tax.

However, although austerity measures seek to enable a government to reduce its budget deficit, they may contribute to a contraction of the economy and underpin a range of social problems that include high levels of homelessness, poverty and unemployment. The latter is an especially serious problem in a number of European countries.

By 2013, the unemployment rate for the 17 countries that used the euro stood at 12 per cent, but in a number of countries was considerable higher than this: 27 per cent of the workforce was unemployed in Greece, 26 per cent in Spain, 18 per cent in Portugal and 14 per cent in Ireland. The young are especially affected by this problem: by the end of April 2013, around 5.6 million people below the age of 25 were unemployed across the EU and in some countries this problem was especially acute: at the beginning of 2013, youth unemployment stood at 59.1 per cent in Greece, 55.9 per cent in Spain, 38.4 per cent in Italy, 38.3 per cent in Portugal (*Guardian Online*, 2013).

Protests against austerity measures have occurred in a number of countries and have taken various forms that include strikes, demonstrations and occupations. The following sections provide a brief account of some of the major actions that have taken place in countries where protests of this nature have been particularly prevalent. It seeks to provide a snapshot of protests that took place between 2010 and 2013.

Greece

In May 2010, the Eurozone countries and the IMF agreed a €110 billion bail-out loan to Greece, to which a number of conditions were attached that included the introduction of austerity measures and the privatisation of government assets worth around €50 billion by 2015. A further loan was provided by the Eurozone leaders in October 2011, amounting to €130 billion, requiring the introduction of further austerity measures. This pattern was repeated in 2013 when austerity measures that included easier procedures to dismiss public sector workers were put forward to obtain additional bail-out funds.

Protests against tax raises and public spending cuts commenced in Greece on 5 May 2011. Further demonstrations organised by the 'Indignant Citizens' Movement' began on 25 May 2011 (Writers for the 99%, 2011: 205). Several hundreds of thousands of people were involved in the demonstration outside the Greek Parliament building in Athens on 5 June 2011 and sporadic protests continued until 7 August. Some of these events witnessed considerable violence involving both demonstrators and police, who were accused of using coercive tactics that included the excessive use of tear gas to break up crowds.

Austerity protests in Greece have since continued against the background of high unemployment and have included a number of general strikes, workers' sit-ins and demonstrations, such as a May Day general strike demanding an end to spending cuts and tax rises that was organised by the trade unions in 2013. Teachers' protests against austerity measures took place in September 2013 and later that month a 48-hour general strike by public sector workers occurred. In April 2014, a trade union-organised march in Athens opposing austerity measures was accompanied by a nationwide walkout of workers, which brought the country to a standstill. Government responses have included the use of emergency laws to get seamen and Athens Metro staff in Athens back to work in early 2013.

Portugal

In Portugal, the government sought to introduce austerity measures of its own in an attempt to avoid a bail-out loan. These triggered protests in March 2011, which were organised by a group that later took the name *Movimento 12 de Março* (12 March Movement). They occurred in a number of cities and primarily involved young people, whose involvement was secured through the use of the social media. The inability of the Prime Minister, José Sócrates, to secure the passage of his government's austerity budget, which included spending cuts and tax rises, led to him tendering his resignation on 23 March 2011. This action triggered legislative elections that were held in June 2011.

In the interim period, in May the government secured a bail-out loan from the EU and the IMF that amounted to €78 billion. This prompted further protests in Portugal and also meant that the new government that was formed after the elections (headed by Pedro Passos Coelho) was required (as a condition of the loan negotiated by the previous government) to implement austerity measures similar to those rejected by Parliament in March 2011. This situation ensured that austerity protests continued, including major demonstrations that took place in Lisbon and Porto in October 2011.

Austerity measures provoked protests which included major demonstrations throughout Portugal in September 2012. In February 2013 protests occurred in 24 of Portugal's cities that were organised by the country's largest trade union, the General Confederation of the Portuguese Workers (CGTP). Further protests occurred in Lisbon and around 20 other cities in March 2013, involving hundreds of thousands of demonstrators (Newlands, 2013). The participants of these protests were mainly young people, whose presence was facilitated by the use of social media by a group of activists known as *Que Se Lixe a Troika* ('Screw the Troika') and who viewed mass participation in protests as a motion of popular censure of the government.

The measures that were put forward by the government included steep tax rises and cuts in public spending. However, in April 2013, the Constitutional Court ruled some of the austerity measures put forward by the government to be illegal, which promoted the introduction of an alternative raft of proposals that included increasing the retirement age and making public sector employees work for an extra hour a day.

A further series of protests took place across the country, culminating in an anti-poverty march in Lisbon on 12 April 2013, which was organised by the CGTP. This was followed by a further event organised by the CGTP on 25 May in Lisbon, which called for the resignation of the government. Protests in the form of industrial action were threatened by the teaching unions during the national examination period in June 2013 and the CGTP called a general strike for 27 June in protest against austerity measures that included public sector pay cuts and the laying-off of employees.

The government sought to cut around 30,000 public sector jobs (from around a total of 500,000) in order to produce savings of around €4.7 million by the end of 2014. However, in August 2013, the Constitutional Court ruled that government proposals to make it easier to dismiss civil servants breached the job safety guarantees and thus were unconstitutional.

Protests occurred in November 2013 against the background of MPs approving the first reading of the Budget that contained additional austerity measures. This budget was finally approved later that month. Portugal left the bail-out in May 2014.

Spain

Spain's initial response to the economic crisis was to use national finances to recapitalise its banking system, which had been adversely affected by bad debts arising from the collapse of the housing market in 2008. This internal bail-out mechanism was termed the *Fondo de reestructuración ordenada bancaria* (the Fund for Orderly Bank Restructuring or FROB), which was initiated in 2009. However, the strain that this imposed on the country's finances forced the government to accept a loan of around €100 billion from the Eurozone countries that was negotiated in July 2012.

In Spain, protests sometimes referred to as the *indignados* ('the outraged') occurred in opposition to austerity measures that were initially imposed by the Spanish government in order to reduce public spending. These included cutting public wages, freezing salaries and pensions and raising the retirement age from 65 to 67. Protesters objected to the manner in which the economy was being run for the benefit of the banks rather than the people (Ainger, 2013). Major events occurred across Spain in May and June 2011 protesting against unemployment and cuts in social spending. In May, police efforts to clear protesters from Barcelona's Plaza de Cataluna included the firing of rubber bullets into the crowd.

Protests against austerity measures associated with conditions attached to the 2012 bail-out loan have since occurred throughout Spain, social networking playing a prominent role in mobilising demonstrators. In September 2012, the imminent announcement by the government of a new round of austerity measures triggered protests in which demonstrators formed a human chain around the Parliament building in Madrid. Their grievances included reductions in the salaries of public sector workers and cuts in the health and education budgets. They were confronted by around 1,500 police in riot gear who fired rubber bullets into the crowd and beat protesters with truncheons.

Further protests in Spain included marches that took place in a number of cities in February and March

2013, in which opposition to austerity cuts, tax rises, unemployment and the privatisation of public services was voiced. A political corruption scandal in Prime Minister Mariano Rajoy's Popular Party was an additional grievance that fuelled events in March 2013. The following month, demonstrators (who were mobilised under the slogan of 'besiege Congress') congregated outside the Spanish Parliament building in Madrid and called upon the government (which was about to announce a further raft of austerity measures) to resign. Around 1,400 police officers were used to quell the demonstration and responded to the bottles and rocks thrown at them by the crowd with batons and firing blank shots into the air.

Opposition to austerity measures continued into 2014, a major event being the rally in Madrid in March 2014, termed the 'march for dignity', which attracted terns of thousands of protesters from across Spain.

A new political party, *Partido X* (Party X), has emerged out of the *indignados* movement, offering the electorate radical progressive alternative to the economic policies pursued by the government (Gerbaudo, 2013). It polled 100,000 votes (0.64 per cent of the total votes cast) in the May 2014 elections for the European Parliament.

The severity of the financial crisis also had an adverse impact on the popularity of the monarch, Juan Carlos, who abdicated in June 2014 in favour of his son, Felipe.

Ireland

In Ireland, austerity measures occurred against a decision made by the government on 29 September 2008 when, following a run on Irish bank deposits, it guaranteed all deposits and liabilities in Irish banks. This decision to recapitalise the banks was initially estimated to cost €5.5 billion, but 'within two years, the bill was over €46 billion, tax receipts declined and a deficit of €20 billion opened in public finances. The state was effectively bankrupt' (Electoral Reform Society, 2011: 8). This required the government to seek a bail-out from the EU and the IMF, the price of which was a requirement to initiate austerity measures.

A large protest against austerity that was coordinated by the Irish Congress of Trade Unions took place in Dublin on 27 November 2010 following the announcement by the Prime Minister of a four-year package to cut spending (that included reductions in spending on welfare programmes and state pensions), reduce the number of public sector jobs and raise taxes. On 7 December, protesters clashed with police outside the Irish Parliament (the Dáil).

The association of austerity measures with the *Fianna Fáil* party cost it dearly in the 2011 general election, when its representation in the Dáil was cut from 78 seats to 20 and *Fine Gael* and Labour took power. The Green Party (which had governed in Coalition with *Fianna Fáil* until it withdrew from government in January 2011) lost its entire parliamentary representation.

Enda Kenny became the new Prime Minister. His mandate was to renegotiate the €85 billion loan that had been secured by the previous government. However, spending cuts and tax increases (and consequent high levels of unemployment) remained a feature of the new government's policies, although in April 2013, Eurozone Finance Ministers agreed to grant Ireland (and also Portugal) more time to repay their bail out loans.

Further austerity protests took place in Ireland, including marches and rallies that occurred in Dublin and five other cities on 9 February 2013. These protests occurred following a deal that the Irish government had reached with the ECB, which enabled the state to pay back the debts accrued by the defunct Anglo-Irish Bank over a lengthier period than had originally been agreed. A particular demand of the protesters was for the European authorities to deliver on an agreement to separate bank debt from sovereign debt.

Subsequent protests (such as that held on 13 April 2013) focused on opposition to the additional taxes that had been imposed by the government. These had given rise to the Campaign Against Household and Water Taxes, which organised this protest. This organisation (which made considerable use of the social media) used methods of protest that included civil disobedience (calling on householders to boycott the property tax forms that were distributed across Ireland in March 2013) and petitions.

Ireland left the bail-out in December 2013.

The UK

Whereas austerity measures in many countries were driven by supranational bodies, in the UK they were put forward by the Coalition government that was formed after the 2010 general election. This government proposed an austerity programme that was intended to significantly reduce, if not entirely eliminate, the nation's budget deficit by 2015. The measures that were put forward entailed major cuts in public spending, which translated into reductions in the number of workers employed throughout the public sector and a freeze on their pay.

Opposition to these measures was voiced from a number of quarters. The trade unions were concerned that workers were bearing the burden of cuts, while big business and financial institutions such as the banks (who they blamed for causing the crisis) were relatively immune from them, and many of their leading executives continued to benefit from large bonus payments. It was also believed that the pace with which spending cuts were being implemented was too rapid.

On 26 March 2011, the Trades Union Congress (TUC) organised a major demonstration in London which involved around 500,000 protesters. Although peaceful in character, the event witnessed episodes of violence by anti-capitalist protesters in central London entailing attacks on shops and the police. A further series of rallies took place on 30 June 2011 (termed J 30) across the country, accompanied by strike action organised by trade unions representing teachers and other public sector workers. A key concern was proposed changes to pensions that entailed basing them on a final salary as opposed to a career average.

An additional strike of public sector workers took place on 30 November 2011. It was organised by trade unions, but involved activists from other organisations such as Occupy London, who pursued direct action tactics which included storming the headquarters of the international mining company, Xstrata, to highlight the high salaries of company chief executives. Localised protests were also organised by unions such as Unison and the GMB, often in connection with measures pursued by local authorities to cope with spending cuts that included axing services and cutting jobs. Subsequent protests included the demonstration in London organised by the TUC in October 2012 that utilised the slogan 'A Future that Works'.

International austerity protests

Austerity protests have also taken an international dimension. On 14 November 2012, a Day of Action (or general strike) was coordinated across a number of countries by the European Trade Union Confederation in protest against the social and economic inequalities that were claimed to be arising from austerity measures. This event also entailed the use of other forms of protest that included demonstrations. Spain and Portugal (both of which had experienced high levels of unemployment) were at the forefront of these events and confrontations between police and protesters took place in cities such as Lisbon, Barcelona and Madrid (where police fired rubber bullets into the crowd). In Italy, students played a prominent role in actions that included marches, occupations and blockades.

Related protests

The austerity protests have also inspired other campaigns against the operations of the global financial system. These include the Occupy movement, which was initiated in New York in September 2011 and which gave rise to the Blockupy movement in Europe. In the UK, the UK Uncut movement has been prominent in protests against tax avoidance by large commercial and financial concerns. Student protests that have taken place in a number of countries have also been in response to the impact of austerity measures on education, especially higher education.

See also: anti-globalisation/anti-capitalist protests (UK), Occupy movement, riots, states of emergency, riots, student protests (England) 2010

Sources and further reading

Ainger, K. (2013) 'In Spain They are All *Indignados* Nowadays', *The Guardian*, 28 April.

Electoral Reform Society (2011) *The Irish General Election 2011*. London: Electoral Reform Society of Great Britain and Ireland.

Gerbaudo, P. (2013) 'Why it's Time to Occupy the State', *The Guardian*, 10 December.

Guardian Online (2013) 'Youth Unemployment in Europe – How is it Affecting You?', 7 May, www.guardian.co.uk/world/2013/may/07/youth-unemployment-europe-your-experiences (date accessed 22 April 2014).

Newlands, P. (2013) 'Portuguese Protesters Take to the Streets over Austerity Measures', *Sunday Times*, 3 March.

Writers for the 99% (2011) *Occupying Wall Street: The Inside Story of an Action that Changed America*. New York: OR Books.

B

BANLIEUE RIOTS (PARIS) 2005

In 2005 France was rocked a series of riots (*émeutes*). While unprecedented in scale, these disturbances were not in any significant unparalled (Hargreaves, 2005; Hamidi, 2009: 140). Violence in the suburbs and the isolation of French youths are not new phenomena (Cesari, 2005) and 'there have been similar disorders in disadvantaged urban areas containing dense concentrations of ethnic minority populations (neighbourhoods generally referred to as the *banlieues* – a term which is defined below) since the late 1970s' (Hargreaves, 2005).

In 1981, a police raid in the Cité de la Cayolle in Marseilles resulted in a number of women, children and elderly residents being injured. In response, young male residents fire-bombed the shopping centres and police stations throughout the area. Also in 1981, a series of violent confrontation between young males and the police occurred in the Lyon suburb of Les Minguettes (Lyon) in 1981. Here, 'In an estimated 250 separate incidents generally referred to as "rodeos" by their participants, groups of young men would steal a car, engage police in a chase, and then abandon and burn the vehicle' (Silverstein and Tetreault, 2006). This was done in the glare of television crews (Body-Gendrot, 2013: 8). Further violence occurred in this district in 1983 and in neighbouring Venissieux (Lyon), leading to the week-long occupation of the housing project by a regiment of 4,000 police officers. These events gave rise to social reform policies directed at disadvantaged neighbourhoods, an approach termed *politique de la ville.*

These events continued in the 1990s and were characterised by confrontations between local youths and the police. It has been observed that: 'By the 1990s, such confrontations began to take on a regular, if generally contained, character' (Silverstein and Tetreault, 2006). These included clashes between youths and the *Compagnies Républicaines de Sécurité* (the CRS or riot police) in November 1990 in the Mas-du-Taureau *cité* of the Lyonnais suburb of Vaulx-en-Velin after the death of one resident, 21-year-old Thomas Claudio, in a motorcycle chase with police. Previous events of this nature served to 'contribute to the infernal spiral of social marginalization and the racialization of their residents as "other". To a great extent, the current violence needs to be understood as the logical extension of such earlier, localized incidents' (Silverstein and Tetreault, 2006).

The disorders that occurred in 2005 form the focus of the account below. These questioned the health of French society, which was revealed to have 'a crisis of citizenship and of unity, the very kinds of problems it believed that its republican ideology immunized it against' (Suleiman, 2005).

On 27 October 2005, two youths of Turkish, Malian and Tunisian descent (17-year-old Zyed Benna and 15-year-old Bouna Traoré) were electrocuted (and another, Muhuttin Altun, was seriously injured) by an electric transformer as they hid from police in order to avoid being subjected to a police ID check. This incident occurred in the eastern Parisian suburb of Clichy-sous-Bois. This led to intermittent rioting over the following two nights, which eventually subsided, and a peaceful protest march then took place. However, more prolonged violence was triggered three nights later when a tear-gas canister fired by the police landed at the entrance to a mosque in Clichy. The police were accused of disrespecting Islam and large-scale violence then broke out, initially in a number of localities north of Paris and then more widely throughout the Paris region (Body-Gendrot, 2013: 13).

Subsequently, the violence spread to the rest of the country (including Toulouse, Lille, Bordeaux and Lyon) and involved 274 localities, which included middle-sized cities with deprived neighbourhoods (Body-Gendrot, 2013: 13). These events caused the government to declare a state of emergency on 7 November, which covered around one-quarter of France. The 2005 riots witnessed '18 nights of destructive violence' (Body-Gendrot, 2013: 13) and resulted in over €200 million of damage, including to buildings, schools and cars. One person (a bystander) was killed in these events and around 3,000 rioters were arrested in nearly 100 municipalities across France. Around 9,000 vehicles were torched during the disturbances (Silverstein and Tetreault, 2006), and in total some 70,000 incidents of urban violence were committed after January 2005 (Withol de Wenden, 2005).

A profile of these disorders suggested that they constituted a 'youth underclass uprising from destitute neighbourhoods. Rioters are youngsters (and males), between 12 and 25 years old; roughly half of the arrested people are under 18' (Roy, 2005). Those involved in the riots were mainly second- and third-generation unemployed ethnic-minority teenagers, principally of North African heritage and mainly Muslims, who were housed in suburban government-sponsored low-income housing projects, *Habitation à Loyer Modéré* (HLMs), located in the *banlieues* (a term which means 'suburbs' and which are not always impoverished neighbourhoods). The HLMs were constructed during the 1950s, but had become 'a formidable trap for immigrant populations and their children' (Cesari, 2005) whose spatial segregation from mainstream French society had been aggravated by a process of white flight from these areas after the 1970s. Segregation was a key issue affecting persons of African origin who lived in these deprived areas (Lagrange, 2009: 121). Specific locations within the *banlieues*, (termed *cités* or housing estates) were the focus of the 2005 disorders.

The context within which these disorders occurred is important to any analysis of their causes. Deindustrialisation and the economic downturn that started in the 1970s contributed towards the marginalisation of those living in the *cité*. This has been exacerbated by fiscal reforms arising from France's participation in the European Monetary Union, 'reforms that have slashed the social welfare budget and the funding for neighborhood associations, after-school programs, community policing, and internships' (Silverstein and Tetreault, 2006). This averse climate was aggravated by the Interior Ministry's 'hard-line policies towards urban crime and more recent "war on terror"', which since the mid-1990s had 'resulted in the de facto militarization of the housing projects, with national riot police and military gendarmes conducting repeated sweeps for suspected terrorists, closing down basement prayer rooms, detaining and deporting undocumented immigrants, performing millions of "random" identity checks on local youth occupying public spaces, and even arresting residents for congregating in the entryways of their own buildings' (Silverstein and Tetreault, 2006).

Consequently, 'the French state has come to be equated with repression in the minds of many *cité* inhabitants' (Silverstein and Tetreault, 2006), a view reinforced by the March 2005 ban on Muslim headscarves and other 'ostensible' religious symbols in public schools.

One feature of the riot-affected areas was the existence of multiple deprivations. These areas evidence 'academic failure, delinquency, drug use, and the highest rate of youth unemployment in all of Europe'. Particular attention was drawn to the 'obscenely low employment rate of the young in France, and especially of low-skilled young men' (Salanié, 2006). Unemployed rates for those aged 15–24 in the places affected by riots included '41.1% in the Grande Borne neighborhood in Grigny, 54.4% in La Revnerie and Bellefontaine in Toulouse, 31.7% in L'Ousse de bois in Pau, 37.1% in the Grand ensemble of Clichy-sous-bois/Montfermeil, 42.1% for Bellevue in Nantes/Saint Herblain' (Poupeau, 2006). These areas were characterised by the absence of opportunities for social mobility (Hargreaves, 2005) and geographical immobility. They constitute 'dormitory towns' physically separated from the main cities whose 'lack of shops, cultural spaces, cafés, etc., means that the HLM are places devoid of what constitutes communal city life' (Cesari, 2005). The lack of local capital for inward investment along with overcrowding and physical dilapidation caused by the demolition of uninhabitable properties that have not subsequently been replaced further worsened this situation (Silverstein and Tetreault, 2006).

However, it has also been argued that poverty per se should not be exaggerated, since some who live in these areas often have 'expensive clothing, *iPads*, and sometimes new cars' (Roy, 2005). This may suggest that factors that include employment discrimination ('young Algerians who spent time in college are four times less likely to have an executive job than comparable French men' and 'it is ... more difficult for teenagers born from immigrants to obtain and keep a job': Salanié, 2006), relative deprivation or the inability to fully participate in a consumerist economy are important underpinnings to the violence – those involved 'want to be part of the consumer society, even as predators' (Roy, 2005).

In addition, rioting did not occur in all areas of deprivation (whatever indicators are used to measure it), which suggested that local conditions were of importance either in encouraging such activities to occur or acting as restraining influences to prevent them from breaking out. An example of the former is 'the importance of street culture and gangs in triggering specifically masculine forms of action' (Poupeau, 2006). Gangs consisting of *'bandes'* or 'groups' were commonplace in areas that experienced disorder. These were 'based on neighbourhood identity and a loose affiliation with a hard core nucleus of local *"caïds"* or leaders; they don't recruit beyond the neighbourhood' (Roy, 2005). The influence wielded by these gangs helped to explain differences in terms of the scale of disorders that took place in localities with a similar demographic profile (Mohammed, 2009: 162). Moreover, factors that include the existence of formal structures through which local concerns could be channelled (including involvement in urban renewal schemes; Epstein, 2009: 132) could reduce the potential for the outbreak of violence and the presence of 'go-betweens' could help to minimise the extent of disorder once it had broken out (Kokoreff, 2009: 153).

Accordingly, it has been argued that 'the underlying issues were far more complex, involving social and economic exclusion, racial discrimination, and most importantly the capacity of the French Republic to respond to these challenges while maintaining its distinctive model of and formal commitment to the social integration of individuals, no matter what their color or creed' (Sahlins, 2006). Cultural inequality in which 'an Arab or Muslim background becomes a symbol over-determined with all the negative imagery built up over decades of colonialism' reinforced social marginalisation and translated into 'institutionalized discrimination in areas such as housing, employment, educational opportunities, and political representation' (Cesari, 2005).

Political marginalisation accompanying spatial segregation was also put forward as an explanation of disorder. It was suggested that the national urban renewal programme that began in 2003 and sought to restructure the most deprived neighbourhoods and attract new populations by carrying out major work on housing illustrated this problem, since although residents were asked to give their consent to the projects, they were not always actively involved in their subsequent development, which might be perceived as seeking to expel residents from their areas. This perhaps served to reinforce the 'distrust felt by the people towards public authorities who appeared to be refusing to listen to them' and created a breeding ground for the riots (Epstein, 2009: 128 and 132–3).

Race and culture featured prominently in explanations put forward by the government to explain the outbreak of violence in 2005. It has been argued that: 'Since the 1980s right-wing and centrist politicians have deliberately blamed French children of immigrants for their purported failure to integrate as a means of mobilizing conservative voters and deflecting responsibility for social inequities' (Silverstein and Tetreault, 2006). It was thus unsurprising that the response of the centre-right government to these events sought to criminalise the violence (Kokoreff, 2009: 148) and adopt an uncompromising, zero-tolerance attitude towards it. The Interior Minister, Nicolas Sarkozy, spoke of 'racaille' (scum) and 'promised to clean popular areas from delinquency with a Karcher' (Wieviorka, 2005). The time-honoured French police strategy of 'space saturation techniques' in riot-affected areas as opposed to 'negotiation, mediation and prevention' (Mouhanna, 2009: 175) was compatible with the government's desire to solve social problems through coercive means.

A state of emergency was declared on 7 November 2005. This measure was dubbed the 'last-ditch instrument of colonial governance' (Silverstein and Tetreault, 2006) and gave prefects the ability to impose curfews within their regions, as well as enabling the Interior Minister to close public spaces and permit search-and-seizures, house arrests and impose press censorship. It was initially imposed for 12 days and was later (on 15 November) extended for a further period of three months. The government's view was to associate rioting with Muslim separatism, illegal immigration and polygamous practices, echoing a view that 'suburban youth are ... a threat: a dangerous social class made up of people who do little but steal and engage in all sorts of illegal activity' (Cesari, 2005). Sentiments of this nature reflected the view that the state bore no responsibility for these events, which were caused by the chosen habits and lifestyles of those who engaged in them.

Orchestration by radical Islamists was put forward as a reason for these disturbances. However, the role of Islamic militancy in the riot-affected areas was questioned, for although the disappearance of the *Beur* associations (which were set up with official financial support in the 1980s in the wake of the youth marches to neutralise further outbreaks of violence) created space for religious figures to exert influence, conservative religious groups associated with the Tabligh or Salafi sects 'are not generally popular among the youth of the suburbs. The proof is given by the rioters themselves, whose actions were in no way motivated by the orders of religious authorities' (Cesari, 2005). In particular, it has been argued that conservative religious groups 'advocate living aloof from mainstream society, and precisely reject the main motivations of the young rioters (they don't push for full citizenship, they don't support claims like non-discriminatory access to night-clubs and they request youth to reject Western "street culture")' (Roy, 2005). Although it was conceded that 'certain religious figures or groups who specifically target young people ... may potentially serve to create an atmosphere of hate and frustration in the suburbs' (Cesari, 2005), it was concluded that the violence was not underpinned by religious motives and that the aim of those involved was to 'collectively express their resentment and frustration regarding social inequalities, their desire for dignity, and the denial of equality of rights and opportunities' (Withol de Wenden, 2005).

The view that the disorders constituted protests against the many forms of injustices suffered by those who resided in the *banlieus* suggests that these events were purposeful in the sense that they 'functioned as a kind of a catalyst for facing many injustices encountered by a significant number of French youth when they live in suburbs: violence from the police, racism, law and order policy, anti-Muslim feelings' (Dufoix, 2005). In particular, the failure to meaningfully tackle racial discrimination has been cited as a key source of the 'simmering unrest' which has characterised the *banlieues* since the late twentieth century (Hargreaves, 2005). In this sense, these riots were 'meaningful to those involved ... they represented profound feelings of injustice and a collective demand for respect' (Kokoreff, 2009: 147).

However, the extent to which these outbreaks constituted a meaningful form of protest has been questioned – 'another feature of the riots is ... the complete absence of claim-making by the rioters as well as the non-existence of any kind of organized movement advocating the right to speak for them ... It seems that any interpretation of the situation in terms of a social movement, or of a revolt, or even a revolution, is questionable, for it lacks the expression of any articulated voice' (Dufoix,

2005). The violence in 2005 might thus be understood more in terms of a negative response to social injustices: 'The issue at stake ... is the actual violent (re)appropriation of a territory by young people who, perhaps more than protesting against their being marginalized in society, just show their rejection of the order of society and demonstrate violently that their place is not society, but the neighborhood over which they claim some kind of power' (Dufoix, 2005).

In the wake of the 2005 disorders, the government announced a series of measures that were designed to improve job and other opportunities in the *banlieues*, although it was unclear whether these constituted new forms of state activity or an acceleration of existing programmes (Hargreaves, 2005). The creation of a new agency to help city mayors tackle poverty and discrimination was announced and a new type of national voluntary service was created, which was open to youths in the *banlieues* (Hargreaves, 2005). However, a pessimistic later assessment argued that despite the expenditure of $57 billion over the past decade to raise living conditions and employment in the *banlieues*, 'the situation in places like Clichy-sous-Bois looks even dimmer today than it did when rioting began in 2005' (Crumley, 2012).

Similarly, the French legal system has also moved slowly to provide justice for the families of the two youths who were killed in 2005. Two officers were subsequently charged with 'non-assistance to a person in danger' – an obligation placed on all French citizens. However, no speedy trial took place and in 2010 the regional prosecutor's office tried (unsuccessfully) to get the charge dropped on the grounds that there was insufficient evidence that the officers knew the youths were hiding in the power sub-station where they died (Le Roux, 2010). Further attempts were made to get the trial dropped, but in October 2012, France's highest court ruled that it should go ahead. In the meantime, the officers involved were not suspended from duty and were not subject to any disciplinary procedures. This trial had not proceeded by the beginning of 2014.

Civil unrest in the *banlieues* has frequently occurred since 2005. It flared up, for example, on 1 October 2006 in the Parisian suburbs of Les Mureaux and Yvelines, again as a result of an incident with the police. In 2010, a crowded bus was attacked in the suburb of Tremblay-en-France by a gang of hooded youths, who threw Molotov cocktails at it. This followed a successful drugs raid by the police in the area.

On 19 July 2013, riots broke out in Trappes, a *banlieue* of Paris. This was triggered by an assault made by a man (who was subsequently arrested) on a police officer who tried to make an identity check on his wife who was wearing a Muslim full-face veil (the wearing of which, in public places, became illegal by a law passed in 2010). This was the first time that this ban had resulted in an occurrence of violence. The riot saw the police station attacked in an attempt to free the arrested man and the burning of bus shelters and cars. Rioting spread to other areas, including Guyancourt, Maurepas and Elancourt. It was observed that this event was caused by police ID checks, a procedure which the socialist government had intended to reform but then shied away from because of opposition from the French police unions. Until this practice is drastically reformed, 'relations between the police and a part of the French population will remain execrable. And with the certainty of more riots' (Arun, 2013).

See also: August riots (England) 2011, Islamic terrorist groups, kettling (containment), public order policing (France), riots, states of emergency

Sources and further reading

Arun, (2013) 'The Trappes Riot', *Arun with a View*, 26 July, http://arunwithaview.wordpress.com/2013/07/26/the-trappes-riot (date accessed 25 April 2014).

Body-Gendrot, S. (2013) 'Urban Violence in France and England: Comparing Paris (2005) and London (2011)'. *Policing and Society: An International Journal of Research and Policy* 23(1): 6–25.

Cesari, J. (2005) 'Ethnicity, Islam, and Les Banlieues: Confusing the Issues', *SSRC Riots in France*, http://riotsfrance.ssrc.org/Cesari (date accessed 25 April 2014).

Crumley, B. (2012) 'The Problem of Clichy: After 2005 Riots, France's Suburbs are Still Miserable', *Time World*, http://world.time.com/2012/12/07/the-problem-of-clichy-after-2005-riots-frances-suburbs-are-still-miserable (date accessed 25 April 2014).

Dufoix, S. (2005) 'More than Riots: A Question of Spheres', *SSRC. Riots in France*, http://riotsfrance.ssrc.org/Dufoix (date accessed 25 April 2014).

Epstein, R. (2009) 'Urban Renewal+ Riot Revival? The Role of Urban Renewal Policy in the French Riots', in D. Waddington, F. Jobard and M. King (eds), *Rioting in the UK and France: A Comparative Analysis*. Cullompton: Willan Publishing.

Hamidi, C. (2009) 'Riots and Protest Cycles: Immigrant Mobilisation in France, 1968–2008', in D. Waddington, F. Jobard and M. King (eds), *Rioting in the UK and France: A Comparative Analysis*. Cullompton: Willan Publishing.

Hargreaves, G. (2005) 'An Emperor with No Clothes?', *SSRC. Riots in France*, http://riotsfrance.ssrc.org/Hargreaves (date accessed 25 April 2014).

Kokoreff, M. (2009) 'The Political Dimension of the 2005 Riots' in D. Waddington, F. Jobard and M. King (eds), *Rioting in the UK and France: A Comparative Analysis*. Cullompton: Willan Publishing.

Lagrange, H. (2009) 'The French Riots and Urban Segregation' in D. Waddington, F. Jobard and M. King (eds), *Rioting in the UK and France: A Comparative Analysis*. Cullompton: Willan Publishing.

Le Roux, G. (2010) 'Five Years after Riots, Paris Suburb is a Neglected Powder Keg', *France 24 International News*, www.france24.com/en/20101027-2005-riots-paris-suburbs-neglected-powder-keg-clichy-sous-bois-france (date accessed 25 April 2014).

Mohammed, M. (2009) 'Youth Gangs, Riots and the Politicisation Process' in D. Waddington, F. Jobard and M. King (eds), *Rioting in the UK and France: A Comparative Analysis*. Cullompton: Willan Publishing.

Mouhanna, C. (2009) 'The French Police and Urban Riots: Is the National Police

Force Part of the Problem or Part of the Solution?' in D. Waddington, F. Jobard and M. King (eds), *Rioting in the UK and France: A Comparative Analysis*. Cullompton: Willan Publishing.

Poupeau, F. (2006) 'French Sociology under Fire: A Preliminary Diagnosis of the November 2005 "Urban Riots"', *SSRC. Riots in France*, http://riotsfrance.ssrc.org/Poupeau (date accessed 25 April 2014).

Roy, O. (2005) 'The Nature of the French Riots', *SSRC Riots in France*, http://riotsfrance.ssrc.org/Roy (date accessed 25 April 2014).

Sahlins, P. (2006) 'Civil Unrest in the French Suburbs', *SSRC. Riots in France*, http://riotsfrance.ssrc.org (date accessed 25 April 2014).

Salanié, B. (2006) 'The Riots in France: An Economist's View', *SSRC. Riots in France*, http://riotsfrance.ssrc.org/Salanie (date accessed 25 April 2014).

Silverstein, P. and Tetreault, C. (2006) 'Postcolonial Urban Apartheid', *SSRC. Riots in France*, http://riotsfrance.ssrc.org/Silverstein_Tetreault (date accessed 25 April 2014).

Suleiman, E. (2005) 'France: One and Divisible', *SSRC. Riots in France*, http://riotsfrance.ssrc.org/Suleiman (date accessed 25 April 2014).

Wieviorka, M. (2005) 'Violence in France', *SSRC. Riots in France*, http://riotsfrance.ssrc.org/Wieviorka (date accessed 25 April 2014).

Withol de Wenden, W. (2005) 'Reflections "À Chaud" on the French Suburban Crisis', *SSRC. Riots in France*, http://riotsfrance.ssrc.org/Wihtol_de_Wenden (date accessed 25 April 2014).

BATTLE OF THE BEANFIELD (WILTSHIRE, ENGLAND) 1985

The Battle of the Beanfield refers to an event that occurred on 1 June 1985, when police in Wiltshire (England) prevented a convoy of around 140 vehicles containing a group of around 600 New Age travellers (a description applied to a diverse range of groups that included peace protesters, green activists and festival-goers) from setting up the 12th Stonehenge Free Festival at Stonehenge. Many of those in the convoy were women and children. Police actions sought to enforce a High Court (at the request of the custodians of Stonehenge, English Heritage) injunction that imposed a four-mile exclusion zone around the site.

The police presence consisted of around 1,300 officers drawn from six counties and from the Ministry of Defence Police. They established a roadblock around seven miles from Stonehenge at a location called Shipton Bellinger. This forced the vehicles to stop and what was effectively an ambush was followed by attacks by the police on the vehicles. Most of the convoy moved into an adjacent field and a subsequent police operation to arrest all members of the convoy (on the presumption that they intended to defy the High Court exclusion zone) resulted in many of its members attempting to escape through a location known as the Beanfield. This was unsuccessful and resulted in the arrest of most convoy members and the destruction of most of the vehicles. The 537 arrests constituted the most arrests that had taken place in a single day since 1945.

The main significance of the event was the degree of violence displayed by the police towards members of the convoy and their vehicles. This was perhaps partly founded on inaccurate police intelligence that indicated the travellers were armed with a variety of weapons. One reporter at the scene recorded that their actions constituted 'some of the most brutal police treatment of people that I've witness in my entire career as a journalist' (Sabido, 1985). Another journalist at the scene stated that the police 'were like flies around rotten meat ... there was no question of trying to make a lawful arrest. They crawled all over, truncheons flailing, hitting anybody they could reach. It was extremely violent and very sickening. The number of people who have been hit by policeman, clubbed whilst holding babies in their arms in coaches around this field, has yet to be counted' (Davies, cited in Thompson, 1985). Many of the officers who were involved in the violence wore riot gear without identification numbers.

Further confrontations between the police and new age travellers occurred in the New Forest, Hampshire, in 1986 and the Battle of the Beanfield became the forerunner of further attacks on the gypsy and travelling community of which the Dale Farm evictions in 2011 provide a relatively recent example. It also set in motion legislation such as the Criminal Justice and Public Order Act 1994, which was designed to restrict the ability of groups of people from freely gathering. However, new forms of protest underpinned by the desire of large numbers of people to reject the values of mainstream society and to live their lives according to alternative moral standards emerged in new directions that included grassroots environmentalism, the acid house movement, rave culture and opposition to globalisation.

In 1990, 21 members of the 1985 convoy were successful in an action taken against Wiltshire Police for wrongful arrest, assault and criminal damage. They received £24,000 in damages, but the judge refused to grant them costs. In 1999, the Law Lords ruled the exclusion zone that had been annually imposed around the area of Stonehenge illegal.

See also: counterculture protest, Dale Farm evictions (Essex, England) 2011, environmental protest groups, public order legislation (England and Wales), public order policing (England and Wales)

Sources and further reading

Sabido, K. (1985) quoted in Maconie, S. (2014) *The People's Songs: The Story of Modern Britain in 50 Records*. London, Ebury Press, p. 355.

Thompson, T. (2005) 'Twenty Years After, Mystery Still Clouds the Battle of the Beanfield', *The Observer*, 12 June.

Worthington, A. (ed.) (2005) *The Battle of the Beanfield*. Teignmouth: Enabler Publications.

BATTLE OF THE BOGSIDE (DERRY, NORTHERN IRELAND) 1969

The Bogside was a Catholic enclave in the city called Londonderry by superseded the more moderate Derry Citizens' Action Committee, which was associated with but was not part of the NICRA (Scarman, 1972: para. 1.16). The most important of these subsequent events was the march of the Apprentice Boys of Derry on 12 August.

The march in Derry was preceded by outbreaks of sectarian violence in Belfast, which led senior police officers there to conclude that the RUC could not contain further serious outbreaks of violence in the city and that the time had come to call in the Army (Scarman, 1972: para. 1.18). The Northern Irish Minister for Home Affairs refused to ban the march. The DCDA asked the Apprentice Boys to cancel or re-route the march, but they refused to do so. The march (which involved thousands of Apprentice Boys) went through Derry city centre and although it did not pass through the Bogside, it went close to the edge of it. Lines of RUC officers were deployed, facing the Nationalist community, suggesting that they viewed their role to be that of defending the marchers. It has been observed that 'there is no question that the Catholic crowd behind the crush barriers was hostile to the march. They resented what they regarded as official hypocrisy in banning a series of civil rights marches while declining to interfere with a Protestant march' (Stetler, 1970).

Violence broke out at the junction of Waterloo Place and William Street. Taunts between Loyalists and Bogsiders escalated into the throwing of missiles. Although those initially involved from the Bogside were branded as 'young hooligans' (Scarman, 1972: para. 1.19), their actions unleashed the pent-up feelings of many in the crowd that the stewards were unable to control. The police came under attack and were pelted with stones and Molotov cocktails. Initially the violence was contained to this area, but it spread to other areas of the Bogside.

The Apprentice Boys' Parade lasted for around two hours and then dispersed peacefully, but by then the violence was spiralling out of control and was spreading to other areas in the Bogside. The action of the Bogsiders was coordinated, with the DCDA playing a prominent role, although the involvement of many of the protesters was a spontaneous reaction to the events as they unfolded, fearing that actions undertaken by the police and Loyalists constituted an attack on their community. One aspect of this response was the existence of pre-prepared barricades, which the police tried to remove with armoured cars. Loyalist gangs were also involved in this violence in support of police actions to clear the barricades and they also attacked Nationalist homes in the area. Their motivation for involvement was a perception that the violence was an IRA plot designed to overthrow the Northern Irish state. The extent to which the police welcomed their involvement is, however, subject to debate (Stetler, 1970).

In 1969, the total strength of the RUC was 3,200 officers (Scarman, 1972: para. 1.9). Deficiencies in police numbers led the RUC to use CS gas (the first time this had been used in the UK) on 12 August. This was mainly used to disperse crowds, but the indiscriminate nature of its application could potentially injure anyone who lived in the area, whether they were involved in the violence or not. This helped to radicalise large numbers of people in the community, who became involved in subsequent events. A news-sheet, the *Barricade Bulletin*, kept people up to date on developments in the area and provided instructions on how to throw petrol bombs and to minimise the effects of CS gas.

Subsequently, police were drafted in from all over Northern Ireland, but their equipment was inadequate to prevent many of them from being injured, especially by petrol bombs. Initially, they were forbidden to use their firearms and sometimes resorted to stone-throwing. However, by 14 August, the use of firearms policy was altered and rioters were shot in Belfast. In addition, the Northern Ireland reserve police force, the Ulster Special Constabulary (commonly called the B-Specials), was mobilised on 14 August, although they were not used in the Bogside.

As the violence continued, calls were made by the DCDA to the NICRA for assistance in the form of demonstrations elsewhere in Northern Ireland that would limit the extent to which police reinforcements could be despatched to the Bogside from other areas in Northern Ireland. The authenticity of this tactic was accepted by a subsequent Tribunal of Inquiry (Scarman, 1972: para. 1.22). This resulted in protests occurring on 13 August in Belfast, Newry, Armagh, Lurgan, Strabane, Dungannon and Dungiven.

Events in Northern Ireland caused concern in the Irish Republic. On 13 August, the *Taoiseach*, Jack Lynch, declared that the RUC could no longer be regarded as an impartial force and called on the British government to request a United Nations Peacekeeping Force. Although the Irish government's direct involvement was limited to providing medical aid to those injured in the violence, Lynch's speech served to further heighten tensions. Loyalists became concerned that the Irish Army would become involved, which led a mob to take to the street on 13 August. The perception that they intended to burn St Eugene's Roman Catholic Cathedral secured further Nationalist support for the violence. The weaponry available included petrol and other devices designed to puncture the tyres of vehicles.

The violence in Derry and elsewhere in Northern Ireland continued for three days. It was characterised by sectarian clashes that escalated into serious violence involving the destruction of homes, business premises and shops. On occasions, firearms were also discharged by those involved in the violence.

On 14 August, the Inspector General of the RUC made a formal request to General Freeland, the General Officer Commanding in Northern Ireland, for the deployment of troops in Derry. This request had the approval of the Northern Irish Prime Minister, James Chichester-Clark, and the UK government's Home Secretary, James Callaghan. This request was agreed to on that day under what was termed 'Operation Banner'. On their arrival in Derry on 14 August, the RUC withdrew from the area and the B-Specials were also stood down. The Army did not, however, attempt to enter the Bogside or remove the barricades. The involvement of the Army was seen as a temporary measure, but lasted for the next 29 years. Troops were deployed on 15 August in Belfast following fierce sectarian riots that entailed Catholics being burned out of their homes by Loyalist mobs in Bombay Street. A separate incident on 15 August resulted in the destruction of around 48 homes in the predominantly Catholic Conway Street in Belfast.

A subsequent investigation into the role played by the RUC in all episodes of violence that occurred in 1969 argued that 'the great majority of the members of the RUC was concerned to do its duty, which, so far as concerned the disturbances, was to maintain order on the streets, using no more force than was reasonably necessary to suppress rioting and protect life and limb' (Scarman, 1972: para. 3.3). Although accusations of sectarian bias arose, it was argued that 'since most of the rioting developed from action on the streets started by Catholic crowds, the RUC were more often than not facing Catholics who, as a result, came to feel that the police were always going for them, baton-charging them – never "the others"' (Scarman, 1972: para. 3.3). It was argued that 'the Shankill riots of the 2/4 August establish beyond doubt the readiness of the police to do their duty against Protestant mobs, when they were the disturbers of the public peace' (Scarman, 1972: para. 3.4). The investigation concluded that 'overall, the RUC struggled manfully to do their duty in a situation which they could not control. Their courage, as casualties and long hours of stress and strain took their toll, was beyond praise; their ultimate failure to maintain order arose not from their mistakes, nor from any lack of professional skill, but from exhaustion and shortage of numbers' (Scarman, 1971: para. 3.10).

See also: Bloody Sunday (or the Bogside Massacre) (Derry, Northern Ireland) 1972, Burntollet Bridge (Derry, Northern Ireland) 1969, Northern Ireland: security policy during the 'Troubles', Provisional IRA, terrorism

Sources and further reading

Bew, P., Gibbon, P. and Patterson, H. (2002) *Northern Ireland 1921–2001: Political Power and Social Classes*. London: Serif.

Kennedy-Pipe, C. (1997) *The Origins of the Present Troubles in Northern Ireland*. Harlow: Longman.

Scarman, Rt. Hon. Lord (1972) *Violence and Civil Disturbances in Northern Ireland in 1969. Report of a Tribunal of Inquiry.* Belfast: HMSO, Cmnd. 566.

Stetler, S. (1970) *The Battle of Bogside: The Politics of Violence in Northern Ireland.* London: Sheed & Ward.

BLOODY SUNDAY (OR THE BOGSIDE MASSACRE) (DERRY, NORTHERN IRELAND) 1972

What was termed 'Bloody Sunday' or 'the Bogside Massacre' took place in Derry (Northern Ireland) on 30 January 1972 during a march to protest against internment that was organised by the Northern Ireland Civil Rights Association. It took place against heightened tensions in the city arising from attempts by the Army in late 1971 to undertake operations that were designed to challenge the grip exerted by the IRA on Creggan and the Bogside, and to re-impose the rule of law in those areas.

This march was technically illegal since all parades and processions had been banned throughout Northern Ireland since August 1971. Estimates of the numbers of protesters vary – one estimate was between 3,000 and 5,000 persons (Widgery, 1972: para. 24).

During the march, a breakaway group from the main event attacked an army barricade that was designed to enforce a route on the protesters to keep them away from the centre of Derry, Guildhall Square having been the organisers' preferred destination at which speeches would be made. Soldiers responded with water cannons and rubber bullets, following which soldiers from the First Battalion of the Parachute Regiment were deployed on an arrest operation; in conducting this, they fired live rounds. This resulted in the death of 12 people (and a further two who were run down by Army vehicles). Seven of these were teenagers and five were shot in the back, suggesting that they were running away to avoid confrontation with the Army.

An inquiry conducted under the 1921 Tribunals of Inquiry (Evidence) Act chaired by Lord Widgery (1972) cleared the authorities and soldiers of most of the blame and laid the prime responsibility for events on that day on the organisers of the march – 'there would have been no deaths in Londonderry on 30 January if those who organised the illegal march had not thereby created a highly dangerous situation in which a clash between demonstrators and the security forces was almost inevitable' (Widgery, 1972: Summary of Conclusions 1). Widgery asserted that although 'none of the deceased or wounded is proved to have been shot whilst handling a firearm or bomb', there was 'no reason to suppose that the soldiers would have opened fire if they had not been fired upon first'. He accepted, however, that in some locations 'firing bordered on the reckless' (Widgery, 1972: Summary of Conclusions, 7, 8 and 10) and that 'in the light of events the wisdom of carrying out the arrest operation is debatable' (para. 32).

However, a subsequent inquiry chaired by Lord Saville asserted that 'the organisers of the civil rights march bear no responsibility for the deaths and injuries on Bloody Sunday (Saville, 2010: vol. 1, para. 4.33). This inquiry confirmed that all those who had been shot were unarmed and concluded that 'there was no justification for the shooting of the civilian casualties' (Saville, 2010: vol. 1, para. 3.76). Its findings included that there had been no warning to any civilians before the soldiers opened fire, that no soldiers fired in response to attacks by nail or petrol bombers or stone-throwers, that none of the casualties were acting in a manner that justified their shooting, that some of those killed or injured were either fleeing or going to help those injured or dying, and that many of the soldiers lied about their actions.

The local commander of the RUC was of the opinion that the march should not be interfered with, but that leaders should be photographed with a view to being subsequently prosecuted (Widgery, 1972: para. 17). This view illustrates the problems that are inherent in using the military as a civil force to police public disorder. Those who are depicted as the enemy (in this case those dubbed the 'Derry Young Hooligans') are likely to be on the receiving end of lethal force. A particular problem with this is over-reaction, whose consequences may serve to legitimise violence and subsequently intensify it:

> what happened on Bloody Sunday strengthened the Provisional IRA, increased nationalist resentment and hostility towards the Army and exacerbated the violent conflict of the years that followed. Bloody Sunday was a tragedy for the bereaved and the wounded, and a catastrophe for the people of Northern Ireland. (Saville, 2010: vol. 1, para. 5.5)

Bloody Sunday has been depicted as an example of state crime in relation to the deaths and subsequent attempts to cover up actions that amounted conspiracy to murder (Rolston, 2010). The responsibility of the state was accepted by Prime Minister David Cameron, who delivered a formal apology on behalf of the British government in the House of Commons on 15 June 2010 in which he declared that 'what happened on Bloody Sunday was both unjustified and unjustifiable. It was wrong' (Cameron, 2010). In July 2012, the police and the Public Prosecution Service in Northern Ireland announced that a murder investigation would be launched in the light of Saville's findings.

See also: Burntollet Bridge (Derry, Northern Ireland) 1969, 'dirty protest' (Northern Ireland) 1978–81, Northern Ireland: security policy during the 'Troubles', Provisional IRA

Sources and further reading

Cameron, D. (2010) Speech in the House of Commons, 15 June. HC Debs, vol. 511, col. 739.

Murray, D. (2011) *Bloody Sunday: Truth, Lies and the Saville Inquiry*. London: Biteback Publishing.

Rolston, B. (2010) 'The Saville Report: A Personal Reflection', International State Crime Initiative, http://statecrime.org/online_article/the-saville-report-a-personal-reflection (date accessed 25 April 2014).

Saville, Rt Hon Lord, with Hoyt, W. and Toohey, J. (2010) *Report of the Bloody Sunday Inquiry*. London: TSO, House of Commons Paper 29.

Widgery, Rt Hon Lord (1972) *Report of the Tribunal appointed to inquire into the events on Sunday, 30 January 1972, which led to loss of life in connection with the procession in Londonderry on that day*. London: HMSO, House of Commons Paper 220. Available at: http://cain.ulst.ac.uk/hmso/widgery.htm (date accessed 25 April 2014).

BRADFORD RIOTS (MANNINGHAM, BRADFORD) 1995

On 9–11 June 1995, disorders occurred in the Manningham district of Bradford, England and the neighbouring areas. These events are commonly referred to as the Manningham Riots, but although this classification was used for the purposes of dealing with claims under the Riot Damages Act 1886, no one involved was prosecuted for the offence of rioting.

It was reported that during the disturbances, 102 premises were attacked (most of which were owned by members of the white and Sikh communities), some looting occurred, 66 vehicles were damaged, ten members of the public were injured (all of whom were white) and nine police officers received injuries (Bradford Commission, 1996: para. 4.25.1). The cost of the damage was estimated to be £500,000 and the extra policing costs were £214,000 (Bradford Commission, 1996: para. 4.25.5). At the height of the disturbances on the night of 10 June, it was estimated that 300 youths were involved, mainly from the Kashmiri community (Bradford Commission, 1996: para. 4.26.1), who constituted the majority of the area's population. Subsequently, members of other Asian communities (and a very small number of white youths) became involved in the disorders on 11 June, many of whom were not Manningham residents (Bradford Commission, 1996: paras. 4.29.4–4.29.6).

The disorders were triggered following a localised altercation between two police officers and a small group of young Asian men on 9 June 1995, which led to the arrest of four people. This led to a larger crowd assembling on the street where the arrests occurred, who were dispersed by police reinforcements. It was argued that the explanation for the violence that took place on the weekend following 9 June was not 'simply a case of alienated youths responding violently in disapproval of a minor policing incident. It is also the anger of the responsible, law-abiding adults ... in protest at what had happened to some of them ... and which unintentionally encouraged many of the young men who expressed their anger violently' (Bradford Commission, 1996: para. 4.8.12).

Subsequently, the magistrates dismissed charges brought against the four defendants who had been arrested, casting doubt on the reliability of the evidence presented by the two arresting police officers, although not vindicating the defendants (Bradford Commission, 1996: paras. 4.8.6–4.8.9). Criticism was also levelled at the nature of the police response to the small crowd that gathered in relation to the arrests, arguing that the coercive response (which included the use of a dog handler) as opposed to 'intelligent conversation' was at variance with the concept of policing with the consent of the community (Bradford Commission, 1996: paras. 4.8.18–4.8.19).

The events on the evening of 9 June led to subsequent disorders that lasted until 11 June. These occurred against the background of 'individual experiences of racial insensitivities by the police, accumulated over many years', an indignation that was 'widely felt by older, respected members of the local community' (Bradford Commission, 1996: para. 4.9.1) and was fuelled by rumours that suggested a police attack had taken place against an Asian woman and her baby as well as an assault that involved a police van driving over the foot of an Asian male teenager. The original arrests and subsequent rumours served to encourage other members of the local community to take to the streets to protest against police actions, which led to the escalation of disorder and resulted in police actions to disperse and crowds and make arrests. Although at that stage it was possible for the police to quell the disorders (which were viewed to be spontaneous), their refusal to engage with those members of the community who had taken to the streets was an important factor in the resulting escalation of violence (Bradford Commission, 1996: paras. 4.11.4 and 4.12.8). Instead, police reinforcements who appeared on the streets in riot gear were brought in from other divisions in Bradford to disperse the crowds. Accusations were made of the absence of identification numbers on some of the overalls worn by the police (Bradford Commission, 1996: para. 4.12.7).

Contact between the police and representatives of the local community occurred at around midnight on 9 June, as a result of which (as a goodwill gesture) police vans withdrew from the area. However, this decision resulted in attacks on property becoming more serious and the demands of the crowd were that all of those arrested (who were held in two separate police stations) should be released. This was eventually done once the police had completed the relevant paperwork, but what was perceived as delay by the crowd exacerbated an already inflamed situation and also suggested to them that assurances regarding the speedy release of prisoners given by local councillors who mediated between the community and the police were worthless.

Discussions between the police and bodies representing the local community (including the Bradford Racial Equality Council, representatives from the Council for Mosques and elected politicians) took place on the afternoon of 10 June 1995. The police aimed to prevent a repetition of the violence that had taken place on the previous day, although it was argued that discussions with community leaders were not a 'permanent substitute for speaking directly and confidently with the local people involved in a tense situation' (Bradford Commission, 1996: para. 4.18.6) However, the police could not accept the demands made by community representatives, which included dropping all charges against those arrested the previous day and the suspension of the two officers who were involved in the original incident that caused the violence. Subsequently, in 1996, the Police Complaints Authority ruled that no officer should be disciplined in connection with the disorders.

Although the police agreed to investigate speedily any complaints made about the behaviour of police officers, the meeting broke up with nothing achieved and the communication of this failure to the crowd who had gathered outside the meeting place triggered further violence which on 10 June was joined by outsiders whose interest in events had been stimulated by the media focus on the events of the previous night (Bradford Commission, 1996: para. 4.17.1). The policing of the area was not initially heavy-handed, but by early evening, a change of tactics was adopted that involved the deployment of police in full riot gear to disperse the crowds. Their presence provoked the crowd into acts of hostility and police lines were pelted with stones and petrol bombs. This violence later became directed at cars (stationary or static) and property that included public houses. Looting also occurred. 'Some estimates were of 700 youths on the rampage, but official police figures are less than half of that. There were 300 police officers deployed to restore order' (Bradford Commission, 1996: para. 4.17.21). The violence petered out at around 2 am.

The following day, against the background of genuine concerns within the local communities (especially the Kashmiri community; Bradford Commission, 1996: para. 4.19.1) regarding the violence, further talks took place between the police and community representatives, and the operational policing of the area was less confrontational than that of the previous day, with officers on the streets not wearing riot gear. Attempts were made by members of the local community and by leading Bradford dignitaries, including the Bishop of Bradford, to defuse the situation on the streets, and the violence that occurred during the day was both limited and sporadic.

However, the potential for more serious violence arose in the evening when a larger crowd numbering several hundred gathered outside Manningham police station for an impromptu meeting to protest against alleged police racism. Speakers at this event (including the Bishop of Bradford) urged that grievances within the community that had provoked the violence should be carefully examined. The day's events ended when a small group of Interfaith Women for Peace arrived to call for peace. No further violence occurred in the area.

In the aftermath of the riots, criticisms were made by some local people of police behaviour and demands were made for charges to be dropped against people arrested on the first day of the disturbances. Subsequently, the Crown Prosecution Service for West Yorkshire determined that although the arrests were justified, the public interest did not require prosecutions to take place (Bradford Commission, 1996: para. 4.23.1). However, the police subsequently set up a specific inquiry team to identify those engaged in criminal actions during the disorders, as a result of which some prosecutions took place.

However, other local people, especially members of the white community in the area, were critical of the failure of the Kashmiri community to apologise for the riots and for the failure of elders in that community to control the actions of its younger members. These views were also articulated by members of other Asian communities in Bradford (Bradford Commission, 1996: paras, 4.26.3 and 4.27.2).

The violence that occurred was said to be spontaneous and not pre-planned (Bradford Commission, 1996: para. 4.28.2). There was no evidence of central direction or leadership (Bradford Commission, 1996: para. 4.29.1), although pre-existing gangs became involved once the violence broke out. It was observed that although 'there was a longstanding and increasingly obvious sense of grievance amongst younger men in particular', there was nothing to suggest that disorders would occur when they did. It was, however, noted that the involvement of persons in these events was facilitated by mechanisms that included informal grapevines and modern technology, especially mobile phones (Bradford Commission, 1996: paras. 4.28.3–4.28.5). Accusations were also made of media manipulation in terms of encouraging violence by participants and bystanders in order to get a newsworthy story (Bradford Commission, 1996: paras 4.31.1–4.31.3). However, the media were not viewed as a cause of the disorders (Bradford Commission, 1996: para. 4.18.2).

In the wake of the disturbances, attempts were to identify their root causes. Adverse socio-economic conditions derived from the decline of the wool textile industry. Bradford 'lost 80% of the jobs in textiles over the period 1960–90 – 60,000 jobs in a population of 295,000' (Bühler et al., 2002: 6). This resulted in poverty which, although widespread throughout Bradford, especially affected ethnic minority communities, who provided the unskilled labour in this industry: 45 per cent of the youths in the local Asian population in Manningham were unemployed (Bradford Commission 1996: para. 5.27.1). This led to the conclusion that 'the grossly different levels of deprivation suffered by different ethnic groups raise very serious doubts about the fairness and effectiveness of political and organisational programmes', even if the problems did not necessarily stem from discrimination (Bradford Commission, 1996: paras. 5.1.1–5.1.2). However, racial discrimination by some local employers was noted (Bradford Commission, 1996: para. 5.1.4).

Social segregation was identified as a major factor underpinning the 1995 disturbances, a situation that provoked inter-racial tensions. It was argued that this situation arose in part as a result of involuntary factors that included 'greater parental choice in education, and the decline in the provision of social housing – both driven by national government – and locally by the irresponsible activities of estate agents' (Bühler et al., 2002: 6) who had abetted the process of 'white flight'. This left 'those in some areas of multiple deprivation in a vicious circle of limited housing values, limited education and quality of services' (Bühler et al., 2002: 7), 'an underclass of relatively poor white people and visible ethnic minority communities' (Ouseley, 2001: 9).

Segregation further arose from voluntary factors, a positive rejection of what is viewed as a discriminatory and oppressive society and/or the desire of 'groups of people who want to be treated as identifiably separate' (Bradford Commission, 1996: para. 5.14.1) and who formed an attachment to a particular locality which 'for the insecure represents the security of familiarity in which the chances of being humiliated, or excluded, are much reduced because of the presence of relatives, friends and familiar associates' (Bradford Commission, 1996: para. 5.11.3). It was alleged that the segregation that this situation gave rise to resulted in a racial motivation on the part of some of the protesters who targeted business premises owned by members of the white and Sikh community, which might be seen as an attempt to drive them out of the area (Bradford Commission, 1996: paras. 4.30.1–4.30.2) and thus justify the term 'race riot' being applied to these events. However, it was argued that factors of a more pragmatic nature may have dictated the targets chosen – the desire not to be recognised and the choice of premises that were unoccupied (Bradford Commission, 1996: para. 4.30.5).

Segregation, whether caused by involuntary or voluntary factors, was a key factor in the 1995 disorders. It was concluded that when there was 'some degree of hostility and mutual suspicion which causes communities to pull apart, social contacts and connections will decline, which may offer greater apparent reason to move even further apart' (Bühler et al., 2002: 7). Negative assumptions concerning the lifestyles and habits of those living in such enclaves (including street behaviour, prostitution and drugs) further serve to marginalise these communities and the perception by the police that these are 'problem' areas may result in a more coercive style of policing being delivered.

Antagonism towards the police was cited as a major explanation of these events: 'Antagonisms between local young men and the police, based upon a longer memory within the community of inappropriate, unfair, or racist treatment by individual police officers was ... undoubtedly a most powerful motive for the indignation of the Kashmiri community' (Bradford Commission, 1996: para. 6.17.6). It was argued that 'an inadequate relationship between the police and the people of Manningham created ... a clear predisposition to violence' (Bradford Commission, 1996: para. 6.15.3), a key explanation for which was 'an institutional capacity to understand, and to relate to, other cultural groupings than the traditional White culture, and in particular to the local Kashmiri community' (Bradford Commission, 1996: para. 6.17.2). This led to the conclusion that 'the present basis of policing in an area such as Manningham was fundamentally flawed' (Bradford Commission, 1996: para. 6.17.3).

The extent to which police racism underpinned the disorders was considered by the Bradford Commission. Although it was argued that police officers were not in general racist, 'there are some police officers who are "racist" and who cannot see the need for even elementary courtesy and consideration in dealing with the City's multi-ethnic population' (Bradford Commission, 1996: para. 6.19.1). Attention was also drawn to 'a racist "canteen culture" which was "unconstructive, divisive and hurtful"' (Bradford Commission, 1996: para. 6.19.5).

Other issues that were raised included local political leadership. It was argued that this had been 'weak in kowtowing to community leadership and operating within a "doing deals" culture to avoid "disturbances" and to "keep the peace"' (Ouseley, 2001: 10). One example of this was the discriminatory local authority housing allocation policies 'which allocated specific ethnic groups to specific new housing estates', thereby effectively enforcing 'the establishment of segregated housing areas' (Allen, 2003: 17). Overall, there was the 'lack of a clear strategy which can be used to prioritise the direction of scarce funds and other resources, to knit together the separate strategies of the various agencies and sub-agencies involved, and to monitor success with a view to further prioritisation' (Bradford Commission, 1996: para. 7.6.2). It was argued that 'a powerful unifying vision for the District and strong political, municipal and community leadership' was required and that: 'In addition, the District needs a people programme that creates social harmony, rejects racial hatred, brings communities together and shows them how to value people of all backgrounds' (Ouseley, 2001: 1). In the absence of such a strategy, 'most political discussion will inevitably degenerate into competition for local or sectarian advantage ... it is inevitable that people will seek to maximise their own bit of the action, leading to accusations of favouritism or political opportunism' (Bradford Commission, 1996: para. 7.7.1).

Although the events that occurred in 1995 were confined to the Manningham area of the city and were relatively brief in duration, the issues that underpinned them – in particular segregation – re-surfaced in 2001 when disorders broke out more widely across the city and elsewhere in northern England.

See also: Northern English towns riots (Bradford, Burnley, Oldham) 2001, public order policing (England and Wales), riots

Sources and further reading

Allen, C. (2003) *Fair Justice: The Bradford Disturbances, the Sentencing and the Impact*. London: Forum Against Islamophobia and Racism.

Bradford Commission Report (1996) *The Report of an Inquiry into the Wider Implications of Public Disorders in Bradford which Occurred on 9, 10 and 11 June 1995*. London: TSO.

Bühler, U, Bujra, J., Carling, A., Cumming, L., Hannam, M., Lewis, P., Macey, M., Nias, P., Pankhurst, D., Pearce, J., Samad, Y. and Vine, I. (2002) 'Bradford: One Year On. Breaking the Silence', University of Bradford, www.brad.ac.uk/admin/pr/pressreleases/2002/silences.PDF (date accessed 29 April 2014).

Ouseley, Sir H. and Race Review Team (2001) 'Community Pride, Not Prejudice', Bradford Vision, http://resources.cohesioninstitute.org.uk/Publications/Documents/Document/Default.aspx?recordId=98 (date accessed 19 May 2014).

BROADWATER FARM ESTATE RIOTS (HARINGEY, LONDON) 1985

A wave of riots took place in England in 1985, the most serious of which occurred at the Broadwater Farm Estate in Tottenham, London.

The first of these riots occurred in Handsworth, Birmingham and lasted from 9 to 11 September. This disorder was triggered by an attempted arrest of a black man in Lozells Road. The man fled to a cafe in the same vicinity and police attempts to arrest him there escalated into a riot in which petrol bombs were used against the police. Two brothers were burned to death seeking to protect the post office that they managed, over 100 people were injured and 45 shops were looted and burnt.

Although persons of all races were involved in the disturbances, it was observed that in that area, 'people of different races live in approximately equal numbers – but with unequal access to scarce resources. And since they coexist by force of circumstances and not from choice, every encounter is fraught with conflict' (Henry,

1987: 111). This suggests inter-racial tensions were simmering below the surface, which became a more significant underpinning to the later disturbances that took place in 2005.

These events were followed by an incident in Brixton, London, on 28 September 1985, in which armed police looking for a man in connection with a robbery raided the house where he suspected of hiding and accidentally shot his mother, Cherry Groce, who was in bed. This incident occurred against a background of tensions between the police and the public (especially black youths) and rumours that Mrs Groce had been killed in the incident. This resulted in attacks being made on the police, the erection of barricades, the use of petrol bombs and looting. The disorder lasted for around 48 hours. One person (a photo-journalist) was killed during the disturbances, 50 people were injured and 200 were arrested. Mrs Groce remained in hospital for two years and was crippled by the shooting. In July 2014, the Metropolitan Police issued a public apology for its failings over this incident following criticism of its actions by an inquest jury.

On 5 October 1985, four police officers embarked on a search of a flat in the Broadwater Farm Estate in Tottenham, north London. It was occupied by Mrs Cynthia Jarrett and the search was in connection with offences committed by her son, Floyd Jarrett. Mrs Jarrett, who had a weak heart, died as a result of this police intervention.

The following day, a number of sporadic attacks were made against the police. This led to the deployment of riot police to clear the streets by mounting baton charges, but instead led to more intense attacks being mounted involving the use of barricades and petrol bombs. Fires were also started and shots were fired at police officers. Police support to fire crews tackling a blaze on the estate resulted in the murder of an officer, PC Keith Blakelock, who was hacked to death in a frenzied mob attack. Fifty-eight police officers and 24 other people were taken to hospital. A strong police presence remained on the estate for the following months. In 1987, three men were convicted of the murder of PC Blakelock, but the convictions were overturned on appeal in 1991.

Although (as in 1981) these disturbances took place in areas that were socially and economically deprived, the common factor in these episodes was that a police intervention prompted disorder. This suggested that strained relationships between the police and the public (and especially African-Caribbean youths) were a feature of the riot-affected areas. In the wake of these riots, a number of changes were introduced into police practices.

Events in Brixton prompted the Metropolitan Police Service (MPS) to review its firearms policy, which led to a ban on Criminal Investigation Department (CID) officers being armed. Henceforth, only centrally controlled specialist squads would carry firearms. The Broadwater Farm riots prompted the MPS to examine its tactics in dealing with public disorder and resulted in the subsequent introduction of armoured Land Rovers and the creation of fast-moving police units whose role was to nip riotous behaviour in the bud. This event also prompted attempts by the police to re-engage with the local community in that area.

It was argued that half of the people on the Estate had little confidence in the way in which it was policed (Broadwater Farm Inquiry, 1986: 166). A particular problem that needed to be addressed was a mismatch between what local people expected of the police and what they chose to prioritise (Broadwater Farm Inquiry, 1986: 162–3). The senior leadership in the division were criticised for failing to have 'recognised, encouraged and responded wholeheartedly to the community organisations on Broadwater Farm' (Broadwater Farm Inquiry, 1986: 190) and for failing to be willing to discuss local concerns regarding policing with the Broadwater Farm Panel. It was argued that 'there must be genuine cooperation – which means a real exchange of information about the problems which are troubling wither the police or community, and about the operations which may have to be mounted to deal with them' (Broadwater Farm Inquiry, 1986: 194).

See also: Bradford riots (Manningham, Bradford) 1995, copycat riots (England) 1981, public order policing (England and Wales), riots

Sources and further reading
Brain, T. (2010) *A History of Policing in England and Wales from 1974: A Turbulent Journey.* Oxford University Press.
Broadwater Farm Inquiry (1986) *Report of the Independent Inquiry into Disturbances of October 1985 at the Broadwater Farm Estate, Tottenham.* London: Karia Press.
Henry, I. (1987) 'Racial Disadvantage, Unemployment and Urban Unrest', in J, Benyon and J. Solomos (eds), *The Roots of Urban Unrest.* Oxford: Pergamon.

BUILDING WORKERS' STRIKE (ENGLAND AND WALES) 1972

In 1972, the Union of Construction, Allied Trades and Technicians (UCATT) was involved in an industrial dispute with two other trade unions (the General and Municipal Workers' Union and the Transport and General Workers Union) that affected the building industry. This was the first ever national strike in that industry.

The strike took place against the backdrop of industrial militancy in other industries (especially by miners and dockers) in the early 1970s, which has been dubbed the 'long hot summer' of industrial strife (Clutterbuck, 1980: 77). Twenty-three million working days were lost in 1972 due to strike action (Haslam, 2007: 106) This situation was a reaction to the Industrial Relations Act 1971, which unions viewed as an attempt to undermine their ability to defend their members' interests, especially in relation to pay and conditions. One additional factor behind this dispute was that the leaders of the UCATT (which had been formed in 1971) felt the need to display to their members that the mergers that had taken place to create this Union provided a more effective mechanism to safeguard the interests of those in the building trade, who had previously been represented by a myriad of smaller unions. The union leaders may also have felt the need to assert their power in the face of displays of earlier militancy in the building industry that were promoted by bodies outside the established trade union structure.

Actions of this nature entailed the formation of local organisations such as the Manchester Building Workers' Forum and the Merseyside Shop Stewards Building Operatives' Committee. Members of the Communist Party played prominent roles in these bodies, which came together at a national level through the mechanism of the Building Workers' Charter Group, which was established in Manchester in April 1970. This operated in parallel with the established trade unions (Clutterbuck, 1980: 80) and was responsible for instigating a range of actions (including demonstrations, strikes, sit-ins and raids on sites). Its demands included the nationalisation of the building industry, a single trade union for the industry which required 100 per cent membership and the banning of the Lump (a term which is defined below) (Clutterbuck, 1980: 81).

This new-found militancy prompted the established trade unions to take action through the formation of a National Joint Council by the vast array of unions employed on building sites. This made a pay claim to the National Federation of Building Trades Employers for £30 per week and a basic 35-hour week for all trades. The national minimum rate for the building trade then was £20 for a skilled worker and £17 for labourers for a 40-hour week. The employers rejected these demands and a national strike was called, which began on 26 June 1972 and lasted for 12 weeks.

The strikers also demanded an end to the 'Lump Labour Scheme', which trade unionists viewed as a major source of contention in the building industry. This entailed workers being treated as self-employed and paid a lump sum for the work they performed (on a daily or weekly basis). They, rather than the employer, were responsible for the payment of tax and National Insurance contributions. This practice was accentuated following the introduction of Selective Employment Tax in 1966. The use of self-employed labour in the construction industry (as opposed to the employer using a directly employed workforce) made it difficult to organise trade unions, which was seen as detrimental both to pay and conditions in the industry, especially in relation to health and safety issues on building sites.

The strikers initially used selective tactics characterised by 'guerrilla strikes' in which pickets would be sent to different sites, urging the workers to join the dispute. In general, this action was targeted at the bigger and well-organised building sites that were located in major towns and cities. This tactic persuaded some employers to concede to the demands, but in order to make this concession apply universally throughout the industry, unofficial, grassroots action took place in August, which was sanctioned by the unions involved in the strike, thus creating an all-out strike in this industry.

The strikers' tactics continued with the use of flying pickets, but became characterised by acts of violence. In September 1972, the unions agreed a settlement with the employers that resulted in an immediate increase in basic rates of pay of £6 a week for craftsmen and £5 for labourers. This was the largest single pay increase ever negotiated in the building industry.

The most prominent incident in the dispute took place on 6 September 1972 when the UCATT and the Transport and General Workers' Union (TGWU) bussed members from north Wales and Chester to picket building sites in Shrewsbury and Telford. Although no arrests were made on that day, a number of workers were subsequently investigated for acts of sabotage and vandalism. This led to 24 pickets being charged with over 200 offences, including unlawful assembly, intimidation and affray.

Six pickets were also charged with conspiracy to intimidate under the provisions of the Conspiracy and Protection of Property Act 1875, a measure which 'many lawyers thought dead and buried'. It had been designed to protect unions from civil actions arising from disputes and had never been used against strikers (Cox, 1975: 47). In 1973, these 24 workers were convicted and six were jailed. The longest prison sentences were given to Des Warren and Ricky Tomlinson (three years and two years respectively), who became known as the 'Shrewsbury Two'. The convictions for affray were subsequently overturned on appeal, but this did not reduce the length of the sentences since they ran concurrently.

The justification for the punitive measures taken against the strikers (which earlier in the dispute had included prosecuting five members of the UCATT and an accompanying TV crew who had occupied the Birmingham offices of an agency employing Lump workers with conspiracy to trespass, thus turning a civil charge into a criminal one) was that the strike witnessed 'some very ugly intimidation, and an underlying viciousness ... the hatred between regular building workers and the "Lump" workers ... was particularly bitter' (Clutterbuck, 1980: 77). One account of the episodes at Shrewsbury and Telford suggested that 'one man was pulled down from the scaffolding and a stone or brick dropped on his head, leaving him blind in one eye; and a number of other men were injured. In these incidents, which spread to several sites, there was mass intimidation by a flying picket of some 250 men' (Clutterbuck, 1980: 83). It was argued that 'there was no question of peaceful persuasion' being used by these pickets (Clutterbuck, 1980: 85).

However, it has been argued that employers also adopted aggressive tactics towards strikers, including the formation of an anti-picketing squad in Shrewsbury (Haslam, 2007: 106). Many trade unionists viewed the prosecutions as an act of political malice on the part of the then Conservative government, which wished to criminalise dissent and make an example of trade union activists who had earlier in the year achieved success outside Saltley gas works: they wished 'to teach the "militants" a political lesson' (Cox, 1975: 48). The Conservative Party's actions may also have been influenced by the close links it had with the building industry. The view that the prosecutions were inspired by the government was heightened by the decision of the Justice Secretary in 2013 to delay the release to the National Archives of documents (in the form of government and police papers) relating to the case for a further period of ten years. This decision was based on section 23 of the Freedom of Information Act 2000 that applies to issues affecting national security.

This decision has been challenged by the view that: 'We were building workers who were trying to get decent wages and working conditions. What's that got to do with "national security"? ... The government continue to throw a security blanket over what really happened during the 1972 dispute and the role of the security forces. We believe that the prosecutions were directed by the government' (Tomlinson, quoted in Taylor, 2013).

Warren died in 2004, but in 2006 the Shrewsbury 24 Campaign was set up with the aim of having the convictions overturned. In April 2012, Tomlinson applied to the Criminal Cases Review Commission to have the cases of the 24 convicted men referred to the Criminal Cases Review Commission and in June of that year an e-petition to Downing Street was launched to support this demand. An early day motion tabled by John McDonnell MP calling on the government to release the documents that were being withheld was approved on 23 January 2014 by 120 votes to three.

See also: miners' dispute (Britain) 1972, miners' dispute (Britain) 1973–4, miners' dispute (Britain) 1984–5, News International dispute (Wapping, London) 1986, workplace protest

Sources and further reading

Clutterbuck, R. (1980) *Britain in Agony: The Growth of Political Violence.* Harmondsworth: Penguin.

Cox, B. (1975) *Civil Liberties in Britain.* Harmondsworth: Penguin.

Haslam, D. (2007) *Young Hearts Run Free: The Real Story of the 1970s.* London: HarperPerennial.

Taylor, M. (2013) 'Ricky Tomlinson Calls on Government to Lift "Veil of Secrecy" on Shrewsbury 24', *The Guardian*, 20 January.

BURNTOLLET BRIDGE (DERRY, NORTHERN IRELAND) 1969

On 1 January 1969, civil rights protesters from the group People's Democracy (an offshoot of the Northern Ireland Civil Rights Association) embarked on a four-day march from Belfast to Derry in Northern Ireland. Many of the participants were students at Queen's University Belfast. This event was designed to highlight the lack of civil rights in Northern Ireland and in particular to address issues that included fairer council house distribution, more jobs and the abolition of extra votes for wealthier citizens. It was modelled on the 1966 civil rights march from Selma to Montgomery in Alabama that highlighted violent racism in America's Deep South and prompted the federal government to address it. The protesters subscribed to the principles of non-violence that were endorsed by the Northern Ireland Civil Rights Association.

Loyalists adopted an aggressive response to the march in the belief that it was seeking to undermine the authority of the Unionist government in the province. The march was subject to constant harassment, which came to a head at Burntollet Bridge, around seven miles from Derry, on 4 January, when the march (which now numbered around 500 people) was ambushed and protesters were attacked by around 200 people armed with an array of weapons that included bottles, stones and iron bars. One participant recalled how 'from lanes at each side of the road a curtain of bricks and boulders and bottles brought the march to a halt. From the lanes burst hordes of screaming people wielding planks of wood, bottles, laths, iron bags, crowbars, cudgels studied with nails, and they waded into the march beating the hell out of everyone' (Devlin, 1969). A number of protesters required hospital treatment.

Subsequent attacks were made on the march when it entered Derry and the Royal Ulster Constabulary (RUC) broke up a rally that was to be held in the city when the march arrived there. Further disorder ensued and, in response, the police mounted an operation directed against Nationalists living in the Bogside area. This led to serious rioting, which culminated with the area sealing itself off. Radio Free Derry was launched and the area effectively became a police no-go area. In the absence of the RUC, residents created their own patrols which remained until the police returned on 12 January.

Following the event, the Prime Minister of Northern Ireland, Terence O'Neill, blamed the violence on some of the protesters and their supporters, and suggested that increased use might have to be made of the B-Specials to carry out normal police duties. The Governor of Northern Ireland, Lord Grey, set up an inquiry (chaired by Lord Cameron) to investigate the causes of the disturbances that occurred in Derry and elsewhere on or after 15 October 1968. It subsequently rejected any suggestion of institutional sectarianism in policing and asserted that 'in the majority of cases we find the police acted with commendable restraint under very great strain and provocation from various quarters' (Cameron, 1969: para. 177).

This view was later echoed by a review conducted by Lord Scarman into the disturbances that occurred during 1969. This stated that 'undoubtedly mistakes were made and certain individual officers acted wrongly on occasions. But the general case of a partisan force cooperating with Protestant mobs to attack Catholic people is devoid of substance and we reject it utterly' (Scarman, 1972: para. 3.2). He further stated of the officers involved in policing these disturbances that: 'Their courage, as casualties and long hours of stress and strain took their toll, was beyond praise' (Scarman, 1972: para. 3.10).

Nonetheless, the Nationalist community was less sympathetic to the stance displayed by the RUC at Burntollet Bridge. Although the RUC accompanied the march, no action was taken to stop the attacks or to protect protesters from the violence. No arrests were made by the police of the ambushers and off-duty members of the Ulster Special Constabulary (usually referred to as the B-Specials) were involved in meting out the violence towards the marchers.

Despite official denials to the contrary, this event (which came on top of similar episodes that included the aggressive handling by the police of a banned civil rights march at Craigavon Bridge, Derry, in October 1968, when a water cannon was used against protesters, some of whom were assaulted by members of the RUC) reflected the sectarian nature of policing in Northern Ireland and further eroded the legitimacy of the police in Nationalist areas. This led to many Nationalists questioning their allegiance to the Northern Irish state and helped to create latent support for the subsequent campaign mounted by the Provisional IRA that was designed to remove the British presence from Northern Ireland for good. The events that occurred at Burntollet Bridge were thus an important milestone in initiating the 'Troubles' that lasted from 1969 until the Good Friday Agreement signed in Belfast in Easter 1998.

See also: Battle of the Bogside (Derry, Northern Ireland) 1969, Bloody Sunday (or the Bogside Massacre) (Derry, Northern Ireland) 1972, 'dirty protest' (Northern Ireland) 1978–81, Northern Ireland: security policy during the 'Troubles', Provisional IRA

Sources and further reading

Cameron, Lord (1969) *Disturbances in Northern Ireland Report of the Commission Appointed by the Governor of Northern Ireland.* Belfast: HMSO, Cmd. 532.

Devlin, B. (1969) *The Price of My Soul.* London: Pan Books.

Scarman, Lord L. (1972) *Violence and Civil Disturbances in Northern Ireland in 1969: Report of Tribunal of Inquiry.* Belfast: HMSO, Cmd. 566.

C

CHICAGO DEMOCRATIC NATIONAL CONVENTION RIOT (CHICAGO) 1968

The National Convention of the American Democratic Party took place in the International Amphitheater in Chicago, Illinois, between 26 and 28 August 1968. The main purpose of this meeting was to select the Party's candidate for the Presidency, as the incumbent, Lyndon B. Johnson, had announced his intention not to seek a further term in office on 31 March following challenges to his candidacy mounted by Senators Robert Kennedy and Eugene McCarthy. These reflected deep divisions within the Party, most notably over the escalation of the war in Vietnam that had occurred during Johnson's term of office.

The Convention took place against the background of protest across America following the assassination of Martin Luther King on 4 April 1968. This event resulted in riots in around 100 cities.

The decision to hold the Convention in Chicago was heavily influenced by its Mayor, Richard Daly, who convinced President Johnson that this would help the Democrats to win the state (and its 27 votes in the Electoral College) in the Presidential election.

The Convention occurred in the context of political uncertainty in the Democratic Party arising from the assassination on 5 June of one of the main contenders to secure the nomination, Senator Robert Kennedy. This meant that a considerable number of delegates attending the Convention were pledged to support Kennedy and it was uncertain how they should act following his death. The front-runner to secure the nomination at the outset of the Convention was Vice President Hubert Humphrey, although the combined votes of Kennedy and McCarthy (standing on a peace platform) outnumbered those of Humphrey. Humphrey declined to enter any of the primary elections and stood only in the states where delegates to the Convention were chosen in party caucuses, controlled by party leaders. Ultimately, Humphrey was chosen as the Democratic candidate (with Senator Ed Muskie as his running mate for the office of Vice President), which led to accusations of strings being pulled by President Johnson.

Prior to the Convention taking place, a number of groups, principally the National Mobilization Committee to End the War in Vietnam (MOBE) and the Youth International Party (known as the 'Yippies'), began to plan a youth festival that would be held in Chicago to coincide with the Democratic National Convention. These were joined by other groups that included the Students for a Democratic Society (SDS).

MOBE was an umbrella organisation that embraced a number of groups that were opposed to the war in Vietnam. Its tactics were more conventional than those employed by the Yippies in the sense that it used demonstrations and civil disobedience to articulate its protest. It had planned to hold two demonstrations in Chicago, which would be supplemented by a number of workshops situated in parks throughout the city.

The Yippies had been formed in 1967 as a counterculture protest movement that included a loose alliance of hippies, activists opposed to the war in Vietnam and left-wing radicals. They aspired to the creation of what was termed a 'new nation' characterised by decentralisation and communal living and based upon anarchist traditions. Their main tactic was the use of direct action, which took the form of stunts and pranks of a theatrical nature that were designed to ridicule key social institutions and the authority with which they were associated in a manner that would secure media attention. One example of this was a mock attempt to levitate the Pentagon Building during the 1967 March on the Pentagon, which was led by Jerry Rubin and Abbie Hoffman, who became key members of the Yippies when it was formed later that year.

Events prior to the Chicago Convention that had taken place in New York in 1968 (one of which was the 'Yip In') led to strained relations between those involved in the event and the police. A large volume of advance publicity announced the intention of the Yippies to come to Chicago, where they planned to hold a six-day Festival of Life, which was designed to include a folk-rock music festival, theatre performances and educational workshops. A number of threats were also made that included intentions to block roads, storm the Convention and dump LSD in the city's water supply. A further concern to the authorities in Chicago was the fear that there were plots to assassinate political leaders who were gathering in the city for the Convention.

The intention of diverse groups to mount protests in Chicago was viewed as an attempt to disrupt the Convention and as a direct challenge to the authority wielded over the city by the Mayor, who refused to grant permits for the Yippies or MOBE to protest legally and who had previously promised (when addressing the American Legion in July 1968) to uphold law and order in the city (Kusch, 2008). To do this, Daley organised a robust force to counter the possibility of disturbances, which included 6,000 Illinois National Guardsmen and 12,000 police officers from the Chicago Police Department, whose efforts were spearheaded by the Chicago Police Department Task Force. A further contingent of 6,000 troops were airlifted to Chicago on 26 August (Walker, 1968). Additional public order training was provided to the police during the summer of 1968. Extreme security measures were also adopted both outside and inside the Convention Hall when this event began.

A number of protests occurred before the Convention was formally opened on 26 August and in total the disorders lasted for eight days. These included an event on 23 August at which the Yippie leader, Jerry Rubin, and folk singer Phil Ochs held a mock presidential nominating convention at which a pig ('Pigasus the Immortal') was nominated. An attempt to parade the pig around Chicago's Civic Center resulted in the arrest of Rubin, Ochs and six other people (as well as the apprehension of the pig). On 24 August, a small demonstration organised by the SDS resulted in some arrests.

A number of protests were planned for Sunday 25 August. These included MOBE's 'meet the delegates' march and picket of the Conrad Hilton Hotel (the main hotel used by delegates at the National Convention) and the Yippie's Festival of Life in Chicago's Lincoln Park. This event witnessed a confrontation between the police and protesters that spilled over from the Park into the surrounding streets and was not quelled until the following morning. Violence subsequently occurred on the following days, the original protesters being joined by others that included the Poor People's Campaign.

On 28 August, a boy lowered an American flag at MOBE's rally that took place in Grant Park following news that McCarthy's peace platform had been defeated in the Convention Hall. This consisted of around 10,000 protesters. The police responded by breaking through the crowd and the boy was beaten. This event triggered an attempt by several thousand of the protesters to march on the Convention Hall. As they had no permit to undertake this protest, the police sought to prevent the march, which ultimately triggered a violent response from the crowd, who pelted the police with whatever material they could lay their hands on, and running battles between the police and protesters characterised an event that became known as the 'Battle of Michigan Avenue'. Tear gas and mace were used to clear the streets of protesters and anyone else who happened to be in the vicinity. The violence was conveyed nationwide by television crews who were stationed outside the Hilton Hotel to cover the Convention's proceedings.

While this violence occurred on the streets of Chicago, the National Convention got on with its job of selecting a Presidential candidate.

Senator Abraham Ribicoff used his speech, which nominated George McGovern, to draw attention to events outside of the meeting, highlighting what he described as 'Gestapo tactics on the streets of Chicago'. Daley, who was inside the Convention Hall, was seen to vent his fury at Ribicoff, appearing to use a string of expletives and anti-semitic remarks. Television cameras constantly switched between events in the Convention Hall and the violence on the streets, which served to highlight the deep divisions within the Party and helped to secure the victory of Richard Nixon in the November Presidential contest.

Subsequently, the National Commission on the Causes and Prevention of Violence appointed Daniel Walker to head the Chicago Study Team that investigated the violence that had occurred in 1968. The report stated that:

> During the week of the Democratic National Convention, the Chicago police were the targets of mounting provocation by both word and act. It took the form of obscene epithets, and of rocks, sticks, bathroom titles, and even human feces [sic] hurled at police by demonstrators. Some of these acts had been planned; others were spontaneous or were themselves provoked by police action. Furthermore, the police had been put on edge by widely published threats of attempts to disrupt both the city and the Convention. (Walker, 1968)

However, it was argued that:

> The nature of the response was unrestrained and indiscriminate police violence on many occasions, particularly at night. That violence was made all the more shocking by the fact that it was often inflicted upon persons who had broken no law, disobeyed no order, made no threat. These included peaceful demonstrators, onlookers, and large numbers of residents who were simply passing through, or happened to live in, the areas where confrontations were occurring. Newsmen and photographers were singled out for assault, and their equipment deliberately damaged. Fundamental police training was ignored; and officers, when on the scene, were often unable to control their men. (Walker, 1968)

It was concluded that: 'To read dispassionately the hundreds of statements describing at first hand the events of Sunday and Monday nights is to become convinced of the presence of what can only be called a police riot' (Walker, 1968). The report also deduced that:

> There has been no public condemnation of these violators of sound police procedures and common decency by either their commanding officers or city officials. Nor (at the time this report is being completed – almost three months after the convention) has

any disciplinary action been taken against most of them ... If no action is taken against them, the effect can only be to discourage the majority of policemen who acted responsibly, and further weaken the bond between police and community. (Walker, 1968)

Following the end of the Convention, the American Justice Department charged eight people, including Yippies and others from the New Left, with conspiracy and incitement to riot. These (the 'Chicago Eight') were Abbie Hoffman, Jerry Rubin, Lee Weiner, Tom Hayden, David Dellinger, Rennie Davis, John Froines and Bobby Seale. Demonstrations organised by the Young Lords and the Black Panthers were held throughout the five-month trial and the courtroom witnessed a considerable degree of acrimony which at one stage led to Seale (a founder of the Black Panthers) being gagged and chained to his chair to prevent his outbursts in court. In February 1970, five of the defendants from Iowa were convicted of the charge of intent to incite a riot whilst crossing state lines, but none was found guilty of conspiracy. The judge, Julius Hoffman, sentenced the defendants and two of their attorneys to lengthy sentences of imprisonment for contempt of court. These convictions were, however, reversed on appeal.

The Yippies were involved in a number of other protests during the 1970s, many of which (such as the block party at the end of their New Nation Conference in Madison, Wisconsin in April 1971) led to clashes with the police. The Yippies also took part in protests that opposed the war in Vietnam, which included the May 1971 occupation of strategic areas of Washington DC in an attempt to close down the American government.

See also: counterculture protest, Grosvenor Square (London) 1969, riot, riot police, student riots (Paris) 1968, third force

Sources and further reading

Farber, D. (1988) *Chicago '68*. University of Chicago Press.
Kusch, F. (2008) *Battleground Chicago: The Police and the 1968 Democratic National Convention*. University of Chicago Press.
Walker, D. (1968) *Rights in Conflict: The Violent Confrontation of Demonstrators and Police in the Parks and Streets of Chicago During the Week of the Democratic National Convention of 1968. A Report submitted by Daniel Walker, Director of the Chicago Study Team to the National Commission on the Causes and Prevention of Violence*. Available at: http://chicago68.com/ricsumm.html (date accessed 24 April 2014).

CIVIL DISOBEDIENCE

Civil disobedience has been described as an act undertaken by a person in his or her capacity as a citizen under government, entailing disobedience which is 'passive', 'non-violent', 'courteous' and 'not uncivil' (Bedau, 1969: 19). It is also referred to as non-violent direct action and although it involves physical actions that result in 'a degree of disruption and confrontation' (Smith, 2013: 79), it entails 'a non-revolutionary encounter with the state not seeking to challenge the legitimacy of its legal or political systems' (Walzer, 1970: 24). Civil disobedience is typically motivated by moral, religious or political impulses (Walzer, 1970: 4) and is directed against actions undertaken by governments (and also those of commercial organisations) that are viewed as unjust or immoral.

An important aspect of civil disobedience os 'the deliberate and open act of breaking an unjust law' (Carter, 1983: 13) The tactics associated with civil disobedience are broad and have historically included marches, vigils, sit-ins and trespass or other actions which openly defy the law (such as the burning of draft cards in America by opponents of the Vietnam War in the 1960s and the 'can't pay, won't pay' stance of those opposed to the introduction of the Poll Tax in England and Wales in 1990). Civil disobedience entails non-cooperation with the government and the refusal to pay taxes is viewed as the last stage in this process since 'it is to deny to government its capacity to govern, to administer and enforce any of its laws' (Bedau, 1969: 22).

Civil disobedience eschews the use of violence and it is hoped that 'the dignity of the protest will aid the cause with which it is associated' (Joyce, 2002: 18), especially if violence is displayed towards protesters by those who represent the cause to which they are opposed. However, displays of violence towards protesters may provoke them into retaliation, at which point it becomes difficult to differentiate between civil disobedience and direct action (especially as many of the tactics used by both forms of protest – such as sit-ins, trespass and the setting-up of blockades – are similar).

There are many historical examples of the use of civil disobedience, which include actions undertaken by Mohandas Gandhi and his Indian Independence Movement (including the March 1930 Salt March) and protests undertaken by the African-American Civil Rights Movement in the 1950s and 1960s. More contemporary examples in India entailed the actions of villagers in the Khandwa district in 2012, who stood neck-deep in water for several days in their quest for compensation and rehabilitation arising from the decision of the state government of Madhya Pradesh to raise the water level in the Omkareshwar Dam, which would submerge houses in the low-lying villages in the area. A similar action that involved standing in the sea in boats was undertaken by protesters in an attempt to prevent the loading of fuel at the Kudankulum nuclear plant in the Southern Indian state of Tamil Nadu in 2012.

Civil disobedience has also been used by the Peace Movement. The Committee of One Hundred used sit-down protests in the early 1960s to articulate their opposition to Britain's independent nuclear deterrent and at its annual conference held in Sheffield in 1982, the Campaign for Nuclear Disarmament (CND) voted to use non-violent direct action in pursuance of the movement's aims.

Civil disobedience has also been directed against the commercial activities of private companies. Examples of this include 'open rescue' by animal liberation groups of mistreated animals, such as the freeing of hens kept in battery cages (Milligan, 2013: Chapter 11). This form of protest has also been embraced by environmentalist protest groups such as Greenpeace in their campaign against genetically modified crops. One example of this took place in Norfolk, England, in 1999, when six acres of genetically modified maize were destroyed.

In more recent years, the tactics associated with civil disobedience have become more diverse. Technology has facilitated aspects of this in the forms of hactivism and whistleblowing, which are dealt with under separate headings in this volume.

A different form of contemporary civil disobedience is associated with the movement Reclaim the Streets (a loose collection of environmentalists, anarchists and anti-capitalists). This has used the tactic of street parties to prevent car access to particular vicinities. The first of these actions occurred in London in 1995 when Camden High Street was closed.

Similar activities are conducted by a movement known as Critical Mass. This operates on a global context and its activities entail using bicycles to block road access to cars. This tactic is known as 'organised coincidence', whereby the direct action tactic is put into operation when a sufficient number of cyclists turn up at a specific location and time.

Reclaim the Streets subsequently broadened its agenda opposing global capitalism and widened its use of tactics to include activities such as guerrilla gardening. This activity entails activists taking over a plot of land (public or privately owned) which has been abandoned or otherwise neglected and turning it into flowerbeds or vegetable plots. The collective name for actions that embrace guerrilla gardening and streets parties carried out by this movement is 'creative occupation'. These may take place at a variety of locations that include public parks, motorways and the London Underground system.

The modern origins of guerrilla gardening have been traced back to the activities undertaken by the artist Liz Christy and her Green Guerrilla Group, which cultivated an abandoned site (that they called the Bowery Garden) in New York in 1973, and it has been subsequently developed across the globe. It is political in that it empowers participants to exercise control over their local environment and also because it targets 'industrialization, commercialization of nature, capitalist food production, unequal land ownership, and the disappearance of public green spaces' (Dauvergne, 2009: 88). A nutritional benefit (as well as a political aspect) of guerrilla gardening is that when vegetables are cultivated, it enables the gardeners to exercise control over the quality of the produce which is not produced using farming methods adopted by large-scale manufacturers (including the use of pesticides).

Guerrilla gardening is usually conducted at the local community level, but groups such as Reclaim the Streets have directed the tactic at more symbolic targets (such as Parliament Square on 1 May 2000) to draw attention to its political ramifications in connection with anti-capitalism and self-reliance.

A further form of civil disobedience entails the use of street theatre in which actors or puppets are used to ridicule those who wield power within society. Actions of this nature attract crowds and thus publicise the views of the protesters. This form of protest has historical roots that date back to forms of public humiliation for those who had transgressed society's standards of behaviour in Ancient Greece (Forsdyke, 2008: 3). In more recent years, this has been used by the Yippies in America during the 1960s in connection with their protests against the Vietnam War and by anti-road campaign groups in Britain in the 1990s.

The use of actions that amount to publicity stunts designed to ridicule the establishment is also a feature of the organisation Fathers4Justice in Britain, which viewed 'family law in this country as a perversion of the course of natural justice' (O'Connor, 2007: 1) This organisation 'grabbed the media spotlight by dressing up as superheroes to show that they are real-life heroes fighting against a family court system that will disenfranchise them from their children if the mother decides, for whatever reason, she doesn't want dad around' (Fatherhood Coalition, 2006).

See also: animal rights protest groups, anti-globalisation/anti-capitalist protest (UK), anti-globalisation/anti-capitalist protest (worldwide), direct action, hactivism, peace movement, whistleblowing

Sources and further reading

Bedau, H. (ed.) (1969) *Civil Disobedience: Theory and Practice*. New York: Macmillan.

Carter, A. (1983) *Direct Action*, 3rd edn. London: Housmans.

Dauvergne, P. (2009) *Historical Dictionary of Environmentalism*. Lanham, MD: Scarecrow Press.

Fatherhood Coalition (2006) 'Fathers Rights Activists to Stage Boston Custo-Tea Party', *The Fatherhood Coalition*, www.fatherhoodcoalition.org/cpf/newswire/2006/PR_061210_Custo-Tea_Party.htm (date accessed 21 April 2014).

Forsdyke, S. (2008) 'Street Theatre and Popular Justice in Ancient Greece: Shaming, Starving and Stoning Offenders Inside and Outside the Courts'. *Past and Present*, 201(1): 3–50.

Joyce, P. (2002) *The Politics of Protest: Extra-parliamentary Politics in Britain since 1970*. Basingstoke: Palgrave.

Milligan, T. (2013) *Civil Disobedience: Protest, Justification and the Law*. London: Bloomsbury Academic.

O'Connor, M. (2007) *Fathers 4 Justice: The Inside Story*. London: Weidenfeld & Nicolson.

Quill, L. (2009) *Civil Disobedience: (Un) Common Sense in Mass Democracies*. Basingstoke: Palgrave Macmillan.

Smith, W. (2013) *Civil Disobedience and Deliberative Democracy*. London: Routledge.

Thoreau, H.D. (1998). *Civil Disobedience, Solitude and Life without Principle*. New York: Prometheus Books.

Tracey. D. (2007) *Guerrilla Gardening: A Manualfesto*. Gabriola Island, British Columbia, Canada: New Society Publishers.

Walzer, M. (1970) *Obligation – Essays on Disobedience, War and Citizenship*. Cambridge, MA: Harvard University Press.

COPYCAT RIOTS (ENGLAND) 1981

Serious disorder occurred on 10–12 April 1981 in Brixton, south London, 'the like of which had not previously been seen this century in Britain' (Scarman, 1981: 1). It occurred against the background of a police stop and search operation (termed 'Swamp 81') targeting street crime (or 'mugging'). The police identified this crime with black youths, who were targeted in this operation. This served to intensify the already-tense relationship between the police and the black communities in parts of London. This dated from perceived police inaction to deal with the 1958 race riots in Notting Hill and, more recently, in connection with the New Cross fire in January 1981 in which 13 black youths were killed.

As in the August 1980 riot in the St Paul's area of Bristol, the riot was triggered by a police intervention. On this occasion, a police officer (who was subsequently joined by a colleague) observed a black youth being chased by other black youths. When it became apparent that the youth being chased had been stabbed, the officers sought to provide help, but their actions were misunderstood by onlookers, who perceived that the youth was being arrested. The injured youth was taken from the police and was conveyed to hospital. Other police officers who attended the scene were attacked.

The initial violence petered out, but resumed the following day, triggered by a police search of a black mini-cab driver and his vehicle on suspicion of possession of drugs. This resulted in a hostile crowd gathering, whose mood was further inflamed by rumours (which were untrue) that the youth who had been stabbed the previous day had subsequently died. Police attempts to arrest those involved further escalated the violence until it turned into a full-blown riot. The police were attacked with petrol bombs (the first time this weapon had been used outside Northern Ireland). Violence was at its worst on 11 April, when 279 police officers and at least 45 members of the general public were injured, a large number of police and other vehicles were damaged or destroyed and 28 buildings were destroyed or damaged by fire. The scene of the riot was described as 'comparable with the aftermath of an air raid' (Scarman, 1981: 1). Widespread looting also occurred in the shopping centre of Brixton.

The government's response to the Brixton riot was to ask a senior judge, Lord Scarman, to conduct an inquiry. This took the form of an investigation under the provisions of the Police Act 1964, suggesting that police–public relations were considered by the government to be an important reason for the occurrence of violence.

As Lord Scarman collected evidence, a further wave of rioting occurred in July 1981. This took place in a number of areas, principally Toxteth (Liverpool), Moss Side (Manchester), Handsworth (Birmingham), Chapeltown (Leeds) and Brixton. Disorder was especially severe in Toxteth, where mutual aid was used. Almost 500 police officers were injured and considerable looting and destruction of buildings and cars occurred. The spread of these disorders led to them being dubbed 'copycat riots', which implied that disorders were caused by people imitating actions that had occurred elsewhere.

All of these areas shared certain demographic characteristics that included a relatively large ethnic minority population and social and economic deprivation (especially unemployment, which had risen to 2.5 million across England and Wales in the summer of 1981). With the exception of Handsworth (Brown, 1982), police–public relations were also strained in the places where riots occurred. As already mentioned, this was the case in Brixton and was also the situation in Toxteth, where violence was triggered by a police intervention to arrest a black youth. Problems of this nature were also alleged to have existed in Moss Side, where the police were accused of delivering 'an intimidatory style of policing, deeply stained with racial prejudice', which was allegedly directed at all sections of the black population, including the older generation (Moss Side Defence Committee, 1981: 3).

Police officers in England Wales had not faced violence of this nature in the twentieth century and a number of problems arose in their response to it. One related to weaponry. CS gas was deployed in Toxteth for the first (and only) time on mainland Britain during the disturbances and in some cases was shot directly at those suspected of being involved in the riots. Police vehicles were also used offensively in an attempt to break up crowds in Moss Side and in the second wave of riots that occurred in Toxteth towards the end of July.

Differences were also evident in connection with public order tactics, in particular whether the police should adopt high-profile policing in an attempt to regain control of the streets or should withdraw. Although the latter tactic might help to defuse tense situations, it also left areas vulnerable to attack by rioters and to criticisms of police inaction by those who became victims of violence in the absence of the police. There were also dilemmas as to whether the best approach was to try and arrest rioters at the scene (thereby running the risk of inflaming an already-tense situation) or to identify participants with a view to arresting them subsequently when the violence had subsided. These differences in approaches were particularly important when mutual aid was used.

A number of varied explanations were offered for the riots. Conservative politicians regarded the violence as mindless hooliganism and the extent of looting in these events was cited as evidence of the criminal mentality of the rioters. Those who were involved were *depraved* rather than *deprived*. The media was also argued to be a contributing factor accounting for 'copycat' riots. This view explained the spread of these disorders arising from intense media coverage, whereby 'televising acts of vandalism and violence' contributed 'to the spread of riots by creating excitement, encouraging imitation, and ... teaching the techniques of violence' (Whitehouse, cited in Tumber, 1982: 7).

However, these views were challenged by other opinions, which held that society was responsible for having caused these actions. Political marginalisation and social problems such as unemployment, poor housing and inadequate educational and recreational facilities were put forward as the context that triggered these disorders. Although there were many white participants in these events (which rendered the designation of these events as 'race riots' inappropriate), it was observed that disorder was aggravated by racial discrimination. This led to the conclusion that 'where deprivation and frustration exist on the scale to be found among young black people in Brixton, the probability of disorder must ... be strong' (Scarman, 1981: 16).

The view that society could be held responsible for these events underpinned Lord Scarman's report, which also took into account the disorders that had occurred in the summer of 1981. However, the bulk of the report considered the relationship between police and public in the areas affected by riots, especially police relations with ethnic minority communities.

Scarman rejected the view that the police were institutionally racist, but accepted that a minority of officers harboured racist feelings – there existed a few rotten apples in the barrel. However, he did accept that the police had failed to adequately adapt themselves to operate in multi-ethnic communities (Scarman, 1981: 79). His report thus put forward a number of reforms to policing that were designed to improve the relationship between the police service and ethnic minority communities, and his main theme was the need to reconstruct the principle of policing by consent in these areas.

His proposals included recruiting more police officers from ethnic minority communities (although he rejected the use of quotas to achieve this objective), improving training programmes by the introduction of multicultural components, making greater utilisation of community policing methods, introducing safeguards to the use of stop and search powers, which he argued should be rationalised across the country rather than being subject to local variation (to enable their use by officers on the streets to be monitored by supervising officers), creating formal consultative mechanisms to enable police–public dialogue to occur and reforming the police complaints machinery by enabling an independent body to supervise the police investigation of the more serious complaints. He also suggested (in his 'consent and balance' principle of policing) that rigid, inflexible law enforcement could be counterproductive if this endangered a key role of the police to maintain public tranquillity (Scarman, 1981: 76–120).

Many of Lord Scarman's proposals were included in the Police and Criminal Evidence Act 1984, which created a national raft of police powers. Other recommendations, which included changes to police training programmes, were left to the police to implement. Additional initiatives (termed 'tension indicators') were also developed within the police service to assess the mood of local communities. These included the use of District Information Officers by the Metropolitan Police Service (Brewer *et al*., 1996: 22; Waddington, 1992: 183).

In addition, the possibility that riots might occur in the future and that mutual aid might be necessary to quell them prompted the Association of Chief Police Officers (ACPO) to seek to standardise public order weaponry, tactics and the training that underpinned their use across police forces through the publication of the ACPO *Public Order Manual of Tactical Operations and Related Matters* in 1983.

See also: Bradford riots (Manningham, Bradford) 1995, Broadwater Farm Estate riot (Haringey, London) 1985, housing estate riots (England) 1991–2, northern English town riots (Bradford, Burnley, Oldham) 2001, public order policing (England and Wales), riots

Sources and further reading

Benyon. J. (ed.) (1984) *Scarman and After: Essays Reflecting on Lord Scarman's Report, the Riots and their Aftermath*. Oxford: Pergamon Press.

Benyon, J. and Solomos, J. (eds) (1987) *Policing the Riots*. Oxford: Pergamon Press.

Brewer, D., Guelke, A., Hume, I., Moxon-Brown, E. and Wilford, R. (1996) *The Police, Public Order and the State: Policing in Great Britain, Northern Ireland, the Irish Republic, the USA, Israel, South Africa and China*, 2nd edn. Basingstoke: Macmillan.

Brown, J. (1982) *Policing by Multi-racial Consent: The Handsworth Experience*. London: Bedford Square Press of the National Council for Voluntary Organisations.

Cowell, D., Jones, T. and Young, J. (1982) *Policing the Riots*. London: Junction Books.

Hytner, B. (1981) *Report of the Moss Side Enquiry Panel to the Leader of the Greater Manchester Council*. Manchester: Moss Side Enquiry Panel.

Moss Side Defence Committee (1981) *The Hytner Myths*. Moss Side Defence Committee.

Scarman, Lord (1981) *The Brixton Disorders 10–12 April 1981: Report of an Inquiry by the Rt Hon Lord Scarman, OBE*. London: HMSO, Cmnd. 8427.

Tumber, H. (1982) *Television and the Riots*. London: British Film Institute Broadcasting Research Unit.

Waddington, D. (1992) *Contemporary Issues in Public Disorder: A Comparative and Historical Approach*. London: Routledge

Wain, N. and Joyce, P. (2012) 'Disaffected Communities, Riots and Policing: Manchester 1981 and 2011'. *Safer Communities*, 1(3): 125–34.

COUNTERCULTURE PROTEST

Counterculture constitutes a rejection of the dominant society and its culture (Nelson, 1989: 8) and typically entails an attack on the moral standards and material values on which the existing social order is based.

Contemporary forms of counterculture protest developed in America and the UK during the 1960s and 1970s. These protests were especially associated with opposition to American involvement in the war in Vietnam and with the campaigns that sought to extend civil rights to black Americans, where what was at stake went beyond the specific issues that were involved and entailed a critique of the social values and attitudes that had given rise to these forms of injustice. Accordingly, those engaged in protests of this nature also 'embraced an alternative lifestyle characterized by long hair, brightly colored clothes, communal living, free sex, and rampant drug use' (Johnson, undated). Events that included the 1967 'Summer of Love' in San Francisco and the 1969 Woodstock Festival in New York were especially associated with American counterculture protests.

The aims with which counterculture protest has been associated are broad. They are typically anti-establishment in character and have included the demand for radical political changes, attempts by marginalised groups to achieve liberation or to redress their misrepresentation by mainstream society, the promotion of social structures that are based upon values different from those embraced by mainstream society and protests associated with specific issues that include demands to liberalise drug laws and protect the environment. Some environmental groups have endorsed the cultural transformation of society into an ecological one based on the philosophy of social ecology (Purkis, 1996: 205).

Counterculture protest may be promoted through a wide range of actions. It may promote philosophies that form the basis of alternative lifestyles, which include communes, various forms of cooperative endeavours and the way of life embraced by the travelling community. An example of the latter are New Age travellers (a description applied to a diverse range of groups that shared a common desire for freedom and a rejection of the state).

Counterculture protest may also be delivered by various art forms that include music, literature, satirical cartoons and the underground press. Important examples of the latter in England were signalled by the launch of the *International Times* in October

1966 (later renamed the *IT*) and, the following year, of *Oz Magazine*. Other examples that were associated with specific causes included *The Black Panther* (associated with the Black Panther Party), *Come Together* (associated with the Gay Liberation Front) and *Shrew* (associated with the UK Women's Liberation Workshop). These publications sought to challenge the negative stereotyping of the communities with which they were associated and to provide platforms for these groups to represent themselves and through which campaigns to advance their values could be promoted.

Music has often been used to deliver counterculture protest and punk rock in particular has been associated with an iconoclastic culture which urged young people to stop consuming a culture that was made for them and instead to create their own. Although protests of this nature may primarily entail an attack on those who control the music industry, punk rock may also contain a political message. One example of this in Britain was the release by the punk rock group, the Sex Pistols, of their version of the UK national anthem 'God Save the Queen' to coincide with the Elizabeth II's Silver Jubilee celebrations in 1977. More recently, the Russian female punk rock group Pussy Riot staged a protest in Moscow Cathedral in 2012 to protest against President Vladimir Putin and the close attachment of the state with the Russian Orthodox Church.

Counterculture protest, whatever form it takes, is often responded to robustly by the state. In England, both *IT* and *Oz Magazine* were subjected to numerous police raids and prosecutions on charges of obscenity and conspiracy to corrupt public morals. A similar response occurred in India, where Aseem Trivedi was charged with sedition in 2012 for his cartoons, which sought to highlight the corruption amongst India's political elite.

The response by the state may also involve clashes between the police and those engaged in some form of counterculture protest, an example of which in Britain is the clashes that have taken place between the police and New Age travellers, usually in connection with attempts to prevent them from occupying common land or to evict them from private land. One of these events that took place in June 1985 was referred to as the 'Battle of the Beanfield' and is generally regarded as an important milestone in the development of grassroots environmentalism.

Similar conflict between police and counterculture protesters occurred regularly in connection with attempts headed by the druids to celebrate the summer solstice at Stonehenge, which led to an exclusion zone being established around the site between 1985 and 2000. Legislation in the form of the Criminal Justice and Public Order Act 1994 was brought forward to outlaw activities associated with counterculture protest and other manifestations of youth subculture.

Counterculture protest may be differentiated from other forms of popular subculture embraced by young people in that it contains a distinct political element (Joyce, 2002: 21). Examples of youth subculture in the UK include clashes between 'mods' and 'rockers' that occurred in a number of south coast seaside towns during the 1960s, based upon differences that were reflected in items that included the style of clothes worn by the participants to these disorders, their choice of music and their mode of transport.

Nonetheless, youth subcultures may also contain an implicit political element in the sense that manifestations of popular culture in 'elaborated societies' constitute 'the culture of the subordinate who resent their subordination' (Fiske, 1989: 169). Examples of youth subculture included the 'swinging sixties' (when a large number of young people rejected society's dominant values, in particular its moral values) and the adoption of rave as the culture of a large number of young people in the 1990s. The latter blended the 1970s festival movement with urban youth culture and was particularly associated with participation at events at which loud music was played and the drug ecstasy was taken. The provision of powers contained in the Criminal Justice and Public Order Act 1994 that enabled the police in England and Wales to take action against raves had the effect of associating 'ravers' with other forms of counterculture protesters.

See also: Battle of the Beanfield (Wiltshire, England) 1985, Dale Farm evictions (Essex, England) 2011, protest songs, public order legislation (England and Wales), public order policing (England and Wales), Pussy Riot protests

Sources and further reading

Fiske, J. (1989) *Understanding Popular Culture*. London: Routledge.
Johnson, K. (undated) 'Summer of Love and Woodstock', Cold War Museum, www.coldwar.org/articles/60s/summeroflove.asp (date accessed 27 April 2014).
Joyce, P. (2002) *The Politics of Protest: Extra-parliamentary Politics in Britain since 1970*. Basingstoke: Palgrave.
Nelson, E. (1989) *The British Counterculture 1966–1973*. Basingstoke: Macmillan.
Purkis, J. (1996) 'Daring to Dream: Idealism in the Philosophy, Organisation and Campaigning Strategies of Earth First', in C. Barker and P. Kennedy (eds), *To Make Another World: Studies in Protest and Collective Action*. Aldershot: Avebury.

COUNTER-TERRORISM

Counter-terrorism refers to a wide range of activities that are designed to enable the state to respond to threats posed by terrorists.

A state's response to terrorism cannot be manufactured in a vacuum. It has to take into account both the dynamics of the policy-making process (which requires constantly adjusting responses to terrorist activities) and external pressures that may influence the nature of anti-terrorist policies. The response to violence of this kind has been depicted in a cyclical fashion: the *threat* posed by terrorism emerges, from which a *perception* develops that impacts on the state's *decision-making machinery*. This results in the initiation of *policy*, which becomes translated into measures that are *implemented*. Implementation creates a reaction by those who use violence, which causes the cycle to begin again. This cycle progresses in both directions, emphasising the fluid nature of the tactics used both by those who carry out violence and by the state, and the manner in which either participant in the struggle has the ability to influence the policies pursued by the other. In addition to the cycle of activities is the 'envelope of influences', which comprises variables such as a country's environment, history or culture. These external factors influence the component parts of the decision-making cycle (Davidson Smith, 1990: 29–31).

Some of the key approaches pursued by counter-terrorist policy are considered below.

Counter-terrorism entails initiatives that seek to win over the hearts and minds of those who might be tempted to either become terrorists or to lend support to others who adopt this course of action. In the UK, this is delivered through the Preventing Violent Extremism programme operated by the Department for Communities and Local Government, which focuses on securing community cohesion and resilience, and tackling underlying grievances that might contribute towards terrorism.

In America, the Department for Homeland Security works with a number of other agencies that include the National Counterterrorism Center to advance the Countering Violent Extremism policy, which has as its aims providing. positive alternatives to those most at risk of radicalisation and recruitment into violent extremism, countering violent extremist narratives and messaging, and increasing international partner capacity (civil society and government) to address the drivers of radicalisation (US Department of State, undated). In Canada, the Prevent element of its counter-terrorist strategy also seeks to tackle the root causes and factors that contribute to terrorism, while in Australia, a Countering Violent Extremism unit located within the Attorney General's Department is responsible for developing approaches that are designed to address radicalisation and tackle home-grown extremism.

Counter-terrorism entails gathering intelligence on terrorist groups which can be used to disrupt their activities and also to prevent attacks from being launched. Much of this activity is conducted covertly by the national security agencies, such as MI5 in the UK and the National Security Agency and the Federal Bureau of Investigation (FBI) in America, which make use of a wide range of surveillance methods to carry it out. The powers of the FBI in relation to surveillance (for example, in connection to gaining access to telephone, email and financial records without a court order) were significantly strengthened by the 2001 USA PATRIOT Act (an acronym of its full title, Uniting and Strengthening America by Providing Appropriate Tools Required to Intercept and Obstruct Terrorism), although legal challenges subsequently reduced the scope of powers of this nature.

In addition, regular police forces may also perform work of this nature in a more overt manner.

Gathering intelligence by the police using time-honoured practices such as questioning usually requires changes to the law to extend the period during which a suspect can be held in a police station for the purposes of being questioned. This procedure is referred to as 'pre-charge detention'. In the UK, the Terrorism Act 2000 permitted a person to be held for a period of up to seven days for these purposes, but this was subsequently increased to 14 days by the Criminal Justice Act 2003 and to 28 days in the Terrorism Act 2006. The Terrorism Prevention and Investigation Measures Act 2011 subsequently reduced it to 14 days. Gathering intelligence also entails cooperation with intelligence and law-enforcement agencies throughout the world, which share the common objective of seeking to defeat terrorism.

Counter-terrorist policy generally includes legislation that provides law-enforcement agencies with additional powers with which to combat terrorism and which itself is deemed to constitute a specific criminal offence.

In the UK, anti-terrorist legislation is contained in a number of measures. These include the Terrorism Act 2000, which unlike its predecessor (the Prevention of Terrorism (Temporary Provisions) Act initially introduced in 1974) is a permanent measure. It provided the police with a vast array of powers with which to combat terrorism, which included measures contained in section 44 of the legislation empowering the police to set up zones within which stop and search procedures (without the requirement of there being 'reasonable suspicion') could be used for a period of up to 28 days, enabling a police officer to order a person and/or his or her vehicle to leave the area. A person reasonably suspected by a police officer of being a terrorist could be stopped and searched and the Act also provided new powers of arrest whereby a police officer could arrest any person without a warrant who was reasonably suspected of being a terrorist. Stop and search powers contained in section 44 of this Act were subsequently replaced by provisions contained in the Protection of Freedoms Act 2012, which contained safeguards that included the stipulation that a specified location where such powers were to be applied should be an area where a senior police officer reasonably suspected that an act of terrorism would take place.

New offences created by the Terrorism Act 2000 were directed at foreign-based individuals or groups that were operating n the UK and made it illegal to incite others to commit criminal acts abroad. Domestic organisations could be banned (or 'proscribed') – previously this provision only applied to groups associated with the politics of Northern Ireland. The Act also made it an offence to provide money or other property which could be used for the purposes of terrorism, for a person not to tell the police if he or she suspected others of terrorist involvement and for a person to possess any 'article' or 'information' in circumstances which gave rise to reasonable suspicion that they could be used for terrorist purposes.

The 2000 Act was supplemented by the Criminal Justice and Police Act 2001 (which was especially directed at the activities such as 'doorstepping' that were associated with animal rights groups) and the Anti-terrorism, Crime and Security Act 2001. The latter was enacted following the 9/11 terrorist attacks in New York and Washington, and was especially directed at countering the threat posed by international terrorism. It contained provisions to provide for the forfeiture of money intended to be used for the purposes of terrorism and enabled the Treasury to make a freezing order to prohibit persons from making funds available or for the benefit of a person or persons named in the order. Powers were also provided in connection with acts of terrorism involving the use of biological, chemical or nuclear weapons, which included making it an offence to aid, abet, counsel, procure or incite a person who was not a citizen of the UK to commit an act of this nature outside of the UK.

Police powers were also extended in the 2001 Act in relation to identifying terrorist suspects through means that included fingerprinting, searching, photographing and the removal of disguises. Powers were also introduced that were designed to improve the safety of the aviation industry, which included unauthorised presence in a restricted zone, in an aerodrome or on an aircraft. Further powers were provided in the Terrorism Act 2006 related to the possession of radioactive devices or materials that were to be used in connection with terrorism.

Counter-terrorism measures also commonly make alterations to a country's judicial procedures. People suspected of terrorism may be denied entry to the country by a procedure known as 'exclusion decisions' in the UK. Speedy procedures to remove suspected terrorists from the UK include the use of exclusion orders that were contained in the Prevention of Terrorism (Temporary Provisions) Act 1974 and subsequent anti-terrorist legislation.

Counter-terrorist policy may also entail changes to a country's trial procedure. The Israeli Prevention of Terrorism Ordinance 1948 provided that terrorist suspects would be tried by a military court, a provision that remained in force until the Ordinance was amended in 1980 to allow such persons to be tried as civilians.

One example of amendments to trial procedures to combat terrorism in the UK was the creation of the

'Diplock Courts' in Northern Ireland during the 1970s so that a judge sitting without a jury would try cases related to terrorism. Internment may also be introduced as a counter-terrorist measure. In America, the 2001 USA PATRIOT Act permitted the indefinite detention of persons who were terrorist suspects in the sense of being enemy combatants or providing them with support. This measure has been subject to legal challenges, but remained part of the government's counter-terrorism strategy in the 2012 National Defense Authorization Act.

The most contentious power contained in the UK's Anti-terrorism, Crime and Security Act 2001 was that of detention without trial, whereby the Secretary of State could issue a certificate that was applied to a person whose presence in the UK was deemed to be a risk to security and who was suspected of either being directly concerned or associated with international terrorism. This person was then detained without trial, which in theory lasted until deportation, but in practice could entail an indefinite period of detention. This power was ruled to be incompatible with the European Convention on Human Rights by the Law Lords in 2004 and was replaced by control orders in the Prevention of Terrorism Act 2005.

Control orders were designed to restrict the movements of any person (including British nationals) who are suspected of terrorist involvement with terrorism. They may entail restrictions that include home curfews enforced by tagging or placing bans on who a suspect can meet and, exceptionally, could be used to restrict a person's movements during a situation of public emergency. These were in turn replaced by terrorism prevention and investigation measures (TPIMs) under provision contained in the Terrorism Prevention and Investigation Measures Act 2011. TPIMs are similar to control orders in that they seek to restrict the actions of individuals who are subject to them, but they contain additional safeguards to the recipient's civil liberties whereby an individual subject to them cannot forcibly be relocated to another part of the country. The restrictions that could be imposed were more limited than those permitted under control orders and TPIMs are time-limited and cannot last for more than 24 months in total.

Counter-terrorism also embraces pre-emptive measures that are designed to protect vital installations and infrastructure from terrorist attacks.

In May 1998, President Bill Clinton signed Presidential Directive 62, which included mechanisms to coordinate federal responses to terrorist threats for events of national interest, which were termed National Special Security Events (NSSEs). The NSSE designation made the US Secret Service the lead agency in designing and implementing an operational security plan which included the formation of partnerships with other federal, state and local law-enforcement agencies. Although used sparingly,

NSSE status can be applied to a large number of large-scale public order events if it is felt that these would attract criminals or terrorists (Narr et al., 2006: 9).

One example of this approach in the UK was the 'ring of steel' policy, which entailed the use of checkpoints on main thoroughfares to stop, question and if necessary search people and vehicles seeking to enter city centre locations. This was pioneered in Belfast and was deployed in Manchester in 1992 and on a more permanent basis around the City of London in 1993. Powers related to these actions in connection with terrorism were provided in the Criminal Justice and Public Order Act 1994 and could be exercised regardless of whether there was reasonable suspicion of a person's involvement in terrorism.

Censorship may also be used as an aspect of counter-terrorist policy. One example of this in the UK was the broadcasting ban introduced in 1988 by powers contained in broadcasting legislation. It was designed to deny terrorist the 'oxygen of publicity' and prohibited the live broadcasting of interviews given by persons associated with organisations suspected of involvement in terrorism or of being associated with such organisations. It was especially directed against spokespersons from Sinn Féin, the political wing of the IRA.

Although the response to terrorism may be delivered by all members of law-enforcement agencies, most states also develop specialist anti-terrorist units that possess expertise in this area of work. This specialism may relate to areas that include weaponry, bomb disposal or responding to hostage and hijack situations. In the UK, the Bomb Squad was initially set up within the Metropolitan Police in 1971 to respond to terrorism that was associated with the Angry Brigade. In 1976 this was renamed the Anti-terrorist Squad, which in 2005 was merged with the Metropolitan Police Special Branch to form the Counter Terrorism Command (SO15). Elsewhere in England and Wales, regional Counter Terrorism Units (CTUs) were set up under the auspices of the Terrorism and Allied Matters initiative by the Association of Chief Police Officers (ACPO) to deliver aspects of the CONTEST programme (which is discussed below), including the gathering of intelligence and evidence to help prevent, disrupt and prosecute terrorist activities and other forms of domestic extremism. Local force Special Branches were incorporated into these new arrangements and CTUs also contain financial investigators, community contact teams, intelligence analysts, forensic specialists and high-tech investigators (ACPO, 2011).

Counter-terrorist policy is typically coordinated at the national government level. In America, the Department for Homeland Security was established by the 2002 Homeland Security Act, whose key purpose is to keep America safe from terrorist attacks.

In the UK, when a terrorist act occurs or is anticipated, coordination will entail the use of the Cabinet Office Briefing Room (Cobra), whereby ministers can be kept abreast of events as they unfold and on the responses that are made. This procedure was put in motion following the murder of soldier Lee Rigby outside Woolwich Royal Artillery Barracks, London, in 2013. Dealing with incidents of this nature also includes the use of organisational structures to deal with emergencies which are laid down in the Civil Contingencies Act 2004.

Pre-emptive aspects of counter-terrorism policy are coordinated by the Office for Security and Counter-Terrorism, which is located in the Home Office. The strategy that underpins its work is known as CONTEST. This was initially developed in 2003, the third and most recent version being issued in 2011. This is organised around four areas, termed 'workstreams', each of which contains a number of objectives.

These workstreams are Pursue (to stop terrorist attacks), Prevent (to stop people becoming terrorists or giving their support to terrorists), Protect (to strengthen the nation's protection against a terrorist attack) and Prepare (to mitigate the impact of a terrorist attack) (HM Government, 2011). These areas provide a context within which specific programmes are implemented. Canada adopts a similar approach with a counter-terrorism strategy entitled 'Building Resilience Against Terrorism'. Like the UK strategy, this also has four strands: Prevent, Detect, Deny and Respond.

An important aspect of counter-terrorist policy is advanced planning. This takes the form of risk assessment to enable anti-terrorist measures to be put in place or to deal with the aftermath of a terrorist attack. In the UK, the National Risk Assessment (NRA) captures 'the range of emergencies that might have a major impact on all, or significant parts, of the UK. These are events which could result in significant harm to human welfare: casualties, damage to property, essential services and disruption to everyday life. The risks cover 3 broad categories: natural events, major accidents and malicious attacks' (Cabinet Office, 2013). The NRA is designed to facilitate preparations to cope with emergencies of this nature.

The approach embodied by the NRA was augmented in 2010 by the publication of the National Security Risk Assessment (NSRA), which seeks to establish the priority tasks for UK national security. Risks are categorised under three tiers, tier 1 embracing hostile attacks on UK cyberspace, international terrorism conducted through the use of chemical, biological, radiological or nuclear materials, an international military crisis between states in which the UK became involved and a major accident or natural hazard such as widespread coastal flooding (HM Government, 2010: para. 0.18). The NSRA informs the decisions made by the Strategic Defence and Security Review, which is conducted by the

National Security Council, a body that was set up in May 2010. Its work is supported by the National Security Secretariat, which also services the Joint Intelligence Committee.

Counter-terrorism policy also embraces international dimensions. This cooperation may be required because terrorist groups work together. Examples of this included the claim that the Hamas suicide bombers who were responsible for a wave of violence in Israel in 2001 had been supplied with explosives by the Basque separatist group ETA and suggestions that in the early years of the twenty-first century, a three-way link existed between the IRA, ETA and the Colombian guerrilla movement, the Armed Revolutionary Forces of Colombia (FARC). In addition, terrorist organisations such as Al-Qaeda do not confine their activities to any specific geographical location, but have activists located throughout the world.

International cooperation on counter-terrorist policy may include international treaties or conventions, and international police and criminal justice cooperation entailing the creation of supranational police organisations such as Europol. This organisation was the creation of the European Union and became formally operational in 1998. It is concerned with combating various forms of organised crime, which includes crimes related to terrorism. Its original function was to pool and share data rather than perform an operational role (Joyce, 2011: 208–30).

Counter-terrorism may also embrace bilateral agreements, especially in areas such as extradition.

Liberal democracies face particular problems in delivering counter-terrorist policy. Terrorists are able to make use of fundamental civil and political liberties to plan and implement terrorist attacks. In addition, measures that embrace counter-terrorism have to draw a careful balance between the considerations of security and liberty. This is especially important as measures that are put forward to combat terrorism (especially where they entail the erosion of civil liberties) face the scrutiny of a judiciary that is independent of the executive branch of government. Courts may declare counter-terrorist measures that erode civil liberties to be unconstitutional (in countries such as America that possess codified constitutions) and thus render them null and void.

The UK does not have a codified constitution, but the courts are required to uphold the provisions of the European Convention on Human Rights, which since 1998 has been incorporated into domestic law, although interventions by the European Court of Human Rights may still take place. One example of this occurred in 2010 when the European Court ruled (in the case of *Gillan and Quinton v UK*) that the stop and search powers contained in the Terrorism Act 2000 were in breach of the Convention since they failed to provide safeguards against abuse and thus violated the respect for private life.

Although courts in the UK cannot set aside law that has been passed by Parliament, they may (through the procedure of issuing a 'declaration of incompatibility' certificate) alert Parliament and the government to its inconsistency with the Convention, which will have the effect of securing changes to counter-terrorist policy.

This judicial power was exerted in connect with detention without trial that had been introduced by the Anti-terrorism, Crime and Security Act 2001 and also in connection with control orders, which replaced detention without trial. In 2009, judges of the Supreme Court of the UK ruled that three people who had been made subject to control orders had been treated unfairly as they were not made aware of the evidence that had been amassed against them to justify a control order being implemented. This situation had arisen because much evidence of this nature had been gathered by the Security Services using a wide range of sources which the government wished to keep secret and not placed in the public domain.

See also: Anti-National Security Agency protest (Germany) 2013, Northern Ireland: security policy during the 'Troubles', political policing, states of emergency, subversion, terrorism, urban guerrilla groups

Sources and further reading

ACPO (2011) 'Terrorism and Allied Matters', www.acpo.police.uk/ACPOBusinessAreas/TerrorismandAlliedMatters.aspx (date accessed 27 April 2014).

Cabinet Office (2013) 'Risk Assessment: How the Risk of Emergencies in the UK is Assessed', https://www.gov.uk/risk-assessment-how-the-risk-of-emergencies-in-the-uk-is-assessed (date accessed 27 April 2014).

Davidson Smith, G. (1990) *Combating Terrorism*. London: Routledge.

HM Government (2010) *A Strong Britain in an Age of Uncertainty: The National Security Strategy*. London: TSO, Cm. 7953.

——. (2011) *Contest: The United Kingdom's Strategy for Countering Terrorism*. London: Home Office.

Joyce, P. (2011) *Policing: Development and Contemporary Practice*. London: Sage.

Narr, T., Oliver, J., Murphy, J., McFarland, M. and Ederheimer, J. (2006) *Police Management of Mass Demonstrations: Identifying Issues and Successful Approaches*. Washington DC: Policy Executive Research Forum. Available at: www.policeforum.org/assets/docs/Critical_Issues_Series/police%20management%20of%20mass%20demonstrations%20-%20identifying%20issues%20and%20successful%20approaches%202006.pdf (date accessed 27 April 2014).

US Department of State (undated) 'Programs and Initiatives', www.state.gov/j/ct/programs/index.htm#CVE (date accessed 27 April 2014).

D

DALE FARM EVICTIONS (ESSEX, ENGLAND) 2011

Dale Farm is located in Crays Hill, Essex, England. It became home to the largest concentration of Travellers in the UK, numbering around 1,000 people at the height of its occupation. However, their presence at this location was illegal as the encampment was set up without planning permission being granted by the local authority (Basildon District Council) in whose boundaries the Farm lay.

After around ten years of legal arguments, a clearance order was executed in October 2011. In order to give bailiffs access to the Travellers' camp, a number of residents and activists were removed by the police.

Dale Farm first began housing Travellers in the 1980s following a successful appeal by two families to reside there, after which the local authority granted permission for 40 families to reside there. However, the influx of Travellers persuaded the Council to cease granting further permissions for the site to be occupied. In 1996, the site (which had been used as a scrapyard located on greenbelt land) was sold to an Irish travelling family, which led to a further influx of caravans and semi-permanent chalets which did not have planning permission. Many of those who came to Dale Farm in around 2001–2 were of Irish origin.

The substantial increase in the number of families at the site in 2001 prompted the Council to serve enforcement notices that year which ordered the land to be restored to its original state. This procedure was challenged by the Travellers, who sought retrospective planning permission. In 2003, the Secretary of State gave the Travellers a two-year period of grace before eviction. However, the site continued to expand (although many of those with pitches there occupied them for only part of the year). This further expansion prompted the Council to decide in 2007 to proceed with the execution of its enforcement notices and evict 14 families. Further delay was caused by a Traveller application for judicial review of this decision. The Travellers were successful in this application before the High Court in 2008, but this decision was overturned by the Court of Appeal in 2009. This gave the Council the right to clear the disputed portion of Dale Farm for which planning permission did not exist. Accordingly, in July 2011, eviction notices were served on families living in around 50 unauthorised plots on the site. They were given until 31 August 2011 to leave and the eviction date was set for the week beginning 19 September 2011.

These actions prompted the creation of Camp Constant within Dale Farm on 27 August 2011. It was organised by a group called Dale Farm Solidarity with the support of the Travellers. Its purpose was to resist the evictions and monitor human rights. It attracted a number of political activists, who viewed actions undertaken by the Council as racially aggravated persecution of the Travelling community: 'Racism towards Gypsies is something that settled communities like to pretend doesn't exist, but it remains virulent and disgraceful, and is clearly at the heart of the conflict over Dale Farm' (Worthington, 2011).

However, on 19 September, on the applications of Travellers' representatives, an injunction was issued by the High Court to prevent the execution of the enforcement notices on the grounds that the Council was required to inform each family individually of the precise nature of the enforcement actions planned against them and must also give them the chance to respond. Judicial permission for the Council to proceed with the evictions was granted on 3 October. Subsequent attempts by the Travellers to launch judicial appeals against the evictions were rejected by the Court.

Meanwhile, residents at Dale Farm took a number of measures to resist the evictions, including locking the large metal gates at the front of the site and using metal fencing and barbed wire to prevent access by the bailiffs and police. A 12-metre-high scaffold tower was also erected at the main gate.

The evictions began on 19 October 2011. Protesters were outnumbered by the police and riot police were deployed, including officers from the Metropolitan Police Service. This operation was justified by the belief that 'bottles, liquids and bricks had been stockpiled and this was a threat to the public, including bailiffs and council workers' (BBC, 2011) and on entering the camp, the police were pelted with items of this nature. Hand-to-hand fighting took place and officers deployed tasers on five occasions (BBC, 2012a). The police insisted that this was in self-defence (Essex Police, quoted in BBC 2012a), although protesters viewed the use of this weaponry as a crowd control technique.

Following the police operation, bailiffs entered the site and began removing illegally erected buildings. Some residents left voluntarily and others were forcibly removed. In total, around 80 families were evicted (BBC, 2012a), numbering around 400 people. On 20 October, Dale Farm Travellers and supporters left the site and bailiffs began removing mobile homes that were left there. On 5 November, the Council was awarded an order at the High Court to prevent the former illegal residents from re-occupying the site.

A total of 45 arrests were made during the eviction operation (BBC, 2012a) and it was estimated that the cost of the eviction to Basildon Council was £7 million (BBC, 2012b). Police involvement amounted to £2.4 million (BBC, 2012a). Dale Farm was subsequently filled with rubble to prevent Travellers returning there and was frequently used for fly-tipping. By April 2012, 83 families displaced by the eviction camped at a site adjacent to the former site and also in the authorised site. Initially the Council determined to evict them, but in February 2013, it instead approved planning permission for 15 double caravan pitches at a government-owned site which the Council leased around 700 yards from Dale Farm.

In the wake of the evictions, Dale Farm Solidarity became renamed the Traveller Solidarity Network. In September 2012 it launched a Fight for Sites Campaign, which was described as 'a confrontational and much-needed challenge to local and national Government, bailiff companies and the Media, who together construct a cycle of homelessness, evictions and racism' (Traveller Solidarity Network, 2012). Amnesty International further expressed its outrage at the failure of Basildon Council 'to ignore the advice of Amnesty, a wide range of UN and Council of Europe bodies and experts, and other UK-based civil society organisations about the human rights impact of these evictions'. It concluded that: 'The eviction at Dale Farm represents a failure on the Council's part to comply with international human rights standards on housing and evictions' (Amnesty International, 2011).

See also: Battle of the Beanfield (Wiltshire, England), counterculture protest, public order policing (England and Wales)

Sources and further reading

Amnesty International (2011) 'Dale Farm Evictions', http://action.amnesty.org.uk/ea-action/action?ea.client.id=1194&ea.campaign.id=11724 (date accessed 27 April 2014).

BBC (2011) 'Dale Farm Traveller Site Eviction Starts with Violence', 19 October, www.bbc.co.uk/news/uk-england-essex-15357932 (date accessed 27 April 2014)

——. (2012a) 'Police Used Tasers Five Times at Dale Farm Eviction', 7 March, www.bbc.co.uk/news/uk-england-essex-17284949 (date accessed 27 April 2014)

——. (2012b) 'Dale Farm Traveller Site Evictions "were Justified"', 16 October, www.bbc.co.uk/news/uk-england-essex-19968784 (date accessed 27 April 2014)

Traveller Solidarity Network (2012) 'Fight for Sites Campaign Launched', http://dalefarm.wordpress.com (date accessed 27 April 2014)

Worthington, A. (2011) 'The Dale Farm Eviction: How Racism Against Gypsies and Travellers Grips Modern-Day Britain', 29 September, www.andyworthington.co.uk/2011/09/29/

the-dale-farm-eviction-how-racism-against-gypsies-and-travellers-grips-modern-day-britain (date accessed 27 April 2014).

DEMONSTRATIONS

A demonstration typically entails a number of people who are united in support of a particular cause and who seek to make others aware of their opinions by undertaking a procession in a public space. Demonstrations are a collective form of protest which 'implies some physical action – marching, chanting slogans, singing – through which the merger of the individual in the mass, which is the essence of the collective experience, finds expression' (Hobsbawm, 2003: 73). The ability to engage in actions of this nature have been facilitated by technology, especially the Internet, which enables demonstrations to be organised easily and on a global scale.

The demonstrators' actions may be guided by a desire to promote a cause in which they believe or to oppose a course of action to which they object. This objective is achieved by mobilising public opinion behind the cause supported by the demonstrators. It is intended to affect the actions of policy makers (whether politicians or business leaders) through the weight of opinion. This may be measured in terms of the numbers who attend the event, but also includes those who become aware of the issue because of the publicity that the demonstration attracts in the media. Typically, the protest is concerned with an aspect of policy (whether conducted by the private or public sectors) that is internal to the country where the demonstration is being held, but it may be directed against the actions of an external state.

Demonstrations are an important aspect of the operations of liberal democratic political systems, enabling citizens to articulate their concerns and grievances and to voice their opinions on issues that arise in periods between general elections. The ability to protest in this manner is safeguarded in the basic law or similar enactments in many countries. For example, it is enshrined in the first amendment to the US Constitution (with respect to the freedom of speech and assembly) and in Article 11 of the European Convention on Human Rights (which relates to the freedom of assembly and association). Although tolerance is not given in equal measure to all forms of protest (especially towards the violent aspects of direct action), it might be argued that the health of a liberal democracy is indicated by the tolerance that it accords to demonstrations and related forms of protest.

However, demonstrations and related activities may result in serious public disorder, sometimes because 'extremist or anarchist groups have instigated violence at organized protests in an attempt to gain publicity or to further their political aims' (Narr et al., 2006: 3). In recent years, many events of this nature have taken place on a global scale at world political gatherings and summits (Narr *et al*. 2006: 2). One objective by such protesters is to provoke robust responses by law-enforcement agencies in the hope that the public will view this as unnecessary violence and thus undermine confidence in the fairness of the state. For this reason, activities of this nature 'often create an inherent risk to public safety and pose particular challenges to law enforcement agencies tasked with protecting life and preserving peace' (Narr *et al.*, 2006: 3).

Such considerations require considerable attention to be devoted to the management of large-scale protests. In America, the key issues that need to be addressed have been identified as effective inter-agency cooperation (since no single agency can effectively manage large events), the need for all agencies to address critical planning issues and processes prior to the event taking place, the importance of planning and training processes considering 'what-ifs' and worst-case scenarios, and plans for mid-course corrections, the need to strike a balance between the right to protest and interventions that are required to protect public safety and property, the devising of policies to guide officers on the degree of force that can be used in response to perceived risks to themselves, the addressing of the issue within operating procedures as to when full body armour and special weapons should be issued (since their appearance could have a negative effect on the crowd), the need for the agency to make the best use of real time and strategic intelligence (which should be managed both internally and via the media) and the determination by the agency of how best to educate and reassure citizens about police professionalism and proportionate responses (Narr *et al.*, 2006: 5).

Of particular importance are police tactics dealing with large-scale demonstrations where it is necessary to ensure that these do not alienate public opinion. It has been asserted that in America, the mass detention at demonstrations of protesters not actively engaged in violence can create 'significant problems' for law-enforcement agencies, especially when non-violent protesters and passers-by are rounded up and detained in 'overly broad sweeps'. Actions of this nature draw into question 'the reasonableness and proportionality of the police response' (Narr *et al.*, 2006: 55). Similar criticisms have been voiced in regard to the use of kettling by police at demonstrations that have been held in the UK.

A further issue of this nature concerns the deployment of officers in riot gear and armed with special weapons. It has been argued that while the appearance of 'Robocop' officers sends a clear message to the assembled protesters and thus exercises a deterrent effect, 'this image can also have a negative effect on the public. Media accounts of protected officers facing off against peaceful demonstrators can lead to a public perception that the police are being heavy handed and overreacting' (Narr et al., 2006: 58). In Britain it has been similarly argued that the British model of policing 'can be easily eroded by premature displays of formidable public order protective uniform and equipment which give the perception – inadvertent or otherwise – of a hardening of the character of British policing' (O'Connor, 2009: 31).

It has also been observed that police operations at large-scale protests increasingly take place in the glare of the media. This highlights the importance of cultivating good relationships with these sources of public information and requires the utilisation of a proactive stance which is typically delivered by the police in briefing sessions to journalists that take place before the event has taken place. These are, however, often selective and may not include freelance journalists who cover events of this nature. In Britain, perceptions of police harassment of journalists arose in connection with protests that included the Kingsnorth Power Station in 2008/9 and the G20 protests in 2009. These included the police filming of journalists (an activity sometimes conducted by surveillance operations by police Forward Intelligence Teams) and preventing them from leaving areas that had been kettled. The General Secretary of the National Union of Journalists pointed out the shortfalls of such activities before the Home Affairs Committee, arguing that 'the police rely very heavily ... on the media in order to get their message out ... and, therefore, there is a common interest between the police and the media in having a good working relationship' (Dear, 2009).

In America, use is made of Joint Information Centres that are set up for large-scale events to provide a single point of contact that the media and members of the public can call to receive information and secure answers to any specific questions that they may have. These include representatives of all key agencies that are involved in handling the protest. These are typically not physically accessible to the media during an event (Narr et al., 2006: 65). In Britain, use has been made of Protest Liaison Officers to aid the communication between protesters and demonstrators before, during and after protests have taken place.

However, although constructing good relations with the traditional media is an important consideration, social media has also been used to highlight police actions. An important example of this occurred at the G20 protests in London in 2009 and emphasises the need for police officers engaged in public order situations to conduct themselves in a professional manner at all times.

There are a number of related actions which are associated with demonstrations:

- A *rally*: this entails a demonstration that is concluded by protesters being addressed by speakers in support of their cause. It is, of

course, possible for speakers to address a rally without any prior demonstration.
- *Static demonstrations*: events of this nature are characterised by protesters being immobile. This is often a feature of *counter-demonstrations*, in which protesters line the route of a demonstration mounted by an organisation to which they are opposed. Their stance is negative and they may seek to physically drive their opponents from the street (in which case they would view the demonstration as a form of direct action). The use of counter-demonstrations was a feature of activities used by opponents of the National Front in England during the 1970s and frequently led to violence and police intervention.
- *Vigils*: these involve protesters mounting a presence outside a target that is the source of their grievance. This is similar to a static demonstration, save that the presence of the demonstrators is usually constant over-lengthy periods of time. An important example of this was the vigil mounted outside Greenham Common Air Force Base between 1981 and 2000 by women who were opposed to the presence of cruise missiles that had been placed there. Vigils may also promote forms of direct action that include trespass or blockades.
- *Sit-ins*: actions of this nature involve demonstrators occupying an area (which may be a private or public space) in order to draw attention to their grievances or to perceived injustices that they wish to publicise. Sit-ins may involve trespassing or they may be designed to assert people's right to be in a particular location. This tactic was one form of protest that was used by supporters of the deposed Egyptian President, Mohamed Morsi, in Cairo and Giza to protest against his ousting following military intervention in 2013.

See also: anti-globalisation/anti-capitalist protests (UK), anti-globalisation/anti-capitalist protests (worldwide), Chicago Democratic National Convention (Chicago) 1968, G20 protests (London) 2009, Greenham Common (Berkshire, England) 1981–2000, kettling, Lewisham disorders (Lewisham, London) 1975, paramilitary policing, post-Arab Spring, Protest Liaison Officers (England and Wales), public order legislation (England and Wales), public order policing (England and Wales), Red Lion Square (London) 1974

Sources and further reading

Dear, J. (2009) Minutes of Evidence, 5 May 2009 in *Policing of the G20 Protests*. Home Affairs Committee, Eighth Report, Session 2008–9. London: TSO, House of Commons Paper 418.

Hobsbawm, E. (2003). *Interesting Times: A Twentieth-Century Life*. London: Pantheon.

Narr, T., Toliver, J., Murphy, J., McFarland, M. and Ederheimer, J. (2006) 'Police Management of Mass Demonstrations: Identifying Issues and Successful Approaches', Policy Executive Research

Forum. Available at: www.policeforum.org/assets/docs/Critical_Issues_Series/police%20management%20of%20mass%20demonstrations%20-%20identifying%20issues%20and%20successful%20approaches%202006.pdf (date accessed 19 April 2014).

O'Connor, D. (2009) *Adapting to Protest: Nurturing the British Model of Policing*. London, HMIC.

DIRECT ACTION

Direct action goes beyond articulating a grievance and/or promoting a cause and aims to advance the protesters' cause by undertaking some form of positive physical action to advance it. Such action may be designed to right the wrong that protesters are concerned with, but may also seek to educate the general public regarding the issue that is the focus of the protest in order to motivate them to endorse an alternative course of action. It has been associated with a greater willingness by citizens to assert their rights and a decreased degree of respect for authority (Carter, 2005: 2).

Direct action has a long historical pedigree and has been raised in connection with actions undertaken by both employers and workers in connection with the struggle for control over the economic life of society, utilising tactics that include industrial sabotage, strikes and lock-outs (Mellor, 1920). It is associated with a wide range of groups espousing a vast array of issues operating at both local and national levels, and has been politically associated with anarchism since it places political power directly in the hands of the people by enabling all persons directly affected by an issue to come together on an equal footing and resolve how best to deal with it. In recent years, direct action has been used as a tactic by social movements.

The positive physical action associated with direct action may embrace a number of forms.

It may entail the formation of organisations whose role is to alert the general public to the existence of a problem and use this awareness to raise money with which to combat it without necessarily involving governments. Typically, these organisations function as charities and also perform the role of pressure groups, lobbying governments for changes in legislation relevant to the cause they are promoting and mobilising public opinion to challenge the practices of commercial enterprises. The tactic of direct action is implemented through members of the public donating money who are thus empowered by playing a part in tackling a serious social problem.

In Britain, action of this nature has been undertaken by organisations that include Shelter (which was established in England and Wales in 1966 and in Scotland in 1968, whose concern is with homelessness), Oxfam (which was initially set up in 1942 in England and is now part of a confederation of 17 organisations which operate in around 90 countries, seeking to combat poverty and related injustices) and Women's

Aid (which was set up in 1974, entailing the merger of a number of existing women's refuge services and was inspired by the Women's Liberation Movement of the late 1960s and early 1970s). The latter sought to provide practical and emotional support to women and children experiencing violence and now supports a range of domestic and sexual violence services across the UK.

Established organisations such as Shelter and Oxfam sometimes seek to raise money in response to a specific humanitarian crisis. Examples of this include Shelter's 2013 Christmas Emergency Appeal directed at child homelessness and Oxfam's 2013 Christmas appeal to provide aid for those affected by the civil war in Syria. However, money-raising in response to a particular humanitarian crisis is also the concern of direct action carried out by groups that are formed specifically for that purpose. An important example of this was Band Aid, which was set up in 1984 by pop artists Bob Geldof and Midge Ure to draw attention to the famine in Ethiopia and raise money from the general public to send food and medical supplies to this country. One vehicle through which this was achieved was the release of a song, 'Do They Know it's Christmas?', which sold 1 million copies in the first week of its release on 29 November 1984.

The song inspired charity records released in other countries, including 'Tears are Not Enough' by Northern Lights (Canada) and 'We are the World' by USA for Africa (USA). New versions of the Band Aid song were released in 1989 and 2004 and also led to the creation of the Band Aid Charitable Trust in 1985, which sought to raise money to relieve hunger and poverty in Ethiopia and the surrounding countries.

A different form of direct action takes the form of consumer boycotts in which activists seek to alert the public to the existence of a social problem that arises in connection with a company's commercial activities (especially in connection with ethical considerations that include environmental issues, the exploitation of labour in developing nations and the treatment of employees) and to elicit their support in combating it by the threat to exert economic pressure against those who are responsible for the action. Petitions are frequently used as the mechanism to mobilise public opinion against a company's commercial practices (in which a boycott may be an implicit or explicit undertaking by the signatories). One recent example of this is Oxfam's Sugar Rush petition, which seeks to stop land grabs in developing nations such as Brazil and Cambodia whereby communities are displaced to make way for sugar production which First World manufacturers put in soft drinks.

The Internet is also an important way through which the activities of multinational corporations can be scrutinised and for facilitating action to be taken against them in the form of consumer boycotts (Hertz,

2001: 148). However, it has been observed that 'consumer and shareholder activism empowers those with greater purchasing power and those with an ability to change their patterns of consumption with relative ease. It is a form of protest that favours the middle class' (Hertz, 2001: 153).

Typically, consumer boycotts are directed against the commercial practices of private companies, although they can be directed against governments that endorse practices to which protesters object. One example of this arose in 1995, when consumer groups called for a boycott of all French products as a protest against French nuclear testing in the South Pacific (Hertz, 2001: 121).

Direct action is frequently associated with some form of physical obstruction that seeks to prevent an action taking place to which protesters object. This particular form of direct action embraces a wide range of activities that include sit-down protests, mass obstruction, mounting blockades, burrowing underground and building treehouses, which has been a feature of campaigns that have sought to prevent motorway construction.

The first of the campaigns using direct action to oppose motorway construction took place at Twyford Down (near Winchester) in 1992 in connection with the extension of the M3 motorway. This threatened several Sites of Special Scientific Interest and ecological sites (the area being one of the few habitats of the rare Chalkhill Blue butterfly). The protest took the form of protest camps on the areas designated for clearance, and construction work and protesters also chained themselves to trees and to construction machinery. A mass trespass also took place on the site of the motorway in July 1993. The first camp was evicted in December 1992, an event termed 'Yellow Wednesday' after the colour of the uniforms worn by the Group4 security guards who performed the action. However, other camps were set up to continue this aspect of the protest.

Among those involved in this protest were Earth First! and the Dongas Tribe. The latter were a group of travellers opposed to road construction who also participated in later events elsewhere. Although small in number, the Dongas were important in influence and it was later observed that: 'They called themselves Dongas, lived outdoors through a bitter winter, threw themselves in front of bulldozers, got beaten up by security guards and sent to prison, and eventually failed to stop the M3 being carved through chalk downland outside Winchester. But the 15–20 urban youths who camped out to try to defend Twyford Down in 1992 are recognised to have fired up British environmental protest and kickstarted a major shift in green attitudes in both government and the public' (Vidal, 2012).

Although these forms of direct action did not prevent the road being built, it inspired other similar protests elsewhere, one of which occurred in connection with the construction of the Newbury bypass in Berkshire in 1996: 'at the protest's height the site included 26 camps made of homemade shelters, treeehouses and networks of underground tunnels' (Learning Dreamers and Dissenters, undated). It was argued that the occupation of tunnels and treehouses (which became developed into 'sky villages') was a particularly effective disruption strategy: 'Protesters relied on knowledge that the government was responsible for their safety; occupied trees could not be felled without risk to the protesters occupying them; construction machinery could not safely drive on land that had been tunnelled without risk of collapse' (Learning Dreamers and Dissenters, undated). Direct action was accompanied by other forms of protest (including a march on the route of the bypass). In response to these protests, the police made use of new powers (especially that of aggravated trespass) derived from the Criminal Justice and Public Order Act 1994. The protests failed to stop the road being built and work was completed in 1998.

Protests against these road building schemes considerably added to the cost of construction (especially in the form of costs of policing and payment to private security companies): it was estimated that the actions of the Dongas at Twyford Down added an additional £3 million to the cost of the project (Bryant, 1996: 308). In addition, the tactics developed in these protests were utilised at other similar protests – tunnelling, for example, being utilised in connection with the building of the extension to the A30 road at Fairmile, Devon in 1996 and to prevent the building of the second runway at Manchester Airport in 1997. A key participant in both of these two episodes was the environmentalist activist Daniel Hooper (then known as 'Swampy').

Physical obstruction may result in some form of confrontation either with those conducting an activity to which protesters object (or with security personnel employed by them) or with the police who attend an event with the aim of keeping the peace or upholding the law if the activities of activists threaten to breach it. This may mean that violence arises when protesters adopt some form of physical obstruction to further their cause even when their own actions are non-violent and constitute civil disobedience. This activity is discussed as a separate entry in this book.

However, some direct action campaigns seek to further their ends by using coercive tactics to achieve it, an example of this in Britain being the campaign waged between 1999 and 2005 against the breeding of guinea pigs for medical research at Darley Oaks Farm, Newchurch, Staffordshire, in which animal liberation groups used violence or the threat of it to isolate the farmer engaged in this form of commercial enterprise. What was dubbed a 'terroristic campaign' was directed at the farm, its owners, employees and suppliers (Kannard, 2009: 157). One extreme form of this direct action entailed digging up the body of the farm-owner's mother-in-law from the local cemetery.

When violence is intentionally used to further a cause (whether political, commercial or moral), the dividing line between terrorism and direct action becomes a thin one and in the UK, recent anti-terrorist legislation has been directed at all groups who seek to achieve their objectives by coercive means.

See also: animal rights protest groups, counter-terrorism, civil disobedience, environmental protest groups, fuel crisis (Britain) 2000, live animal export protests (England) 1994–5, Occupy movement, terrorism

Sources and further reading

Bryant, B. (1996) *Twyford Down: Roads, Campaigning and Environmental Law.* London: E & F Spon.
Carter, A. (2005) *Direct Action and Democracy Today.* Cambridge: Polity Press.
Direct action groups:
 Oxfam – www.oxfam.org
 Shelter – www.shelter.org.uk
 Women's Aid – www.womensaid.org.uk
Hertz, N. (2001) *The Silent Takeover: Global Capitalism and the Death of Democracy.* London: William Heinemann.
Kannard, B. (2009) *Skullduggery: 45 True Tales of Disturbing the Dead.* Nashville, TN: Grave Distractions Press.
Learning Dreamers and Dissenters (undated) 'Treehouses and Tunnels', www.bl.uk/learning/histcitizen/21cc/counterculture/disruption/treehouses/treehousesandtunnels.html (date accessed 30 April 2014).
Mellor (1920) *Direct Action.* London: Parsons, subsequently reprinted by BiblioLife, Charleston, SC in 2009.

Vidal, J. (2012) 'Twyford Down's Dongas Return 20 Years after M3 Protest', *The Guardian*, 28 September.

'DIRTY PROTEST' (NORTHERN IRELAND) 1978–81

Persons convicted of crimes of violence associated with paramilitary organisations in Northern Ireland were initially treated in the same manner as other criminals. However, a hunger strike by a number of IRA prisoners in July 1972 resulted in the introduction of Special Category Status, as a result of which these prisoners were accorded a number of privileges that included not having to wear prison uniforms or undertake prison work and being allowed extra visits and food parcels. They were also housed according to their membership of paramilitary organisations, resulting in a situation that was akin to that of prisoners of war.

In January 1975, the Gardiner Committee considered measures to combat terrorism in Northern Ireland. It concluded that the introduction of Special Category Status for convicted prisoners had been 'a serious mistake' (Gardiner, 1975: para. 107) and recommended that it should be ended at the earliest practicable opportunity (para. 108). The new system would apply to those convicted of a crime associated with a paramilitary organisation after 1 March 1976, who would be treated as ordinary criminals, thus requiring them to wear a prison uniform and undertake prison work. The sentence would be served in a regime that was completely separate from the remainder of the prison estate in Northern Ireland in what became known as the H-Blocks of the newly constructed Maze Prison that was constructed on the site of the former Long Kesh Detention Centre around nine miles from Belfast.

The abolition of Special Category Status was opposed by the IRA on a number of grounds. Acts of violence were viewed as motivated by political rather than criminal concerns and the legitimacy of the Diplock Courts was disputed. This new judicial procedure was introduced under provisions contained in the Northern Ireland (Emergency Provisions) Act 1973 and constituted a key aspect of the criminalisation process. It entailed crimes associated with political violence (the 'scheduled offences') being tried by a judge but no jury. The abolition of Special Category Status also undermined the authority that the paramilitary leadership inside prisons had been able to exert over their own men and was resisted for that reason.

The decision to end Special Category Status thus triggered a range of actions that included a request by IRA leaders in prison to the IRA Army Council to commence a policy of assassinating prison officers, the first victim being Patrick Dillon in April 1976. Inside prison, the initial action was the 'blanket protest' initiated by a newly convicted paramilitary prison Kieran Nugent on 14 September 1976. This entailed the refusal of prisoners belonging to the IRA (and also the Irish National Liberation Army (INLA)) to wear prison uniforms and instead to go about prisons either naked or wearing clothing fashioned from prison blankets. This was known as the 'blanket protest' (which subsequently became the 'dirty protest' in April 1978). By August 1976, around 300 prisoners were involved in this protest (Dickson, 2010: 279).

The dirty protest arose from events that occurred in the Maze Prison in March and April 1978, in which prisoners refused to leave their cells to shower or use lavatory facilities because of concerns relating to attacks on them by prison staff. Instead, the prisoners asked for wash basins to be placed in their cells. This was agreed to, but a further request for showers to be installed was denied, which resulted in prisoners refusing to use the hand basins. This transformed the 'blanket protest' into the 'no wash protest'.

A fight between a prisoner and a prison officer at the end of April 1978 resulting in an escalation of the protest. The prisoner was placed in solitary confinement, but rumours spread across the prison that he had been badly beaten. Other prisoners responded to this news by smashing the furniture in their cells, to which the authorities responded by removing everything save mattresses and blankets in order to prevent prisoners from using prison furniture as weapons. This action led to the prisoners refusing to leave their cells to 'slop out' and commencing the 'dirty protest' in which the cell walls were smeared with excrement. Although the prison authorities sought to maintain standards of hygiene by methods that included breaking cell windows and spraying in disinfectant, and physically removing prisoners from their cells and spraying the walls clean, this was to no avail as the prisoners reverted to the protest as soon as they were returned to their cells.

A situation of stalemate was thus reached. The protest continued (and was joined by most newly arrived prisoners) and the British government refused to make concessions. In January 1980, prisoners issued a list of requirements to end the protest which were called the 'Five Demands'. These were:

- The right not to wear a prison uniform.
- The right of free association with other republican prisoners.
- The right not to do prison work.
- The right to organise their own educational and recreational pursuits.
- The right to one visit, one letter and one parcel per week.

The prisoners also wanted the full restoration of remission they might lose arising from their involvement in the protest (Dickson, 2010: 279).

These demands were not met and the protest further escalated in February 1980, when a number of prisoners at Armagh Women's Prison commenced a dirty protest that included smearing the cell walls with their menstrual blood. The resolve of the British government not to concede to the protest was strengthened by a ruling of the European Commission of Human Rights in June 1980 that rejected as inadmissible a claim by four prisoners that conditions inside the prison constituted a breach of Articles 3 and 8 of the European Convention on Human Rights. The ruling asserted that 'slopping out' and the use of chamber pots in cells were self-inflicted, and that surveillance was necessary to prevent disorder or crime (*McFeeley, Nugent, Huntley and Campbell v UK* (1980)). Judgment was adjourned relating to the complaint regarding interference with prisoners' mail, a complaint that was subsequently upheld as a breach of Article 8 of the European Convention (*Silver and Others v UK* (1983)).

A further attempt by paramilitary prisoners to secure the 'Five Demands' occurred on 27 October 1980 when the IRA and an INLA prisoner embarked on a hunger strike. This was called off on 18 December on the assumption that the government had agreed to make concessions along the lines of the 'Five Demands'. When this proved not to be the case, a further hunger strike was initiated on 1 March 1981 by Bobby Sands. This action prompted the end of the 'dirty protest' on 2 March.

The hunger strike ended on 3 October 1981 and cost the lives of ten men, including Sands, who had been elected as MP for the constituency of Fermanagh and South Tyrone in April 1981. On 5 October, the new Secretary of State for Northern Ireland, James Prior, announced changes to prison policy which allowed paramilitary prisoners to wear their own clothes whilst in jail.

'Dirty protests' have subsequently occurred in Northern Ireland. In May 2011, a group of dissident republicans held in Maghaberry Prison began a protest of this nature in opposition to strip searches, which they wished to be replaced with scanning devices. Actions allied to this protest included the murder of a prison officer in November 2012. Some of those involved ended this protest in that month.

See also: Bloody Sunday (or the Bogside massacre) (Derry, Northern Ireland) 1972, Burntollet Bridge (Derry, Northern Ireland) 1969, Northern Ireland: security policy during the 'Troubles', Provisional IRA

Sources and further reading

Bishop, P. and Mallie, E. (1987) *The Provisional IRA*. London: Corgi.

Coogan, T. (2000) *The IRA*. London: HarperCollins.

Dickson, B. (2010) *The European Convention on Human Rights and the Conflict in Northern Ireland*. Oxford University Press.

English, R. (2003) *Armed Struggle: The History of the IRA*. London: Pan.

Gardiner, Lord G. (1975) *Report of a Committee to Consider, in the Context of Civil Liberties and Human Rights, Measures to Deal with Terrorism in Northern Ireland*. London: HMSO, Cmnd. 5847.

McFeeley, Nugent, Huntley and Campbell v UK (1980) DR 20, 3 EHRR 161.

O'Rawe, R. (2005) *Blanketmen: The Untold History of the H-Block Hunger Strike*. Dublin: New Island.

Silver and Others v UK (1983), Series A, No. 61, 5 EHRR 347.

Taylor, P. (1997) *Provos: The IRA and Sinn Féin*. London: Bloomsbury.

Walker, C. (1984) 'Irish Republican Prisoners – Political Detainees, Prisoners of War of Common Criminals?', *The Irish Jurist*, XIX: 189–225. Available at: www.leeds.ac.uk/law/staff/law6cw/Walker-IrJur.pdf (date accessed 30 April 2014).

E

ENGLISH DEFENCE LEAGUE

Recent years have seen the significant re-emergence of right-wing extremism in Europe. Fuelled by the economic crisis and rising fears of immigration in a number of countries, together with a rising concern about the Islamification of the West, a number of fascist groups have reappeared or evolved in a different guise. The English Defence League (EDL) is a far-right movement that originated in Luton in the aftermath of Islamist protests against UK soldiers returning from Afghanistan in 2009.

The main group evolved through social networks of groups associated with football hooliganism that were attracted to the cause by its combination of patriotic appeal, Islamaphobia and opportunities to engage in violent confrontation that was now more difficult to do at organised sports fixtures (Treadwell, 2012). Far-right groups have had a long association with football supporters, especially hooligan groups associated with national teams (Garland and Treadwell, 2010). Concerns about far-right activity and racist attacks were a major concern for the policing of the Euro 2012 football championships in Poland and Ukraine.

The EDL states that it is a non-racist group that intends to conduct peaceful protest marches and demonstrations to highlight Islamic extremism and oppose Sharia law in England. However, its members have consistently been involved in violent clashes with the police and with Unite Against Fascism (UAF), a group made up of people from diverse backgrounds who aim to oppose the spread of right-wing extremism in the UK. The UAF states that the EDL is a fascist party that has clear links to the British National Party and other 'mainstream' fascist groups. In 2011 it was reported that the EDL had connections to the Norwegian mass murderer Anders Breivik, who was responsible for the killing of 77 people in Oslo and Utøya island.

Whilst some EDL demonstrations have passed off peacefully, many have not and since 2009 the scale and frequency of these protests have increased in intensity, with disorder occurring in many towns and cities.

For the police, the mere potential for a protest creates significant problems in managing community relations as the locations chosen by the EDL have diverse communities and are often areas where riots involving minority groups have previously occurred, such as Oldham and Birmingham.

In September 2009 the EDL declared its intention to demonstrate in Piccadilly Gardens in Manchester city centre. This resulted in the UAF informing the police of its intention to hold a counter-demonstration on the same site. In order to police the protests, Greater Manchester Police (GMP) commenced Operation Foot, which involved significant planning and attempts to communicate with both groups in order to avert disorder. The demonstration, which took place at 5 pm on 10 October 2009, caused significant disruption to city centre commuters, shoppers and businesses, and required the erection of steel barriers to separate the two groups. The EDL adopted tactics used by football hooligan groups by arriving in the city early in the morning by train and then drinking heavily all day in local public houses. GMP deployed over 700 officers to police the event and utilised resources from mounted officers through to a police helicopter. Whilst the actual demonstration only lasted 90 minutes, the policing operation lasted all day. In the main, the police managed to keep the two groups apart and 30 arrests of both EDL and UAF members were made.

The costs of policing this demonstration and keeping apart 2,000 EDL supporters and 1,000 UAF representatives were significant at around £200,000. However, the estimated costs of policing other EDL demonstrations have been much higher. The cost of policing a similar event in Leicester was put at around £850,000, whilst one in Luton in 2011, with a similar number of demonstrators to the event in Manchester, was estimated to have cost £2 million, not including the economic costs to businesses and the city. With at least 56 EDL demonstrations since 2009 in different towns and cities, raising tensions and the question of costs, more calls have come for the police to ban the demonstrations.

The power to ban a march under section 13 of the Public Order Act 1986 was used by the Home Secretary in August 2011 to stop an EDL march through a large Muslim community in Tower Hamlets, which was scheduled just weeks after riots had occurred across the UK. Police and community leaders were concerned that there would be a repeat of the Cable Street riots in 1936, when Oswald Mosley's Blackshirts were opposed by Londoners from the East End.

Some concerns have been raised about the use of the power to ban marches as it is seen as counterproductive, since the power being used to ban the EDL could also be used against other protests and demonstrations. This was suggested by the former Commissioner of the Metropolitan Police, Paul Stephenson, for student demonstrations after violent protests in Parliament Square in December 2010.

A call for a similar ban on an EDL march in February 2012 was made by councillors in Hyde after a white teenager had been attacked by Asian men. Hyde, a small industrial town outside Manchester, had previously seen a National Front march banned in 1977 under the Public Order Act 1936, but this had not prevented the leader of the National Front, Martin Webster, walking up the main street on his own with a union flag escorted by hundreds of police officers. The call to ban the 2012 EDL march was not supported by the GMP, which wished to facilitate a lawful protest. In the event, it passed off relatively peacefully with just 11 arrests.

Whilst the EDL does not currently pose a right-wing threat on the same scale as the British Union of Fascists in the 1930s, some commentators have argued that it presents the most significant challenge to public order since the National Front in the 1970s.

There is a also Scottish equivalent of the EDL called the Scottish Defence League. Its activities have included organising a march in Edinburgh in August 2013 to demand better treatment for British troops returning homes from war zones.

See also: demonstrations, nationalist terrorist groups, paramilitary policing, Protest Liaison Officers (England and Wales), public order legislation (England and Wales), public order policing (England and Wales)

Sources and further reading:

BBC News (2009) 'Protest Police Cost was £200,000', 12 October, http://news.bbc.co.uk/1/hi/england/manchester/8303150.stm (date accessed 1 May 2014).

Daily Mirror (2011) 'English Defence League Demo Cost Police £2million', 25 April, www.mirror.co.uk/news/uk-news/english-defence-league-demo-cost-124640 (date accessed 1 May 2014).

Garland, J. and Treadwell, J. (2010) '"No Surrender to the Taliban!" Football Hooliganism, Islamophobia and the Rise of the English Defence League'. British Society of Criminology. Papers from the British Criminology Conference, 10: 19–35.

Treadwell, J. (2012) 'White Riot: The English Defence League and the 2011 English riots'. Criminal Justice Matters, 87: 36–7.

Walker, P. (2011) 'English Defence League March through Tower Hamlets Banned by Theresa May', 26 August, The Guardian, www.guardian.co.uk/uk/2011/aug/26/edl-march-banned-tower-hamlets (date accessed 1 May 2014).

ENVIRONMENTAL PROTEST GROUPS

Environmental protest groups campaign against a wide array of actions that pose a threat to the environment. This might be the local environment or to the planet as a whole.

Environmental protest groups need to be distinguished from groups that are concerned with the protection of the environment, which enjoy relatively easy access to policy makers and are thus able to advance their cause as 'insiders' to the policy-making process. Environmental protest groups are 'outsiders' to the policy-making process and are forced to campaign to achieve influence, hoping that the cause they champion will succeed in mobilising public support, the weight of which will influence governments to adopt the course of action they are promoting. Environmental activism performed by outsider groups can, however, result in the development of 'a professionalized form of environmental activism that ... builds on cooperative relationships between political authorities and scientific elites', as is stated to have been the case in Brazil in the wake of the United Nations Conference on Environment and Development, known as Rio-92 or the Earth Summit (Alonso and Maciel, 2010: 300).

The tactics utilised by environmental protests groups are wide, although some form of direct action is commonly used to advance their cause. Environmental protest groups have been innovative in their use of direct action and have advanced the tactics of protest through actions that include 'tree sitting' (which has been used by American environmental activists since the mid-1980s to prevent logging and the subsequent destruction of forest lands) and living in treehouses and burrowing underground (which was used in the 1990s by British environmental protesters in an attempt to halt road-building programmes). A novel tactic was used in 2013, when four Spanish environmental protesters from the environmentalist group Mugitu (which was opposed to the development of a high-speed train network that threatened forest land in the Pyrenees) hurled a number of pies at the regional President, Yolanda Barcina Angulo, in what was stated to be 'an energetic fashion'. These actions (which took place in Toulouse, France) left the President 'dazed and disoriented', with damage to her clothes (Hamilos, 2013).

Some environmental protest groups (such as Greenpeace) are highly structured, operate on a global basis and campaign against a range of environmental injustices. Other protests are mounted on a national level and some environmental protests (such as that against fracking) are organised locally on an ad hoc basis and whose formation is stimulated by a specific environmental concern.

Britain has witnessed a range of environmental protests since the 1990s, some of which have enjoyed a degree of success. The road-building programme in the 1990s was disrupted by protests using an innovative range of direct actions. The destruction in 2003 by environmental activists of fields of genetically modified crops alerted the public to the potential dangers of this method of food production. In 2008, environmental protesters campaigned against the proposal to expand Heathrow Airport, which culminated in the shelving of the plan to build a third runway.

Actions that threaten the environment are frequently carried out by commercial concerns that have the support of governments. For this reason, environmental activists may find themselves vilified as 'environmental terrorists' or 'eco terrorists' and may face penalties for their actions. These might range from relatively minor public order offences such as obstruction or trespass (as is often the case in Britain) to more serious charges. In 2013, activists, journalists and crew members of the Greenpeace ship *Arctic Sunrise* ('The Arctic Thirty') were arrested by the Russian Coast Guard. They were engaged in a peaceful protest against Russian oil and gas drilling in the Arctic and wished to highlight the threat it posed to climate change. They were initially charged with piracy (which carried a 15-year prison sentence); this charge was eventually reduced to hooliganism as part of an organised group (for which the maximum penalty was seven years' imprisonment), but all charges were dropped by the end of that year and all of those arrested were freed under the terms of a general amnesty law.

Greenpeace is a major environmental protest group which operates internationally. It is a non-governmental organisation (NGO – an organisation that promotes social objectives that have political dimensions, but which is not a political party). It was founded in 1971 and now has a presence in over 40 countries. Its structure is provided by regional offices and there is a coordinating body (Greenpeace International, set up in 1979) in Amsterdam, although local groups are not compelled to join it. Greenpeace is funded by donations from its almost three million members and has a general consultative status with the United Nations Economic and Social Council.

The origins of Greenpeace derive from the anti-nuclear protests mounted by the Don't Make a Wave Committee in 1971, which entailed chartering a ship, the *Phyllis Cormack*, to oppose the testing of nuclear devices by America in Amchitka, Alaska. This Committee subsequently adopted the name 'Greenpeace'. Seaborne forms of direct action have continued to be used as a tactic by Greenpeace, using the vessels that include the *Rainbow Warrior*.

Greenpeace's vision is:

> to transform the world by fundamentally changing the way people think about it. We want governments, industry and each and every person to stop viewing the Earth as an inexhaustible resource and start treating it as something precious that needs our protection and careful management. We all need a planet that is ecologically healthy and able to nurture life in all its diversity. (Greenpeace, 2014a).

It seeks to achieve this aim by promoting positive change through action:

> This action takes many forms – from investigating and exposing environmental abuse and lobbying governments and decision makers to championing environmentally

responsible and socially just solutions and taking nonviolent direct action. Throughout, we always hold true to our core values of independence, internationalism and personal responsibility. (Greenpeace, 2014a)

The campaigns with which Greenpeace is associated include 'climate change, protecting forests, defending oceans, working for peace, challenging nuclear power, promoting sustainable agriculture and eliminating toxic chemicals' (Greenpeace, 2014b). This has led Greenpeace activists to become involved in a number of specific activities, including the occupation of power stations using coal and obstructing coal shipments to them, publicising through graphic images the actions of states who defy the global ban on commercial hunting of whales (such as Iceland in 2013), uprooting genetically modified crops (such as a raid carried out in Manila, the Philippines in 2011) and placing pressure on companies whose commercial practices contribute to deforestation in countries such as Brazil and Indonesia.

Direct action has also been used to disrupt nuclear tests by sailing into the zone where they are to take place. One response to this activity was the bombing of the *Rainbow Warrior* by agents from the French intelligence agency (the *Direction Générale de la Sécurité Extérieure*) in Auckland's Waitemata Harbour in 1985, which killed a photographer who was on board the ship at the time of the attack. The French government wished to prevent the ship being used to interfere with a planned nuclear test it intended to conduct in Moruroa.

In 2011, Greenpeace initiated a campaign against the use of toxic chemicals in the manufacture of clothing. This arises from the use of hazardous dyes and chemicals, which pollute water sources and remain in the finished product. It sought to mobilise public opinion against such practices and its activities included a petition (the Fashion Manifesto) that called on brands and suppliers to act immediately to stop poisoning waterways around the world with hazardous chemicals, as well as mounting protests outside stores that sold such clothing.

Earth First! is another example of an environmental protest group. It originated in America in 1980 and there are now similar groups in a large number of other counties, including France, Germany and the UK. Its first main focus in America during the 1980s was on logging and its tactics to prevent this entailed the use of a new tactic, tree sitting, as opposed to mounting blockades or other forms of obstruction to prevent the movement of logs. It subsequently broadened its activities to protest against construction developments (such as the building of dams) that threatened the wildlife habitats or the character of the rural environment.

The tactics of Earth First! in America have often sought to slow down a threat posed to the environment by the target of the protest while a lawsuit to end the activity is being prepared. Sabotage (sometimes termed *ecotage*) is also used against equipment and machinery used in activities such as tree felling. Earth First! has also been involved in opposition to fracking in America and in 2012, activists managed to temporarily close down a fracking site in Pennsylvania by blocking the access road by tree sitting. In America, Earth First! embraces rural and urban activists and the agenda of the latter extends to anti-oppression work directed against racism, sexism, transphobia, homophobia and ageism (Longenecker, 2012).

Earth First! in the UK originated in 1990, entailing action directed at a nuclear power station in Dungerness in Kent. Subsequent campaigns were directed at the importation of tropical hardwood and entailed actions at the Tilbury and Merseyside docks. The latter action entailed the occupation of Liverpool Docks for two days. Earth First! was also involved in protests against road construction, alongside other groups that included the Dongas Tribe and Reclaim the Streets.

Earth First! is associated with the philosophy of Deep Ecology, which maintained that all forms of life on earth had equal value and that their worth should not be measured solely in relation to their utility to human needs. It has also become increasingly influenced by anarchist political philosophy, which promoted a rejection of organisation and leadership and an endorsement of grassroots activism at a local level performed by autonomous groups who subscribe to Earth First! principles. There are, however, annual gatherings of activists. Divisions have also appeared between Earth First! activists who wish to use peaceful protest to further their aims and those who endorse the use of more violent tactics that involve criminal damage. The latter formed an offshoot of Earth First! Called the Earth Liberation Front, which originated in Britain.

The organisation Friends of the Earth International is a further example of an environmental protest group. It was set up in 1971, bringing together under one umbrella a number of existing groups that were promoting environmental issues. Other groups subsequently aligned themselves with Friends of the Earth International, which thus became a network of environmental groups operating in over 70 countries. These typically take the name 'Friends of the Earth' followed by the location (town, city or country) in which they are active. Friends of the Earth International has a secretariat in Amsterdam that supports this network and the campaigns with which it is associated. By 2008, the combined number of members and supporters of Friends of the Earth groups was more than two million and Friends of the Earth International comprised more than 5,000 local activist groups (Friends of the Earth International, undated).

Friends of the Earth stands for 'a beautiful world ... a good life ... a positive relationship with the environment' (Friends of the Earth, 2012). The focus of its campaigns go beyond concerns that are strictly environmental and include seeking to address the social, political and human rights issues that these embrace: 'We campaign on today's most urgent environmental and social issues. We challenge the current model of economic and global corporate globalization, and promote solutions that will help create environmentally sustainable and just societies' (Friends of the Earth International, 2013). Its campaigns have thus included promoting economic justice and opposition to neoliberalism alongside environmental issues such as deforestation, climate change and opposition to genetically modified crop farming, nuclear power and fracking. In 2014 it directed its attention to the human rights abuses and environmental destruction resulting from the palm oil industry.

See also: civil disobedience, direct action, fracking protests, Monsanto protests (worldwide) 2013, Occupy movement

Sources and further reading

Alonso, A. and Maciel, D. (2010) 'From Protest to Professionalization: Brazilian Environmental Activism after Rio-92'. *Journal of Environment Development*, 19(30): 300–17.

Friends of the Earth (2012) 'What We Stand For', www.foe.co.uk/what_we_do/about_us/friends_earth_values_beliefs (date accessed 1 May 2014).

Friends of the Earth International (undated) 'A Short History of FoEI', www.foei.org/en/who-we-are/about/history (date accessed 1 May 2014).

——. (2013) 'What We Do', www.foei.org/en/what-we-do (date accessed 1 May 2014).

Greenpeace (2014a) 'About Greenpeace', www.greenpeace.org.uk/about (date accessed 1 May 2014).

——. (2014b) 'Global Campaigns', www.greenpeace.org.uk/global (date accessed 1 May 2014).

Hamilos, P. (2013) 'Spanish Environmental Activists Could Face Lengthy Jail Terms for Pie Protest', *The Guardian*, 17 November, www.theguardian.com/world/2013/nov/17/spanish-activists-trial-pie-protest (date accessed 1 May 2014).

Longenecker, C. (2012) 'Fracking Site Bows to Earth First! Convergence', *Waging Nonviolence*, http://wagingnonviolence.org/feature/fracking-site-bows-to-earth-first-convergence (date accessed 1 May 2014).

Rootes, C. (ed.) (2003) *Environmental Protest in Western Europe*. Oxford University Press.

F

FRACKING PROTESTS

The process of fracking (or hydraulic fracturing) entails drilling several miles down into the ground and injecting water, sand and chemicals into shale rock at high pressure in order to release the oil and gas that is trapped inside. This process is generally performed by horizontal drilling. Shale gas is a form of natural gas and the use of this form of fuel can lessen worldwide dependence on fossil fuels and thus aid the tackling of global warming.

It is also seen in the UK as a way of lowering energy bills: 'In the US, shale gas has replaced a lot of coal in power stations for generating electricity as the local price of natural gas has plunged from $15 per thousand cubic feet in 2005 to below $2 at one stage. Gas in the US is one-third the cost in Europe, while electricity is half the price' (Macalister, 2014). However, a parliamentary investigation in the UK concluded that 'it is too early to say whether domestic production of shale gas could result in cheaper gas prices in the UK' (Energy and Climate Change Committee, 2013: para. 61). Nonetheless, the industry could benefit the economy in other ways by creating jobs, both directly and indirectly.

The UK Coalition government has firmly committed itself to shale gas extraction. In 2013, it was announced that affected communities would receive £100,000 for a test well and one per cent of revenue from viable sites. The Prime Minister subsequently announced in January 2014 that local authorities that granted planning permission for fracking projects would receive 100 per cent of the business rates collected from shale gas schemes as opposed to the usual 50 per cent. It was also reported that in 2013 the UK government had spearheaded opposition to the introduction of binding EU regulations on fracking that were designed to safeguard the environment and had succeeded in getting these substituted for a set on non-binding recommendations covering protection against water contamination and potential earthquakes (Carrington, 2014).

In the UK, fracking will occur on onshore sites and has led to opposition. This is mounted by environmental protesters whose alternative approach is to encourage energy efficiency and to invest in renewable sources of energy. Their concerns are that the potentially carcinogenic chemicals used in fracking may pollute surface and underground water supplies, and that the process can lead to leaks of methane (a potent greenhouse gas) from wells that have been abandoned. The location of drilling sites in the countryside would also lead to the industrialisation of the countryside and would harm the natural beauty of affected areas and the wildlife living there. The need to transport large amounts of water to the fracking site presents further environmental hazards.

In addition, economic arguments against fracking have been produced querying whether the energy that is produced will be for home consumption or will be exported and the extent to which foreign-owned companies will derive the most financial benefit from operations based in the UK.

These concerns are also shared by local communities where test drilling has taken place, whose concerns also extend to the possible damage to their property. In 2011, fracking was linked to an earthquake in Oklahoma and to two minor earthquakes in the Blackpool area, which led to the temporary suspension of test drilling.

Accordingly, a number of protests in the UK have occurred where test drilling has been scheduled to take place. This has to be sanctioned by the local authority, which grants planning permission to conduct exploratory drilling to companies that have obtained a licence from the Department of Energy & Climate Change. These have taken place at Balcombe (West Sussex) in 2013 and Barton Moss (Greater Manchester) in 2013/14. At Balcombe, a test drilling site operated by the company Cuadrilla Resources was opposed by protesters using direct action tactics that included setting up a camp on a roadside verge, blocking the entrance to the site. The local police force made use of mutual aid arrangements to police this protest. The major protest at Barton Moss (Greater Manchester) in 2013 and 2014 came about as a result of the energy company IGas being granted permission to build a test well. Protests have been organised by the local group Frack Free Greater Manchester and involved tactics that included demonstrations and direct action that sought to prevent the access of the energy company's lorries to the site. On one occasion, two protesters superglued themselves inside a car to block entrance to the site. Although the company stated that the drilling was designed to see what type of gas could be found at the site and that it had no plans to commence fracking, protesters believed that if shale gas was found, the company would subsequently seek to extract it using the fracking method (BBC, 2013).

These two protests have resulted in police interventions. The policing of them has been costly, and it was estimated that policing the protests in Barton Moss cost around £750,000 and that protests in Balcombe cost around £4 million (BBC 2014). Numerous arrests were made at both of these protests for offences that included obstruction and trespass, including that of the Green MP Caroline Lucas at Balcombe on 19 August 2013.

Fracking is banned in France and Germany, but protests have occurred in those countries where it is permitted. One example of this is the protests that have taken place in Northern Alberta, Canada, in late 2013, where the Lubicon Lake Nation objected to fracking being carried out on its traditional lands, which its members used to hunt, fish and trap.

In America (where fracking is a matter for states to determine), it has been observed that 'the impact shale gas has had on the US energy market and its wider economy has been described in terms of a "revolution" which could have impacts globally' (Energy and Climate Change Committee, 2013: para. 4). However, fracking it is not universally welcomed, having, for example, been banned (albeit not permanently) in New York since 2008. Demonstrators have put pressure on the state governor to keep this ban in place. Where it is not banned, protesters have sought to make it so. In January 2014, a rally at the state legislature in Annapolis, Maryland sought to secure a moratorium on fracking from the state legislature. In California, it was reported in January 2014 that Governor Gerry Brown received boxes filled with 100,000 public comments urging him to refrain from expanding fracking operations throughout the state (Cherot, 2014).

See also: civil disobedience, direct action, environmentalist protest groups, public order policing (England and Wales)

Sources and further reading

BBC (2013) 'Four Arrested at Barton Moss Fracking Protest', *BBC News Manchester*, 27 November, www.bbc.co.uk/news/uk-england-manchester-25123294 (date accessed 1 May 2014).

——. (2014) 'Barton Moss: Government "Must Pay Anti-fracking Demo Bill"', *BBC News Manchester*, 16 January, www.bbc.co.uk/news/uk-england-manchester-25745788 (date accessed 1 May 2014).

Carrington, D. (2014) 'UK Defeats European Bid for Fracking Regulations', *The Guardian*, 14 January, www.theguardian.com/environment/2014/jan/14/uk-defeats-european-bid-fracking-regulations (date accessed 1 May 2014).

Cherot, N. (2014) 'Governor Gets 100,000 Anti-fracking New Year Wishes', *Mission and State*, 15 January, www.missionandstate.org/blog/governor-gets-100000-anti-fracking-new-year-wishes (date accessed 1 May 2014).

Energy and Climate Change Committee (2013) *The Impact of Shale Gas on Energy Markets*. Parliamentary Session 2012/13. London: TSO, House of Commons Paper 785.

Macalister, T. (2014) 'Anti-fracking Protests Fail to Halt Interest in Shale Gas', *The Guardian*, 12 January, www.theguardian.com/environment/2014/jan/12/anti-fracking-protests-corporation-interest (date accessed 1 May 2014).

FUEL CRISIS (BRITAIN) 2000

The background to the 2000 fuel crisis in the UK was the rising price of fuel. Between January 1999 and July 2000, the average price of a litre of unleaded petrol in the UK increased from 62.9 pence to 84.7 pence (Seely, 2011: 1).

During 1999, the Organization of the Petroleum Exporting Countries (OPEC) sanctioned cuts in oil production in order to raise the price of crude oil, which had fallen due to factors that included the Far East recession. This triggered protests by those affected by rising fuel costs. Protest action against escalating fuel prices was initiated in France on 30 August 2000, when the Channel Tunnel and Channel ports were blockaded by French fishermen. This action secured concessions, but inspired protests from others, including farmers, lorry drivers and taxi drivers, who blockaded oil refineries and fuel distribution depots. This action meant that most petrol stations throughout France ran out of fuel and prompted the French government on 10 September to grant concessions on fuel tax to industries that were heavily dependent on fuel, such as fishing, farming and haulage. Actions of this nature also occurred in Belgium, Germany, the Netherlands and Spain. These inspired similar episodes to occur in the UK.

The main forces directing the protests in the UK were a disparate group based around road hauliers, farmers and others associated with rural interests, who used the Internet and mobile phones as their main sources of organisation and communication. Although elements associated with established organisations that included the Countryside Alliance and the Road Haulage Association participated in the protest, it operated under the banner of the People's Fuel Lobby, in which the group Farmers for Action was a key component. The main protests took the form of direct action that entailed mounting blockades outside oil refineries and oil distribution depots in order to prevent the collection and distribution of fuel. The first of these took place outside Stanlow Oil Refinery in Cheshire on 7 September. Other forms of direct action were also undertaken that included lorry drivers driving slowly to obstruct the flow of traffic. The aim of the protesters was to force the government to reduce the taxation imposed on fuel, which they viewed as a 'stealth tax': approximately 77 per cent of the cost of a gallon of fuel was accounted for by fuel tax and VAT.

The protests assumed a fast momentum. A considerable number of oil-tanker drivers were unwilling to either leave refineries with a cargo of oil or enter refineries to collect one. These feelings were fashioned by motives that included the desire to display solidarity with farmers and lorry drivers, and thus not to cross what they regarded as a picket line, or the fear of intimidation (especially whilst on open roads or when delivering fuel to petrol stations) if they did so. The problem of supply shortages was supplemented by panic buying by motorists, usually in response to an announcement by protesters regarding their intention to blockade a refinery. Accordingly, by 13 September, 90 per cent of filling stations in the UK had run out of fuel and the country ground to a halt. People who relied on private transport were unable to get to work, schools had to be closed and access to food distribution centres and deliveries to supermarkets were affected, causing some to ration the sale of essentials such as bread and milk.

The ability of the protest to cause widespread disruption was explained by additional factors. The government initially adopted a laid-back approach to the protests and considerably underestimated their potential impact. It waited until 11 September to initiate procedures (via an Order in Council obtained from the Privy Council) whereby it could invoke emergency powers under the Energy Act 1976 to secure the delivery of fuel to essential services. This enabled a number of petrol stations to be designated as priority suppliers (a task that was undertaken by local authorities in conjunction with the police: Liddell, 2000) to which oil companies were asked to ensure deliveries so that individuals designated as 'essential users' were able to obtain fuel.

A particular weakness of the government's response was its failure to communicate with the police service regarding its views as to how the protest should be handled. This form of dialogue (which in the miners' dispute of 1984/5 was in the nature of informal instructions) meant that the police were able to use their own discretion as to what action should be taken.

The police took the view that as the protests were peaceful and those involved obeyed police instructions when these were given (for example, not to block the highway), there was no need for coercive action to ensure that tanker drivers were able to enter and leave oil refineries if they wished to do so. This non-intervention was also influenced by the fact that protests outside individual oil refineries were controlled by officers from the local police force. There was no central coordination of police responses and mutual aid was not used. Police officers who were deployed outside oil refiners had no desire to create friction between themselves and protesters (many of whom were from a 'respectable' middle-class background).

Other issues also accounted for the disruption caused by the protest. Although oil companies were soon aware of the potential impact of the protest, they were conscious that a protest directed at the high level of taxation on fuel diverted attention away from their own high profit margins. In addition, it emerged during the strike that many fuel-tanker drivers were employed by haulage firms rather than directly by the oil companies. The Shell Oil Company, for example, subcontracted this work to P&O. Haulage companies would financially benefit from a reduction in fuel duty and thus placed no pressure on their drivers to cross blockades, and in many cases continued to pay them their wages whilst not working. This situation meant that oil companies were often not in a position to instruct tanker drivers to collect and deliver fuel, although they could have exerted pressure on their employers, for example, by threatening legal action to force haulage firms to honour their contracts. However, the oil companies did not embark on such action and did not take remedial measures by increasing deliveries from oil refineries not subject to blockades.

Ultimately, the government was spurred into action. Ministers were irked by scenes outside oil refineries in which protesters determined when to temporarily lift the blockade to enable supplies of fuel to reach essential targets such as hospitals. A twin approach was then launched. This entailed placing the National Health Service (NHS) on 'red alert' (a procedure that would be employed in response to a terrorist attack) in order to warn the public of the seriousness of the protesters' actions on the health and welfare of the nation. Second, the Transport and General Workers' Union (then led by Bill Morris) was mobilised and union officials were sent to Grangemouth in Scotland to persuade tanker drivers to break the blockade of the refinery and deliver cargoes of fuel. The arrangement that was struck entailed providing tankers with a police escort for the duration of their shift or enabling each tanker to be 'double-crewed' as a safeguard against random acts of violence that could be directed against them.

The protesters were perhaps taken by surprise by the impact of their actions and anticipated that the government and the police would eventually adopt a more robust response. This prompted the Stanlow protesters to abandon their action on 14 September – but on their own terms. The protest was ended on the understanding that the government had 60 days to concede to its demands to considerably lower fuel taxes. If this was not done, the protesters threatened to return and continue with their actions.

Although the government had taken the view throughout the protests that decisions regarding taxation were taken by budgets and not as the result of protests, some concessions were made to the fuel protesters in the November 2000 pre-Budget Report. These included a freeze on fuel duty until April 2002 and a reduction in the cost of vehicle excise duty. These changes were implemented in the 2001 Budget. Furthermore, more coercive measures were initiated that were designed to limit the impact of future episodes of this nature. These included establishing a Fuel Task Force in the Cabinet Office whose work resulted in the devising of a Memorandum of Understanding signed on 29

September by four Cabinet Ministers (the Home Secretary, the Secretary of State for Trade and Industry, the Chief Secretary to the Treasury and the Minister for Transport), leading ministers of the Scottish Executive and the Welsh Assembly, the Trades Union Congress, the Association of Chief Police Officers, major oil companies and haulage firms, which pledged them to cooperate in order to ensure the supply of fuel in future protests of this nature (Office of Fair Trading, 2001).

Various explanations have been put forward to explain the motives of those involved in the protest. Some ministers viewed it as an extra-parliamentary challenge to the authority of the government that was mounted by political interests who believed 'there is something terribly, terribly wrong about having a Labour government' (Beckett, quoted in Hetherington, Hencke and White, 2000). Although this protest did not succeed in bringing the government down, its capacity to govern was undermined and the standing of both the government and the Prime Minister temporarily slumped in opinion polls. Protesters were keen to downplay the protest as a political challenge to the government and instead depicted it as a 'people's protest', which was designed to articulate the concerns of ordinary people regarding fuel prices to a government which it viewed as being out of touch with public opinion.

Alternative perspectives have viewed the protest as more sectarian in nature, seeking to articulate the concerns of rural England which were viewed as being ignored by a 'towny-led' Labour government. The countryside was especially reliant on transport and the rise in fuel prices was seen as the latest injustice that had been inflicted on rural interests in the wake of others. These included the 1996 bovine spongiform encephalopathy (BSE) crisis, the closure of rural facilities such as schools, post offices and shops, the inadequacies of rural public transport in the wake of bus deregulation, and the extent of rural crime that was highlighted following the conviction of a Norfolk farmer in 2000 for shooting and killing a burglar.

It has further been suggested that the protest was motivated by the imminence of legislation to outlaw fox hunting – an issue which assumed symbolic importance to many who lived in rural England, the banning of which was viewed as an assault on the rural way of life. This measure had spurred major demonstrations in London in 1997 and 1998. However, such a cause was unlikely to secure much support outside the countryside, which therefore needed an issue to attract support from a broader segment of public opinion with which to challenge the government (Joyce, 2002: 23). A reduction in fuel duty potentially appealed to the bulk of the nation and the rise in fuel prices caused by OPEC provided the trigger for a taxpayer's protest to take place.

Similar protests in connection with fuel prices occurred in 2005 and

2007, but their impact was relatively limited.

See also: direct action, paramilitary policing, public order policing (England and Wales), states of emergency

Sources and further reading

Doherty, B., Peterson, M., Plows, A. and Walls, D. (2003) 'Explaining the Fuel Protests', *British Journal of Politics and International Relations*, 5(1): 1–23.

Hetherington, P, Hencke, D. and White, M. (2000) 'Ministers Vent Fuel Fury', *The Guardian*, 16 September.

Joyce, P. (2002) *The Politics of Protest: Extra-parliamentary Politics in Britain since 1970*. Basingstoke: Palgrave.

Liddell, H. (2000) Speech in the House of Commons, 13 November, HC Debs, Session 1999–2000, vol. 356, col. 772.

Office of Fair Trading (2001) 'Memorandum of Understanding on the Supply of Fuel Oils in an Emergency', www.oft.gov.uk/shared_oft/ca98_public_register/decisions/fuel.pdf (date accessed 1 May 2014).

Seely, A. (2011) *Taxation of Road Fuels: Policy Following the 'Fuel Crisis' (2000–2008)*. House of Commons Library, Standard Note SN/BT/3016, www.parliament.uk/briefing-papers/SN03016.pdf (date accessed 1 May 2014).

G

G20 PROTESTS (LONDON) 2009

The focus of the G20 protests was the G20 summit held in London on 2 April 2009. Those involved in the protests held on 1 and 2 April came from a wide variety of groups with diverse agendas that included economic policy, the operations of the banking system and bankers' pay and bonuses, climate change and the War on Terror. The banner of 'anti-capitalism' served as an umbrella under which these groups could coordinate a protest. On 1 April, there were ten separate protests over seven sites in London. In excess of 5,500 Metropolitan Police officers were deployed on 1 April and 2,800 on 2 April. The Metropolitan Police Service (MPS) estimated the cost of the G20 event as £7.5 million (HMIC, 2009a: 22).

The events on 1 and 2 April were preceded by a 'March for Jobs, Justice and Climate' that took place on 28 March. It was organised by the 'Put People First' coalition, which originated from earlier campaigns that included the Jubilee Debt Campaign and the Trade Justice Movement. Around 35,000 people were involved and the event culminated in a rally in Hyde Park.

In addition to a police security operation mounted outside the ExCel Centre which hosted the G20 summit, a number of other protests occurred on 1 April. There were three key events.

The G20 Meltdown Protest embraced four separate marches focusing on war, climate change, financial crimes and land enclosures and borders, which converged outside the Bank of England. This protest was inspired by radical anti-capitalist sentiments. Some damage was caused to property, principally at a branch of the Royal Bank of Scotland, following which confrontations between the police and protesters took place. A branch of HSBC Bank was also attacked. Direct action associated with this protest also included a small number of squats, which were used for diverse purposes such as accommodating protesters and acting as workshops.

A second protest that took place in Bishopsgate was the 'Camp in the

City', which sought to draw attention to environmental issues, especially carbon trading. Prior to the event, protesters met with the police. However, some scuffles took place between the police and protesters in connection with police actions to clear the camp.

A third event was a march by the Stop the War Coalition, which attracted support from other organisations that included the Campaign for Nuclear Disarmament and the Palestine Solidarity Committee.

A total of 9–11,500 persons were involved these three protests (HMIC, 2009a: 23). The police operation to deal with them was code-named 'Operation Glencoe', evoking unfortunate images of violence associated with the massacre of the MacDonalds in Glencoe in 1692. An important aspect of the protests was the role played by 'citizen journalists', who were 'members of the public who play an active role in collecting, analysing and distributing media themselves' (HMIC, 2009a: 25). Considerable use was made of mobile phones to record and disseminate the events that occurred, especially police actions.

Following these events, a number of complaints were made regarding police actions, which included 185 referrals to the Independent Police Complaints Commission. One person (a newspaper vendor whose way home from work took him through the path of the Meltdown Protest) was pushed to the ground by a police officer and subsequently died. Although an inquest jury returned the verdict of unlawful killing in 2011, the officer concerned was subsequently found not guilty of his manslaughter in 2012. He was, however, dismissed from the police service.

A number of criticisms were made concerning the use of police powers. The main issues included the absence of clear standards governing the use of force by individual officers involved in events of this nature, the interpretation of public order law and the use of public order powers covering actions such as stop and search, photography and obtaining the names and addresses of demonstrators. The treatment by the police of the media was a particular concern at the G20 protests, whose members were sometimes on the receiving end of coercive police interventions (especially those derived from section 14 of the Public Order Act 1986, which gave the police powers to end or limit a protest) when seeking to report events (Home Affairs Committee, 2009: para. 17). It was concluded that the police needed to 'demonstrate explicit consideration of the facilitation of peaceful protest throughout the planning and execution of the operation or operations'. The starting point for the police in responding to events of this nature 'is the presumption in favour of facilitating peaceful assembly' (HMIC, 2009a: 47).

Containment ('kettling' or 'coralling') was used as a police response to these protests. It was argued that since the use of containment involved a shift in power and control from the protesters to the police, it 'should be used sparingly and in clearly defined circumstances', which should be codified and linked to police intelligence to ensure that there were reasonable grounds to suggest that those who were subject to it were likely to cause disturbance elsewhere (Home Affairs Committee, 2009: para. 16) A further parliamentary report argued that containment should be used only when it was 'necessary and proportionate' and for 'the minimum period of time necessary' (Joint Committee on Human Rights, 2009b: para. 29). In 2011, the High Court ruled that the Metropolitan Police broke the law in the way they 'kettled' protesters at the G20 demonstrations in 2009, although this ruling was overturned by the Court of Appeal in 2012. In 2012, the European Court of Human Rights also ruled this tactic to be lawful.

It was observed at the G20 protests that some officers had removed their identification numbers, making it extremely difficult for subsequent identification in the event of questions being raised regarding their conduct. It also gave the impression that the police were taking, or intended to take, actions that they wished to hide (Home Affairs Committee, 2009: para. 17). This practice was unambiguously condemned by HMIC (2009a: 11 and 62) and national standards regarding officer identification were subsequently agreed in September 2010.

The debates occasioned by the G20 protests also highlighted the importance of communication to the successful outcome of a police operation, which might on occasions be adversely affected by 'mutual distrust' between police officers and protesters. The adoption of a 'no surprises' communication philosophy with protesters, the media and the wider public was called for in order that protesters and the public were aware of likely police actions and could then make informed choices and decisions (HMIC, 2009b: 7–8). In response to these comments, use has been made of contact points in events that included demonstrations involving the English Defence League, and more recently Police Protest Liaison Officers have been introduced.

However, communication is not a one-sided activity, but also requires those engaged in protest to enter into meaningful dialogue with those who are charged with policing such events. It was therefore recommended that protest groups should 'put ideological concerns to one side and do everything they can do to aid communication both before and during the protest' (Home Affairs Committee, 2009: para. 34).

One of the most important consequences of the policing of the G20 protests related to the need to ensure that the future policing of protests reflected the core values of British policing. These were identified as being 'an approachable, impartial, accountable style of policing based on minimal force and anchored in public consent' whose key purpose was 'to ensure the safety of the public and the preservation of the peace within a tolerant, plural society' (HMIC, 2009b: 5 and 11). It was argued that when dealing with protests, this model could be eroded by police actions that included 'premature displays of formidable public order protective uniform and equipment' (HMIC, 2009b: 5), which might give the perception of a hardening of the character of British policing. It was further jeopardised by 'poor police communication, uncontrolled instances of force and the confused and inappropriate use of police powers' (HMIC, 2009b: 12).

A number of recommendations were put forward to ensure that the future policing of protest strengthened and reinforced the core values of the British model of policing. These included the adoption of a set of fundamental principles governing the use of force, the codification of public order policing to ensure consistency in training and the use of equipment, tactics and powers (in particular, the human rights obligations imposed on the police service by the Human Rights Act 1998) and clarification of the legal framework for the use of overt photography by the police during public order operations and the subsequent collation and retention of photographic images (HMIC, 2009b).

See also: anti-globalisation, anti-globalisation movement, anti-globalisation/anti-capitalist protest (UK), anti-globalisation/anti-capitalist protest (worldwide), direct action, kettling (containment), peace movement, protest liaison officers (England and Wales), public order legislation (England and Wales), public order policing (England and Wales), student protests (England) 2010

Sources and further reading

Home Affairs Committee (2009) *Policing of the G20 Protests.* Eighth Report, Session 2008–09. London: TSO, House of Commons Paper 418.

HMIC (2009a) *Adapting to Protest.* London: HMIC. Available at: www.hmic.gov.uk/media/adapting-to-protest-20090705.pdf (date accessed 1 May 2014).

——. (2009b) *Adapting to Protest: Nurturing the British Model of Policing.* London: HMIC. Available at: www.hmic.gov.uk/media/adapting-to-protest-nurturing-the-british-model-of-policing-20091125.pdf (date accessed 1 May 2014).

Joint Committee on Human Rights (2009a) *Demonstrating Respect for Rights? A Human Rights Approach to Policing Protest.* Seventh Report, Session 2008–09. London: TSO, House of Commons Paper 320.

——. (2009b) *Demonstrating Respect for Rights? Follow-up.* Twenty-Second Report, Session 2008–09. London: TSO, House of Commons Paper 522.

GDAŃSK SHIPYARD PROTESTS (GDAŃSK, POLAND) 1980-9

Economic problems in Poland during the 1970s, characterised by stagnating wages, high food prices and increasing levels of foreign debt, led to a number of strikes in June 1976 in Plock, Radom and Ursus. These prompted the government to implement measures to curb dissent, but led to the formation of underground organisations (which included labour unions) opposed to the government, most notably the *Komitet Obrony Robotników* (KOR – Committee for Defence of the Workers, which was re-named the Committee for Social Self-Defence in 1977). Its initial role was to provide aid to workers who had been victimised for their involvement in the protests.

The events that took place in the 1970s formed the background to the protests at the Lenin Shipyard in Gdańsk, Poland, in 1980 and were triggered by the government's decision to raise the price of meat in July 1980. This led to a wave of strikes and factory occupations that commenced at the State Aviation Works in Świdnik on 8 July 1980 and spread to other areas including Lublin. Initially the industrial action was not coordinated, although the KOR acted as a disseminator of news and information.

The dismissal of a political activist, Anna Walentynowicz, at the Lenin Shipyard in Gdańsk prompted the involvement of workers there in these disputes. A strike began on 14 August 1980. It was organised by *Wolne Związki Zawodowe Wybrzeża* (the Free Trade Unions of the Coast) and was led by Lech Walesa, who had been dismissed in 1976 for his involvement in the disputes. The strikers made a number of demands that included the reinstatement of Walentynowicz and Walesa, and respect for workers' rights.

The government sought to impose censorship on events in Gdańsk, but this aim was subverted by underground forms of communication and Radio Free Europe, whose broadcasts were accessible in Iron Curtain countries. Gdańsk then became the centre of protests in Poland. On 16 August, delegations from other strike committees arrived there and it was agreed to form an Inter-Enterprise Strike Committee whose demands went beyond localised bread and butter issues to include the right to form independent trade unions, the right to strike, the relaxation of censorship, the freeing of political prisoners, improvements in the national health service and additional rights for the Church. The following day, delegates from the KOR arrived at Gdańsk and with their help a newssheet, *Solidarność* (*Solidarity*), was produced at the shipyard. The name *Solidarność* became widely used in reference to the organisation behind the strike at Gdańsk.

Events in Gdańsk encouraged similar protests elsewhere. On 18 August, Szczecin Shipyard joined the strike and within a few days most of Poland was affected by strikes, bringing the economy to a halt. This forced the government to make concessions. Governmental commissions were despatched to Gdańsk and Szczecin, and on 3 September representatives of the workers and the government signed an agreement (the *Porozumienia sierpniowe* or Gdańsk agreement). Similar agreements were signed in other areas. These accepted many of the workers' demands, including legal recognition of the right to strike and the ability to form a labour union independent of the control of the Communist Party. In addition, the agreements enabled citizens to introduce democratic changes within the communist political structure – a development that was latterly viewed as the first step in dismantling the Party's monopoly of power.

The success of the August strikes resulted in the formation of a nationwide labour union that was independent of the Communist Party. It was called *Niezależny Samorządny Związek Zawodowy Solidarność* (*NSZZ Solidarity*) and was effectively the merger of Solidarity with other free trade unions from other parts of the country.

The philosophical inspiration behind these protests was provided by the works of Leszek Kolakowski, most notably his essay 'Thesis on Hope and Hopelessness' (1971), which suggested that the internal contradictions of 'bureaucratic despotic socialism' made it susceptible to pressure exerted from below. He thus suggested that the Poles should 'organize themselves outside the structures of the Party-state. These "self-organised" social groups and movements would then gradually expand the areas of negative liberty and self-determination open to the citizen', resulting in the transformation of Polish society 'in an increasingly open, democratic and pluralist way' (Spencer, 1991).

His works were banned in Poland, but copies obtained through the underground were available and exerted an influence on the Polish intelligentsia. Support for *Solidarity* was also provided by the Catholic Church under the leadership of Pope John Paul II. He had previously been Bishop of Kraków and became Pope in 1978. He conducted a pilgrimage to Poland in 1979 and his masses were attended by hundreds of thousands, during which he called for freedom and human rights and denounced violence.

In addition, *Solidarity* secured vocal foreign support (most notably from America) in the early 1980s. This arose because *Solidarity* was fighting for values of 'individual freedom, democratic government, the rule of law' (Ash, 2002: 327), which were compatible with American values, and also because dissent of this nature served to weaken the Soviet Union. Nonetheless, there were reservations in America arising from the socialist aspects of *Solidarity*'s economic reform programme (Ash, 2002: 327). Reservations of this nature also affected the support given by the UK government: although vocal encouragement was given, reservations were privately expressed that the activities undertaken by *Solidarity* might spiral out of control and there was also the desire not to upset the Soviet government, in case this threatened British business interests that were involved with the construction of a gas pipeline in Siberia (Kapturek, 2013).

Solidarity's initial status was that of a trade union. However, following the Gdańsk agreement, a number of other unions that included the Independent Student Union and the Independent Farmers' Trade Union (or Rural Solidarity) attached themselves to *Solidarity* through sub-organisations. This gave *Solidarity* a mass nationwide membership. In April 1981, it began the publication of its own newspaper, *Tygodnik Solidarność*. Its programme also extended beyond bread-and-butter issues affecting workers to embrace political reforms and changes to government policy. This was apparent in the document the 'Self-governing Republic' that was adopted at the first national congress of *Solidarity*, which was held in Gdańsk in September and October 1981, and where Lech Walesa was elected as the movement's chairman. This marked the transition of *Solidarity* from a trade union to a political movement.

The tactics adopted by *Solidarity* were non-violent, as it sought to avoid provoking repressive action by the government. Hunger marches and strikes (often of a wildcat nature) were important features of its activities. Its methods were effective: when a number of supporters were attacked by security forces on 19 March 1981, a strike was called that involved around 12 million workers – the largest event of this nature that had ever occurred in the Eastern Bloc. This forced the government to make concessions (including an investigation into the attacks) in return for an agreement to defer further strikes.

Agitation, however, continued at a grassroots level in the form of street protests and local strikes, which included hunger strikes in 1981, triggered by deteriorating economic conditions. Such occurrences made it inevitable that the government would eventually respond coercively (in part because such activities had adverse repercussions on the economy) and were under increasing pressure from the Soviet Union to do so.

The pretext for action arose on 12 December 1981 when a number of *Solidarity* radicals meeting in Gdańsk called for a national referendum on the future of the Communist government and a re-examination of Poland's military alliance with the Soviet Union. The following day, 13 December 1981, the new First Secretary, Wojciech Jaruzelski, adopted a hardline approach and by doing so forestalled potential Soviet intervention.

Martial law was declared, a Military Council of National Salvation was created and a large number of *Solidarity* supporters (including Walesa) were rounded up and arrested. The regional and national headquarters of *Solidarity* were closed down and censorship was extended, which included the banning of *Solidarity* publications. The military appeared on the streets and the paramilitary riot police (ZOMO) took a leading role in suppressing strikes, occupations and demonstrations that involved protesters being shot at, some of whom were killed. A sit-in protest by striking miners at the Piast Coal Mine ended on 28 December. These events towards the end of 1981 severely affected the vitality of *Solidarity*: 'the once-mighty

Solidarity ... was reduced to a collection of local resistance groups putting out clandestine publications and endlessly feuding over goals and tactics' (Zirakzadeh, 2006: 117). It was banned on 8 October 1982.

Actions taken against *Solidarity* forced it to become an underground movement whose activities included broadcasting through Radio Solidarity, which was set up in April 1982. Leadership was provided through several bodies that included the Interim Coordinating Commission that was set up in April 1982, which enabled protests to continue, including a series of strikes in May 1982. However, activities undertaken by *Solidarity* were subject to state intervention by the Security Service (SB), which resulted in a number of protesters being killed in demonstrations that took place throughout 1982. Although Walesa was released in November 1982, repression continued – a large number of activists were arrested in December 1982 and the assets of *Solidarity* were transferred to a pro-government trade union, the All-Poland Alliance of Trade Unions. However, repression of this nature failed to crush *Solidarity*. Street protests were frequent during the first part of 1983 and a large number of underground newspapers evidenced the continued vitality of the opposition. Martial law was ended on 22 July 1983 and later that year Walesa was awarded the Nobel Peace Prize. The government's refusal to issue him with a passport meant that his wife had to receive it in Oslo on his behalf.

The murder of a pro-*Solidarity* priest, Fr. Jerzy Popieluszko, in October 1984 resulted in large numbers of protesters taking to the streets to attend his funeral in Warsaw. The government initially sought to appease such sentiments by releasing thousands of political prisoners, although new waves of arrests occurred the following year. However, although international economic sanctions that were imposed on Poland had failed to make any impact on the repressive policies carried out towards the movement by the Polish government, the tide then began to turn in favour of *Solidarity*.

On 11 March 1985, Mikhail Gorbachev assumed power in the Soviet Union against the background of severe economic difficulties that affected the Soviet Union and the entire Eastern Bloc. The economic and political reforms pursued by Gorbachev in the Soviet Union served to encourage dissidence in the Eastern Bloc, although the key significance of this change of power in the Soviet Union was that it became apparent that it would abandon the Brezhnev Doctrine and would not use military force to keep communist parties in power in satellite states.

The Polish government thus became aware that it needed to make concessions towards *Solidarity*. Accordingly, in September 1986, the last political prisoners associated with *Solidarity* were released, and at the end of that month, it came into the open with the creation of the *Tymczasowa Rada NSZZ Solidarność* (the Temporary Council of *NSZZ Solidarity*). This act encouraged a large number of local underground *Solidarity* organisations to emerge and on 25 October 1987, the *Krajowa Komisja Wykonawcza NSZZ Solidarność* (National Executive Committee of *NSZZ Solidarity*) was set up. Although government repression had not entirely ended, it was less severe than had been the case in the early 1980s.

The further deterioration of economic conditions (characterised by inflation and ever-rising foreign debt) made Jaruzelski's government unpopular. Economic (and also limited political) reforms were the subject of a referendum held in November 1987, but failed to quell political dissent or ameliorate economic difficulties. Long queues and empty shelves created antagonism towards the government, which was forced to export food products to help pay towards its foreign debt that amounted to $38 billion in 1989. The government's decision to raise food prices in February 1988 was the trigger for a further wave of strikes. Those that took place in August (which included the Gdańsk Shipyard) induced the government to negotiate with *Solidarity*. This culminated in the Roundtable Talks that took place in Warsaw from 6 February to 4 April 1989. These were instigated by the government and included a range of opposition groups, including *Solidarity*. These resulted in the conclusion of an agreement, the *Contract Sejm* (or Roundtable Agreement). This Agreement legalised independent trade unions, established a bicameral legislative and a President who would be the country's chief executive (a reform that was at the expense of the power formerly wielded by the General Secretary of the Polish Communist Party). *Solidarity* was also legalised and was thus able to participate (albeit in a limited manner, restricted to contesting 35 per cent of the seats in the *Sejm*) in the forthcoming legislative elections.

These elections were held in June1989 and resulted in a crushing defeat for the Communist Party. *Solidarity* secured victory in every seat save one that it was allowed to contest for in the lower House of the Polish Parliament (the *Sejm*) and also won 99 of the 100 seats in the newly formed upper House of the Polish Parliament, the *Senat* (Senate). Anti-communist parties in Parliament came together through the formation of *Obywatelski Klub Parliamentarny 'Solidarność'* (Solidarity Citizens' Parliamentary Club) and this led to the election on 24 August 1989 by the *Sejm* of a *Solidarity* representative, Tadeusz Mazowiecki, as Prime Minister, the first non-communist Prime Minister in Eastern Europe for over 40 years. By the end of August 1989, a *Solidarity*-led coalition government had been formed. In April 1990, Walesa was elected chairman at *Solidarity*'s second national congress and in December 1990 he was elected President of the Republic of Poland, an office he held until 1995.

Solidarity's victories set in train a series of political reforms both within and outside of Poland that resulted in the collapse of communist rule in Central and Eastern Europe. This was symbolically demonstrated by the collapse of the Berlin Wall on 9 November 1989.

See also: direct action, riot police, states of emergency, Tianamen Square protest (Beijing) 1976 and 1989, workplace protest

Sources and further reading

Ash, T. Garton (1993) *The Magic Lantern: The Revolution of '89 Witnessed in Warsaw, Budapest, Berlin, and Prague*. New York: Vintage Books.
——. (2002) *The Polish Reveolution: Solidarity*, 3rd edn. New Haven: Yale University Press.
Kapturek, C. (2013) 'Thatcher, Poland and a False Dichotomy', http://theredandblackstork.wordpress.com/2013/04/29/thatcher-poland-and-a-false-dichotomy (date accessed 1 May 2014).
Osiatyński, W. 'The Roundtable Talks in Poland' in J. Elster (ed.), *The Roundtable Talks and the Breakdown of Communism*. University of Chicago Press.
Spencer, M. (1991) 'The Soviet Peace Movement at the Time of the Coup', http://metta.spencer.name/?Papers:Academic_papers:The_Soviet_Peace_Movement_at_the_Time_of_the_Coup (date accessed 1 May 2014).
Stokes, G. (1993) *The Walls Came Tumbling Down: The Collapse of Communism in Eastern Europe*. New York: Oxford University Press.
Zirakzadeh, C. (2006) *Social Movements in Politics: A Comparative Study*, expanded edn. Basingstoke: Palgrave Macmillan.

GREENHAM COMMON (BERKSHIRE, ENGLAND) 1981–2000

On 5 September 1981, a small Welsh group, Women for Life on Earth, embarked on a protest march from Cardiff to the RAF Greenham Common Airbase in Berkshire, England. This had been loaned to the US Air Force in 1943, which had retained occupancy thereafter. Their march was occasioned by the decision taken by the North Atlantic Treaty Organization (NATO) in 1979 that the base was to house Tomahawk Cruise missiles. Eventually, 96 of these weapons were located there, commencing in 1983.

The initial intention of the protesters was to challenge the Base Commander to enter into a debate concerning the anticipated arrival of the missiles. When this request was ignored, they established a peace camp on the perimeter fence surrounding the base. This tactics had been used by members of the peace movement during the 1920s, involving a temporary presence that was mounted outside military bases. It became known as the Women's Peace Camp and consisted of nine camps that were sited at various gates around the base. The camp was run by women (becoming women-only in February 1982) and had a strong feminist following. Its existence inspired other peace camps both in the UK and abroad. These included the Faslane Peace Camp (set up in 1982) and the Aldermaston Women's Peace Camp (set up in 1985).

The Peace Camp lasted for 19 years and provided a permanent protest to nuclear weapons that was in the nature of a vigil. Support was given by feminist and anti-nuclear groups and from the Women's Peace Alliance. Chain-letter writing (in the context of *Greenham Women Everywhere*) was also used to create support for the protest.

The protesters pursued a number of non-violent actions. These included blockading the base (initially to stop site preparations and then to disrupt its day-to-day operations). Key events included *Embrace the Base* in December 1982, when around 30,000 women linked hands around the entire perimeter fence. This action was repeated the following year involving 50,000 women. Activities of this nature were also held in conjunction with the Campaign for Nuclear Disarmament (CND): during Easter 1983, around 70,000 campaigners joined hands to form a 14-mile human chain that linked the nuclear warhead factories at Aldermaston and Burghfield with Greenham Common.

Other activities entailed women chaining themselves to railings, trespassing on the base and disrupting training exercises by laying down in front of lorries. In December 1983, paper doves, baby clothes and other symbols of peace were woven into the fabric of the perimeter fence. On occasions, bolt cutters were used to remove sections of the fence. An additional target was the ground-launched cruise missiles. The intention of these was that they could be moved from Greenham Common into the countryside and the Soviets would not know of their whereabouts. Exercises involving this tactic were tracked by the Greenham protesters ('Cruisewatch'), thus defeating its purpose of secrecy and serving to disrupt dispersal exercises (Fairhall, 2006: 188–9 and 197).

The policing of the Greenham Common protest was often violent and characterised by sexual harassment and intimidation. One woman, Helen Thomas, died in 1989 after being struck by a police vehicle. Large numbers of women involved in the wide range of actions that were associated with these protests were arrested. By 18 January 1984, 1,175 arrests had been made at the base or in relation to activities associated with the protest there. Of the 623 cases that were brought before the courts, 608 people were convicted and the most common penalty was a fine of around £20 (Brittan, 1984). Many women went to prison rather than accept bail conditions that would prevent them from future involvement in the Peace Camp.

Numerous attempts were made by the local authority, Newbury District Council, to evict the women using police or bailiffs. The first action of this nature took place in May 1982 and a mass eviction occurred on 4 April 1984. However, these actions proved abortive as new camps immediately took the place of those that had been cleared. In 1983, bylaws that designated Greenham Common as common land were revoked by the local authority, which made itself the private landlord of the site. In 1985, the Secretary of State for Defence issued bylaws that made it a criminal offence to be inside the base without permission. The protesters' response was to enter the base at the stroke of midnight when they came into force. In 1990, the Law Lords ruled these bylaws to be invalid (although damaging the fence to secure access was deemed to be a criminal offence). It was also later revealed that the Security Service (MI5) opened a file on the Greenham Common Peace Camp on the grounds that it was subject to penetration by subversive groups (Andrew, 2009).

The Intermediate-Range Nuclear Forces (INF) Treaty signed by the USA and the Soviet Union in 1987 initiated the removal of cruise missiles in 1989. In 1990, the USA announced that Greenham Common was no longer an operational base and remaining missiles and US Air Force personnel left in 1991. The Peace Camp remained as a symbol of opposition to nuclear weapons (in particular the UK's Trident Programme), but closed in 2000 after planning permission had been granted for the erection of a memorial to the activities of the Camp.

The Greenham protest raised awareness of nuclear weapons, although the extent to which it succeeded in securing the signing of the INF Treaty earlier than might otherwise have been the case and hastening the end of the Cold War is debatable. However, the protest achieved other objectives, in particular that of empowering women (Fairhall, 2006: 191–202) and inspiring later non-violent protests, including that of the Occupy movement.

See also: civil disobedience, Occupy movement, peace movement, political policing

Sources and further reading

Andrew, C. (2009) *The Defence of the Realm: The Authorized History of MI5*. London: Allen Lane.

Brittan, L. (1984) HC Debs, 19 January, vol. 52, col. 429, OQ.

Fairhall, D. (2006) *Common Ground: The Story of Greenham*. London: I.B. Tauris.

Hipperson, S. (2005) *Greenham: Non-violent Women-v-Crown Prerogative*. London: Greenham Publications.

Jones, L. (1983) *Keeping the Peace*. London: Women's Press.

Junor, B. and Howse, K. (1995) *Greenham Common Women's Peace Camp: A History of Non-violent Resistance*. London: Working Press.

Pettitt, A. (2006) *Walking to Greenham: How the Peace Camp Began and the Cold War Ended*. Aberystwyth: Honno.

Roseneil, S. (1995) *Disarming Patriarchy: Feminism and Political Action at Greenham*. Buckingham: Open University Press.

GROSVENOR SQUARE (LONDON) 1968

The protest that occurred in the vicinity of the US Embassy in Grosvenor Square, London was an aspect of the international and domestic political turmoil that was a feature of 1968. Protests occurred in Eastern Bloc countries such as Yugoslavia and Poland, and political reform in Czechoslovakia was met by a Russian invasion of the country in 1968. In Western countries, disturbances occurred in Paris, Chicago and Northern Ireland, and in America, Robert Kennedy and Martin Luther

King, widely regarded as radical leaders of forces seeking political change, were assassinated. In the UK, economic problems encountered by Harold Wilson's Labour government and political divisions articulated in Enoch Powell's 'Rivers of Blood' speech and the resignation of Foreign Secretary George Brown added to this air of uncertainty. Young people, especially students, were in the vanguard of protest movements, whose actions were characterised by occupations of universities. Their behaviour displayed a desire to break away from the obedience and respect for authority that had characterised post-war society. It was subsequently observed that this event took place around 20 years after the first post-war baby-boom peak (Willetts, 2011: 129) and at the time the role played in violence by foreign students was unfavourably commented upon (Taverne, 1968: col. 750).

Estimates of the number of protesters taking part in the protest march vary, with figures ranging from 10,000 (Taverne, 1968: col. 751) to 50,000 (Clutterbuck, 1979: 251). The event began in Trafalgar Square and culminated in a rally at Hyde Park. En route, a petition signed by around 75,000 people, asking the UK government to cease supporting the American policy in Vietnam, was handed into 10 Downing Street. A group led by the Maoist Britain-Vietnam Solidarity Front, numbering between 3,000 and 6,000 people broke away from the main body of the march and sought to attack the American Embassy in Grosvenor Square. Their actions were more akin to a riot than to a demonstration.

Around 9,000 police were deployed at the event (Clutterbuck, 1979: 309) and the Square was defended by around 1,000 police, whose main tactic was to stand shoulder-to-shoulder in a cordon that was designed to prevent the protesters gaining access to the Embassy. This cordon came under attack from protesters, who formed a human wall which charged the police lines. The police were pelted with stones, banners and improvised weapons such as fencing, in response to which they supported the cordon with mounted police officers who sought to break up the demonstrators and prevent them securing access to the Embassy. The mounted police, in turn, came under attack from fireworks that were designed to frighten the horses as well as marbles and ball bearings that were thrown under their hooves in order to incapacitate them. Ultimately, around 86 people were injured and around 200 were arrested. It was claimed that three times as many police officers as demonstrators required hospital treatment (Taverne, 1968: col. 747).

It was argued that police tactics had contributed to the disorder by their last-minute decision to change the route that had been agreed in prior negotiations with the protest organisers. This allegedly created confusion and also created a bottleneck in the vicinity of Grosvenor Square that broke up the orderly progress of the demonstration (Jackson, 1968: col. 732).

The event in Grosvenor Square evidenced an anti-statist aspect in the attitude of some demonstrators that placed the police at the forefront of targets which protesters wished to physically confront and defeat. A nebulous cause became replaced in the minds of some demonstrators with a physical target that could be attacked. This would be replicated in future events of this nature.

In hindsight, the police seemed ill-prepared to deal with the event. They were organised in serials (consisting of one inspector, two sergeants and 20 constables) and arrived at the event in coaches (then painted green). Although they anticipated some disorder (one indicator of this being that coaches conveying demonstrators to London were stopped and searched for offensive weapons), the level of violence that subsequently occurred took the police by surprise. The key significance of Grosvenor Square was that it influenced the attitudes that both the police and demonstrators would adopt towards each other in future events. It also placed on the policing agenda the need for the service to consider the tactics (offensive and defensive) that they would use at future events of this nature to replace the on-the-spot improvisation that had been witnessed in 1968, which included accusations of gratuitous violence by some police officers towards demonstrators who were not participating in violent actions (Jackson, 1968: cols. 734–7).

Among the deficiencies that needed to be addressed were issues that included the equipment, weaponry and tactics that were appropriate to policing disorderly crowds, together with associated training and organisational matters such as the need to give briefings to officers who were required to deal with volatile crowd situations. There was, however, a disinclination to use weaponry such as water cannons in the belief that this would mark a departure from traditional methods of British policing (Taverne, 1968: col. 752).

See also: Chicago Democratic National Convention (Chicago, 1968), public order policing (England and Wales), student protests (England) 2010, student riots (Paris) 1968, Trafalgar Square anti-Poll Tax rally (London) 1990 riot

Sources and further reading
Clutterbuck, R. (1979) *Britain in Agony*. Harmondsworth: Penguin.
Jackson, P. (1968) Speech in the House of Commons, 4 April, HC Debs, vol. 762.
Taverne, D. (1968) Speech in the House of Commons, 4 April, HC Debs, vol. 762.
Willetts, D. (2011) *The Pinch: How the Baby Boomers Took their Children's Future – and Why they Should Give it Back*. London: Atlantic Books.

H

HACTIVISM

Hactivism is 'mainly interpreted by society as the transposition of protest into cyberspace. Hacktivism is the use of technology to express dissent' (Paganini, 2013) and is also known as electronic civil disobedience. The term was initially coined in 1996 by a member of the Cult of the Dead Cow hacker collective known as Omega, although hacking had occurred (whether for financial gain or political objectives) before that date, including the Guy Fawkes Day attack on the UK government on 11 November 1994 as a protest against the proposed Criminal Justice Bill.

Hactivism entails a diverse range of actions. It is usually associated with illegally breaking into computers or computer systems (often those managed by governments, security and law-enforcement agencies or private companies) in order to perform a variety of actions that are collectively referred to as 'cyber-attacks'. The activities associated with cyber-attacks include accessing sensitive or classified information stored on those computers ('information theft'). This information may then be leaked to the general public, an action referred to as 'whistleblowing'.

Other activities associated with cyber-attacks include disrupting the services of the organisation that operates them (termed 'denial of service' (DoS) or sabotage), which entails flooding a website with more traffic than the server can handle, causing it to crash, or leaving political messages or symbols on websites (a form of website defacement sometimes involving parodies).

In order to perform their actions, hactivists may make use of anonymous blogging (whereby software provides anonymity to those wishing to criticise government actions) and encryption software to provide for secure communications between activists that cannot be accessed by outsiders, including the surveillance activities carried out by government agencies.

Hactivism derives from merging the two words 'hacker' and 'activist', thus asserting the political agenda of those engaged in the process of digital incursions. These political objectives are frequently associated with the freedom of speech and the citizen's right to know about government activities. An important group of hactivists who perform actions of this nature is termed Anonymous, 'a leaderless collection of hackers and activists who come together in response to perceived injustices, then work for a time until the operation is over. They have no meet-ups, membership programs, or stated agenda' (Casserly, 2012). Anonymous mounted Operation Payback in 2010 (having previously engaged in actions against the Church of Scientology in 2008). This entailed DoS attacks (initially against recording and media companies that sought to take action against piracy sites, but subsequently in support for the WikiLeaks programme undertaken by Julian Assange based on their opposition to Internet government censorship). The actions of Anonymous in support of WikiLeaks entailed mounting DoS attacks on organisations that had severed links with WikiLeaks, and their actions succeeded in bringing down the websites of Mastercard, Paypal and Visa. These companies were denying services to WikiLeaks, including refusing to process donations to its campaign. Subsequently (in 2011), Anonymous has been associated with activities in support of the Occupy movement.

Hactivism has been associated with a number of important political events including the initiation of the Arab Spring in Tunisia, where hactivism (initially WikiLeaks) was responsible for releasing documents derived from the American Embassy in Tunis that revealed the level of government corruption in that country. Subsequently, other hactivists (especially Anonymous) joined the opposition to the Tunisian government campaign and provided political dissidents with the tools to avoid detection whilst communicating online (Casserly, 2012). Events in Tunisia paved the way for similar protests and regime changes in other Arab countries.

Hactivism can, however, be motivated by other considerations. It has been argued that the activities of the group Lulzsec (which in 2011 included hacking a range of sites such as those of Sony, several game companies and a number of UK and US government agencies) were motivated 'just for laughs' and also to display their technical abilities (Casserly, 2012).

Hactivism can also be used by organised criminal gangs and state-sponsored groups. One example of the latter is the Chinese Red Hacker Alliance, whose origins date to the late 1990s. It emerged from the China Hacker Emergency Meeting Center, which targeted Indonesian government websites following anti-Chinese riots in that country in 1998 and was formed following the accidental attack by a NATO jet on the Chinese Embassy in Belgrade in 1999 (Carr, 2012: 2). In the early years of the twenty-first century, this group incorporated a further group of Chinese hactivists called the Honker Union of China. This latter group (which still conducts activities in its own name) is not officially endorsed by the Chinese government, but its actions (mainly directed against American and Japanese online targets, usually government departments) are motivated by the emotions of patriotism and nationalism. Hactivism conducted in this country enables the nationalist feelings embraced by many young Chinese people to find an outlet and also lends support to the stance of the Chinese government in its conduct of foreign policy.

Hacking (usually in the form of data theft) can also be used by private companies to further their commercial objectives. One example of this was the *News of the World* hacking scandal in the UK, in which voice messages stored on mobile phones were intercepted in order to obtain information to form the basis of sensational stories that would boost the newspaper's sales. Public distaste in the UK towards this illegal activity led the proprietor of the newspaper, Rupert Murdoch, to close it down in July 2011.

See also: Arab Spring, civil disobedience, Occupy movement, whistleblowing

Sources and further reading

Carr, J. (2012) *Cyber Warfare: Mapping the Cyber Underworld*, 2nd edn. Sebastopol, CA: O'Reilly Media.
Casserly, M. (2012) 'What is Hactivism?: A Short History of Anonymous, Lulzsec and the Arab Spring', *PC Advisor*, www.pcadvisor.co.uk/features/internet/3414409/what-is-hacktivism-short-history-anonymous-lulzsec-arab-spring (date accessed 2 May 2014).
Jordan, T. (2001) *Activism! Direct Action, Hactivism and the Future of Society*. London: Reaktion Books.
Paganini, P. (2013) 'Hactivism: Means and Motivations ... What Else?', *Infosec Institute*, http://resources.infosecinstitute.com/hacktivism-means-and-motivations-what-else (date accessed 2 May 2014).

HOUSING ESTATE RIOTS (ENGLAND) 1991–2

Between 1991 and 1995, 28 recorded violent disturbances or riots occurred across England, in which the police, local authorities and the community at large temporarily lost control over public spaces to an often relatively small group of young men (Power and Tunstall, 1997: 1). In 13 areas, serious disorders that constituted riots occurred in 1991 and 1992. In addition, there were three further riots in 1992 and 1993 in places where serious disturbances had previously occurred. These riots lasted an average of three days (Power and Tunstall, 1997: 13) and violence was characterised by arson, attacks on buildings and other property and looting. Around 800 people were arrested, most of whom were charged with offences against the Public Order Act 1986. Convictions were mainly for violent disorder as opposed to the offence of rioting (Power and Tunstall, 1997: 21).

The 13 areas in which riots occurred in 1991–2 shared a number of common characteristics. Twelve of the worst-affected areas were relatively large council housing estates outside of London (Power and Tunstall, 1997: 4), which had been constructed in the 1930s, 1940s and 1950s to re-house slum clearance families. These areas subsequently suffered from poor reputations (which were aggravated by local authority policy to re-locate 'problem families' to them) and evidenced a wide range of economic and social problems coupled with demographic peculiarities (Power and Tunstall, 1997: xi), which provided the underpinning of the riots. Most of those involved in the disturbances in these 13 locations were white British males aged 10–30. Ten of the 13 areas contained a white population in excess of 90 per cent and in only one area (Blackburn) were a significant number of ethnic-minority residents involved (Power and Tunstall, 1997: ix and 11).

The riots occurred against the background of 'an extremely severe recession' (Power and Tunstall, 1997: 13). The main economic problem in the 13 riot-affected areas was high unemployment levels arising from the lack of marketable skills and work experience of local residents. Levels of unemployment were 'three times as high as for the local authority area as a whole and more than twice as high as other areas comprising social housing' (Power and Tunstall, 1997: ix and xi). One consequence of this was that a large majority of households in the riot areas were dependent on income support (Power and Tunstall, 1997: 9). Social problems included poverty, social breakdown and weak social controls (Power and Tunstall, 1997: xi and 7). The main demographic features of the riot-affected areas were 'an unusually youthful population' characterised by a very high concentration of young people below the age of 24 with high levels of transience and very high numbers of single-parent families that comprised over half of all families (Power and Tunstall, 1997: ix, xi and 9). It was concluded that these factors 'made for a dangerous combination of large numbers of out-of-work young males with no status or stake in society, living in low-income, work-poor households, in areas suffering from a high social stigma' (Power and Tunstall, 1997: ix).

A further important feature of the riot-affected areas was the prevalence of crime and other forms of law-breaking. North-eastern England gave birth to the phenomenon of 'ram raiding' and this activity and other forms of criminal activities directed at commercial enterprises away from the riot-affected areas were primarily conducted for economic gain. Other forms of criminal activity conducted within the riot-affected areas (such as 'joyriding' and 'causing trouble') were carried out for non-economic reasons that included the desire to assert 'an alternative, defiant, anti-authority and destructive image to compensate for the inability to succeed or participate in a more organised way in the mainstream society' (Power and Tunstall, 1997: x). Nonetheless, such an atmosphere was conducive to more traditional forms of criminal enterprise as criminals could 'use the estates as safe haven' (Power and Tunstall, 1997: 21).

These situations resulted in a constant state of friction between the police and local residents, which in nine areas assumed the character of 'rumbling disorder or slow riots' (Power and Tunstall, 1997: 14). Police tactics in these areas frequently 'tolerated or failed to stamp out sporadic violence and public law-breaking', which may have led young men to believe 'that *they* were in control rather than the official authorities' (Power and Tunstall, 1997: 14). Attempts by the police to enforce the law were likely to meet with resistance. The riot that occurred in Tyneside's Meadow Well Estate in September 1991, for example, was triggered by the deaths of two youths driving a stolen car that crashed during a police pursuit, and a related event involving a stolen motorcycle triggered violence in Bristol's Hartcliffe Estate in July 1992. It was concluded that serious violence 'frequently followed an unusual level of police intervention in response to a threatened breakdown in order' in which attempts were made to 'reassert control and enforce the law' (Power and Tunstall, 1997: x and 15). The riots had the character of 'chaotic street battles between two groups of young men – the police and the local youths – over control of the area' (Power and Tunstall, 1997: x).

There were various solutions put forward to prevent further outbreaks of this nature. Although the demographic profile of the areas involved in violence in 1991–2 was different from that of previous events in the 1980s, a common factor was deprivation and exclusion from mainstream society, characteristics associated with the underclass.

The structural definition of this term argues that the social structure of society (especially economic conditions characterised by recession and the movement of job opportunities away from traditional manufacturing industries to service industries) created a social grouping located in specific geographical areas which was effectively unemployed and unemployable. However, although this description was frequently associated with ethnic-minority communities (where racial discrimination had an adverse impact on employment opportunities and social status), by the 1990s it extended beyond such communities in England to embrace white (previously working-class) areas. Although a variety of government regeneration programmes had been directed at the riot-affected areas, their impact had been limited (Power and Tunstall, 1997: 23–4). One solution, therefore, was intensified reforms to improve education and training, and the provision of more work opportunities in the areas in which disorder occurred.

The view that the operations of society were the root causes of these disorders is compatible with viewing riots as purposeful forms of protest. This may seek to draw the government's attention to a problem that they might otherwise seek to ignore or to express opposition to government decisions affecting the area. An example of the latter was that the riot in Bristol's Hartcliffe Estate in July 1992 occurred following the area's failure to secure funding from the government's City Challenge programme.

However, Conservative politicians rejected the view that riots were a meaningful protest against the operations of society and instead focused on the behavioural characteristics of the underclass: the problem was seen to be moral depravation as opposed to social and economic deprivation. In the wake of these events, suggestions were put forward to address this issue that were designed to influence the attitudes and behaviour of individuals. Although this approach included expressions of support for the traditional family unit, it also embraced positive action to prevent juvenile delinquency by directing support to individuals whose potential for anti-social behaviour and crime could be detected at an early age. A former Conservative Home Secretary justified this approach by the argument that criminals were characterised by 'young men who have failed to go to school regularly, failed to behave there, failed to achieve at school; have unsatisfactory family and other relationships and so often have poor financial prospects ... If criminal behaviour is to be nipped in the bud it needs to be tackled by those who first observe a problem – parents, teachers, churches, social workers' (Baker, 1992).

This course of action was based upon methods pioneered in the Highscope Institute in Detroit, USA, in which young children were selected by criteria in which prominence was placed on family poverty. These children were then provided with a pre-school programme that utilised teaching methods designed to make the child 'self-motivated and independent' (Joyce, 1992: 245). This programme claimed a high success rate in preventing future delinquency, but a high staff–pupil ratio made it a costly option and pre-emptive action of this nature also raised accusations of surveillance and intrusion of civil liberties.

See also: Bradford riots (Manningham, Bradford) 1985, Broadwater Farm Estate riot (Haringey, London) 1985, copycat riot (England) 1981, public order policing (England and Wales), riots

Sources and further reading
Baker, K. (1992) Speech to the ACOP Annual Conference, 26 February.
Joyce, P. (1992) 'A Decade of Disorder', *Policing*, 8: 232–48.
Power, A. and Tunstall, R. (1997) *Dangerous Disorder. Riots and Violent Disturbances in Thirteen Areas of Britain, 1991–92*. York: Joseph Rowntree Foundation.

I

ISLAMIC TERRORIST GROUPS

The key motive of Islamic terrorism is 'to extend throughout the world the fundamentalist interpretation of Islamic law in Iran and, indeed, to export the revolution that established the Iranian Islamic Republic to other Muslim countries' (Hoffman, 1993: 4). It adheres to a literal interpretation of the Qur'an and Hadith, and of the commands of the Prophet. Islamic terrorism is a form of religious or 'holy terror' and 'is clearly conceived and conducted as a form of Holy War which can only end when total victory has been achieved' (Hoffman, 1993: 4). This Holy War is usually referred to as a *jihad*.

Holy terror is unlike other, more traditional forms of terrorism. It does not seek to achieve its aims by coercing governments into making concessions. The violence with which it is associated constitutes a total rejection of the established social order and a desire to destroy it through acts of violence, and in this sense violence is seen 'as an end in itself' rather than the means to an end' (Hoffman, 1993: 3). In the case of Islamic terror, its enemies will be offered the choice between converting to Islam or dying (Taheri, 1987: 7–8).

This will make for extreme forms of indiscriminate violence that include bombings, suicide bombings designed to cause death and injury to the public at large, hijackings that result in the deaths of those involved in whatever mode of transportation that is seized, and the kidnapping and execution of prisoners, often videoed for propaganda purposes. Violence of this nature is not designed to court or coerce support from the population at large: the aim of holy terror is to destroy its opponents. This will be achieved both through the violent acts that are performed and also from the backlash that such events are likely to cause, which will serve to radicalise those members of the religion not initially involved in the campaign of violence, intensify the violence and tear society apart into warring groups supporting or opposing Islam. It was in this sense that Bill Clinton argued that the purpose of terrorism in diverse societies was to make people 'afraid of each other' (Clinton, 2001).

Holy terror is also underpinned by different value systems from those embraced by secular terrorists: 'violence first and foremost is a sacramental act or divine duty executed in direct response to some theological demand or imperative ... religion serves as a legitimizing force – conveyed by sacred text or imparted via clerical authorities claiming to speak for the divine (Hoffman, 1993: 2–3).

Islamic terrorist groups possess a long historical heritage (dating back at least as far as the eleventh century Assassins), but in the late twentieth century acquired a considerable public profile. The emergence of contemporary Islamic terrorism dates from the 1979 Iranian Revolution and has been fuelled by other factors such as the Soviet invasion of Afghanistan in October 1979.

Islamic terrorism has two key aims. First, it is designed to rid Muslim nations of secular governments which owe their existence to being propped up by Western nations, especially America, thereby liberating Muslim populations from oppression. Leading personnel in such governments are thus a target of Islamic terrorist campaigns, an example being the assassination of President Anwar Sadat of Egypt in 1981.

Second, Islamic terrorism mounts direct attacks on Western nations (or on property, facilities and installations owned by Western nations in other countries such as embassies) and justifies its actions as a response to the injustices inflicted on Muslims throughout the world derived from Western foreign policy, especially the American-led invasions of Afghanistan in 2001 and Iraq in 2003, the political support given to the State of Israel and the propping-up of secular dictatorships in Muslim nations such as Egypt, Algeria and Morocco. It also carries out attacks on Muslim governments that are seen as being too close to America, such as Saudi Arabia. This country had admitted American troops into it in the wake of the 1990 Iraqi invasion of Kuwait. The mosques at Mecca and Medina were located in Saudi Arabia and the presence of American troops there was viewed as a profanity by fundamentalist Muslims. Such events legitimise a perception that Islam is under attack worldwide and needs to be defended by its believers.

Although Western nations are frequently the subject of acts of terror, this is not exclusively the case and it has also been associated with the demands of the Muslim population of Chechnya in Russia for separatism since 1994.

The treatment of the Palestinian Arabs is often used as a rationale for conducting acts of violence that are designed highlight the sufferings caused to Muslims whose denial of access to formal mechanisms to voice their concerns resulted in a 'feeling of impotence derived from degradation and the failure to be heard or understood' (Pamuk, 2001). The focus on injustices is designed to encourage more Muslims to adopt a militant approach and pursue acts of violence, which in addition to the damage inflicted on the target will create martyrs whose sacrifice will spur others to carry out similar acts. Contemporary Islamic terror is especially associated with the tactic of indiscriminate terror caused by the use of suicide attacks. This method of waging war was developed during the occupation of Lebanon by Hezbollah and was based upon an interpretation of Islam that was compatible with this form of martyrdom.

Islamic terrorism has been carried out by a number of organisations and some of the principal ones are briefly discussed below.

Hezbollah (or the Party of Allah) was formed in Lebanon following the Israeli invasion in 1982 (which lasted until 2000), which was designed to remove the Palestinian Liberation Organization (PLO) from southern Lebanon. Hezbollah was formed from existing Shi'a militias whose immediate aim was to rid their country of Israeli occupation and whose longer-term objective was to spread the Islamic revolution and to entirely eliminate the State of Israel. It was funded by Iran and its members were trained by the Iranian Revolutionary Guards. Its ideology was Shi'a radicalism.

Hezbollah's initial actions entailed the use of attacks that were mounted against Israeli soldiers involved in the 1982 invasion and also Israeli targets outside of Lebanon. Soldiers from the multinational force that was dispatched to supervise the removal of the PLO from Lebanon in 1982 were also subject to attacks of this nature. The methods used included suicide bombings, kidnappings (which occurred systematically in Lebanon between 1982 and 1992), hijackings (which included the seizure of the Trans World Airlines flight 847 in June 1985, which sought the release of 700 Shi'ite prisoners held in Israel that subsequently developed into a hostage situation) and assassinations. Indiscriminate violence was also used in the form of rocket attacks directed against Israeli territory.

However, these methods, associated with tactics used by terrorists, were latterly supplanted by more conventional methods of warfare, which transformed Hezbollah into an armed militia that exercised considerable influence in the Shi'ite areas of southern Lebanon that were adjacent to the country's border with Israel. The actions with which Hezbollah was involved included the 2006 military conflict, known as the Lebanon War, in which Hezbollah used rocket attacks against towns in Israel, and Israel responded with artillery fire and air strikes in Lebanon.

Hezbollah has since developed into a major political movement in the Lebanon, with seats in the national unity government that was formed in 2008. Its military wing was engaged in warfare with Israel in 2006 and has more recently been involved in the Syrian civil war, giving support to President Bashar al-Assad's regime.

Hezbollah has been associated with activities carried out by the Islamic Jihad Organisation (IJO). These included an attack on barracks used by American and French soldiers in Beirut in 1982, which killed 241 US marines and 58 French paratroopers, and the attack on the Israeli Embassy in Buenos Aires, Argentina in 1992 that killed 29 and injured over 240. The nature of this link (including whether the IJO is merely a front name used by Hezbollah) is uncertain.

Another Islamic organisation that is viewed as terrorist in some parts of the world, including the European Union (EU) and America, is Hamas (the Islamic Resistance Movement). It is located in Palestine and was formed in 1987 during the first Intifada (a popular uprising in Palestine against the Israeli occupation of Gaza and the West Bank). It has a military wing, the Izz ad-Din al-Qassam Brigades. Hamas adheres to the principles of Islamic fundamentalism and emerged as an offshoot of the Muslim Brotherhood in Egypt. It sought to liberate Palestine from Israeli occupation and establish an Islamic state embracing Israel, the Gaza Strip and the West Bank. Its opposition to Israel's existence as a state and commitment to *jihad* to accomplish this aim was made explicit in the *Islamic Covenant* that was published in 1988.

Since its formation, its military wing, the Izz ad-Din al-Qassam Brigades (or Squads), have been responsible for directing a number of attacks against civilian and military targets in Israel which began in 1992. It used a number of tactics that included suicide bombings in the West Bank and in Israel, mortar attacks across the border and a number of activities directed against Israeli soldiers, such as using explosive charges against tanks and other vehicles, kidnappings and ambushes.

The Izz ad-Din al-Qassam Brigades also launched suicide attacks against military and civilian targets in Israel during the second Intifada, which commenced in 2000 following the failure of the Camp David Summit. They also performed more conventional forms of warfare involving rocket attacks against Israeli settlements in the Gaza Strip and Israeli cities outside of it. These attacks included the bombing of the Sbarro pizza restaurant in Jerusalem in August 2001, in which 15 Israeli civilians were killed. In 2006, a series of suicide bus bombings took place in Israel, which killed over 60 Israelis (*BBC News*, 2012). The response by Israel included targeted assassinations against the leadership of Hamas, which included Hamas founder Sheikh Ahmed Yassin in March 2004 and his successor, Abdul Aziz al-Rantisi, in April 2004.

In 2006, Hamas secured a majority of seats in the Palestinian Parliament. This occurred in the wake of the death in 2004 of Yasser Arafat, the leader of Fatah, which was affiliated with the PLO. The PLO (itself once regarded as a terrorist organisation) had recognised the right of the State of Israel to exist in 1993 and rejected violence and terrorism. This led it to be accepted by Israel as the body that represented the Palestinian people.

Hamas was immediately put under external pressure by the EU, the United Nations, America and Russia to recognise the State of Israel and abandon violence. Hamas refused such demands, which led to foreign economic aid being suspended. Tensions within Palestine led to clashes between Hamas and Fatah in 2007 (the Battle of Gaza), which resulted in the effective division of Palestine into the West Bank (governed by the Palestinian National Authority) and Gaza (controlled by Hamas). Hamas subsequently launched rocket attacks against Israel, which prompted Israel to retaliate, including an invasion of Gaza in December 2008, termed Operation Cast Lead. This resulted in a ceasefire being declared by Israel in 2009 and in 2011 a captive Israeli soldier, Gilad Shalit, was 'swapped' for over 1,000 Palestinian prisoners within Israeli jails. However, this did not end the violence.

Between 2010 and 2012, a series of rocket attacks by Hamas (working in conjunction with other Islamic terrorist groups that opposed the existence of the State of Israel (such as Palestinian Islamic Jihad) directed at Eilat (in Israel) and Aqaba (in Jordan) were fired from Egyptian territory. In addition, rocket attacks against Israel were mounted from within Gaza, to which Israel responded with a ground operation referred to as the 'Pillar of Defense' in November 2012. A ceasefire between Hamas and Israel, mediated by Egypt, came into operation, but peace negotiations between the two sides had failed to yield any positive results by the beginning of January 2014. Following the Egyptian military's overthrow of President Mohamed Morsi (who supported Hamas) in 2013, a clampdown on smuggling tunnels between Gaza and Egypt was initiated, thus depriving Hamas of finance.

In May 2011, a reconciliation pact between Hamas and Fatah was signed in Cairo that entailed Hamas renouncing violence and accepting a Palestinian state based on the borders that existed before the 1967 Six Days' War. However, this failed to produce a government of unity across Palestine, whose control thus remained divided between Fatah and Hamas.

Al-Qaeda ('The Base') is a further example of an Islamic terrorist organisation. Its origins date back to the Soviet invasion of Afghanistan in 1979, but it emerged as an organisation in the late 1980s founded and led by Osama Bin Laden. He had been involved in organising training camps for Muslims who came to Afghanistan from all over the world to fight alongside the Afghanistan *mujahideen* who were fighting against the Soviet invasion of the country. Towards the end of this war (which ended when the Soviets withdrew in 1989), some elements within the *mujahideen* wished to broaden their activities and engage in Islamic struggles in other parts of the world. One such group was led by Osama binLaden became known as al-Qaeda following a meeting in Peshawar,

Pakistan, in August 1988. Other key members included Mohammed Atef, who later became al-Qaeda's military chief.

Al-Qaeda is a radical Sunni Muslim organisation that adopts a strict interpretation of Islam and endorses a jihad on a global basis. All political authority that does not follow their strict interpretation of Islam is regarded as illegitimate and thus justifies attacks on all who do not adhere to this view, whether Muslim or non-Muslim.

Al-Qaeda has conducted attacks globally, including the truck bomb explosions of the American Embassies in Dar es Salaam and Nairobi on 7 August 1988 in which several hundred people were killed. This resulted in bin Laden being placed by the FBI on its ten most-wanted fugitives list. America responded with bombing raids against Afghanistan and the Sudan, which were associated with aiding these attacks.

America was identified as the key enemy of Islam and became a particular target for al-Qaeda attacks. In 1993, the World Trade Center in New York was the subject of a truck bomb attack that caused extensive damage to the buildings and injuries. In October 2000, an al-Qeada operation mounted from the Yemen killed 17 US sailors on board the *USS Cole*.

On 11 September 2001, al-Qaeda carried out its most infamous action, which involved the hijacking of four American planes on internal flights. Two of these were crashed into the Twin Towers Building of New York's World Trade Center and another into the Pentagon in Washington. The fourth plane failed to reach its destination of the White House and crashed in Pennsylvania. This act resulted in the deaths of around 3,000 people and the total destruction of the Twin Towers.

Following these events (which became known as 9/11), America initiated a War on Terror. This was an international military operation that was designed to wipe out al-Qaeda and also to launch attacks on any countries which lent support to this or any other militant Islamic terrorist organisation. It was spearheaded by America, but involved a number of other NATO countries, including the UK. Pakistan (which had previously been supportive of al-Qaeda) also supported this coalition, primarily to avoid American reprisals being directed at it. Afghanistan (then ruled by the Taliban) was invaded in October 2001 and air strikes were directed at both the Taliban and training camps used by al-Qaeda fighters. This succeeded in toppling the Taliban government, but failed to eliminate them as a fighting force. Iraq was invaded in 2003, which led to the overthrow of Saddam Hussein's regime.

The War on Terror had significant implications for the manner in which al-Qaeda was organised. Initially, leadership was relatively centralised in the hands of bin Laden, who was advised by a Shura Council of senior al-Qaeda members. However, following the American attacks on

Afghanistan, al-Qaeda became more decentralised, with attacks being organised by local groups who were inspired by al-Qaeda and perhaps secured financial or logistical support from this organisation but were not directly controlled by them.

Other changes to al-Qaeda's tactics also occurred after 2001. Fighters trained in Afghanistan returned to their home countries where they might perform terrorist acts, but use was also made of individuals who were local to an area where an attack was planned. These had no previous involvement with Islamic militancy and more easily slipped under the radar of the police and security services. The Madrid train bombings in 2004, for example, were carried out by people from such backgrounds.

Thus, after 2001, attacks by al-Qaeda continued. They included:

- the Bali (Indonesia) bombings in 2002: these killed over 200 people and injured around the same number and were carried out by a suicide bomb, a car bomb and a bomb planted outside the American Consulate in Denpasar. This attack was in retaliation for the country's support for the American War on Terror and for Australia's role in the liberation of East Timor (over 80 Australians were killed in this attack);
- the Madrid train bombings in 2004;
- the London bombings in 2005;
- the attack on Glasgow International Airport in 2007.

The constant changes in targets (especially different forms of transportation) and the tactics used to undertake attacks made it difficult for the law-enforcement agencies to devise effective counter-measures. They were forced to use a reactive approach, which put them one step behind of the terrorists. The decentralised nature of al-Qaeda also meant that the death of bin-Laden at the hands of American Special Forces in 2011 was unlikely to halt activities associated with Islamic terrorism.

Other al-Qaeda-inspired groups have been responsible for attacks in recent years. These include the Somali-based al-Shabaab ('The Youth'). Its attacks included the seizure of a shopping mall (Westgate) in Nairobi, Kenya in 2013. A siege then ensued and over 60 people were killed. In Nigeria, the group Boko Haram seeks to establish a pure Islamic state governed by Sharia law and has launched a number of attacks since the beginning of the twenty-first century. It especially directs its violence at government and Christian targets, one example of this being an attack on a boarding school in July 2013 in the Mamudu district of Yobe State in which over 40 people were killed. In April 2014, this group abducted over 250 schoolgirls from the Government Girls Secondary School in the town of Chibok in Borno State. Boko Haram objects to girls being educated, a development which it views as a symptom of the Westernisation of Nigeria, to which it is opposed.

See also: counter-terrorism, nationalist terrorist groups, post-Arab Spring terrorism

Sources and further reading:

BBC News (2012) 'Profile: Hamas Palestinian Movement', *BBC News Middle East*, 6 December, www.bbc.co.uk/news/world-middle-east-13331522 (accessed 2 May 2014).

Clinton, B. (2001) 'The Struggle for the Soul of the Twenty-First Century', Dimbleby Lecture, BBC1, 16 December, http://australianpolitics.com/news/2001/01-12-14.shtml (accessed 2 May 2014).

Hoffman, B. (1993) '"Holy Terror": The Implications of Terrorism Motivated by a Religious Imperative'. Santa Monica, CA: RAND.

Pamuk, O. (2001) 'Listen to the Damned'. *The Guardian*, 29 September.

Taheri, A. (1987) *Holy Terror: The Inside Story of Islamic Terrorism*. London: Sphere Books.

K

KETTLING (CONTAINMENT)

Kettling is a term used by the media and protestors for the UK police tactic of containment. This tactic is normally deployed to prevent serious disorder and contain outbreaks of disorder. It is often used by police commanders to gain control over a crowd during an escalating incident. It is mainly used to control protest crowds, but it has been widely used in the policing of football. In order to implement the tactic, large numbers of police officers are required, so the police will often use building lines and other street furniture to act as one side of the containment.

The tactic is a controversial one that is often described in an emotive way, mainly due to the indiscriminate way it is sometimes employed by the police. Allegations are made that those who are contained are often innocent bystanders who get caught up in the protest and that police are unable or unwilling to discriminatebetween such people and protestors. Its use was initially challenged after the May Day protests in 2001, when about 3,000 demonstrators were contained for over seven hours by the Metropolitan Police outside Oxford Circus. Two protestors brought a claim against the police that they had had their liberty deprived under Article 5 of the European Convention on Human Rights. In the resultant case, the House of Lords ruled that such measures 'fell outside the ambit of Article 5 provided that they were not arbitrary in that they were resorted to in good faith, were proportionate and enforced for no longer than was reasonably necessary'. It was concluded that kettling 'constituted a restriction of liberty, not a deprivation of it' (*Austin and Another v Commissioner of Police of the Metropolis* (2009)).

The use of containment came to wider public attention as a result of the G20 protests in 2009, when it was used to contain a large number of protestors outside the Bank of England after violence and damage to property had occurred. The subsequent report into the protests by HMIC (2009a) suggested that whilst the rationale for the use of the tactic was correct, the Metropolitan Police had not considered the peaceful members of the crowd who got caught up inside the containment, and a lack of communication by the police increased anxiety and resentment amongst those contained. The coverage in the media was heightened by journalists who had also found themselves within the 'Kettle' and were not released due to a lack of understanding of press accreditation by the police officers involved.

The report made a number of recommendations for immediate implementation, including a 'no surprises' approach involving the notification of both protestors and the public of potential police actions, as well as a clear plan to release any vulnerable members of the public who are caught up within the containment and information being given to those contained as to the likely length of time of the containment and the reason for it. In addition, the police now needed to consider basic facilities such as toilets if the containment was to be prolonged. A subsequent report (HMIC, 2009b) recommended that the police improve their intelligence gathering to ensure the proportionality of the containment and continue communication both before and during the containment.

Another review of the same protests by the Home Affairs Select Committee (2010) reinforced all these recommendations and also recommended devolution of command of the containment to allow better understanding of crowd dynamics and decision making. The Metropolitan Police subsequently introduced the functional position of Bronze Cordons to undertake this role and this has now been adopted by most UK police forces.

The controversy over the use of kettling continued. Just before Christmas 2010, student protests in London against rising tuition fees resulted in damage and major disorder, yet once again the police found themselves criticised for, on the one hand, not containing the violence and, on the other hand, for using too much force. Once again, the Metropolitan Police faced questions around their use of containment or, as the media more emotively described it, 'kettling'.

The new phrase in media circles is 'hyper-kettling', recently wrongly attributed to the Association of Chief Police Officers (ACPO) President Hugh Orde. This is described as containing protestors in a cordon and gradually decreasing the space inside.

The issue of 'kettling' illustrates the classic police dilemma in policing protest, which is how to balance the rights of the protestor with the need to protect the public and property. Guidance on kettling provided by the National Police Improvement Agency in the publication 'Keeping the Peace' (discussed in Wain, 2011) focuses on the need for commanders to satisfy the needs of Article 5 of the European Convention on Human Rights (ECHR), the right to liberty and security, especially consideration of the issues raised in recent legal challenges. The guidance also suggests that as far as reasonably practicable, the basic welfare needs of those contained should be addressed, such as the provision of water and toilets. Whilst the latter is clearly a good thing to do and the Metropolitan Police have made such provision in recent times, some police commanders have questioned both the feasibility and cost of such efforts (Wain, 2011).

The use of containment is also used in policing football matches, although the term 'kettling' is not used. It is often used to contain travelling away fans based upon an intelligence assessment that there is the possibility of disorder. This can be seen as disproportionate, as all the fans are corralled and herded to the ground, whether they have violent intentions or not. Perhaps more controversially, the tactic of containment is used inside football grounds to prevent certain sections of the crowd from leaving. This tactic used to be called a 'hold back' and is not specifically referred to within police guidance on football matches. The escorting, holding back and containment of football fans is seen as restrictive and has been described as 'bubbling' by supporters' groups. The court in the *Austin* judgment considered containment at a football match, but observed that the circumstances would not amount to a breach of human rights provided that it was necessary to prevent serious injury or damage and the supporters were kept contained for the minimum period required.

Kettling is used by police forces in other countries. It was deployed against an Occupy Wall Street protest in New York in September 2011, which took the form of demonstrations that sought to close roads and block traffic. Here kettling entailed the use of orange nets to isolate protesters with a view to breaking them up into smaller groups and penning them into confined spaces.

See also: anti-globalisation/anti-capitalist protests (UK), demonstrations, G20 protests (London) 2009, protest liaison officers (England and Wales), public order legislation (England and Wales), public order policing (England and Wales), student protests (England) 2010, Trafalgar Square anti-Poll Tax rally (London) 1990

Sources and further reading:

Austin and Another v Commissioner of the Metropolis [2009] UKHL 5.

HMIC (2009a) *Adapting to Protest*. London: HMIC.

——. (2009b) *Adapting to Protest: Nurturing the British Model of Policing*. London: HMIC.

Home Affairs Committee (2010) *Policing of the G20 Protests: Government Response to the Committee's Eighth Report of Session 2008–2009*. First Special Report, Session 2009–10. London, TSO, House of Commons Paper 201.

Wain. N, (2011) 'Parade Aid'. *Police Review*, 18 February: 16–17.

L

LEWISHAM DISORDERS (LEWISHAM, LONDON) 1977

On 13 August 1977, the National Front intended to hold a march from New Cross to Lewisham in south London. This was designed to highlight the issue of mugging, which demonstrators wished to project as a crime committed by black people (Clutterbuck, 1980: 227). This event was inspired by the police arrest of a number of black youths in south London on 30 May 1977 for this offence, which led to the formation of a defence committee for the 'Lewisham 18' (later becoming the 'Lewisham 21'). It was alleged that this defence committee was inspired by the Socialist Workers' Party (Clutterbuck, 1980: 227), although individuals not associated with this organisation were also involved. On 2 July 1977, this group organised a demonstration in New Cross, which met with violent opposition from National Front supporters and around 80 arrests were made (Brain, 2010: 37).

There were two main sources of opposition to the National Front's march. The first of these was a march called by the All-Lewisham Campaign Against Racism and Fascism, headed by the Bishop of Southwark. The decision to hold this event followed the unsuccessful attempt by Lewisham Council (whose request was supported by the Bishop of Southwark) to get the Commissioner of the Metropolitan Police to recommend to the Home Secretary that the march by the National Front should be banned under the provisions of the Public Order Act 1936. This organisation had been set up in 1976 following the electoral achievements of the National Front and the right-wing National Party, and was composed of local trade unionists and other local groups that included churches who were opposed to fascism and racism. This event attracted a crowd of around 4,000 people and although their route took them close to the vicinity where the National Front assembled, the event passed off peacefully.

The second source of opposition came from a counter-demonstration organised by the defence committee, which was strongly supported by the Socialist Workers' Party, whose aim was to 'drive the Nazis off the streets' and to stop them from marching (Clutterbuck, 1980: 228). Around 6,000 demonstrators turned up, many of whom were members of the local black community. Their tactics were twofold.

First, they attempted to occupy the location from where the National Front march (consisting of around 800 participants, who were at one stage joined by around 200 supporters of Millwall Football Club) was to commence, a place called Clifton Rise, opposite Deptford Town Hall (Clutterbuck, 1980: 228–9). This led to a confrontation between the police, who tried to clear a path for the march to get underway by deploying officers on foot and mounted police, and demonstrators, who sought to attack the National Front with sticks, smoke bombs, rocks and bottles. It was alleged that weapons confiscated from anti-fascist demonstrators included 'carving knives and a large iron pipe studded with bolts for use as a club. Some of demonstrators also carried ammonia with which they attacked the policemen's eyes' (Clutterbuck, 1980: 229). Although the National Front march was initially broken up, police tactics succeeded in enabling it to get underway.

Second, opponents to the National Front gathered in central Lewisham, determined to halt the progress of the march through Lewisham by occupying the area through which it had been intended to march. This tactic was successful, forcing the National Front to abandon its intended route and bringing about the premature end of its march.

Following the cessation of the National Front march, police tactics focused on clearing anti-fascist demonstrators from the streets of central Lewisham. The anger of the latter was intensified by a perception that the police had engineered the safe exit of National Front supporters from the area. This resulted in considerable violence in Lewisham High Street, where property was destroyed and police vehicles were wrecked. Police tactics to clear the demonstrators included the use of mounted police and foot officers with riot shields. There was, however, a lack of coherence to police operations and officers involved were attacked and pelted with bricks. Ladywell Police Station was also attacked.

The police deployed around 3,500 officers on 13 August (Brain, 2010: 37). In total, 134 people required hospital treatment, of whom 56 were police officers. The police arrested 214 people, only 46 of whom came from Lewisham (Clutterbuck, 1980: 230).

Lewisham was significant for a number of reasons. It witnessed the deployment of the police armed with long batons and perspex riot shields, the first time that the latter had been deployed on the streets of mainland Britain. Their use subsequently became routine, the next deployment being two days later in Birmingham in connection with a National Front meeting during the Ladywood by-election campaign (Brain, 2010: 38). It also queried the relevance of police public order powers, for although they had the power to recommend a ban or a re-routing of the National Front march, they possessed no powers to regulate counter-demonstrations, which was the activity used by the anti-fascists on this occasion. Following Lewisham, the Home Secretary, Merlyn Rees, undertook a review of public order law (although legislative change did not occur until 1986).

The events that occurred in Lewisham also illustrated the dilemmas in public order policing. The police took the view that the National Front march was lawful and should thus be protected from those who wished to prevent the legitimate use of the freedoms of assembly and speech. Those opposed to fascism reasoned that but for the presence of the police, the National Front would not have dared to take to the streets and the police were thus acting as the defenders of fascism by ensuring that an event could go ahead that would not otherwise have taken place.

Perhaps most significantly, Lewisham was regarded as a key event in the history of anti-fascism. Until that period, it seemed that the National Front and similar right-wing extremist parties were in the ascendant. There was widespread disillusionment on the part of the left with the record of the Labour government (which included high unemployment and cuts in public spending) and the National Front had polled strongly in local government and parliamentary by-elections. This highlighted the impotence of conventional politics to combat this movement and implied that protest was the method that was more likely to achieve this objective.

Lewisham was a significant defeat for the National Front and right-wing extremism – it:

> knocked the stuffing out of a generation of fascists, splitting the leaders of the National Front in two, between one group who gave up immediately on previous ideas of dominating communities physically, and turned instead to electoralism; and a second group who adopted violence intensely and without political purpose. Each group was far smaller than the previous whole. For anti-fascists, it showed that fascism and racism could be confronted and defeated. It was the start of an upwards curve. (Renton, undated)

See also: demonstrations, English Defence League, public order legislation (England and Wales), public order policing (England and Wales), Red Lion Square (London) 1974, riots, Southall disorders (Southall, London) 1980

Sources and further reading

Brain, T. (2010) *A History of Policing in England and Wales from 1974: A Turbulent Journey*. Oxford University Press.

Clutterbuck, R. (1980) *Britain in Agony: The Growth of Political Violence*. Harmondsworth: Penguin.

Renton, D. (undated) 'August 1977: The Battle of Lewisham', www.dkrenton.co.uk/lewisham_1977.html (date accessed 2 May 2014).

LIVE ANIMAL EXPORT PROTESTS (ENGLAND) 1994-5

Live animal exports became a lucrative trade in Britain during the 1990s. In 1992, 250,000 live calves and 1.4 million sheep were exported to Europe (Erlichman, 1993). A further boost to this trade was provided by the introduction of the European Single Market in 1993, whereby live animals were classified as agricultural products and were not subject to any regulation regarding journey times or conditions, since this would constitute a restraint on trade.

Groups that included Compassion in World Farming (CIWF) and the Royal Society for the Prevention of Cruelty to Animals (RSPCA) expressed opposition to the conditions under which live animals were transported to Europe for slaughter (which they deemed to be cruel and inhumane) and the methods used by farms in Europe concerned with veal production (for which purposes the exported calves were used). The CIWF had, since its inception in 1967, called for an end to this trade and both it and the RSPCA desired that journeys involving animals should last for no more than eight hours (EU regulations permitting journeys of up to 24 hours without the animals being fed or watered). Their view (supported by the British Veterinary Association) was that animals should be slaughtered close to the place where they were reared.

Initially, animals were transported to Europe by the ferry companies operating from major ports such as Dover, but the withdrawal of Brittany Ferries, Stena Sealink and P&O from this trade in 1994 forced animal exporters to find alternative routes. Ports that included Grimsby, Sheerness, Plymouth, Brightlingsea and Shoreham-by-Sea became engaged in this trade, which resulted in these locations becoming the targets of protesters.

Those opposed to the trade in live animals sought to prevent lorries entering the ports by obstructing the highways. Public disorder occurred when protesters engaged in such tactics clashed with police, who sought to keep the highways open. Disorders especially occurred at Brightlingsea and Shoreham-by-Sea and were respectively dubbed 'the Battle of Brightlingsea' and 'the Siege of Shoreham'.

Protests in Shoreham-by-Sea began on 2 January 1995 when protesters succeeded in turning back convoys of lorries loaded with sheep and calves. The protesters were mainly local residents who mounted vigorous, but mainly non-violent opposition to the trade, although on the second night, damage was caused to the trucks transporting animals. The inability of the Sussex police to control the crowds prompted them to invoke mutual aid arrangements and officers from the Metropolitan Police and the Kent and Hampshire Constabularies were used to counter the protests on 4 January. In total, these numbered over 1,000 officers on that night (Penman, 1995).

This arrangement continued for the period of 4–14 January, following which the number of demonstrators decreased, allowing for a reduced police presence. The cost of securing outside aid amounted to £1.25 million and 67 arrests were made (*R v Chief Constable of Sussex ex parte International Trader's Ferry Ltd* (1998)).

Actions undertaken by the police (which in the case of officers from the Metropolitan Police were extremely robust) were a spur to local residents to organise themselves. One aspect of this was the appearance of the publication, *The Shoreham Protester*, in February 1995 to promote non-violent local protest to end the transportation of live animal exports through the port (*The Shoreham Protester*, 1995). However, in January 1995, the Shoreham Port Authority decided to halt live animal exports when existing contracts had expired. Further, on 10 April (as is argued below), the chief constable restricted the number of sailings from the port.

Protests began in the port of Brightlingsea on 16 January 1995 and ended on 30 October of that year. They were orchestrated by an ad hoc local group, Brightlingsea Against Live Exports (BALE), which sought an outright ban on live animal exports. A second local group, Horror Out of Farming (HOOF), was also formed, whose members believed that an export ban was unlikely to happen and thus instead focused on the conditions under which animals were transported. During this period, around 150 convoys conveyed 250,000 animals for export.

The success of the first protest on 16 January in preventing the convoy reaching the docks prompted one exporter to threaten to sue the police and this was one factor in using more robust tactics in future to force convoys through to the port when the next convoy arrived on 18 January. Claims of overly aggressive policing to clear the roads for lorries were made, which included the use of long batons by officers wearing balaclavas, many of whom were dressed in riot gear. One journalist recounted how on 18 January: 'The first group of protesters who sat in the road were dragged out by police and anybody attempting to take their place was stamped on or punched by officers' (Cusick, 1995). Almost 600 people were arrested during the protests, the majority of whom were local residents. It was observed that: 'From Isla Humphreys, 19, who was repeatedly arrested, to Tilly Merritt, 79, it was the women, housewives, mothers, grandmothers, and children, who caught the media's eye. Especially when youngsters staged a protest during the half-term holidays' (Wilson, 2010).

Subsequently, the police made use of the advance notice requirement contained in the Public Order Act 1986, an action that tended to encourage outsiders (some of whom were more prone to use violence to advance the cause of the protests) into the town (Wilson, 2010). The costs of policing were estimated to be £4 million. In addition, in April 1995, the Assistant Chief Constable of Essex wrote to every householder in Brightlingsea advising them to desist from engaging in protests against live animal exports and threatening them with arrest and imprisonment if they failed to heed these instructions. Nonetheless, the protests continued on an almost daily basis until the exporters ceased the trade from the town because of the cost and disruption to their businesses that were caused by the protests. Exports were terminated in August 1995, but continued from other places.

However, police actions did not display a consistent bias against protest, illustrating how the discretionary nature of police powers provided by public order legislation is subject to diverse interpretation. These may also display an awareness of a desire not to inflame opinions in middle England, which is traditionally supportive of the police.

In Kent, the police removed unroadworthy lorries engaged in the trade from the roads and government veterinarians also intervened to assess the welfare of the animals. In Sussex, Chief Constable Paul Whitehouse imposed stringent conditions on those engaged in live animal exports by restricting the number of sailings from the port of Shoreham to two a week and threatened to arrest lorry drivers who attempted to contravene this restriction for obstructing a police officer in the execution of his duty. This action was primarily prompted by financial concerns related to the costs of policing the protest on the police budget. However, in July 1995, the International Traders' Ferry succeeded in obtaining a decision from the High Court that such actions by the police were unlawful under EU law.

However, the success of these protests forced the companies engaged in such trade to fly cattle out of the country, using airports that included Coventry and Swansea. This transferred the protests to these locations and led to the death of protester Jill Phipps in 1995, who was run over by a lorry carrying veal calves to the airport.

The success of the protests can be measured by the decision of the local authorities in Plymouth and Coventry and the Dover Harbour Board to impose their own bans on exporting live animals in order to end the protests. Although these decisions were ruled illegal by the High Court in April 1995, the export of all live animals from Britain ceased in February 1996 as the result of an EU ban designed to prevent mad cow disease from entering the European food chain. This ban remained in force until 2006. The overall cost of policing the demonstrations in 1995 was £6 million (BBC, 2006).

See also: animal rights protest groups, civil disobedience, direct action, public order legislation (England Wales), public order policing (England and Wales)

Sources and further reading

BBC (2006) 'Live Exports that Sparked Protests', http://news.bbc.co.uk/1/hi/uk/4784852.stm (date accessed 2 May 2014).

Cusick, J. (1995) 'Sheep Cargo Sails Despite Clashes', *The Independent*, 19 January.

Erlichman, E. (1993) 'Saying Cheese as the Trade Gap Yawns', *The Guardian*, 16 October.

Howkins, A. and Merricks, L. (2000) '"Dewy-eyed Veal Calves". Live Animal Exports and Middle-Class Opinion, 1980–1995', *Agricultural History Review*, 48(1): 85–103.

Penham, D. (1995) '1,000 Police Drafted to Animal Port', *The Independent*, 5 January.

R v Chief Constable of Sussex ex parte International Trader's Ferry Ltd (1998) judgment by the Lords of Appeal, 11 November.

The Shoreham Protester (1995) Issue 1, Thursday 2 February, www.chaos.org.uk/~maureen/tsp1.html (date accessed 2 May 2014).

Wilson, L. (22010) 'Fifteen Years since Live Animal Exports Divided Brightlingsea', *BBC News Essex*, http://news.bbc.co.uk/local/essex/hi/people_and_places/history/newsid_8506000/8506735.stm (date accessed 2 May 2014).

LOS ANGELES RIOTS (LOS ANGELES, CALIFORNIA) 1992

Riots that took place in Los Angeles, California in 1992 occurred as a protest related to the acquittal on 29 April of three Los Angeles police officers of assault with a deadly weapon and the use of excessive force against a black motorist, Rodney King. A fourth officer was cleared of assault, but the jury could not reach a verdict in connection with the use of excessive force charge. This incident occurred in March 1991 after officers from the California Highway Patrol had attempted a traffic stop, which led to a high-speed chase culminating in the arrest of the occupants of the car, one of whom was Rodney King, who was on parole from prison having been convicted of robbery.

King was subsequently tasered, hit with batons and beaten whilst lying on the ground, but the officers' behaviour had been videotaped by a resident from the area where the arrests took place. The acquittal verdict seemed to be at odds with the available evidence. As the four police officers were white and nine of the 12 jurors were also white, the outcome was perceived to be based on racist prejudices.

The riots (which are sometimes referred to as the Rodney King riots or the South Central riots) started on 29 April and lasted for six days. African Americans formed the main composition of the initial force of rioters, subsequently joined by Hispanic Americans. A key target of the rioters' violence were businesses in the locality owned by Korean and Asian individuals. The anger of the rioters towards successful Korean businesses was fuelled by an event soon after the beating of Rodney King in 1991 in which a Korean shopkeeper shot and killed a 15-year-old black girl in a dispute over a bottle of fruit juice, but received no custodial sentence.

Initial examples of violence also included random attacks on motorists including Reginald Denny, who received serious head injuries on the first day of the rioting, an assault that was captured on film by a news helicopter. Thousands of people were subsequently involved in the disturbances, which were characterised by looting, arson, assault and murder, and the damage caused was officially estimated to be around $750 million (Special Committee of the California Legislature, 1992). The local police were impotent to prevent the outbreak and escalation of the violence, which led to episodes of vigilantism such as the presence of armed Koreans to defend Korean businesses, resulting in gun battles occurring on the streets between looters and those seeking to safeguard property.

In six days of rioting, 2,383 people were injured, 8,000 were arrested, 51 were killed and over 700 businesses were burned. Property damage was estimated at over $1 billion (Webster, 1992: 23). The hardest-hit areas were South Central Los Angeles and Koreatown. Half of those arrested and over one-third of those killed were Hispanic. The riots were eventually quelled by security measures such as curfews, the deployment of the California National Guard and soldiers, including some US Marines.

During the riots, the US Justice Department announced that it was initiating an investigation into the incident and following the cessation of rioting, the original incident was re-visited and the officers were re-tried, charged with federal charges of violating Rodney King's civil rights. On 17 April 1993, two officers were convicted of these charges (for which they were imprisoned) and the other two were acquitted. Rodney King was awarded $3.8 million damages from the City of Los Angeles. He died in June 2012.

A number of reports were written to explain the occurrence of these events. The socio-economic conditions in the riot-afflicted area were highlighted in a report for the California State Legislature, which called for policies designed to end the economic isolation of the inner city (Special Committee of the California Legislature, 1992). A separate investigation echoed these sentiments and observed that little had been done to resolve: '(1) access to economic opportunity, (2) inter-ethnic minority and majority tensions, (3) police-community conflicts, and (4) to revise government policies to address the needs of poor, ethnic minorities' (Farrell and Johnson, 2001: 337). However, other studies argued that the riots were not in the nature of events that occurred during the 1960s (which could be depicted as protests against economic deprivation and political marginalisation), but were more in the nature of a defensive backlash to in-migration initiated by African Americans against those who were moving into their areas (Bergesen and Herman, 1998: 52).

The report for the California State Legislature also drew attention to the existence of 'serious flaws in our criminal justice system' and called for criminal penalties to be established for law-enforcement officers who failed to report assaults committed by another officer (Special Committee of the California Legislature, 1992). Policing matters were further considered in a report written for the Los Angeles Board of Police Commissioners. Although this also discussed socio-economic issues such as poverty and unemployment, it emphasised the need to improve police–public relations by placing a renewed emphasis on basic patrol duties and suggested that field command experience in patrol should become a primary criteria for promotion to the command ranks. It was also urged that more attention should be paid to emergency response planning and training within the Police Department and the city as a whole (Webster, 1992).

See also: Banlieue riots (Paris) 2005, Chicago Democratic National Convention riot (Chicago) 1968, riot police

Sources and further reading

Bergesen, A. and Herman, M. (1998) 'Immigration, Race and Riot: The 1992 Los Angeles Uprising'. *American Sociological Review*, 63(1): 39–54.

Farrell, W. and Johnson, J. (2001). 'Structural Violence as an Inducement to African American and Hispanic Participation in the Los Angeles Civil Disturbance of 1992'. *Journal Of Human Behavior in the Social Environment*, 4(4): 337–59.

Special Committee of the California Legislature (1992) *To Re-build is Not Enough: Final Report and Recommendations of the Assembly Special Committee on the Los Angeles Crisis*. Sacramento: Assembly Publications Office. Available at: www.usc.edu/libraries/archives/cityinstress/reb/i.htm (date accessed 2 May 2014).

Webster, W. (1992) *The City in Crisis*. Los Angeles: Institute for Government and Public Affairs, UCLA. Available at: https://www.ncjrs.gov/App/publications/Abstract.aspx?id=174014 (date accessed 2 May 2014).

M

MINERS' DISPUTE (BRITAIN) 1972

The 1972 British miners' dispute was a strike seeking higher wages for those employed within the industry. It was the first miners' strike since 1926.

An overtime ban in favour of a pay rise had been put in place in November 1971 and the dispute began on 9 January 1972, following a ballot of members of the National Union of Miners (NUM). It arose against a background of pit closures and pay restraint during the 1960s that saw miners' pay decline in relation to that of other working-class occupations, despite rises in productivity. However, the government's incomes policy (which imposed a limit of eight per cent on pay rises) prevented the National Coal Board (NCB) from awarding the major increase in pay sought by the unions: its offer of an increase of £1.80 per week fell far short of the NUM's demand for increases of up to £9.00 on top of the basic wage of £19.00 a week.

The main tactic deployed by the NUM was the use of mass picketing. This was directed at ports and was designed to prevent the importation of fuel from abroad at major coal users (such as the steel industry) and at places housing major fuel stocks in order to prevent its distribution to power stations. The use of this tactic owed much to a leading NUM activist in Barnsley, Yorkshire, Arthur Scargill. Its effective use required a considerable degree of logistical organisation to enable pickets to be shipped to sites where they were needed to enforce the strike and to accommodate them whilst they remained there.

The most significant episode in the 1972 dispute occurred at Saltley Marsh Coal Depot (outside of Birmingham). Saltley (which was owned by the West Midlands Gas Board) housed a very large stock of coke and lorries from across England travelled there to convey it to power stations. Coke shortages elsewhere made Saltley a key battleground in the dispute and the number of lorries arriving there increased significantly towards the end of January 1972. However, the impact of picketing on turning lorries away was negligible since many of the drivers were not members of the Transport and General Workers' Union (TGWU) and refused to support strike action.

Additional pickets from Yorkshire arrived over the weekend of 5–6 February and increased tensions at the Coke Depot resulted in the police rather than gasboard employees manning the gates. Increasingly, lorries could get through the gates only with police aid, which considerably slowed down the rate at which they could be loaded. But some were getting through and the government's tactic was to declare a state of emergency on 9 February and to impose a three-day working week on 11 February in order to conserve coal stocks.

This situation prompted Scargill to increase the number of pickets by getting other unions in Birmingham involved in the dispute. On 10 February, the TGWU and the Amalgamated Union of Engineering Workers (AUEW) in Birmingham called sympathy strikes in support of the miners, a decision that vastly increased the number of pickets, which numbered thousands that morning. Acknowledging that attempts by the police (who numbered around 800) to force lorries through the crowd might result in serious injuries, the Chief Constable of Birmingham, Sir Derrick Capper, asked the depot manager to close the gates.

Following Saltley, Lord Wilberforce was appointed by the government to head a Court of Inquiry, the main recommendation of which was to increase the pay rise from the £1.80 that had originally been offered to £6.00 per week – an increase of around 27 per cent. This was accepted and the strike ended on 25 February.

The episode at Saltley raised the issue of the police handling of large crowds. Saltley had been policed by officers drawn from the city of Birmingham police force, who had been heavily outnumbered in the latter stages of the picketing. Their role was limited to getting lorries through the depot gates. In performing this task, they had operated within the spirit of the principles of policing by consent and the use of minimum force. The Chief Constable might have departed from these principles and used weaponry and reinforcements to prevent pickets from the Birmingham area reaching the Coke Depot on 10 February, but once they had arrived, it became impossible for lorries to get through the gates. His decision to accede to the miners' requests to close the gates was a common-sense decision that exemplified the tactic of 'winning by appearing to lose' that avoided an adverse public reaction to more aggressive police tactics.

Nonetheless, many people at the time, especially those who were on the right of the political spectrum, saw the Chief Constable's decision as tantamount to a surrender to mob rule, which implied that a concerted effort could overawe authority. This view was endorsed by Scargill, who announced that this event was 'living proof that the working class had only to flex its muscles and it could bring government, employers, society to a total standstill' (cited in Clutterbuck, 1980: 70). It exemplified his view that organised labour rather than parliamentary politics was the way to secure a socialist society.

There were a number of longer-term consequences of Saltley. In 1973 the government established the National Security Committee (latterly named the Civil Contingencies Unit and situated within the Cabinet Office) whose role included the devising of contingency plans to counter subsequent strikes (Bunyan, 1977: 269). The National Reporting Centre, whose role was to coordinate the deployment of police officers to areas of the country experiencing public order problems, was established by the Association of Chief Police Officers (ACPO). Picketing, in particular, the presence of pickets outside places of work not directly involved in a dispute, and the extent to which coercive tactics rather than peaceful persuasion were used to enforce a strike were also addressed. The Trade Union and Industrial Relations Act 1974 emphasised the legality of picketing, provided this was conducted peacefully, but the trade union legislation of Margaret Thatcher's government in the early 1980s adopted a more restrictive attitude to events of this nature.

See also: miners' dispute (Britain), 1973–4, miners' dispute (Britain), 1984–5, News International dispute (Wapping, London) 1986, public order legislation (England and Wales), public order policing (England and Wales), workplace protest

Sources and further reading

Bunyan, T. (1977) *The History and Practice of the Political Police in Britain*. London: Quartet Books.

Clutterbuck, R. (1980) *Britain in Agony: The Growth of Political Violence*. Harmondsworth: Penguin.

MINERS' DISPUTE (BRITAIN) 1973–4

In November 1972, the Conservative government led by Prime Minister Edward Heath announced a 90-day wage freeze as the first measure of a statutory incomes policy. Subsequently, in 1973, the Pay Board and Prices Commission was set up to make key decisions relating to the government's counter-inflation policy. This policy was unpopular with trade unions and prompted a number of industrial disputes during 1973 that included the 'Day of National Protest and Stoppage' by the Trades Union Congress (TUC) on 1 May 1973, which entailed a strike by over 1.5 million workers.

The 1973–4 miners' dispute took place against the background of Stage 3 of the Conservative government's counter-inflation policy, which limited pay rises to seven per cent. Although the miners had secured a good wage increase in 1972, it had been subsequently eroded. In response to this situation, the National Coal Board (NCB) 'made use of every loophole in the code' (Clutterbuck, 1980: 105) and put forward an offer that amounted to a significant pay increase of around 16.5 per cent.

Although a pay increase of this amount may well have secured acceptance by the miners, it was put to the leadership of the National Union of Miners (NUM), then headed by Joe Gormley as an entire package. This was argued to have constituted 'a fatal – and ... tactical error' (Clutterbuck, 1980: 105), since it undermined the process of negotiation that the NUM would enter into. Radicals in the NUM leadership viewed strike action as a mechanism to break the Pay Code and bring the government down, and would not be willing to approve any deal that undermined this objective. However, their opposition could be overcome by the acceptance of an offer by moderates in the NUM leadership, but in order to appease such moderates, the union leadership would need to be seen as tough fighters in their members' cause and could not possibly accept the first offer that was put forward. However, by presenting the entire package at the outset, the government was left with no room for manoeuvre – to allow the NCB to improve upon it would undermine its counter-inflation policy and open the floodgates for other trade unions to demand similar concessions in breach of this policy.

Accordingly, the NUM rejected the offer on 8 November 1973 and initiated an overtime ban on 12 November. The purpose of this was to deplete stocks of coal at power stations as a precursor to strike action later (Clutterbuck, 1980: 106). It coincided with a reduction of oil deliveries from the Arab oil states in the wake of the 1973 Middle East (Yom Kippur) War (which served to drive up the price of coal as well as of oil) and also industrial action in the form of a ban on out-of-hours working by the Electrical Power Engineers' Association in support of a pay claim, which could result in power stations being taken of action while essential maintenance work was carried out.

In order to cope with the issues arising from these developments, the government declared a state of emergency on 13 November. The main aim of this course of action was to conserve energy stocks and avoid 'chaotic and unplanned' cuts through advance planning (Clutterbuck, 1980: 107).

A meeting between the NUM Executive and the government took place at Downing Street on 28 November. The government had virtually nothing to offer, save the possibility that the Relativities Report that was due out at the end of 1973 might offer scope for improvement of the offer. Accordingly, the NUM Executive rejected the proposal to hold a ballot as to whether the overtime ban should be continued. The government responded by moving William Whitelaw from the Northern Ireland Office to become Employment Secretary (in place of Maurice Macmillan) in early December. He had a reputation as a conciliator, but his capacity to solve the problem was jeopardised by the strain that seeking to promote the peace process in Northern Ireland had exerted on him (Clutterbuck, 1980: 110). Other problems then faced by the government (including the creation of the power-sharing executive in Northern Ireland and the need to reduce public spending because of the financial crisis that arose from the reduction in oil deliveries) also prevented the government from focusing on this issue to the exclusion of all else. The national situation became further complicated when the train drivers' union (ASLEF) called a work-to-rule and overtime ban on 12 December in support of a wage demand. This action threatened to worsen the energy crisis by imposing restrictions on the movement of coal by freight trains.

An unofficial meeting between Whitelaw and Gormley failed to resolve the situation. It was suggested that a concession in the form of a special energy supplement paid to the miners to counter the reduction in oil supplies from the Arab nations might have secured a settlement (Clutterbuck, 1980: 111) without undermining Stage 3, but this offer was not presented. Accordingly, on 13 December, the government announced the introduction of a three-day working week, to commence on 30 December. This meant that from 1 January 1974, commercial users of electricity would be limited to three specified consecutive days' consumption each week. Television companies were required to cease broadcasting at 10.30 pm during the crisis to conserve electricity. Services that were deemed as essential (such as hospitals, food outlets and the newspaper industry) were exempt from the Three-Day Work Order.

The unions (represented by the Trades Union Congress (TUC)) viewed this step as unnecessary on the basis that adequate coal stocks existed. They feared that unemployment and bankruptcy would result from this action and, at a meeting of the National Economic Development Council on 9 January, proposed that the government should treat the miners as a special case and that, if this happened, other unions would not use this as a precedent to further their own pay claims (Clutterbuck, 1980: 113). The government would not agree to this, however, on the grounds it would be unfair to those unions that had accepted a wage settlement in conformity with Stage 3.

On 24 January, the NUM Executive voted to call a pithead ballot to give it a free hand, with the authority to call a strike if necessary. The last possibility of settling the dispute, the publication of the relativities report on 24 January, was not used, since the Pay Board ruled that the relativities mechanism should not be used during the currency of an industrial dispute. The Prime Minister subsequently offered to re-open the miners' case to the Relativities Board in return for resulting normal working, but by this time a momentum had built up in favour of strike action. On 4 February 1974, the result of the pithead ballot was announced, which gave the NUM Executive a free hand to deal with the dispute. This prompted the Prime Minister to announce the dissolution of Parliament on 7 February and the calling of a snap election on 28 February. A national strike by the miners began on 10 February.

Strikes commonly cost the Labour Party electoral support and in an attempt to minimise this, the NUM adopted a low-key approach to picketing. Preparations made by Scotland Yard to counter the mass picketing that had been seen at Saltley in 1972 thus did not need to be utilised (Clutterbuck, 1980: 115). In addition, the focus of the election as to whether the government or the unions ran the country tended to unify trade union movement behind peaceful actions in support of the miners (for example, unions representing railway, power station, gas and general workers instructed their members not to handle coal or alternative fuels). Violence at picket lines caused by workers from other unions wishing to cross them was not a feature of this strike.

The Conservatives' general election campaign encountered a number of difficulties, the most significant of which was a report by the Pay Board's relativities inquiry on 21 February suggesting (on the basis of new statistics prepared by the Pay Board) that the miners were underpaid in relation to manual workers in the manufacturing industry and were entitled to a further pay increase of around eight per cent on that which was already proposed. Furthermore, although the government sought to focus on the miners' dispute and the issue of trade union power, the Labour campaign sought to highlight Conservative economic mismanagement and its failure to keep its promise made at the 1970 election to reduce prices, especially for food (Joyce, 2004: 330).

The Conservative Party outpolled Labour in the general election, but secured fewer seats in Parliament and Harold Wilson formed a minority Labour government, which was 17 seats short of a overall majority in the House of Commons. Its first priority was to get the miners back to work, a feat accomplished by offering a pay increase of around double that initially put forward by the NCB, but quite similar to the recommendation of the Relativities Report. This was implemented by the new Secretary of State for Employment, Michael Foot. The miners returned to work on 11 March and emergency regulations and the three-day week were ended.

The 1973–4 miners' dispute is a significant episode that indicated the ability of protest to bring governments down. However, the event also illustrated 'the folly of seeking to implement an incomes policy, particularly a statutory one, as opposed to an approach based on free collective bargaining in the context of market forces' (Dorey, 2002: 86).

See also: building workers' strike (England and Wales) 1972, miners' dispute (Britain) 1972, miners' dispute

(Britain) 1984–5, states of emergency, workplace protest

Sources and further reading

Clutterbuck, R. (1980) *Britain in Agony: The Growth of Political Violence*. Harmondsworth: Penguin.
Dorey, P. (2002) *The Conservative Party and the Trade Unions*. London: Routledge.
Joyce, P. (2004) *UK General Elections 1832–2001*. London: Methuen.
Phillips, J. (2006) 'The 1972 Miners' Strike: Popular Agency and Industrial Politics in Britain'. *Contemporary British History*, 20(2): 187–207.

MINERS' DISPUTE (BRITAIN) 1984–5

The British Miners' Dispute 1984–5 was triggered when the Chairman of the National Coal Board (NCB), Sir Ian MacGregor, gave four weeks' notice of the closure of Cortonwood Colliery in Yorkshire on 1 March 1984. On 6 March, MacGregor announced further plans to cut coal production by around 4 million tonnes, the closure of 20 pits and 20,000 redundancies. The rationale for these proposals was that the pits were uneconomic and were supported by state subsidies that amounted to around £1.3 billion, although this figure was contested (Fine and Millar, 1985: 3–4).

In response, the President of the National Union of Miners (NUM), Arthur Scargill, claimed that this plan entailed a greater number of pit closures and higher redundancies – this was the thin end of the wedge that would ultimately result in job losses of 84,000. The NUM leadership shied away from holding a national ballot, perhaps in the belief that support for a national strike would not be forthcoming: on previous occasions when a ballot had been held (October 1982 and March 1983), the 55 per cent majority that was required to sanction a national strike had not been achieved (Pugh, 2011: 376). Thus, instead of calling a national ballot to legitimise strike action, the NUM Executive called on local areas to take strike action from Monday 12 March. Miners in Yorkshire and Kent and most in South Wales and Scotland supported this call, resulting in the closure of large numbers of pits. However, the absence of a national ballot gave the leadership of the Labour Party a rationale for not officially supporting the strike.

A key objective of Margaret Thatcher's Conservative government was to break the power of organised labour, which was regarded as a key contributor to the UK's economic problems (in particular the ability of unions to force wage rises that were not underpinned by productivity, thus resulting in inflation). A clash between the NUM and the government had been a likely occurrence and its timing was influenced by the defeat of trade unions at the dispute by the National Graphical Association at Warrington in 1983, as well as the perception that divisions within the NUM would limit the impact of strike action. The prelude to industrial action came in the autumn of 1983, when the NUM imposed an overtime ban.

In 1977, a productivity deal in the mining industry meant that henceforth workers in the more productive pits earned more than their counterparts in the less productive ones. This created a division in the NUM between those miners who enjoyed high wages and relatively secure jobs and those who were less well paid, working in pits whose long-term prospects were uncertain. The government believed that this situation could be exploited to its advantage. Many of the productive pits and the relatively high-paid miners were situated in Nottinghamshire, which thus became the key battleground in the strike.

Although there were vast stockpiles of coal in March 1984 and contingency plans were in place to import additional stocks from abroad (mainly America, Poland and European Community (EC) countries, which was to be landed at unregistered ports and thus would escape any industrial action from unionised dock workers), the prospect of a long strike, especially if this lasted until the winter months of 1984/5, required some coal to be mined in the UK. Although coal was a declining source of energy (accounting for less than 40 per cent of Britain's energy requirements compared to 55 per cent being provided by oil and natural gas – Odell, 2013: 217), it remained important to the nation's energy needs and if strike action closed pits in Nottinghamshire, the government would be forced to cave into the miners' demands and would lose all credibility.

The miners' tactics were similar to those used in disputes in the 1970s, entailing the use of mass pickets to close pits which remained working in order to prevent the movement of coal stockpiles to power stations and to restrict the movement of coal to other industries (such as steel) that were reliant on it. Although the Conservative government's 1980 and 1982 Employment Acts had sought to outlaw secondary picketing of this nature, civil law injunctions obtained under it were ignored. The early response of the government was thus to use the police force as the mechanism to keep pits open, effectively using the police as an agency to enforce civil law (National Council for Civil Liberties, 1984: 9).

There were two significant developments affecting police tactics during the dispute. One was the use of the National Reporting Centre (NRC) at New Scotland Yard to coordinate the deployment of police officers from police forces across England and Wales to hotspots. This development further gave the government a central mechanism within the police service to which requests and suggestions could be made informally. One of these concerned police tactics to counter picketing.

On 18 March 1984, a large number of police officers were deployed by the NRC to Nottinghamshire. This initiated the 'intercept policy', which effectively sought to seal the borders of Nottinghamshire to pickets by the use of roadblocks. The use of roadblocks to establish the intent of a vehicle user and other occupants was authorised by the Police and Criminal Evidence Act 1984, but this provision did not come into force until January 1986.

Under the policy that was adopted during the strike, those suspected of intending to enter Nottingham in order to picket were instructed to turn back, being threatened with arrest under breach of the peace powers if they refused to do so. In the first 27 weeks of the strike, some 164,508 people were prevented from entering Nottingham on the basis that they were 'presumed pickets' (National Council for Civil Liberties, 1984: 20–1). This policy was also adopted further afield, including at the Dartford Tunnel in Kent, a police action that considerably extended the existing definition of situations to which a breach of the peace could apply. It was, however, latterly approved by the courts in the 1984 in the case of *Moss and Others v McLachlan*.

The police utilised other tactics, including that of infiltrators, to identify strikers who should be arrested on picket lines. The pronounced role of the police gave rise to the accusation of politicisation, that they were being used to enforce Conservative economic policies and to stifle the protest of those who were most adversely affected by them: this was encapsulated in the description of the police as 'Maggie's Boot Boys'. A further problem with this situation was that knowing the government would give its support to any action undertaken by them to defeat the strike may have encouraged acts of violence by police officers against striking miners, especially by those who were deployed under mutual aid arrangements and had no need to adhere to the time-honoured principle of policing by consent in the areas to which they were sent. Thatcher's impassioned defence of police actions at Orgreave on 18 June 1984 (which entailed the use of mounted police officers against strikers and their supporters) was one indicator of this situation.

The role of the police was supplemented by other aspects of state activity. Changes to the system of supplementary benefits introduced by the Social Security Act 1980 enabled deductions to be made from benefits paid to striking miners' families on the presumption – which was false – that they were receiving strike pay from the NUM. The aim of this was to starve the miners into submission.

The Security Service, MI5, was accused of planting a mole in the headquarters of the NUM (Milne, 1994: 391) whose purpose was both to relay information on union tactics and also – if the need arose – to organise 'dirty tricks' to undermine the credibility of the union leadership in the public eye.

Accusations were made that MI5, Special Branch and the Government Communications Headquarters (GCHQ) were involved in activities that included tapping the telephones and opening the mail of striking miners (National Council for Civil Liberties, 1984: 16; Milne, 1994: 438). Some elements of the media, especially the tabloid press, also sought to support the government's desire to defeat the strike by highlighting picket line violence and intimidation (Green, 1990: 157).

The courts, especially those in Nottinghamshire, dealt with those arrested by the police in a systematic way, a common disposal being to use bail provisions to prevent those subject to them to go near premises owned by the NCB. Many of the charges that were brought against picketing miners (such as obstruction of a police officer or of the highway, breach of the peace or threatening behaviour) could be heard in a magistrates' court and did not require witnesses other than a police officer (Miller and Walker, 1984, vol. 1: 13–14). In addition, the ancient charge of 'watching and besetting' defined in the Conspiracy and Protection of Property Act 1875 was used in connection with picketing the homes of working miners: 650 charges were laid for this during the strike (Hardy, 2011: 302).

Aspects of trade union legislation were also utilised, including the sequestration of union funds which was first used against the Welsh NUM in August for its failure to pay a fine for contempt of court in connection with secondary picketing. Scargill was also involved in a High Court action for contempt of court for claiming that the strike was official, for which he was fined £1,000 and the NUM £200,000 in October.

The NUM's refusal to pay the fine resulted in its assets being sequestrated in October 1984 (although foreseeing such an action, many of these had been transferred abroad, making access to them difficult for the accountants acting for the court). In December, leading NUM members Scargill, Peter Heathfield and Mick McGahey were declared by the High Court to be 'unfit persons' to be trustees of NUM funds and a receiver was appointed in their place.

Other tactics that were adopted during the strike were inspired by the NCB. These included 'back to work' initiatives by the NCB that began in July 1984 to encourage striking miners to return to work. This entailed major police operations to enable what was initially a very small number of returning workers to cross picket lines, amounting to no more than a provocative gesture. Towards the end of 1984, miners convicted of damaging NCB property were dismissed.

By late 1984, the strike was turning in favour of the miners. The 'back to work' campaign was faltering, coal stocks were becoming depleted and problems associated with the movement of stockpiles made the government contemplate using troops to transport them – an action that would have escalated strike action. Increased use was made of oil at power stations, which raised the costs of electricity production. On 28 September, the pit deputies union, the National Association of Colliery Overseers, Deputies and Shotfirers

(NACODS), voted to join the strike, which had the potential to close all pits, including those still working. Some members of other unions also undertook sympathetic industrial action relating to the delivery or handling of coal and oil.

However, events then moved against the miners. The threatened strike by the NACODS was averted and public sympathy (and financial aid to striking miners) was adversely affected by media coverage to a trip to Libya by the NUM chief executive officer, Roger Windsor, in which he was filmed embracing Colonel Gaddafi only months after the killing of WPC Yvonne Fletcher outside the Libyan Embassy. The aim of this visit was to ask Gaddafi not to accede to the government's request to increase the supply of oil to the UK in order to counter the impact of the miners' strike.

The 'back to work' campaign was stepped up by the NCB in early 1985 with a limited degree of success and the TUC intervened in February by drafting a document that accepted the NCB's right to close uneconomic pits and agreeing this with the government. Although the NUM Executive Committee opposed this document, it revealed the isolation of the union from the remainder of members of the TUC and at this stage many miners began to return to work.

Accordingly, the NUM accepted the inevitable and on 3 March 1985 a special delegate conference of the NUM decided on a national return to work, but without an agreement.

The 1984/5 miners' dispute was unusual in the sense that industrial action sought not to secure higher wages or improved working conditions, but, rather, to defend jobs and the mining communities that were built upon them.

In 1984 there were 170 pits in Britain employing around 190,000 miners. Twenty years later, the British mining industry consisted of 20 pits and 5,000 miners.

See also: building workers' strike (England and Wales) 1972, miners' dispute (Britain) 1972, miners' dispute (Britain) 1973–4, public order legislation (England and Wales), public order policing (England and Wales), riot police, workplace protest

Sources and further reading

Fine, B. and Millar, R. (1985) 'Introduction: The Law of the Market and the Rule of Law' in B. Fine and R. Millar, *Policing the Miners' Strike*. London: Lawrence & Wishart.

Green, R. (1990) *The Enemy Without: Policing and Class Consciousness in the Miners' Strike*. Oxford University Press.

Hardy, S. (2011) *Labour Law in Great Britain*. Alphen aan den Rijn: Kluwer Law International.

Miller, S. and Walker, M. (1984) *A State of Siege: Policing the Coalfields in the First Six Weeks of the Miners' Strike*, vol. 1. Yorkshire Area NUM.

Milne, S. (1994) *The Enemy Within: The Secret War Against the Miners*. London: Pan Books.

National Council for Civil Liberties (1984) *Civil Liberties and the Miners' Dispute*. London: National Council for Civil Liberties.

Odell, P. (2013 [1986]) *Oil and World Power*. London: Routledge.

Pugh, M. (2011) *Speak for Britain! A New History of the Labour Party*. London: Vintage.

Scraton, P. and Thomas, P. (eds) (1985) 'The State v The People. Lessons from the Coal Dispute'. Special edition of *Journal of Law and Society*, 12(3): 251–436.

MONSANTO PROTESTS (WORLDWIDE) 2013

Protest is often conducted in an attempt to change the direction of public policy. However, it can be directed at business enterprises in an attempt to alter their commercial policies. One example of this was the protests directed at the Monsanto company that were conducted in 2013 on a global basis, reflecting Monsanto's multinational status. This took place against the background of earlier protests that included direct action in the form of the occupation by American safe food advocates of the US Food and Drug Administration's (FDA) Center for Food Safety and Applied Nutrition on 8 April 2013 where an eat-in to label genetically modified organisms (GMOs) was staged.

The cause of these protests was the company's use of genetically modified seeds and the May 2013 protests focused especially on GMOs, which consist of plants, bacteria and animals whose genetic make-up has been scientifically altered by the use of molecular biology techniques. These are the source of genetically modified (GM) food, being designed to produce plants that resist the chemicals contained in insecticides and herbicides and to provide other benefits such as resistance to harsh environmental conditions, increases in nutritional value or improvements in crop yields. Such food thus has the potential to help solve the world's hunger and nutritional problems. However, critics argue that these advantages are outweighed by a range of disadvantages, since GMOs can result in serious health issues and can cause harm to the environment, for example, by harming other organisms or cross-breeding with other species such as weeds, which then become tolerant to herbicides.

Seed producers such as Monsanto deny there is evidence that health is at risk from GMOs. However, their use is subject to ongoing evaluation by a number of bodies. In the EU, for example, the GMO Panel of the European Food Safety Authority provides independent scientific advice concerning GMOs and GM food and feed. Its work is supported by the GMO unit.

On 28 February 2013, Tami Canal created a page on Facebook that called for a rally against the company's practices. This event was termed the 'March Against Monsanto', which took place on 25 May 2013. It was worldwide in scope and involved over two million people in over 50 countries, spanning six continents (*Russia Today*, 2013).

There was a considerable expansion in the production of GM crops in the late twentieth century: the acreage of GM crops 'increased 25-fold in just five years, from approximately 4.3 million acres in 1996 to 109 million acres in 2000 – almost twice the area of the United Kingdom. Approximately 99 million acres were devoted to GM crops in the US and Argentina alone' (Whitman, 2000). Much of the corn, soybean and cotton crops that are grown in America have been genetically modified.

One demand of protesters is for the compulsory labelling of GM food. This demand can be supported on the grounds of 'food democracy' – that consumers should have the right to know what they are eating (Food Democracy Now, 2013). However, although surveys have suggested that around 90 per cent of the American people support the mandatory labelling of GM foods (Walshe, 2013), this has not so far happened in that country, a situation that is complicated by three government agencies having jurisdiction over GM food: the Environmental Protection Agency (EPA), the United States Department of Agriculture (USDA) and the FDA (Whitman, 2000).

Monsanto is an extremely powerful company with an annual turnover of almost $60 billion. In March 2013, President Barack Obama signed an Emergency Budget Bill (the Consolidated and Further Continuing Appropriations Act), which contained a rider, the Farmer Assurance Provision (which is more popularly referred to as the 'Monsanto Protection Act'), whose provisions lasted until the end of the fiscal year in September 2013. This enabled the Secretary of Agriculture to overturn the decision of a court to reverse the approval given by the US Department of Agriculture to a biotech crop, thus enabling the growers to continue to produce it while legal challenges run their course. In the same month, the Center for Food Safety submitted a petition to the US Food and Drug Administration with over a million signatures demanding this reform, but no action followed. In May 2013, the US Senate overwhelmingly voted down a measure that would have allowed individual states to make their own decisions concerning labelling requirements on GM products.

The organisers of the May protests called for consumer boycotts of Monsanto-owned companies that used GMOs and urged supporters to buy only organically produced products. Localised protests that seek to pressurise individual states to adopt laws requiring food manufacturers to label products containing GM ingredients have also taken place, such as that in New York on 30 July 2013. The campaign against Monsanto has also boosted support for alternative ways of food production and distribution, especially those associated with community gardening.

Protests against Monsanto subsequently continued and included the global 'March Against Monsanto', which was held in May 2014.

See also: demonstrations, direct action, environmental protest groups

Sources and further reading

Food Democracy Now (2013) 'GMO Labeling: America's Right to Know', http://action.fooddemocracynow.org/sign/label_gmos_now (date accessed 3 May 2014).

Russia Today (2013) 'Challenging Monsanto: Over Two Million March the Streets of 436 Cities, 52 Countries', 24 May, http://rt.com/news/monsanto-gmo-protests-world-721 (date accessed 3 May 2014).

Walshe, S. (2013) 'We Can't Let Monsanto Win on Genetically Modified Food', *The Guardian*, 29 May.

Whitman, D. (2000) 'Genetically Modified Foods: Harmful or Helpful?', *ProQuest Information and Learning*, www.csa.com/discoveryguides/gmfood/overview.php (date accessed 3 May 2014).

NATIONALIST TERRORIST GROUPS

Nationalism is a sentiment underpinning a people's desire to exercise control over their own political affairs. Those who live in a particular locality are united by a desire to be independent of other nations and live under a political system that they control. This unity may be based on a common ethnic identity or religion, upon a cultural heritage (including the existence of a separate language and literature) or is grounded in a sense of shared citizenship that may transcend ethnic or cultural differences.

Nationalist terrorist groups carry out acts of violence in an attempt to secure a greater degree of political control over the area which they represent. Their objectives range from seeking a greater degree of autonomy from the central state to the desire to create a self-governing independent state, totally divorced from the rule of the country that currently exercises powers of government over them. Nationalist terrorist groups may also seek to rid their country from the rule of an occupying foreign power that exercises political and economic domination over its citizens.

Those who engage in acts of nationalist-inspired violence may reject the label of terrorism and view themselves as freedom fighters, seeking to replace a repressive and illegitimate form of government with one that will enjoy the consent of those who live in the region or country from where the group derives. For this reason, nationalist-inspired terrorist groups frequently enjoy support from populations who share their objectives and approve of their use of violence to attain them.

There are several examples of groups that are inspired by nationalism and that have used violence to pursue their aims. The Provisional IRA (PIRA) is an important example of this (and is discussed in a separate entry in this work).

In the Philippines, the Moro Islamic Liberation Front has been engaged in separatist violence since 1981, when it split from the Moro National Liberation Front. It subsequently engaged in various forms of attacks and assassinations, and in 2000 declared a jihad against the government, its supporters and citizens of the Philippines when the government tore up an agreement that had been reached in 1997 to grant the area the status of an autonomous region. It originally sought the establishment of an independent Muslim state in the south of the country, but accepted self-rule in the form of the creation of an autonomous region to be called Bangsamoro, which would secure a considerable proportion of the taxes on the area's metallic mineral wealth. On that basis, a peace deal was concluded with the government in January 2014.

Another nationalist group that has used terrorist tactics is the *Euskadi Ta Askatasuna* (ETA or Basque Homeland and Freedom), which seeks full independence from Spain for the Greater Basque Country. The aims of ETA and the PIRA are similar in nature and the two groups established contact during the 1970s.

ETA was formed in 1959 and originated as a student protest movement whose main concern was to promote the Basque language and culture in response to the repressive policies adopted towards the Basque Country by Spain's military dictatorship headed by General Franco, which included banning the Basque language. It subsequently evolved into a paramilitary group seeking independence for the Basque Country. Franco's death in 1975 resulted in a transition in Spain to liberal democracy and in 1979, 17 regions (or autonomous communities) were set up, each with an assembly and a president. The 1978 Constitution made Castilian the pre-eminent language in the country, but left regional parliaments to determine the balance between that and regional languages. In 1983, the regional parliament in Catalonia decreed the mandatory use of Catalan in regional government. However, although these new arrangements resulted in the grant of a considerable degree of autonomy to the Basque region (which includes control over policing, education and the power to collect taxes), they fell short of the full independence to which ETA aspired.

In order to achieve the aim of full independence, campaigns of violence have been waged, punctuated by ceasefires (in 1989, 1996, 1998 and 2006) and lengthy cessations of action. The most recent ceasefire was declared on 5 September 2010 and in January 2011 a permanent and 'internationally verifiable' ceasefire was announced (*BBC News*, 2011). One factor influencing this decision was the al-Qaeda-inspired train bombings in Madrid in 2004 (for which ETA was initially blamed). These attacks created public distaste for all forms of political violence. Although successive governments have refused to negotiate with ETA, in 2013 (following a ruling from the European Court of Human Rights), a number of ETA members were released from prison. However, many others (estimated to be 520: Groult, 2014) remain in prison and whose cause was the subject of a large protest march in Bilbao in January 2014 involving over 100,000 people.

The tactics used by ETA have included selective violence directed at members of Spain's national police force, the Guardia Civil and politicians who are opposed to Basque separatism. Its most notable act of this nature during the period of Franco's dictatorship was the assassination in Madrid of Admiral Luis Carrero Blanco in December 1973 by a bomb planted in a sewer over which his car passed. Blanco was President of the government and Franco's chosen successor. Other attacks included the bombing of the Plaza Republica Dominicana in July 1986, which killed 12 members of the Guardia Civil and injured 50.

A highly publicised attack was the July 1997 kidnapping in Ermua of Miguel Angel Blanco, a Popular Party Councillor in the Basque region. ETA demanded the transmission to prisons in the Basque region of its 460 prisoners held in jails across Spain as a condition for his release. When this demand was not met, Blanco was shot twice in the head and died from his injuries. It was estimated that over six million people across Spain demonstrated to demand an end to ETA violence, which led ETA to call a ceasefire in 1998 that was ended in December 1999 as the government refused to discuss its demands for Basque independence (*BBC News*, 2011).

Indiscriminate violence has also been used by ETA, including an attack on the Hipercor shopping centre of Barcelona in June 1987 that killed 21 people and injured over 40. A number of random attacks were also launched in 2001, such as a car-bomb attack in Madrid in November, which injured 65 people. Later attacks of this nature included the bombing of a car park at Madrid Airport in December 2006.

ETA is also associated with actions directed against public and private property, especially that owned by its political opponents and members of law-enforcement agencies. These are referred to as *kale borroka* (street fighting) and include episodes of rioting carried out by younger supporters of ETA. This form of collective action emerged in the 1990s and was inspired by the Palestinian intifada.

This campaign has led to more than 820 deaths in the past 40 years and in the late 1970s, an average of 100 people were killed each year (*BBC News*, 2011).

ETA is banned under anti-terrorist legislation in Spain, France, the UK and America. Its organisation extends to France (where during the Franco era, a degree of tolerance was shown towards ETA because of France's dislike of Spain's fascist regime). Following the Spanish transition to democracy, there has been a greater degree of cooperation against ETA by the law-enforcement agencies of both countries, which began when the French Interior Minister agreed to allow the extradition of ETA suspects from France to Spain in 1984. This has subsequently led to joint action by the French and Spanish police to combat the organisation.

High-profile arrests that took place in France included that of ETA's political commander, Javier Lopez Pena, and its suspected military head, Garikoitz Aspiazu Rubina, both in 2008. The success enjoyed by law-enforcement agencies against ETA have also led it to change its structure, becoming a more decentralised organisation operating under the umbrella of a small directorial committee known as *Zuzendaritza Batzordea*.

The state campaign against ETA has also made use of violent methods, including the 'dirty war' waged by death squads supported by Spanish security forces and intelligence services during the 1970s and early 1980s and later in the 1980s by a paramilitary group, Grupos Antiterroristas de Liberacion (GAL) (Anti-terrorist Liberation Groups), which was also connected to the Spanish authorities. Until the cessation of its activities in 1987, GAL was responsible for kidnappings, torture and assassinations of suspected ETA members.

Like the PIRA, ETA has a political wing which has operated under the names of Herri Batasuna, Euskal Herritarrok and Batasuna. Unlike the situation in Northern Ireland, however, the political wing has been banned in Spain since a 2003 decision by the Supreme Court of Spain relating to the *Ley de Partidos Políticos*, which banned political parties that supported violence or were involved with terrorist groups. This action was taken because it and ETA were regarded as closely intertwined movements so that donations to the political wing might be used to finance ETA attacks. In addition, the government hoped that banning the political wing would hinder the cause of Basque separatism by preventing it from gaining popular support in elections.

However, although objectives such as self-determination, self-rule and freedom from foreign rule may be viewed as worthy political ideals that seek to liberate subjugated people from oppressive foreign rule, the love of one's country may lead to the hatred of other people who do not share this national identity. Xenophobic feelings may inspire ethnic cleansing or genocide, such as that carried out in Bosnia-Herzegovina by the Bosnian Serbs against the Bosnian Muslims in 1992 and subsequently by the Serbs against the ethnic Albanians in Kosovo in 1999.

Nationalist terrorist groups have been associated with violence against immigrants from other places who come to live in their area. In Greece, activities of this nature are associated with a far-right political party known as Golden Dawn (*Chrysí Avgí*), which was set up by Nikolaos Michaloliakos in 1985. It stands for a Greece which belongs to the Greeks and has been associated with racist, anti-immigrant and xenophobic rhetoric and acts, as well as attacks on migrant workers. The murder of an anti-fascist musician in September 2013, which was blamed on a Golden Dawn supporter, prompted the government to take action against the party, which included the arrest of a number of its activists (including its founder and other Members of Parliament) in 2013 and 2014 on charges of belonging to and directing a criminal organisation, which carries a severe sentence under Greek anti-terrorist legislation.

In the UK, an example of a nationalist terrorist group is Combat 18, a racist right-wing extremist group which believed in white supremacy and was also violently anti-semitic.

Combat 18 was set up in 1992, involving members who had been active previously in the East End Barmy Army (some of who had previously been associated with football hooliganism). It carried out attacks on meetings held by opponents of right-wing extremism such as the Anti-Nazi League and also conducted random acts of racially motivated violence. Although it had ties with the British National Party (BNP) and stewarded some of its meetings, 'where C18 differed from previous strong-arm groups of the British Right was that it ran itself' (Lowles, 2001: 18). It was also 'surplus to requirements' when the BNP, following its electoral success at a Council by-election in Tower Hamlets in 1993, aspired to the status of a respectable political party whose attempts to secure electoral support would not be aided by 'a street force hell-bent on confrontation' (Lowles, 2001: 27–38). Combat 18 was thus effectively proscribed by the BNP in December 1993.

Subsequently, Combat 18 became associated with the National Socialist Alliance. It courted support from gangs of football hooligans and its activities included violence at football matches, attacks on Anti-Nazi League activists and racially inspired violence. Examples of this included the riot at the England–Ireland football match at Lansdowne Road in 1995, an incident that induced the police and the security services to take the organisation seriously. This concern was also prompted by the links forged between Combat 18 and Loyalist paramilitary groups, especially the Ulster Defence Association. It moved on from being a street-fighting organisation to adopting an ideology – 'it would describe itself as a revolutionary, national socialist, terrorist organisation. Its enemies were no longer individual blacks or Asians but the political, cultural and economic system which, it claimed, discriminated against white people' (Lowles, 2001: 305). By 1995, it advocated a race war in Britain and, compatible with this, it played a 'major role' in the racial violence that occurred in Oldham in 2001 (Lowles, 2001: 305 and 320).

See also: Islamic terrorist groups, northern English town riots (Bradford, Burnley, Oldham) 2001, Provisional IRA, riots

Sources and further reading

Alexander, Y., Swetman, M. and Levine H. (2001) *ETA: Profile of a Terrorist Group.* New York: Transnational Publishers.

BBC News (2011) 'What is Eta?', *BBC News Europe,* www.bbc.co.uk/news/world-europe-11183574 (date accessed 3 May 2014).

Groult, S. (2014) 'Crowds Defy Madrid to Take Part in Basque Demonstration', *China Post*, 13 January, www.chinapost.com.tw/international/europe/2014/01/13/398221/Crowds-defy.htm (date accessed 3 May 2014).

Lowles, N. (2001) *White Riot: The Violent Story of Combat 18*. Bury: Milo Books.

NEWS INTERNATIONAL DISPUTE (WAPPING, LONDON) 1986

This dispute began on 24 January 1986 and arose against the background of the dismissal of around 6,000 print workers employed by News International (NI) for participating in industrial action prior to a move from Fleet Street to the company's new plant at Wapping, London. This action occurred after protracted negotiations between NI and trade unions relating to attempts by NI to secure a five-year, legally binding agreement that would impose flexible working practices, the use of new technology and the abandonment of the closed shop at the new plant. The dismissals prompted the printworkers' unions (the Society of Graphical and Allied Trades '82 (SOGAT '82) and the National Graphical Association (NGA)) to enter into an official dispute with NI, seeking full reinstatement of their sacked members.

The motives of NI were to remove printworkers from the future publication and distribution of the company's titles, which would henceforth be composed electronically by members of the electrician's union (the Electrical, Electronic, Telecommunications and Plumbing Union (EETPU)) at this new location.

The tactics used by the unions entailed mass picketing of the plant at Wapping in an attempt to disrupt newspaper production and distribution, which it coupled with attempts to organise a consumer boycott of NI titles. The first picket took place on 25 January and occurred regularly thereafter. Pickets were usually preceded by a march to the plant, where a rally was held. The first of these events occurred on 15 February 1986.

Accusations of violence were made by both sides. Some protesters were engaged in actions that included destroying sections of the plant's perimeter fence, throwing missiles and attempting to overturn lorries, and an allegation of arson directed at the NI warehouse in Deptford in June 1986 was also made.

The pickets were met with a considerable police presence (which included the use of the Special Patrol Group), which the Metropolitan Police Commissioner estimated to be around 300 officers a day (Newman, cited in London Strategic Policy Unit, 1987: 33). Protesters encountered the use of charges by foot and mounted police to break up crowds and disperse people, and 'snatch squads' in riot gear were used to clear a path for the company's lorries to enter and leave the plant. This gave rise to accusations of attempts by the police to provoke or intimidate demonstrators.

Specific criticisms of police actions included allegations that they sought to disperse and incapacitate people as opposed to arresting those involved in violence, that police manoeuvres failed to provide room for people to disperse, that demonstrators were often hit on the head, that truncheons (and other equipment such as riot shields) were used in an offensive as opposed to a defensive manner, that unauthorised weapons were deployed by some police officers, that mounted police were employed without prior warning (in order to enable protesters to disperse) and that many officers failed to wear identification numbers.

A major demonstration of around 15,000 people held on 24 January 1987 to mark the first anniversary of the dispute especially gave rise to accusations of aggressive police actions, which involved the alleged use of random and gratuitous violence by officers towards protesters (Haldane Society of Socialist Lawyers, 1987). On that occasion, a separate protest was mounted by residents of the area, whose lives had been disrupted by police roadblocks directed at picketing, leading to accusations of police harassment (National Council for Civil Liberties, 1986). A further key concern was that lorries should observe traffic lights and speed regulations.

Accusations were also made of police assaults on journalists, photographers and news camera crews (London Strategic Policy Unit, 1987: 39, Haldane Society of Socialist Lawyers, 1987). Accusations (which were strenuously denied by the government) of the use of the Continental practice of spraying protesters with red dye (to facilitate subsequent identification and arrest) were also made (Haldane Society of Socialist Lawyers, 1987). Allegations of unwarranted violence used by the police towards protesters were articulated in a debate in the House of Commons on 8 May 1986.

By the first anniversary of the dispute, 1.2 million police hours had been worked in connection with it at an estimated cost of £5.3 million (Haldane Society of Socialist Lawyers, 1987). Mutual aid was not deployed, although officers from surrounding forces were involved in actions that included preventing pickets from obtaining access to Wapping. The dispute also witnessed the first ever use of riot-trained female Metropolitan Police officers.

A total of 1,370 people were arrested during the dispute and 1,238 were charged (Haldane Society of Socialist Lawyers, 1987). Sanctions imposed included bail conditions not to go within a mile of Wapping and the disposal of fines and bindovers to keep the peace. It was alleged that intervention by the police and magistrates drew a distinction between print workers and those who supported them, taking the view that actions of the latter constituted secondary picketing, which was illegal under the government's trade union legislation (London Strategic Policy Unit, 1987: 21–2). A common charge was that of threatening or insulting behaviour.

Trade union law was used during the dispute. In February 1986, a court ordered SOGAT to lift instructions to its members not to handle NI titles. Its refusal to do so resulted in the sequestration of £400,000 from union funds. Attempts to resolve the dispute by NI proved abortive and in July 1986, it obtained an injunction against the unions involved in the picketing. This permitted demonstrations provided they were conducted peacefully and did not block the roads, but limited peaceful picketing to consist of up to six individuals, who were to be sacked workers or trade union representatives. Despite attempts by SOGAT to abide by these conditions, the terms of the injunction were breached. This led NI to commence proceedings, which prompted both unions to end the dispute in February 1987.

Supporters of the trade union activity viewed Wapping as a further episode in the government's attack on trade unions: 'When one matches the methods used at Wapping with the Orgreave operation in 1984, and recalls Mrs Thatcher's call to defeat "the enemy within", the aim of the authorities seems to be clear: to defeat industrial protest at all costs, and thereby to give employers the licence to act as they please.' The leadership of the Metropolitan Police were accused of deciding to use the tactics of war against 'any who may exercise the right to protest against the injustices of our present society' (Haldane Society of Socialist Lawyers, 1987).

See also: miners' dispute (Britain) 1972, miners' dispute (Britain) 1973–4, miners' dispute (Britain) 1984–5, paramilitary policing, public order legislation (England and Wales), public order policing (England and Wales), workplace protest

Sources and further reading

Haldane Society of Socialist Lawyers (1987) *A Case to Answer: A Report on the Policing of the News International Demonstration at Wapping on January 24th 1987*. London: Haldane Society of Socialist Lawyers. Available at: www.oatridge.co.uk/wapping_files/Haldane NI.htm (date accessed 4 May 2014).

London Strategic Policy Unit (1987) *Policing Wapping: An Account of the Dispute 1986/7*. London: Police Monitoring and Research Group, Briefing Paper No. 3.

Melvern, L. (1986) *The End of the Street*. London: Methuen.

National Council for Civil Liberties (1986) *No Way in Wapping. The Effect of the Policing of the News International Dispute on Wapping Residents*. London: Civil Liberties Trust.

NORTHERN IRELAND: SECURITY POLICY DURING THE 'TROUBLES'

Political violence became a feature of the politics of Northern Ireland in the late 1960s and was practised by a number of paramilitary groups on both sides of the sectarian divide. This period is referred to as the 'Troubles', which lasted until a political settlement (the Good Friday Agreement) was reached in 1998. During this period, 3,725 people were killed, approximately 47,451 were injured, and there were 36,923 shootings and

16,209 bombings (Day of Reflection, undated). Security policy sought to combat political violence and was especially targeted at the Provisional IRA (PIRA), whose campaign of violence extended beyond Northern Ireland to mainland Britain.

At the outset of the 'Troubles', the security forces consisted of the Royal Ulster Constabulary (RUC) and the Ulster Special Constabulary (USC, usually known as the B-Specials). The former was the regular police force of Northern Ireland that had been modelled on the former Royal Irish Constabulary that operated throughout Ireland before partition. It was centrally controlled by the Minister of Home Affairs at Stormont and was under the operational control of an Inspector General. The RUC was organised along paramilitary lines.

The USC was formed in 1920 before partition and was composed of members of the Loyalist paramilitary group, the Ulster Volunteer Force. Its members remained almost exclusively Protestant and played a major role in dealing with the civil rights protests during the 1960s in a highly partisan fashion. As the result of the Hunt Committee (Hunt, 1969: para. 171), this force was disbanded and replaced by the Ulster Defence Regiment (UDR), whose status was that of a regiment in the British Army under the control of the General Officer Commanding (GOC) Northern Ireland.

The inability of the police to contain disorder in 1969 led to the deployment of soldiers (initially on the streets of Derry and Belfast and subsequently throughout Northern Ireland) under the concept of Military Aid to the Civil Power. Troops initially performed a key role in policing areas in which the RUC could not operate and also in providing specialist services such as bomb disposal and surveillance and undercover tasks (the latter being performed by the Special Air Service (SAS)).

The subsequent development of security police is Northern Ireland is discussed below under a number of key headings.

Public order powers

The powers available to the security forces during the 'Troubles' consisted of four major pieces of legislation:

- *The Civil Authorities (Special Powers) Act 1922*: this was initially subject to annual renewal, but became permanent in 1933. Its provisions included internment, which rested on a decision of the executive. It was authorised by the Northern Ireland Minister for Home Affairs and was directed against anyone who was acting, had acted or was about to act 'in a manner prejudicial to the preservation of the peace and maintenance or order'. Such a person would remain in detention until the minister who had authorised it ordered his or her release.
- *The Criminal Justice (Temporary Provisions) Act 1970*: this was introduced to deal with rioters and provided a six-month minimum

mandatory prison sentence for anyone convicted of 'riotous behaviour', 'disorderly behaviour' or 'behaviour likely to cause a breach of the peace'.
- *The Northern Ireland (Emergency Provisions) Act 1973*: this legislation (which was replaced by Acts of a similar name in 1978 and 1987) enabled the RUC to detain a person for a period of up to 72 hours without the requirement of being suspected of having committed any offence and also provided soldiers with basic police powers, allowing a member of Her Majesty's forces on duty to arrest without warrant, and detain for not more than four hours, a person who was suspected of committing, having committed or being about to commit any offence. It was based upon the report of a commission concerned with considering legal procedures to deal with terrorist activities in Northern Ireland (Diplock, 1972). This legislation was repealed in 1991.

The 1973 legislation also initiated fundamental changes to the common law test for the admissibility of evidence whereby a confession made by the accused should be admissible as evidence in cases involving the terrorist (termed 'scheduled') offences 'unless it was obtained by torture or inhuman or degrading treatment; if admissible it would then be for the court to determine its reliability on the basis of evidence given from either side as to the circumstances in which the confession had been obtained' (Diplock, 1972: paras. 73–92).
- *The Prevention of Terrorism (Temporary Provisions) Act 1974*: the provisions of this Act applied to Northern Ireland, a key one being the ability to detain a person for 48 hours and then, provided the Secretary of State approved, for an additional period of up to five days in cases where there was a reasonable suspicion of the detainee's involvement in terrorism. The RUC preferred to use powers granted by the 1973 legislation in connection with the detention of a person suspected of involvement with terrorism (Scorer and Hewitt, 1981: 59). The 1974 Act, however, although used more sparingly than the 1973 measure, was a key underpinning of the interrogation procedure, since it enabled individuals to be detained for a period longer than that available under the 1973 Act.

Ulsterisation and criminalisation

During the course of the 1970s, a number of key changes were introduced into security policy which sought to re-establish the RUC as the main policing agency in Northern Ireland and to restore a degree of normality to judicial proceedings. The first of these policies was referred to as 'police primacy' (or Ulsterisation) and the second as 'criminalisation'.

It has been argued that 'the blow to the standing and status of both the RUC and the USC as a result of criticism of their handling of public disorder was enormous. Consequently, reform of policing formed one of the first objectives in intervention by the British government in the situation' (Brewer and Magee, 1991: 50). A further motive underpinning these reforms was to enable the police to take over from the Army most policing functions in Northern Ireland, since there was always a danger that troops would overreact (something that was a feature of 'Bloody Sunday' in 1972).

The blueprint for reform of the RUC was initially directed by the Hunt Committee (1969), whose main aim was to neutralise the political control of the police and re-establish policing on a civilian and non-armed basis (Hillyard, 1983: 36). This led to the (temporary) disarming of the RUC and the creation of a Northern Ireland Police Authority in 1970, which was designed 'to provide a buffer between the police and the Unionist government' (Murphy, 2013: 11).

Subsequent reforms to the RUC included an expansion of its numbers, the improvement of intelligence gathering and the formation of mobile anti-terrorist units (initially set up in 1977 as the Bessbrook Support Unit, but which were eventually re-named as Headquarters Mobile Support Units). In addition, beginning in the 1980s, the RUC initiated a number of reforms that were designed to make the force more 'professional' and less sectarian. These reforms were especially pursued by RUC Chief Constables Kenneth Newman (1976–80) and John Hermon (1980–9).

Attempts were also made to develop community policing in Northern Ireland and to adopt a more even-handed approach to the policing of Loyalist parades. Loyalists had traditionally claimed the right to parade anywhere in Northern Ireland, but in 1985 John Hermon banned a parade from passing through the primarily Catholic Gortalowry housing estate, Cookstown and enforced this ban with a line of RUC officers in riot gear supported by armoured Land Rovers. The 1985 Anglo-Irish Agreement further evidenced police willingness to 'take on' Loyalists who were opposed to this agreement and protested in a disorderly manner.

'Criminalisation' entailed the reform of the Northern Ireland judicial process. An initial response to violence during the 'Troubles' had been the introduction of internment. However, although safeguards against unjust decisions were in place, 'they can never appear to be as complete as the safeguards which are provided by a public trial in a court of law' (Diplock, 1972: paras. 28–33). However, the use of trial by jury was deemed impossible (Diplock, 1972: para. 27) in the early 1970s through fear of intimidation, which justified the development of a special judicial procedure that fell midway between internment and trial by jury. This entailed the trial of terrorist ('scheduled') offences before a judge who would sit without a jury. This was based on proposals contained in the Diplock Report (1972) and such courts were commonly referred to as 'Diplock Courts'. However, Republicans felt that the new judicial process embodied in the Diplock Courts was weighted against them. One aspect of this argument was the high number of convictions of persons charged with terrorist offences, a situation allegedly arising as the result of the 'case hardening' of judges who served in these courts (Walsh, 1983: 94).

Security force tactics

A wide variety of tactics were utilised by the security forces in an attempt to control the extent of politically motivated violence. These included internment, interrogation, the supergrass policy and allegations relating to 'shoot to kill' and the waging of a 'dirty war'.

Internment was introduced in August 1971 and within six months more than 2,000 persons had been arrested, the bulk of whom were released following interrogation. The military performed a leading role in rounding up suspects, acting under the direction of Stormont and making use of RUC intelligence. However, it was argued that this tactic was 'militarily, a complete failure. The IRA had known of it for some time and as a result virtually every senior IRA man was billeted away from home' (McGuffin, 1973: 86). The intelligence on which the process was based was flawed, resulting in veteran IRA members rather than members of the newly-formed PIRA being rounded up. Further, the use of this procedure inflamed tensions and heightened violence. In the four months prior to internment, four soldiers and four civilians were killed, but in the four months following its introduction, 30 soldiers, 73 civilians and 11 RUC and UDR men died (McGuffin, 1973: 112). In total, there had been 174 deaths in Northern Ireland in 1971, but in 1972 this figure rose to 467 (Amnesty International, 1978).

Following the introduction of direct rule in 1972, changes were made to internment procedures. A quasi-judicial procedure was utilised to determine internment, and in 1973 some Protestants became subject to the procedure. The introduction of the Diplock Courts during the 1970s made it possible to phase out internment (which was suspended in February 1975).

Those who were detained (and also those convicted by the courts of politically motivated crimes) were given certain privileges, which became termed 'Special Category Status'. A later report argued that the introduction of Special Category Status for convicted prisoners had been 'a serious mistake' (Gardiner, 1975: para. 107) and this procedure was ended. In protest against the end of Special Category Status, a number of Republican prisoners mounted the 'dirty protest' in 1978 and waves of hunger strikes that resulted in a number of deaths, including that of Bobby Sands in 1981. The resultant increase in support for Sinn Féin led to its adoption of the 'armalite and the ballot box' strategy in 1981.

During the 1970s, interrogation was used both to obtain intelligence and also to extract confessions from a person suspected of involvement in paramilitary activities. This procedure was initially conducted by RUC detectives in a small number of centres at Castlereagh, Omagh and Gough Barracks (Taylor, 1980). However, the methods used (which initially included sensory deprivation) were subject to widespread condemnation, especially when directed against individuals who proclaimed their innocence.

Changes to the methods used were introduced during the early 1970s. In 1972, Prime Minister Edward Heath banned the use of the 'five techniques' (wall standing, hooding, subjection to noise, deprivation of sleep and deprivation of food and drink) following a recommendation made by a committee of inquiry (Parker, 1972). However, the government of the Irish Republic took up the cases of those who had been subjected to such treatment, which led the UK to be found guilty by the European Commission of Human Rights of 'systematic torture', which, on appeal by the UK government to the European Court of Human Rights, was downgraded in 1978 to 'inhuman and degrading treatment'.

Nonetheless, abuses continued, which led Amnesty International to conclude that 'maltreatment of suspected terrorists by the RUC has taken place with sufficient frequency to warrant the establishment of a public inquiry to investigate it' (Amnesty International, 1978). This recommendation led to the establishment of an inquiry into interrogation practice by the RUC. This advised that closed-circuit television (CCTV) should be installed in all interviews used for interrogation (Bennett, 1979: paras. 225–6) and that medical officers should have the means to satisfy themselves that prisoners were not being ill-treated (Bennett, 1979: para. 240). It was also argued that the 'consistent refusal to allow access to a solicitor through the whole period of detention is unjustifiable' (Bennett, 1979: para. 276). Reforms to interrogation procedures that included the use of CCTV to monitor interviews and the Prisoner Arrest Form were subsequently introduced. However, despite these measures, it was argued that 'a suspect in an interrogation centre will still be under extreme pressure to make a confession, whether it be true or false' (Scorer and Hewitt, 1981: 60).

The publication of the Bennett Report also had a crucial bearing on British politics. Two Northern Irish MPs representing the nationalist community (Gerry Fitt and Frank Maguire) abstained in a vote of no confidence in the Labour government held in the House of Commons on 28 March 1979. Fitt customarily voted with the Labour government and had he done so on this occasion, the government would not have been defeated. In the subsequent general election, the Labour government was swept from power by the Conservative Party, led by Margaret Thatcher.

Criticisms that had been made of interrogation resulted in the introduction of a new procedure which did not call for the use of robust questioning techniques. This entailed the use of accomplice evidence and was usually referred to as the supergrass policy, which involved a person who had been apprehended for a terrorist offence giving evidence against his or her accomplices in return for which he or she would be given immunity from prosecution.

Between November 1981 and November 1983, 7 Loyalist and 18 Republican supergrasses were responsible for around 450 people being arrested and charged with offences connected with paramilitary activity in Northern Ireland (Weitzer, 1990: 217). A person named by a supergrass was arrested and usually held in custody until a trial date was set. This could take several months and led to the system being condemned as 'internment on remand'. Other problems included allegations that the RUC 'schooled' supergrasses to name individuals who they were not acquainted with in order to get them off the streets (Gifford, 1984: 26–7). Although this secured convictions, many of these were overturned by the Northern Ireland Court of Appeal (Shetreet and Forsyth, 2012: 421) and the system fell into disuse by around 1986.

Problems associated with the supergrass policy allegedly formed the basis of a new police initiative to respond to terrorism. This was the 'shoot to kill' policy. Between 1 July 1969 and 10 August 1983, 267 individuals were killed by the security forces. Of these, 154 (57.7 per cent) were civilians with no connection to paramilitary organisations or any of the security forces (International Lawyers' Inquiry, 1985: 18). This figure was stated to be 'unacceptable' and was partly attributed to the inadequacy of the law governing the use of deadly force by the police and the Army in Northern Ireland (International Lawyers' Inquiry, 1985: 125).

This situation may have arisen by the inappropriate use of weapons by members of the security forces who perhaps should have been arrested rather than becoming the subject of the use of lethal force. Alternatively, it may have occurred as the result of a deliberate policy of assassination conducted by members of the security forces who targeted suspected members of paramilitary organisations. This latter accusation arose in 1982 following the deaths of six people who were shot by members of the RUC's southern regional Headquarters Mobile Support Unit in south Armagh. The Chief Constable of the RUC, John Hermon, subscribed to the notion of 'an honest mistake' and defended his officers who were implicated in this policy, threatening to resign if court proceedings were initiated.

However, three trials took place in 1984 at which all RUC officers were acquitted, although in each trial evidence was produced of a cover-up by RUC Special Branch officers, allegedly designed to protect the involvement and identities of informants placed in the IRA by the intelligence services. The 'circumstances which had allegedly led police to fabricate cover stories in three incidents where six men had been shot dead by the RUC's anti-terrorist unit in County Armagh in the autumn of 1982' (Taylor, 1987: 29) were subsequently investigated by the Deputy Chief Constable of the Greater Manchester Police, John Stalker.

An interim report was produced in 1985, which concluded that there was no evidence of a 'shoot to kill' policy being conducted by the RUC (Taylor, 1987: 118), but Stalker awaited information derived from a surveillance device that had been previously planted at the scene of one of the shootings by MI5 before producing the final report. Before this was received, he was removed from the investigation in 1986 in connection with an alleged disciplinary offence (of which he was subsequently cleared of any wrongdoing). The investigation was taken over by Colin Sampson and the final report was concluded in 1987. This found evidence of conspiracy to pervert the course of justice and obstruction of the police investigation and criminal charges were recommended (Cunningham, 2001: 59). However, on 25 January 1988, Sir Patrick Mayhew, the Attorney General, announced there would be no further prosecutions in respect of the three 1982 shootings.

Although allegations that the RUC had been involved in a policy of assassination were strenuously denied in police circles, an alternative approach was to use other organisations to conduct such a policy. During the 1990s, accusations were made of security force involvement with Loyalist paramilitary organisations, principally the Ulster Defence Association (UDA).

It was alleged that these were provided with security force intelligence so that suspected members of Republican paramilitary organisations would be targeted by Loyalist organisations. Loyalist paramilitary activity had increased during the 1990s, but much of this activity was initially directed against Catholics in a random way. It is alleged that the security forces sought to make use of this heightened level of activity by Loyalist groups, but targeted it against members of the PIRA. This is known as the 'dirty war'. The bodies involved in such collusion were British Army's Force Research Unit (a branch of Army intelligence which infiltrated agents into Republican and Loyalist paramilitary organisations and which has subsequently been re-named the Joint Support Group) and the RUC, especially its Special Branch. This matter was the subject of three investigations by Sir John Stevens.

The first of these was triggered when the Chief Constable of the RUC, Sir Hugh Annesley, ordered an inquiry into the circumstances surrounding the death of Loughlin Maginn in August 1989 at the hands of the Loyalist paramilitary group, the Ulster Freedom Fighters. Initially, Stevens concluded that collusion between the security forces and Loyalist paramilitary groups had occurred, but that it was 'neither widespread nor institutionalised' (Stevens, 1990: paras. 11 and 27).

A second (unpublished) report was issued in 1994 dealing with the handling by the security services of Brian Nelson, an informant planted in the UDA by the security services who was alleged to have served as a conduit for leaking security force information to this organisation to aid its targeting of Republicans. This led to the arrest of 30 members of the UDA, of whom nine were charged.

Reports from other bodies insisted that collusion had taken place. One alleged that the Force Research Unit (FRU) 'sought out loyalist Brian Nelson and infiltrated him into the Ulster Defence Association, which carried out its campaign of murder under the flag of convenience of the Ulster Freedom Fighters (UFF). FRU used Nelson to enhance the Loyalists' intelligence on people it was targeting for murder, and that intelligence rapidly spread throughout other Loyalist paramilitary groups' (British Irish Rights Watch, 1999). Patrick Finucane, Terence McDaid and Gerard Slane were stated to be three 'innocent victims of this deadly enterprise' (British Irish Rights Watch 1999).

A further report made reference to 'the many credible allegations of deep-seated security force involvement' in the murder of Patrick Finucane, a solicitor who had represented a number of Republicans (Lawyer's Committee for Human Rights, 2002: 68). Accusations of this nature prompted a third investigation to be mounted by Sir John Stevens, which discussed the murders of Brian Adam Lambert in 1987 and Patrick Finucane in 1989. This report acknowledged that 'there was collusion' regarding these murders, which was evidenced in ways that included 'the wilful failure to keep records, the absence of accountability, the withholding of intelligence and evidence, through to the extreme of agents being involved in murder' (Stevens, 2003: para. 4.7).

A later report concluded that on the balance of probabilities, 'an RUC officer or officers did prepare Patrick Finucane ... as a UDA target' and that 'in being tasked by the FRU to target "PIRA activists" for the UDA, Nelson would, to all intents and purposes, properly be considered to be acting in a position equivalent to an employee of the Ministry of Defence' (de Silva, 2012: paras. 74 and 87).

The response to terrorism also entailed cooperation with the Irish Republic's police force, the *Garda Síochána*. This took the form of cross-border cooperation between the RUC and the *Garda* in areas that included sharing intelligence on the activities of suspected subversives (McArdle, 1984: 33). It was also alleged that

RUC undercover units operated in the Republic to keep observations on those suspected of involvement in terrorist activities (McArdle, 1984: 47). However, cross-border contacts between police forces could be a double-edged sword. In 1989, two senior RUC officers (Harry Breen and Robert Buchanan) were ambushed and killed by the IRA after they left a meeting at Dundalk Police Station. It was later argued that collusion between the IRA and the *Garda* based at this police station was 'on the balance of probabilities' a factor in this attack (Smithwick, 2013: paras. 23.2.2, 23.2.3, 23.2.5 and 23.2.7).

See also: Battle of the Bogside, Derry (Northern Ireland) 1969, Bloody Sunday (Derry, Northern Ireland) 1972, Burnollet Bridge (Derry, Northern Ireland) 1969, counter-terrorism, 'dirty protest' (Northern Ireland) 1978–81, Provisional IRA, states of emergency, terrorism

Sources and further reading

Amnesty International (1978) *Northern Ireland. Report of an Amnesty International Mission to Northern Ireland (28 November 1977–6 December 1977*. London: Amnesty International. Available at: http://cain.ulst.ac.uk/issues/police/docs/amnesty78.htm (date accessed 4 May 2014).

Bennett, Judge H. (1979) *Report of a Committee of Inquiry into Police Interrogation Procedures in Northern Ireland*. London: HMSO, Cmnd. 7497.

Boyle, K., Hadden, T. and Hillyard. P. (1980) *Ten Years on in Northern Ireland: The Legal Control of Political Violence*. London: Cobden Trust.

Brewer, J. and Magee, K. (1991) *Inside the RUC: Routine Policing in a Divided Society*. Oxford: Clarendon.

British Irish Rights Watch (1999) 'Deadly Intelligence: State Involvement in Loyalist Murder in Northern Ireland', http://cain.ulst.ac.uk/issues/violence/birw0299.htm (date accessed 4 May 2014).

Cunningham, M. (2001) *British Government Policy in Northern Ireland, 1969–2000*. Manchester University Press.

Day of Reflection (undated) 'Fact Sheet on the Conflict in and About Northern Ireland, www.dayofreflection.com/pdf/fact_sheet_on_the_conflict_in_and_about_northern_ireland_2.pdf (date accessed 4 May 2014).

De Silva, Rt Hon Sir D. (2012) *The Report of the Patrick Finucane Review*. London: TSO, House of Commons Paper 802.

Diplock, Lord K. (1972) *Report of the Commission to Consider Legal Procedures to Deal with Terrorist Activities in Northern Ireland*. London: HMSO, Cm. 5185.

Evelegh, R. (1978) *Peace Keeping in a Democratic Society: The Lessons of Northern Ireland*. London: C. Hurst and Co.

Gardiner, Lord G. (1975) *Report of a Committee to Consider, in the Context of Civil Liberties and Human Rights Measures to Deal with Terrorism in Northern Ireland*. London, HMSO, Cmnd. 5847.

Gifford, Lord T. (1984) *Supergrasses: The Use of Accomplice Evidence in Northern Ireland*. London: Cobden Trust.

Harvey, R. (1980) *Diplock and the Assault on Civil Liberties*. London: Haldane Society of Socialist Lawyers.

Hillyard, P. (1983) 'Law and Order' in J. Darby (ed.), *Northern Ireland: The Background to the Conflict*. Belfast: Appletree Press.

Hunt, Baron J. (1969) *Report of the Advisory Committee on Policing in Northern Ireland*. Belfast: HMSO, Cmd. 535.

International Lawyers Inquiry (1985) *Shoot to Kill? International Lawyers' Inquiry, into the Lethal Use of Firearms*

by the Security Forces in Northern Ireland. Cork: Mercier Press.
Kennedy-Pipe, C. (1997) *The Origins of the Present Troubles in Northern Ireland*. Harlow: Longman.
Lawyer's Committee for Human Rights (2002) *Beyond Collusion: The UK Security Forces and the Murder of Patrick Finucane*. Washington DC: Lawyer's Committee for Human Rights.
McArdle, P. (1984) *The Secret War: An Account of the Sinister Activities along the Border Involving Gardaí, RUC, British Army and the SAS*. Cork: Mercier Press.
McGuffin, J. (1973) *Internment*. Tralee, County Kerry: Anvil Books.
Mulcahy, A. (2006) *Policing Northern Ireland: Conflict, Legitimacy and Reform*. Cullompton: Willan Publishing.
Murphy, J. (2013) *Policing for Peace in Northern Ireland: Change, Conflict and Continuity*. Basingstoke: Palgrave Macmillan.
Parker, Lord Chief Justice H. (1972) *Report of the Committee of Privy Councillors Appointed to Consider Authorise Procedures for the Interrogation of Persons Suspected of Terrorism*. London: HMSO, Cm. 4901.
Ryder, C. (2000) *The RUC 1922–2000: A Force Under Fire*, 2nd revised edn. London: Arrow Books.
Scorer, C. and Hewitt, P. (1981) *The Prevention of Terrorism Act: The Case for Repeal*. London: National Council for Civil Liberties.
Shetreet, S. and Forsyth, C. (eds) (2012) *The Culture of Judicial Independence: Conceptual Foundations and Practical Challenges*. Leiden: Martinus Nijhoff Publishers.
Smithwick, His Honour Judge P. (2013) *Report of the Tribunal of Inquiry into Suggestions that Members of the Garda Síochána or Other Employees of the State Colluded in the Fatal Shootings of RUC Chief Superintendent Harry Breen and RUC Superintendent Robert Buchanan on the 20th March 1989*. Dublin: The Stationery Office.

Stevens, J. (1990) *Summary of the Report of the Deputy Chief Constable of Cambridgeshire John Stevens, into Allegations of Collusion between Members of the Security Forces and Loyalist Paramilitaries 17 May*. Belfast: The Stevens Inquiry.
Stevens, Sir J. (2003) *Stevens Inquiry 3: Overview and Recommendations 17 April 2003*. Belfast: The Stevens Inquiry.
Taylor, P. (1980) *Beating the Terrorists?* Harmondsworth: Penguin.
——. (1987) *Stalker. The Search for the Truth*. London: Faber & Faber.
Walsh. D. (1983) *The Use and Abuse of Emergency Legislation in Northern Ireland*. London: Cobden Trust.
Weitzer, R. (1990) *Transforming Settler States: Communal Conflict and Internal Security in Northern Ireland and Zimbabwe*. Berkeley, CA: University of California Press.

NOTTING HILL CARNIVAL RIOT (NOTTING HILL, LONDON) 1976

On 30 August 1976, a riot occurred at the Notting Hill Carnival in London, in which 300 police officers were injured, 35 police vehicles were damaged and several shops were attacked and looted. Most of those involved were from the African-Caribbean community, although white individuals were involved in some aspects of the disorder. A total of 60 people were arrested in relation to the disturbance.

The violence took place against a background of tensions in the Notting Hill area between the police and the black community. These tensions historically derived from what was perceived as inadequate police action during racial attacks against black people that had occurred in Notting Hill in 1958 and 1959. The contemporary manifestation of distrust arose from stop and search operations (based on the 'sus law') in the area, which were viewed as harassment by those on the receiving end. This situation prompted the Metropolitan Police to seek to exert a strong grip on the Carnival and run it their way, which included encircling each of the steel bands with a serial of 25 police officers. A large number of officers (between 1,600 and 3,000) were deployed (compared to around 200 the previous year) to ensure that they were able to control events.

Although the presence of a large number of police officers might be justified by the increased number of Carnival-goers in the previous year (when around 150,000 people attended from across the country), the size of the police deployment ran the risk of being viewed as provocative. Actions undertaken by the police during the Carnival gave credence to this perception. It was observed that the Metropolitan Police staged a series of raids on all centres of entertainment on day one of the 1976 Notting Hill Carnival, which entailed arresting stallholders for obstructing the highway and arresting or reporting sellers of alcohol: 'this, and more, made for an atmosphere of palpable oppression and not a "carnival" atmosphere' (Gutzmore, 1982: 33).

The riot was triggered by a police action to arrest a pickpocket. People in the immediate area viewed this as a racially motivated police action and several black youths came to his aid. The police soon found themselves under fierce attack from stones and other missiles, and in many places were forced to hastily retreat. They were not prepared for violence of this intensity and were forced to improvise their protection, using traffic cones, dustbin lids and milk crates to fend off objects thrown by the rioters. It was in this sense especially that the Carnival (which had initially been a celebration of West Indian and African culture) was transformed into a symbol of resistance to the police criminalisation of black people.

The disturbance was important in the development of riot gear from police forces in England and Wales. The immediate innovations were riot shields and reinforced helmets. These were first used in connection with policing a demonstration in Lewisham in 1977 involving the National Front and its opponents. Notting Hill also required the Metropolitan Police to view the adequacy of its racial awareness training that had been introduced in 1964.

Seventeen black youths were tried for their part in the 1976 disturbances, but only two were convicted in Carnival-related offences in a trial that cost £250,000 (which was then a record amount of money). Despite reservations from the Metropolitan Police, the Notting Hill Carnival has remained an annual event and generally passes off without serious incident. One explanation for this has been the role played by local consultative groups that meet during the year to plan the event and whose actions help to marginalise disruptive and disorderly groups (Waddington, 2007: 133). Nonetheless, violence has sometimes broken out: in 2000, two men were killed during the Carnival and rioting also broke out in 2008.

See also: Broadwater Farm Estate riot (Haringey, London) 1985, copycat riots (England) 1981, public order policing (England Wales), riots

Sources and further reading

Gutzmore, C. (1982) 'The Notting Hill Carnival'. *Marxism Today*, August, pp. 31–3.

James, W. and Harris, C. (eds) (1993) *Inside Babylon: The Caribbean Diaspora in Britain.* London: Verso.

Moore, T. (2013) *Policing Notting Hill: Fifty Years of Turbulence.* Hook: Waterside Press.

Owusu. K. and Ross, J. (1988) *Behind the Masquerade: The History of the Notting Hill Carnival.* London: Media Arts Group.

Waddington, P. (2007) 'Public Order: Then and Now' in A. Henry and D. Smith (eds), *Transformations of Policing.* Aldershot: Ashgate.

NORTHERN ENGLAND TOWN RIOTS (BRADFORD, OLDHAM AND BURNLEY) 2001

In 2001, a wave of riots took place in a number of towns in northern England, the first of which was in Oldham (26–29 May). Other main areas affected by these disturbances were Burnley (23–25 June) and Bradford (7–9 July, a minor disturbance having occurred there on 14–15 April). Muslim youths of Pakistani and Bangladeshi heritage played a significant role in these disorders. A smaller disturbance also occurred in the Harehills district of Leeds (5–6 June), which entailed a crowd of around 200 white, Asian and black youths attacking the police following the wrongful police arrest of an Asian man.

The riots took place against an economic background of high unemployment amongst Asian youths arising from the decline of the local textile industry and a psychological climate whereby Asian youths were no longer willing to sit back and suffer what they perceived to be oppression waged by the state, its agencies such as the police service or by citizens who harboured racist sentiments or exhibited racist actions.

Their immediate context was the existence of inter-racial tensions between Asian and white communities, which was influenced by local factors such as perceptions that one community was securing a better deal in relation to local authority expenditure than another. These tensions sometimes resulted in acts of racial violence (Home Office, 2001a: 8) that included white individuals being attacked in Asian areas of Oldham and Bradford – actions that were perceived as 'invading their territory'. This gave the events in 2001 the appearance of race riots.

The disorders were triggered by a range of diverse factors that included attacks by Asians on white people in Oldham, a National Front rally in Bradford in which Asian youths clashed with white extremists, and fights between gangs of white and Asian youths in Burnley. In all of these cases, significant confrontations between Asian males and the police occurred, the worst of which was in Bradford, where attacks using missiles and petrol bombs left over 300 police officers injured (Fielding, 2005: 213). Accusations of aggressive police actions towards Asians were made, which included an assault on Shahid Malik in Burnley, son of the town's deputy mayor. Mr Malik subsequently received an apology from the Lancashire police and went on to become the Member of Parliament for Dewsbury between 2005 and 2010.

The disorders witnessed violence directed against property and individuals. Shops were looted and cars were burnt out. The police used mutual aid to quell the disturbances, eight forces sending officers to Bradford (Fielding, 2005: 213). Ministers were genuinely surprised by the occurrence of riots in 2001 and a number of reports were written that sought to explain the causes of these events.

One explanation that was offered by disturbances in Bradford in 1995 was the existence of 'strong pressures ... which prevent young people of different backgrounds from exploring life ... together (Bradford Commission, 1996: para. 2.9.1). This view was forcefully projected as a key explanation of the events that occurred in 2001 when it was observed that 'many communities operate on the basis of parallel lives' (Home Office 2001b: 9). This meant that members of white and Asian communities who lived in adjacent areas 'had very few ways of learning from and understanding one another's culture and beliefs' (Burnley Task Force, 2001b: 9).

This situation resulted in enhanced fear and intolerance, which could split cities into warring camps. This toxic climate could also be exploited by extremist groups (Home Office, 2001b: 9). A further problem with what might be termed 'no-go' areas was that unacceptable forms of criminal activity such as drug trading could be carried out within them. This was alleged to have been a factor accounting for disturbances in Bradford (Sutcliffe, cited in Wainwright, 2001) and Burnley (Burnley Task Force 2001b: 9), although the police service and local drug action teams failed to endorse it as a significant explanation of these events (Home Office, 2001a: 9 and 17).

The 2001 disorders placed the need to tackle segregation at the forefront of the political agenda by promoting the new concept of community cohesion. There were a number of ways whereby this objective could be pursued, a prerequisite of which was effective political leadership within communities that sought to promote the goal of community cohesion. The absence of this was observed as a key factor underpinning the events in 2001: it was noted that Oldham lacked 'strategic direction and a vision for the way it should develop in the future' (Oldham Independent Review, 2001:14) and that in Burnley, 'leadership, vision and civic pride are lacking at all levels of society ... in both Asian and White communities' (Burnley Task Force, 2001b: 9). Overall, the absence of an agreed vision of how things could be made better and an inability to broker relations between key interests and to work up agreed solutions was observed (Home Office, 2001a: 13).

One important consideration in terms of tackling geographical segregation was the adoption of a compulsory approach that entailed enforced integration. Although suggestions of this nature were made in the wake of the 2001 disorders by politicians in riot-affected areas (Woolas, 2001) and by the Chairman of the Commission for Racial Equality (Singh, cited in Ashley and Hetherington, 2002), this approach (which in the 1960s had entailed bussing Asian schoolchildren in Southall into white areas) failed to find official endorsement. Attempts to reverse segregation by compulsory methods fail to address the underlying causes as to why this situation had arisen, which included a conscious attempt by ethnic-minority communities to band together in resistance to racial prejudice and discrimination (including perceived police indifference to acts of racial violence) and the accompanying process of 'white flight' from that location by those who felt that the area had been 'taken over' by 'foreigners'. Accordingly, the favoured approach was to advance initiatives that were designed to develop a sense of understanding between communities.

Following the events in 2001, a number of specific actions were put forward to address segregation and promote social cohesion. Local policy makers were advised to ensure that all of their decisions were informed by an awareness of these objectives (Oldham Independent Review, 2001: 61) and it was suggested that initiatives by the voluntary sector that transcended racial and ethnic boundaries should be endorsed (Burnley Task Force 2001a: 14; Home Office, 2001b: 72). The need to build confidence and trust across all communities was emphasised, which might entail teaching citizenship in schools to educate children to respect and understand diversity (Home Office, 2001b: 74; Ouseley, 2001: 24–8). It was proposed that the existence of monocultural schools could be balanced by initiatives to foster an understanding of other communities by actions that included the twinning of schools of this nature or holding joint sports developments under the auspices of inter-faith networks (Home Office, 2001b: 30). Subsequently, the Education and Inspections Act 2006 imposed a new legal duty on schools to promote cohesion.

Political developments to redress problems of ineffective leadership were also put forward after 2001, designed to break down inter-racial barriers and to tackle the perception of powerlessness that might underpin community fragmentation. In

Blackburn (an area which experienced no disorder in 2001 but which possessed similar demographic characteristics to places where disorder did take place), these included residents' meetings (which were initiated in 2003) and the borough-wide Hundred Voices Cohesion Forum that was set up in 2006.

Historically, the police service had contributed to segregation by pursuing approaches that were perceived to be racist. In particular, ethnic-minority communities experienced over-policing (in the form of the over-zealous use of stop and search powers) and under-protection from racially motivated violence. The need for the police service to redress this situation and become part of the solution to securing community cohesion was emphasised after 2001, the National Policing Plan for 2003–6 acknowledging that 'the promotion of social cohesion should be central to the work of the police' (Home Office, 2002: 22).

Ongoing policies to promote social cohesion included attempts to make police forces more socially representative of the communities that they served, delivering training in diversity, neighbourhood policing and police involvement in multi-agency initiatives.

In addition, a wide range of new initiatives were put forward by the police service to promote community cohesion, the most important being that of community engagement. Police relations with Muslim communities in the wake of 9/11 have required particularly sensitive handling and have taken forms that include regular contact with community leaders (perhaps involving a degree of power sharing) and neighbourhood meetings to explain police actions in connection with terrorism.

Pre-emptive approaches to reduce the likelihood of disorder were pursued, including the creation of the National Community Tension Team in 2005 to monitor tensions across the country and the development of rumour management as a tool to reduce tensions. Initiatives of this nature also included rumour management in which 'gossip, hearsay and myths propagated by sources that include word of mouth, the media and the extreme right can be dispelled' before they have the opportunity to instigate or intensify disorder (Joyce, 2007: 23). Neighbourhood Policing Teams could also play an important role in pre-emptive approaches to combat terrorism.

See also: Bradford riots (Manningham, Bradford) 1995, riots

Sources and further reading

Ashley, J. and Hetherington, P. (2002) 'Force the Races to Mix Says CRE Chief', *The Guardian*, 18 March.

Bradford Commission (1996) *The Bradford Commission Report: Report of an Inquiry into the Wider Implications of Public Disorders which Occurred on 9, 10 and 11 June 1995*. London: HMSO.

Burnley Task Force (2001a) *Burnley Speaks, Who Listens? Burnley Task Force Report on the Disturbances in June 2001*. Burnley Task Force.

——. (2001b) *Burnley Speaks, Who Listens? A Summary of the Burnley Task Force Report on the Disturbances in June 2001.* Burnley Task Force.

Fielding, N. (2005) *The Police and Social Conflict: Rhetoric and Reality*, 2nd edn. London: Athlone Press.

Flint, J. and Robinson, D. (eds) (2008) *Community Cohesion in Crisis?* Bristol: Policy Press.

Home Office (2001a) *Building Cohesive Communities: A Report of the Ministerial Group on Public Order and Community Concern.* London: Home Office.

——. (2001b) *Community Cohesion: Report of the Independent Review Team Chaired by Ted Cantle.* London: Home Office.

——. (2002) *National Policing Plan 2003–2006.* London: Home Office.

Joyce, P. (2007) 'A Lesson from Lancashire'. *Policing Today*, 13(2): 23–5.

Oldham Independent Review (2001) *One Oldham, One Future.* Manchester: Government Office for the North West.

Ouseley, H. (2001) *Community Pride Not Prejudice: Making Diversity Work in Bradford.* Bradford Vision.

Waddington, D. (2001) 'Trouble at Mill Towns', *The Psychologist*, 14(9): 454–5.

Wainwright, M. (2001) 'Riot-torn City Voices Dismay at "Lawless Idiots"', *The Guardian*, 10 July.

Woolas, P. (2001) 'Beating the BNP', *The Guardian*, 15 June.

OCCUPY MOVEMENT

The Occupy movement originated from the Occupy Wall Street protests in 2011. It is an international protest movement that uses direct action to further its demands. In America, the designation of Occupy Wall Street is commonly used and elsewhere the name of the city or country where the group focuses its activities is usually added. Although its early activities were associated with the physical occupation of open spaces, it has subsequently adopted a broader range of tactics and has also formed alliances with other like-minded groups.

The Occupy movement focuses on economic and social injustice, which is manifested in problems that include poverty, unemployment, political corruption and the growing gap between society's 'haves' and 'have-nots'. In common with anti-globalisation protests, the Occupy movement is opposed to the operations of the global financial system and the power wielded over it by multinational corporations, which the movement feels benefits the many at the expense of the few and undermines democracy as the institutions that manage and benefit from the global economy are impervious to the normal operations of liberal democracy.

Some Occupy actions (including the protest in January 2012 at a meeting of the World Economic Forum) reflect those associated with anti-globalisation protests and some of the participants at anti-globalisation protests have also been involved in Occupy movement protests. The protest in Rome on 15 October 2012, for example, was joined by anarchists using Black Bloc tactics who 'torched cars, broke windows and clashed with police' (Karimi and Sterling, 2011). The association of Occupy movements with violence has provoked a hostile reaction from law-enforcement agencies – in the period from 17 September 2011 to 17 September 2013, 7,765 documented arrests of Occupy Wall Street activists had taken place in 122 American cities (OccupyArrests, 2013).

The Occupy movement was inspired by a number of other protests that included the Arab Spring and Spain's Los Indignados movement in Spain, both of which demonstrated the people's rediscovery of 'their collective power, their ability to act' (Schneider, 2013). The Los Indignados movement also used camps as a tactic of direct action. It frequently uses the slogan 'we are the 99 per cent', which refers to the concentration of wealth in the hands of the top one per cent of income-earners.

The Occupy movement is essentially leaderless, but this does not mean that it lacks structure or organisation. The structure of the movement is typically based around working groups which feed into (and, in many cases, direct) the decisions taken by general assemblies which are held at local levels across the world. Considerable use is made by Occupy movement activists of social media to organise their protests, whose aims are diverse. Use has also been made of media coordinators to get the movement's message across to the media, especially when confrontations with the police have occurred.

Although earlier protests (including the Democracy Village, set up outside the UK House of Commons in London in December 2010) were compatible with the concerns articulated by the Occupy movement, the first significant Occupy protest was the Occupy Wall Street protest that began on 17 September 2011 in Zuccotti Park, New York. It sought to highlight what it regarded as an unjust and greedy financial system, and took the form of a protest camp. It was observed that: 'In occupied Zuccotti Park, thousands of people ate, slept, met, talked, argued, read, planned, and were dragged away to jail. Many came to protest the most abstract of wrongs – the deregulation of high finance, the funding of electoral campaigns, the erosion of the social safety net, the logic of mass incarceration, the failure to address climate change' (Schneider, 2013: 5–6).

Activists involved in this protest also participated in demonstrations. In one of these (on 24 September), arrests were made for blocking traffic and disorderly conduct, and some officers used pepper spray against the demonstrators. Significantly more protesters were arrested on 1 October in an attempted march across Brooklyn Bridge. This was followed by a much larger march on 5 October that included Occupy activists, trade unionists, students and the unemployed. This march was mainly peaceful, although scuffles occurred in the late evening involving a small number of protesters who attempted to storm barricades designed to keep them out of Wall Street and the Stock Exchange. Pepper spray was again used by the police. The American police version of kettling (entailing the use of orange nets to pen demonstrators in and disperse them into small groups) was also used as a response to this (and earlier) protests in New York.

The events in New York in September–October 2011 associated with Occupy Wall Street spawned similar protests throughout the world, one of which was an attempt to occupy the London Stock Exchange. This event was organised by Occupy London and was associated with worldwide protests that took place on 15 October 2011. Although the police managed to prevent Occupy movement protesters from gaining access to the Stock Exchange, a number of protesters set up a camp outside St Paul's Cathedral.

Initially the authorities adopted a relatively tolerant approach to the Occupy movement's camps, but a harder line was subsequently taken towards them. On 11 November, 2011, police in Nova Scotia, Canada forcibly ejected Occupy campers in Victoria Park, Halifax and law-enforcement agencies throughout the world adopted a similar approach, including the closure of the camp in Zuccotti Park, New York (which was briefly re-occupied in March 2012 until it was cleared by the police), These actions resulted in the closure of most camps by February 2012, although the one outside St Paul's Cathedral, London, remained until June 2012, when protesters were evicted at the behest of the City of London Corporation. These evictions sometimes led to clashes with law-enforcement agencies, which threatened to undermine the Occupy movement's initial commitment to non-violence, although displays of violence towards peaceful protesters might secure public sympathy towards those who are perceived to be subjected to unjust treatment by the authorities.

Outside of America, Occupy groups voice concerns related to issues that are specific to their own countries (and, in this sense, the movement constitutes a loose collection of diverse groups inspired by similar motives). Occupy Nigeria, for example, was triggered by the decision of the country's President to end fuel subsidies in January 2012, but which also voiced opposition to corruption and human rights violations conducted by the government. In other countries, the Occupy movement was supported by those opposed to austerity measures that were imposed on them by bodies such as the troika.

In addition to camps and demonstrations, the Occupy movement has carried out a number of other forms of direct action. On 5 November, Occupy protesters in America marched on the banks and other financial institutions to urge Americans to move their money from big corporate banks to the smaller community credit unions. This event was dubbed 'Bank Transfer Day'. Also in November 2011, Occupy the Roads was initiated to bring the Occupy message across to the general public across the USA.

In December 2011, Occupy Homes was initiated in America as a protest against the practices used by banks that resulted in people losing their homes. The protest included the occupation of foreclosed homes, the disruption of bank auctions and attempts to prevent evictions from taking place.

Some of these actions entailed seeking to cooperate with groups not associated with the Occupy movement but whose aims were seen to be compatible with it. This was the case with the Occupy the Ports demonstrations and blockades, which succeeded in closing a number of ports on America's west coast in December 2011, actions that entailed lending support to workers in dispute with their employer, Export Grain Terminal, and terminal operator SSA Marine on the grounds that such actions would serve to 'disrupt the economic machine that benefits the wealthiest individuals and corporations' (Pearson, 2011). However, the unions and workers involved expressed reservations concerning the involvement of outside protesters in their dispute, mainly because of the loss of wages entailed by port closures (Pearson, 2011).

Occupy activists were also willing to engage in other forms of direct action, which represented a movement away from the Occupy movement's core message of income inequality and its symbolic focus on Wall Street (Maslin, 2013). This was the case with Occupy Sandy, which provided disaster relief in the wake of Superstorm Sandy in October 2012. This had caused considerable damage in the American states of New York and New Jersey, following which Occupy activists 'played a leading role in grassroots disaster relief across the city. They organized donation hubs, delivered food and medications to elderly storm victims and helped people repair their homes, among other volunteer efforts' (Barr, 2013). Subsequently, Occupy Sandy merged with another organisation, The Working World, to form Worker-Owned Rockaway Cooperatives, which seek to stimulate the development of locally owned cooperative business ventures in the Rockaway area of New York, which was especially devastated by the storm (Occupy Sandy 2013).

However, although these examples illustrate the involvement of the Occupy movement in a diverse range of activities, this situation could be considered a weakness rather than a strength. It has been observed that: 'Without leaders or specific demands, Occupy turned into an amorphous protest against everything wrong with the world' (Barr, 2013).

Although the Occupy movement seeks to influence public opinion through its activities, it has also succeeded in gaining support from big business. One example of this was the statement of support given to Occupy Wall Street by the Board of Directors of ice-cream makers Ben and Jerry's, which expressed 'our deepest admiration to all of you who have initiated the non-violent Occupy Wall Street Movement and to those around the country who have joined in solidarity'. The statement condemned as 'immoral' the 'inequity that exists between classes in our country' (Ben and Jerry's Board of Directors, 2011). Personal (as opposed to corporate) support has also been given to the Occupy movement by prominent members of the business community, including Seth Goldman, President of Honest Tea (a subsidiary of Coca-Cola) (Hines, 2012).

The influence wielded by the Occupy movement has also been endorsed in England by the Bank of England's Executive Director for Financial Stability, Andrew Haldane, who stated that Occupy had been 'successful in its efforts to popularise the problems of the global financial system for one very simple reason: they are right'. He added that protesters who camped out near St Paul's Cathedral in London and dozens of other cities including New York 'touched a moral nerve in pointing to growing inequities in the allocation of wealth'. He also credited the Occupy movement with stirring a 'reformation of finance' (Haldane, 2012).

The Occupy movement has more recently contemplated the use of conventional politics to supplement direct action – an objective that seeks to 'Occupy the State' (Gerbaudo, 2013). This would position it as a progressive alternative to the right-wing response to the financial crisis put forward by the American Tea Party (which also blends conventional political action with protest).

See also: anti-austerity protests, anti-globalisation, anti-globalisation movement, anti-globalisation/anti-capitalist protests (UK), anti-globalisation/anti-capitalist protests (worldwide), Arab Spring, civil disobedience, demonstrations, direct action, kettling

Sources and further reading

Barr, M. (2013) '3 Occupy Wall Street Protesters Arrested', *Associated Press*, http://abclocal.go.com/wabc/story?section=news/local/new_york&id=9251246 (date accessed 5 May 2014).

Ben and Jerry's Board of Directors (2011) 'To Those who Occupy: We Stand with You', www.benjerry.com/activism/occupy-movement (date accessed 5 May 2014).

Byrne, J. (ed.) (2012) *The Occupy Handbook*. Boston, MA: Back Bay Books.

Chomsky, N. (2012) *Occupy*. London: Penguin.

Gerbaudo, P. (2013) 'Why it's Time to Occupy the State', *The Guardian*, 10 December.

Haldane. A. (2012) Speech to an Occupy Economics meeting, London, 28 October, quoted in *The Independent*, 29 October.

Hines, A. (2012) 'Ben and Jerry's Occupy Wall Street Love Affair Turning Cold', *Huffington Post*, 10 February, www.huffingtonpost.com/2012/10/02/ben-jerrys-occupy-wall-street_n_1932499.html (date accessed 5 May 2014).

Karimi, F. and Sterling, J. (2011) 'Occupy Protests Spread Around the World; 70 Injured in Rome', *CNN*, 15 October, http://edition.cnn.com/2011/10/15/world/occupy-goes-global (date accessed 5 May 2014).

Maslin, S. (2013) 'Storm Effort Causes a Rift in a Shifting Occupy Movement', *New York Times*, 30 April.

OccupyArrests (2013) 'Number of Occupy Arrests', http://stpeteforpeace.org/occupyarrests.sources.html (date accessed 5 May 2014).

Occupy Sandy (2013) 'Who Will Own the Rockaways?', http://occupysandy.net (date accessed 5 May 2014).

Pearson, M. (2011) 'Occupy Protesters Try to Disrupt Ports; Police Make Arrests', *CNN*, 13 December, http://edition.cnn.

com/2011/12/12/us/occupy-ports (date accessed 5 May 2014).

Schneider, N. (2013) *Thank You, Anarchy: Notes from the Occupy Apocalypse*. Berkeley, CA: University of California Press.

Welby, E., Bolton, M., Nayak, M. and Malone, C. (eds) (2012) *Occupying Political Science: The Occupy Wall Street Movement from New York to the World*. New York: Palgrave Macmillan.

P

PARAMILITARY POLICING (ENGLAND AND WALES)

The term 'paramilitary policing' as applied to England and Wales refers to changes affecting the tactics, weaponry and equipment used by the police at public order events and the way in which the deployment of police resources was organised in advance of a specific event and controlled on the day of it. These changes were incrementally introduced during the 1980s, often as reactive responses to events such as the 1981 inner-city disorders and the 1984/5 miners' dispute.

Paramilitary policing has been described as 'the application of (quasi) military training, equipment and organisation to questions of policing (whether under central control or not)' (Jefferson, 1990: 16). It has often been associated with aggressive policing in which those on the receiving end are viewed as the enemy and are subjected to a violent police response. The presence of police officers at a specific incident who are dressed and equipped as if they were 'looking for trouble' may serve to deter protesters or provoke or legitimise the use of violence by a crowd (Jefferson, 1987: 51–3).

It has been argued that paramilitary policing is contrary to the traditional ways in which the police responded to protest, in that the time-honoured notion of minimum force that underpinned policing since the early years of the nineteenth century (Brewer *et al.*, 1996: 22) has given way to a style of policing that favours the use of coercion to quell manifestations of dissent, similar to methods associated with colonial policing tactics (Northam, 1989: 59).

However, arguments that equate paramilitary policing with an aggressive police response at public order events present an incomplete account of the range of developments with which paramilitary policing was associated.

Particular attention has been drawn (Waddington, 1987 and 1993) to the contribution made by command and control systems to paramilitary policing that enabled 'a more disciplined approach to disorderly and violent situations than was possible by traditional methods' (Waddington

1993: 353). These enhanced the degree of control that senior officers were able to exert over officers deployed in public order situations and served to suppress the discretion of individual officers and undermine the influence that subcultural values might otherwise exert over their actions (Waddington, 1993: 357). Other developments associated with paramilitary policing included intelligence gathering and planning and the use of tension indicators (Waddington, 1987), which sought to avoid confrontation rather than to provoke it.

In addition, the opinion that paramilitary policing characterised a more aggressive form of policing that set aside the time-honoured principle of minimum force has been challenged by arguments that suggest that changes to police methods in the latter decades of the twentieth century were prompted by the violence to which police officers were often subjected. These changes did not undermine the concept of minimum force but the base line was altered so that the level of force that constituted 'minimum' was pushed upwards in response to the violence associated with protest (Reiner, 1998: 46).

See also: copycat riots (England) 1981, miners' dispute (Britain) 1984–5, public order policing (England and Wales), riot police, third force

Sources and further reading:

Brewer, J., Guelke, A., Hume, I., Moxon-Browne, E. and Wilford, R. (1996) *The Police, Public Order and the State*, 2nd edn. Basingstoke: Palgrave Macmillan.

Jefferson. T. (1987) 'Beyond Paramilitarism'. *British Journal of Criminology*, 27: 47–53.

——. (1990) *The Case Against Paramilitary Policing*. Buckingham: Open University Press.

Northam, G. (1989) *Shooting in the Dark: Riot Police in Britain*. London: Faber & Faber.

Reiner, R. (1998) 'Policing Protest and Disorder in Britain' in D. Della Porta and H. Reiter (eds), *The Control of Mass Demonstrations in Western Democracies*. University of Minnesota Press, pp. 35–49.

Waddington, P. (1987) 'Towards Paramilitarism? Dilemma in the Policing of Public Disorder'. *British Journal of Criminology*, 27: 37–46.

——. (1993) 'The Case Against Paramilitary Policing Considered'. *British Journal of Criminology*, 33(3): 353–73.

PEACE MOVEMENT

The peace movement embraces a wide range of organisations dedicated to opposition to war and the pursuit of world peace.

An important organisation associated with the peace movement in the UK is the Campaign for Nuclear Disarmament (CND), which was formed in 1957 under the chairmanship of Canon John Collins. Its main objective is unilateral nuclear disarmament by the UK, a call that was made following Britain's testing of hydrogen bombs at locations that included the Maralinga test site in the south Australian desert and Christmas Island in the Pacific Ocean.

CND sought the unconditional renunciation of the use, production of or dependence upon nuclear weapons by Britain and the bringing about of a general disarmament convention. Its current policies relating to this objective include the call to cancel the Trident programme and the advocacy of a nuclear-free and less militarised Europe, which includes the removal of US military bases and nuclear weapons in Europe. It has promoted its beliefs by various forms of protest. These included the march from the Atomic Weapons Establishment near Aldermaston to Trafalgar Square in London that was held over the Easter weekend between 1959 and 1965. It also highlighted its views by organising protests in relation to events that emphasised the dangers of nuclear weapons, including demonstrations that were held against the background of the 1962 Cuban Missile Crisis.

CND's commitment to lawful protest created an early schism in the movement that resulted in the formation of the Committee of 100 in 1960, whose leading figure was the philosopher Bertrand Russell. The Committee endorsed the tactic of civil disobedience and its main form of protest were mass sit-down demonstrations that were staged in London and outside military bases. The first of these took place outside the Ministry of Defence building in London on 18 February 1961.

A further demonstration on 17 September 1961 led to Russell, then aged 89 and a holder of the Order of Merit and Nobel Prize for Literature, being imprisoned in Brixton for seven days for inciting civil disobedience. He was offered the opportunity to be bound over on a promise of good behaviour for 12 months, but refused.

Following this protest, further actions were planned at air-force bases where nuclear weapons would be deployed. It was intended to walk onto these bases and sit down on the runways. In response, 3,000 military and civilian police were mobilised at one of the protest sites (Wethersfield) and around 850 arrests were made. Six members of the Committee of 100 who were deemed to be the organisers of this event were charged with conspiracy and incitement to breach the Official Secrets Act 1911. These ('the Wethersfield six') were imprisoned, five for 18 months and one for 12 months. The Committee of 100 was dissolved in 1968 and CND subsequently itself utilised direct action as a tactic of protest.

CND also promotes a number of other aims. It endorses international nuclear disarmament, tighter international arms regulation through agreements that include the Nuclear Non-Proliferation Treaty and is opposed to military action that may result in the use of nuclear, chemical or biological weapons of mass destruction. It is also against the construction of nuclear power stations in the UK and wants Britain to withdraw from the North Atlantic Treaty Organization (NATO). It has opposed wars (such as the Vietnam War) and has sometimes voiced its objections in conjunction with other organisations, such as the collaboration with the Stop the War Coalition, which opposed the war against Iraq in 2002. It also seeks to mobilise public opinion behind the concerns that it raises in ways other than demonstrations. For example, its current opposition to Trident has been mounted through a petition calling on the government to scrap Trident and cancel its replacement, and by organising a nationwide series of public meetings under the umbrella of 'the new ban the bomb tour'.

Support for CND has ebbed and flowed since its formation. The conclusion of the 1963 Test Ban Treaty served to diminish its support, which picked up during the 1980s with the intensification of the Cold War, one aspect of which was the deployment of US nuclear missiles in Europe. In response to this situation, the government issued its plans for home defence during the 1970s and 1980s, and an important aspect of this was the pamphlet *Protect and Survive*, published in 1980. This advised citizens how to defend themselves in the event of a nuclear attack and added further weight to opposition to nuclear weapons. In October 1983, CND organised a major demonstration in London to oppose cruise missile deployment in the UK, which was attended by around 300,000 protesters. Opposition to nuclear weapons was also popularised by other protests, including that at Greenham Common and Molesworth.

CND has been subjected to various forms of state surveillance on the grounds that it was viewed as a subversive organisation. This charge primarily arose from the involvement of a number of its activists (including John Cox who was Chairman from 1971 to 1977) with the Communist Party of Great Britain. MI5 initially viewed it as a communist-controlled organisation, which was downgraded towards the end of the 1970s to that of a communist-penetrated organisation. The surveillance operations mounted against CND and its leading activists included telephone tapping and the placing of informants within its organisation. Revelations in 1985 by an MI5 officer, Cathy Massiter (who had been responsible for monitoring CND), also revealed that concern by the intelligence agencies was also provoked by fears as to its political influence.

Another organisation associated with the peace movement is the Stop the War Coalition. This was initially formed in September 2001 in opposition to the declaration by President George W. Bush of the 'War on Terror':

It has since been dedicated to ending wars in Afghanistan and Iraq, bringing the troops home and forcing the British government to change its disastrous foreign policies. We have initiated campaigns around these issues and are also committed to opposing sanctions and military attacks on Iran, supporting Palestinian rights, opposing racism and defending civil liberties. (Stop the War Coalition, 2014)

Its tactics have included organising demonstrations (one of which on 15 February 2003 in London attracted around 750,000 participants) (*BBC News*, 2003), holding public meetings and direct action in the run-up to war in 2003, which included walk-outs from workplaces, colleges and schools. The Coalition has also lobbied Parliament and convened peace conferences and People's Assemblies.

Organisations associated with the peace movement exist throughout the World. In America, protests against the Vietnam War included civil disobedience in the form of draft dodging and the burning of draft cards. Organisations such as Students for a Democratic Society were involved in protests that included demonstrations and marches. Major protests were mounted at the 1968 Democratic National Convention in Chicago and a protest against the invasion of Cambodia in 1970 resulted in the deaths of four students at Kent State University at the hands of the Ohio National Guard.

The National Nuclear Weapons Freeze Campaign emerged during the 1980s, arising out of a concern of the increased threat of a nuclear war following the Senate's failure to ratify the SALT II arms control agreement that had been negotiated with the Soviet Union in 1979. It called on the USA and Soviet Union to adopt a mutual freeze on the testing, production and deployment of nuclear weapons and of missiles, and of new aircraft designed primarily to deliver nuclear weapons.

The actions undertaken by the Freeze Campaign included a 'disarmament week' in 1981 in which local organisations carried out a number of activities such as lectures, films, exhibitions and press conferences to advertise the dangers of nuclear war. In June 1982, it participated in a rally in June 1982 held in New York's Central Park that attracted around one million demonstrators and called for an end to the Cold War arms race and the abandonment of nuclear weapons.

A political action committee, FREEZEPAC, was formed in 1982 that endorsed candidates for the House of Representatives and the Senate in the November 1982 elections who advocated a bilateral nuclear weapons freeze between the USA and the Soviet Union. This effectively provided for a national referendum on this topic. A subsequent political action committee, Freeze Voter '84, campaigned for candidates supporting the freeze and opposing those who did not.

The views of the Freeze Campaign bore fruit in agreements relating to the testing, development and deployment of nuclear weapons concluded between the USA and the Soviet leader, Mikhail Gorbachev, beginning in the mid-1980s. In 1987, the Freeze Movement merged with the National Committee for a Sane Policy to form Peace Action, which continues to campaign for nuclear disarmament. In 2003, Peace Action launched a Campaign for a New Foreign Policy, which sought to mobilise public opinion in support of a US foreign policy based upon nuclear disarmament, human rights, democracy and international cooperation.

The invasions of Afghanistan in 2001 and Iraq in 2003 were further spurs to the activities of the peace movement in America, which included organisations such as Act Now to Stop War and End Racism (ANSWER), an umbrella group that organised rallies and demonstrations against the war in Afghanistan.

In addition to the organisations located in specific countries, others operate on a wider geographical basis. One of these is European Nuclear Disarmament (END), which was formed in 1980 following the escalation of the Cold War in which NATO deployed Cruise and Pershing II missiles in a number of European countries as a response to the Soviet Union's upgrading of its intermediate nuclear missiles in Europe. It aims for a nuclear-free Europe 'from Poland to Portugal' and a key feature of its actions entailed convening European Nuclear Disarmament Conventions, the first of which was held in Brussels in 1982. It also closely worked with dissidents in the Soviet Union and the Eastern Bloc. The 1987 Intermediate-Range Nuclear Forces Treaty accomplished the key concerns of END. In the UK, END became incorporated into the European Dialogue in 1989.

Peace Direct is an organisation that operates on a global basis. It is a charity that seeks to support those engaged in local peace building:

In the world's most fragile countries, we seek out local peacebuilders who are making a real difference – building peace from the grassroots up, preventing conflict in the places where it starts – locally. They are disarming rebels, resettling refugees, healing communities, reviving economies. They work at great personal risk on crucial problems like child soldiers, women and conflict, youth and peace, political violence. They are the key to preventing conflicts and creating a lasting peace. (Peace Direct, 2014)

See also: civil disobedience, demonstrations, direct action, Greenham Common (Berkshire, England) 1981–2000, Islamic terrorist groups, political policing, public order policing (England and Wales), subversion

Sources and further reading

The website for CND is www.cnduk.org.

The website for Peace Direct is www.peacedirect.org/uk/landing-page/world-peace/?gclid=CKO725DdwbwCFaQfwwodqSEAXQ.

The website for the Stop the War Coalition is www.stopwar.org.uk.

BBC News (2003) '"Million" March Against Iraq War', 16 February, http://news.bbc.co.uk/1/hi/2765041.stm (date accessed 5 May 2014).

Minnion, J. and Bolsover, P. (1983) *The CND Story: The First 25 Years of CND in the Words of People Involved*. London: Allison and Busby.

Parkin, F. (1968) *Middle Class Radicalism: The Social Bases of the British Campaign for Nuclear Disarmament*. Manchester University Press.

Peace Direct (2014) 'Taking a Lead from Locals', www.peacedirect.org/uk/about (date accessed 5 May 2014).

Stop the War Coalition (2014) 'About' (date accessed 5 May 2014).
Wittner, L. (2003) *The Struggle Against the Bomb*. Stanford University Press.

POLITICAL POLICING

Political policing is concerned with the policing of ideas and opinions, primarily by gathering information on those who hold or who articulate ideas that the state labels 'subversive'. The rationale for this is that these ideas or opinions may be translated into actions that cause harm to the state or the citizens who live within it.

Although political policing may seem incompatible with fundamental civil and political liberties enjoyed by citizens in liberal democracies, most states of this nature possess agencies that perform this type of work. In America, the National Security Agency (NSA) was set up in 1952, bringing all US communication intelligence operations under one body, which operates under the control of the Department of Defense. It is concerned with signals intelligence (SIGINT) and its focus is on gathering and analysing intelligence derived from intercepting electronic forms of communication, such as microwave and radio transmissions, much of which is from outside America, although it also conducts internal surveillance. The NSA makes considerable use of computer technology to carry out its tasks.

The Federal Bureau of Investigation (FBI) and the Central Intelligence Agency (CIA) also perform related tasks. The former is a federal law-enforcement agency that also gathers intelligence related to domestic crime, including threats to national security and the CIA evaluates information that is gathered from across the world in relation to threats to national security. Unlike the NSA, both of these agencies can derive information directly from human sources.

In Canada, the Canadian Security Intelligence Service (CSIS) performs the task of political policing and in Australia this work is carried out by the Australian Security Intelligence Organisation (ASIO).

In the UK, a number of agencies are involved in seeking to counter subversion. The main police unit whose role was to counter subversion was Special Branch, which was a specialist branch of the police service whose origins can be traced to 1883 in connection with the bombing campaign waged on mainland Britain by Irish Republican groups (called Fenians). Historically, Special Branch was based in London, but subsequently all police forces possessed special branches that were technically answerable to individual chief constables. Special Branch played a major role in surveillance work directed at foreign communities living in Britain and in the enforcement of anti-terrorist legislation, and also played a key role in the process of positive vetting. Subsequently, Special Branch has been incorporated in the eight counter-terrorist units that operate on a regional basis across England and Wales (the Welsh unit being called the Welsh Extremism and Counter-terrorist Unit).

Specialist squads involving police officers (some of whom may be members of Special Branch) may also carry out specific activities of this nature, one aspect of which is the planting of undercover officers in organisations engaged in protest. Three police units – the Special Demonstration Squad (SDS) of the Metropolitan Police (which was housed within Special Branch), the National Public Order Intelligence Unit of the Metropolitan Police Service and the National Extremism Tactical Coordination Unit (set up by the Chief Constable of Cambridgeshire) – were involved in activities of this nature.

These units were placed under the control of the Association of Chief Police Officers' National Coordinator for Domestic Extremism in 2006 and then transferred to the Metropolitan Police Service in 2010 and was collectively re-named the National Domestic Extremism Unit. This action was prompted by revelations concerning the activities of an undercover officer of the National Public Order Intelligence Unit, PC Mark Kennedy, who had infiltrated a number of protest groups in the early years of the twenty-first century and whose activities allegedly bordered on acting as an *agent provocateur*.

An example of their methods occurred in 2001, when eight women announced they were bringing a case against the Metropolitan Police Service in relation to the actions of five of its officers who were engaged in infiltrating environmental and social justice campaign groups between the mid-1980s and 2010. The targets of such activities included London Greenpeace, the Animal Liberation Front, Reclaim the Streets, Globalise Resistance, Dissent!, anti-racist and anti-roads campaigns, anti-capitalist movements and hunt saboteurs (Jones, 2013: 21). The officers involved were accused of having had relationships with the women, one of which lasted for nine years (Jones, 2013: 17).

Additional practices used by undercover police officers included the appropriation of the identities of dead infants to create false identities for undercover officers, a practice that the Home Affairs Committee stated to be 'ghoulish and disrespectful' and which could 'potentially have placed bereaved families in real danger of retaliation' (Home Affairs Committee, 2013, para. 22). The SDS had been disbanded in 2008, but subsequently, in 2013, a revelation arose that the SDS had been involved in an attempt to smear the family of Stephen Lawrence, who had been murdered in 1993 and his friend, Duwayne Brooks, who was with him at the time of the attack. The aim of this action was designed to counter racially motivated public order issues in the event of these arising (Evans and Lewis, 2013a).

Revelations of this nature resulted in the Metropolitan Police Service conducting a review of the use of undercover officers by the now-disbanded Special Demonstration Squad, which commenced in October 2011 and was known as Operation Herne.

The policing of groups deemed to be subversive is also conducted by bodies divorced from mainstream policing. One of these is the Civil Nuclear Constabulary that (following the enactment of the Energy Act 2004) replaced the Atomic Energy Authority Constabulary. This body does not guard nuclear establishments (a task performed by the Ministry of Defence police and the military), but it does carry out covert intelligence operations against anti-nuclear protesters.

In addition to the role of the police in countering subversion, another agency concerned with this task is the Government Communications Headquarters (GCHQ), which derives from Signals Intelligence (SIGINT) that was established during the First World War and adopted the GCHQ designation during the Second World War, when it played a major role in code-breaking.

Its main role became that of monitoring a wide range of electronic forms of communication through the use of devices that included listening posts and spy satellites. This remained known as Signals Intelligence (SIGINT). It was designed to focus on external affairs (initially communications made between and within communist countries), although allegations have been made regarding its use in domestic events involving the use of extra-parliamentary forms of political activity, in particular the 1984/5 miners' dispute, where it was alleged that 'large scale misuse of GCHQ and its outstations in Britain' had taken place 'to track the activities of NUM officials and the movement of the miners' funds around the European banking system' (Milne, 1995: 4).

It has been estimated that by the early 1980s, more than 80 per cent of Britain's intelligence related to national security derived from signals intelligence (Aldrich, 2010: 441). Its work is similar to that performed by the American NSA, with whom it has cooperated in connection with both gathering intelligence and the technological means through which such work is conducted. One aspect of this cooperation related to the Zircon spy satellite programme. This had been intended as a unilateral British venture, but was cancelled in 1987 on the grounds of expense. Following this cancellation, Britain made use of spy satellites designed for the use of NSA by effectively buying a one-third time share in the American SIGINT satellite system (Aldrich, 2010: 460).

A key body concerned with combating subversion is MI5. It was established in 1909 to foil the spying activities of foreign governments within Britain. It is controlled by a Director General appointed by the Prime Minister and is operationally accountable to the Home Secretary. It had no legal status until the enactment of the Security Service Act 1989, a situation that presented a number of problems relating to accountability and funding.

MI5 is primarily an intelligence-gathering body. Historically it has collected information organisations and individuals deemed to be subversive through a number of methods, including:

- mail interception;
- interception ('tapping') of telephone calls and other forms of electronic communication;
- placing bugs in a target's home or premises (which relays by either radio frequencies or telephone wires conversations that take place in the location where the bug is planted);
- planting informants or agents in organisations.

MI5's main role is to gather intelligence and pass this over to other organisations to whom it might be relevant. MI5 agents lack police powers and it historically worked closely with Special Branch should arrests be required. In 1975, a proposal was made (but which was not acted upon) to create a centralised intelligence agency to coordinate the work of a number of intelligence-gathering agencies including Special Branch and MI5 (Geary, 1985: 95–6). The intelligence that MI5 gathers (for example, derived from telephone taps) is often not admissible as evidence in court.

Occasionally, the role of MI5 has extended beyond intelligence gathering to embrace other forms of activity. These include accusations regarding the use of 'dirty tricks' designed to sabotage or destabilise an organisation that has been targeted as subversive. One example of this was the allegation that MI5 planted a mole in the upper echelons of the National Union of Miners during the 1980s (Milne, 1995: 190–241).

A key consideration affecting the operation of agencies concerned with political policing is the degree of external control that is exerted over their operations. In some countries, ministers or their equivalent may give directions to such agencies regarding how they should conduct investigations. This is the case in Australia and Canada in connection with investigations conducted by the ASIO and the CSIS. In America, Attorney-General Edward Levi produced guidelines in 1976 to govern the conduct of investigations undertaken by the FBI (Ross, 2000: 93).

Specific activities concerned with information gathering may also be subject to external control. In America, the Omnibus Crime Control and Safe Streets Act 1968 placed telephone-tapping activities undertaken at a state or federal level under judicial control so that only a state court (or, in the case of the FBI, a federal judge) could sanction these activities. The activities of the NSA were largely outside the scope of this Act, which did not cover electronic monitoring (Fitzgerald and Leopold, 1987: 171).

However, in the wake of Watergate, Congress passed the Foreign Intelligence Surveillance Act 1978, which required the NSA to secure authorisation from federal judges convened in a special court (the Foreign Intelligence Surveillance Court) when intercepting communications within America of citizens who were suspected of involvement in activities such as espionage or terrorism. The Act does not apply to work of this nature conducted abroad and has been amended in the wake of 9/11 by the Terrorist Surveillance Act 2006, the Protect America Act 2007 and the FISA Amendments Act 2008. However, the President may authorise electronic surveillance without a court order for a period of one year, provided it is used only for the purposes of foreign intelligence information.

In the UK, a number of important developments have taken place since the middle of the twentieth century in connection with external control exerted over MI5.

A key consideration concerning MI5 is the extent to which this agency is accountable for its actions. However, in seeking to assess the adequacy of external control exerted over the activities of MI5, it is necessary to balance the requirements of the agency to exercise a degree of operational independence against the need to ensure that it functions in accordance with the principles of liberal democratic political systems.

Insufficient external control may mean that the agency effectively becomes self-tasking, engaging in a range of activities that might threaten to undermine liberal democracy: this may result in democratically elected governments themselves (or individual members of governments) being targets of MI5 (allegations of this nature being made in connection with Labour governments in the 1970s – Wright, 1987). Historically, this problem was compounded by the manner in which MI5 recruited its agents – primarily through the use of an 'old boy' network rather than through the use of civil service rules and procedures, giving rise to the perception that it was a socially unrepresentative self-perpetuating elite. The conviction of Michael Bettaney for spying in 1985 ultimately led to the open recruitment of graduates in 1995.

On the other hand, too much external control may result in MI5 effectively being used as a tool to advance the political interests of the government. Although the 1952 Maxwell Fyfe Directive emphasised that MI5 should be kept 'absolutely free from any political bias or influence' (quoted in West, 1982: 243), accusations have been made that it strayed from this remit, especially during the 1980s.

The perception that controls over the operations of MI5 were inadequate prompted a number of reforms during the 1980s to place the agency under a more effective form of external control.

The Interception of Communications Act 1985 placed telephone tapping on a statutory basis by requiring it to be authorised in a warrant signed by a minister. This Act was enacted to comply with the European Court of Human Right's verdict in the *Malone* case, whereby evidence used against the defendant in court in 1977 had been obtained from a telephone tap. The Act contained safeguards for individuals who felt that their rights were being infringed: a tribunal (to establish that correct procedures had been followed) and a commissioner (to oversee the legislative arrangements). This legislation did not, however, apply to bugging, which was regulated by guidelines from the Home Office, the first of which were issued in 1977 (Fitzgerald and Leopold, 1987: 182–3).

Increased openness concerning the work of the agency was theoretically provided by the Data Protection Acts of 1984 and 1998. This legislation allowed citizens to access information stored on them by the state, but exceptions were made in the interests of national security. The 1998 Act permitted an appeal to the National Security Appeals Panel against a decision by a minister to refuse access to personal data on the grounds of national security.

A major development concerning the operations of MI5 was the Security Service Act 1989. This was passed following revelations by a former MI5 operative, Cathy Massiter, in relation to the tapping of the telephone of Dr John Cox, a vice-president of CND and a Communist Party Councillor. This measure placed MI5 on a statutory basis and defined its sphere of operations. It also authorised the issuance of 'property warrants' to enable the agency to 'bug and burgle' in order to gather intelligence – the first legislation to formally acknowledge the practice of bugging. The Police Act 1997 gave the police service similar powers in connection with combating serious crime. A Security Services Tribunal was established to consider complaints by members of the public and the operations of the legislation in connection with property warrants was overseen by a Security Services Commissioner.

Subsequent legislation (the Intelligence Services Act 1994) placed the Secret Service (MI6) and GCHQ on a statutory footing. The 1994 Act also created the Intelligence and Security Committee composed of MPs and peers to scrutinise the expenditure and administration of MI5, MI6 and GCHQ.

The work performed by MI5 was expanded by the Security Services Act 1996, which extended the role of MI5 into 'serious crime'. This was defined as an offence that carried a sentence of three or more years on first conviction or any offence involving conduct by a large number of individuals in pursuit of a common purpose. This definition could embrace groups using various forms of protest to further their aims.

The current legislation governing the operations of MI5 is contained in the Regulation of Investigatory Powers Act 2000. The Human Rights Act 1998 (which tranposed the European Convention on Human

Rights into UK domestic law) established the right to privacy and family life and the freedoms of expression and peaceful assembly and association with others.

Article 8 (which was concerned with privacy) required policing methods that infringed privacy to be founded on statute. Thus, the government enacted the Regulation of Investigatory Powers Act 2000. This developed existing safeguards related to intrusive surveillance (which referred to surveillance conducted in a private location that included a person's home or property such as a car where a presumption of privacy would normally apply). Safeguards were provided through warrants in relation to telephone tapping to other forms of electronic communication (such as emails and the Internet) and enabled bodies that in 1985 were either not established (such as the NCIS) or not officially in existence (such as MI5 and GCHQ) to apply for warrants to intercept communications. Warrants required the authorisation of a Secretary of State.

Covert intelligence gathering (or directed surveillance) was also authorised by the Act, including the use of informants. Covert intelligence typically took place in a public place to obtain private information about a person. However, covert intelligence is not authorised by warrants, but is authorised by police officers whose actions are subject to a Code of Practice.

The safeguards established by the Act included a tribunal to hear complaints from members of the public. The work performed by the existing Interception of Communications Commissioner (Interception of Communications Act 1985) and the Intelligence Services Commissioner (Official Secrets Act 1989) was coordinated by the new post of Chief Surveillance Commissioner.

However, although a number of reforms affecting the external control of MI5 have been introduced since the 1980s, there remain deficiencies. Safeguards introduced in legislation affecting the operations of MI5 have proved to be ineffective. For example, warrants are issued by the executive branch of government rather than the judiciary and tribunals established under the 1985/1989/2000 legislation have proved to be ineffective – in particular because they have not been required to produce evidence to a complainant or to justify the decision that they reach. In 1996 (in connection with a complaint made by Alison Halford), the European Human Rights Commission ruled that the refusal of a tribunal to clarify whether her home and office telephones had been tapped and whether the Home Secretary had authorised it gave her no effective redress, as was required by Article 13 of the Convention.

Increased openness in relation to the affairs of MI5 has to some extent been thwarted by the Official Secrets Act 1989. This sought to place more severe limits on whistleblowing by declaring it to be an offence for a past or present member of the security or intelligence services without any lawful authority to disclose any information, document or other article relating to intelligence or security which was (or had been) in that person's possession by virtue of his or her employment. This imposed a lifelong duty of confidentiality on such individuals. The Freedom of Information Act 2000 also contained a blanket ban on the disclosure of information relevant to national security regardless of any public interest consideration.

A key issue that relates to the activities of state security agencies is the impact of technology to enable material to be intercepted and assessed with regard to its relevance to national security. Historically, telephone tapping was directed at individuals and organisations that were deemed to be subversive by listening into conversations or, following the introduction of magnetic tape recorders in the 1940s, sifting through intercepted material that was stored on tape. These functions were conducted at the level of local telephone exchanges until the creation of an integrated national tapping centre during the 1960s (nicknamed 'Tinkerbell') to which telephone intercepts to any local exchange could be transmitted. MI5 made considerable use of this facility (Fitzgerald and Leopold, 1987: 75).

The focus on specific targets could be extended through the process of trawling, which enabled a number of telephone calls to be intercepted and then filtered in order to ascertain information of interest to security services (Fitzgerald and Leopold, 1987: 84). This was customarily directed at telephone traffic abroad and was conducted by GCHQ. This form of interception was initially conducted by intercepting links between telephone exchanges which were conveyed by microwave radio relay transmission.

This initially required the physical installation of antennae on ground locations, but during the 1970s, satellite technology was developed by the Americans (the Rhyolite satellites) to conduct this work from above the surface of the earth. Technology of this nature was subsequently developed and included the interception of satellite communications which in the UK were relayed back to a GCHQ facility that was close to the village of Bude in Cornwall. This was operational in the late 1960s. Communications that were carried by underground and submarine cables were also subject to interception. Work of this nature within Britain is also conducted by America's National Security Agency (NSA), which has a facility at Menwith Hill, Yorkshire.

Other forms of communication that are subject to interception include telegrams (often referred to as 'cables') and telex transmissions. The key technology that was developed to aid this process were computer systems that could sift through traffic of this nature that had been recorded on magnetic tape and which would then identify items of interest (defined in terms of containing key words or phrases or being sent to or received by selected addresses). This task was carried out by a computer system (initially HARVEST) that developed in America and used by the NSA towards the end of the 1960s, and was also used in conjunction with a joint NSA–GCHQ operation known as MINARET, which sifted through international commercial traffic and targeted political activists. Developments in computer technology in the form of voice or keyword recognition have also been applied to sifting through intercepted telephone calls. It was alleged that technology of this nature was installed at the Tinkerbell facility and was used during the 1984/5 miners' dispute (Fitzgerald and Leopold, 1987: 111).

Developments affecting technology have considerably added to the capacity of agencies such as America's NSA (acting in concert with foreign counterparts) to conduct surveillance on a global basis. Material leaked by the whistleblower Edward Snowden indicated the extent of such activities, including the Prism programme, which collected stored Internet communications from companies such as Google and Apple.

Internal and external concern over the extent of NSA spying activities prompted President Barack Obama to deliver a speech on 17 January 2014 in which he stated that new technology and new times required the balance between protecting national security and eroding individual liberty to be re-visited. He proposed ending the current system of bulk collection of domestic phone records by restricting analysts' searches of the database that would be transferred to the telecommunication companies or to a third party (McCarthy, 2014). He also stated that he had made it clear to the intelligence community that unless there was a compelling national security motive, the USA would not monitor the communications of heads of state and government of its close friends and allies (Zurcher, 2014).

See also: anti-National Security Agency protests (Germany) 2013, miners' dispute (Britain) 1984–5, public order policing (England and Wales), subversion, whistleblowing

Sources and further reading

Aldrich, R. (2010) *GCHQ: The Uncensored Story of Britain's Most Secret Intelligence Agency*. London: HarperPress.

Andrew, C. (2009) *Defend the Realm: The Unauthorised History of MI5*. New York: Knopf.

Bunyan. T. (1977) *The History and Practice of Political Policing in England and Wales*. London: Quartet Books.

Evans, R. and Lewis, P. (2013a) 'Police "Smear" Campaign Targets Steephen Lawrence's Friends and Family', *The Guardian*, 24 June.

———. (2013b) *Undercover: The True Story of Britain's Secret Police*. London: Faber & Faber.

Fitzgerald, P. and Leopold, M. (1987) *Stranger on the Line: The Secret History of Phone Tapping*. London: Bodley Head.

Geary, R. (1985) *Policing Industrial Disputes, 1893–1985*. London: Methuen.

Gill, P. (1994) *Policing Politics: Security Intelligence and the Liberal Democratic State*. Abingdon: Frank Cass.

Home Affairs Committee (2013) *Undercover Policing: Interim 13th Report*. Session

2012/13. London: TSO, House of Commons Paper 837.

Jones, C. (2013) 'Secrets and Lies: Undercover Police Operations Raise More Questions than Answers', *Statewatch*, www.statewatch.org/subscriber/protected/statewatch-journal-vol23n2-august-2013.pdf (date accessed 5 May 2014).

Lustgarten, L. and Leigh, I. (1995) *In from the Cold: National Security and Parliamentary Democracy*. Oxford University Press.

McCarthy, T, (2014) 'Obama Announces New Limits on NSA Surveillance Programmes – Live Reaction', *The Guardian*, 17 January, www.theguardian.com/world/2014/jan/17/obama-nsa-surveillance-reforms-speech-live (date accessed 5 May 2014).

Milne, S. (1995) *The Enemy Within: The Secret War Against the Miners*, 2nd edn. London: Pan Books.

Rimington, S. *The Open Secret*. London: Hutchinson.

Ross, J, (ed) (2000) *Controlling State Crime*, 2nd edn. New Brunswick, NJ: Transaction Publishers.

Thomas, G. (2009) *Secret Wars: Inside British Intelligence: 100 Years of MI5 and MI6*. New York: Tomas Dunne Books.

West, N. (1982) *MI5 1945–1972: A Matter of Trust*. London: Cornet Books.

Wright, P. (1987) *Spycatcher: The Candid Autobiography of a Senior Intelligence Office*. New York: Heinemann.

Zurcher, A. (2014) 'Obama's NSA Speech Reflects American Apathy', *BBC News Echo Chambers*, 17 January, www.bbc.co.uk/news/blogs-echochambers-25787468 (date accessed 5 May 2014).

POST-ARAB SPRING

The events that were termed the 'Arab Spring' did not bring stability to the countries that were affected by these events. Violence and protest continued to be a feature of countries that experienced regime changes and also in those where existing regimes managed to retain power. This violence took numerous forms and was inspired by a variety of motives, underpinned by the inability of governments to assert their authority throughout the countries which they governed. This entry briefly summarises events that have taken place up to the beginning of 2014.

Tunisia

The involvement of members of the former President Zine El Abidine Ben Ali's political party, the Rally for Constitutional Democracy (RCD), in a new government failed to halt protests in the early weeks of 2011, which now demanded the dissolution of this organisation. The police and the Army struggled to keep control of protests and the curfew remained in place. The demands of the protesters were met by the resignation of the newly installed Prime Minister, Mohamed Ghannouchi, in February 2011 and the subsequent dissolution of the RCD in March. On 23 October 2011, elections took place to a constituent assembly whose key function was to draw up a new constitution to replace the document that had been in operation since 1956. Elections took place under new legislation that required male and female parity of parties' election lists, although the tendency for most parties to place men at the top of their lists ensured that men and women were not elected in equal numbers (FIDH, 2012).

Ennahda, the moderate Islamist Party, secured 37 per cent of the vote in this contest, which fell short of an absolute majority in the new assembly. In December 2011, Moncef Marzouki (a human rights activist) was elected President by the constituent assembly, and the leader of Ennahda, Hamadi Jebali, was sworn in as Prime Minister.

This situation did not, however, end the violence, a new aspect of which was that it assumed a religious dimension. Hardline Islamists who wanted the introduction of Sharia law in Tunisia clashed with security forces in May 2012.

The key task of the Ennahda-led government was to perform a political balancing act between the country's secular opposition and more radical Islamist groups in the country that had been banned by former President Ben Ali. These comprised the Salafists, Sunni Muslims who believe that Islam should be practised in the way that it was in the earliest days of the faith.

Political dissent following the 2011 uprising was especially associated with the opposition of many young people to the soft approach which they perceived the government was adopting towards hardline Islamist groups. These Tunisians endorsed a secular society and their concerns were aggravated by the publication of the draft constitution in August 2012, which proposed reducing the rights of women (who were referred to as 'complementary to men'). This sparked a major protest in Tunis.

This dissent was also influenced by the government's failure to tackle the country's economic problems. Concerns regarding lack of jobs and government investment have also caused violence. One example of this was the action by a local trade union in Siliana to call a general strike that witnessed clashes between demonstrators and police in 2012 that were reminiscent of the coercive methods of the Ben Ali era.

In February 2013, a prominent secular political figure, Chokri Belaid, was assassinated. His supporters blamed his murder on Ennanda (*BBC News*, 2013). This provoked mass protests and led to the resignation of Prime Minister Hamadi Jebali. Jebali had proposed pursuing a conciliatory line towards the secular opposition and Ennahda's unwillingness to compromise for fear that this would result in its core supporters turning towards the more militant Salafists resulted in his fall from power.

Protests re-occurred following the assassination of Mohamed Brahmi on 25 July 2013. He was the leader of the Movement of the People Party and his supporters blamed his death on the ruling Ennahda Party. Both of these killings were attributed to the Salafist Ansar al-Sharia group, which had also been responsible for attacks against government forces in the Chaambi region that borders Algeria. These attacks prompted the government to launch artillery and air strikes against these militants in early August 2013.

The murder of Brahmi led the country's largest trade union to call for a general strike against terrorism, violence and murder, and a number of opposition parties withdrew from the National Constituent Assembly and called for the replacement of Ennahda by a national unity administration.

These demands were maintained in August 2013, during which opponents of the Islamist government demanded the dissolution of the National Constituent Assembly that was drawing up a new constitution and the resignation of the government. The task of drawing up the new constitution had commenced in 2011 and had dragged on since, to the detriment of tackling the day-to-day issues facing the country.

Mass protests (including agitation in a number of Tunisia's economically marginalised interior towns) occurred on 24 August, fuelled by the country's economic problems and accusations of political corruption. These were designed to force the government to step down and make way for a neutral government of technocrats. In response, Ennahda offered to form a government of national unity drawn from all the main political parties.

These protests eventually provoked National Dialogue Talks to be held in an attempt to end the country's political crisis. These began on 25 October 2010 against the background of continued demonstrations and violence, which caused the government in November 2013 to extend the state of emergency until June 2014. The key purposes of the talks were to form a caretaker government and set a date for elections. On the first day of these talks, the Ennahda Prime Minister Ali Larayedh signed a written pledge to dissolve the government within three weeks in an attempt to secure the involvement of the opposition in the negotiations.

In December 2013, agreement was reached on the appointment of a new prime minister (the current Minister of Industry, Mehdi Jomaa), who would head a caretaker government until elections were held in 2014.

The National Constituent Assembly subsequently completed its task of drawing up the draft of a new constitution in January 2014. This guaranteed freedom of worship, but decreed that Islam was the state religion. It also recognised equality between men and women. Following this approval, Prime Minister Jomaa formed a government that consisted of independents and technocrats. This would run the country until new elections were held.

Egypt

The appointment on 4 March 2011 of a civilian, Essam Sharaf, as Prime Minister was widely applauded by many demonstrators. However, violent protests continued in opposition to the power wielded by the Supreme Council of the Armed Forces and the slow pace of reform. Demonstrators returned to Tahrir Square in July 2011 to express dissatisfaction with the transitional government and they returned there in November to protest against the failure of the military to hand over power. This culminated in the resignation of the Prime Minister and the Cabinet on 21 November. Violent clashes occurred between the police, soldiers and protesters in November, and the violence meted out to women protesters led to a demonstration by Egyptian women in Cairo in 20 December.

Elections for the People's Assembly of Egypt took place between November 2011 and January 2012, and Egypt's first democratically elected Parliament for over 50 years met on 23 January 2012. The Muslim Brotherhood's Freedom and Justice Party (which was the dominant partner in a loose coalition of a number of parties that adopted the name of the Democratic Alliance for Egypt) emerged with the largest number of representatives following these elections and in February the Freedom and Justice Party emerged as the largest party following dominated elections for the Upper House, the Shura Council. In May, elections for the presidency took place and Mohamed Morsi of the Muslim Brotherhood was declared victor by the country's election commission in June.

The election that led to the victory of Mohamed Morsi arose in part as the opposition to him had been fragmented, leaving a former Mubarak supporter as his main opponent. However, following the election, the opposition re-united, which sparked protests against the new President.

The key concern was that following his election victory, Morsi had sought to advance the sectional interests of the Muslim Brotherhood and to pursue an ever-narrowing Islamist agenda rather than attempting to provide an inclusive government and rule in the national interest, focusing on key problems that included high unemployment and inflation.

Late June and early July 2013 saw a wave of demonstrations involving supporters and opponents of President Morsi, the latter demanding that he quit his office. He refused to do this and violent clashes occurred between the two sets of protagonists. Morsi belatedly offered to form a government of national consensus, yet the level of civil unrest prompted the military to intervene on 3 July 2013 in an event that might legitimately be described as a military coup, but which the US government carefully described as 'military intervention'. The Army claimed that its intervention was in support of democracy since the government's actions in office had made it undemocratic.

On 4 July, the military swore in the Egypt's Chief Justice, Adly Mansour, as interim President and a panel of experts was set up to write a new constitution, since the military intervention amounted to a suspension of the existing document. Warrants for the arrest of senior members of the Muslim Brotherhood were subsequently issued. However, forming an interim government failed to be an easy task.

Following military intervention, supporters of the ousted President took to the streets to demand his re-instatement. This provoked a coercive response from the military and in one event in Cairo on 5 July 2013, the Army used tear gas, water cannons and blank rounds of ammunition against them. Almost 40 protesters were killed and 1,000 were injured in these clashes. In a subsequent clash in Cairo on 8 July, around 50 supporters of President Morsi were killed. Such violence provoked the Muslim Brotherhood to call for a popular uprising. In response, the interim President announced that new parliamentary elections would be held in early 2014 and also that a judicial investigation would be set up to examine the violence that took place in Cairo on 8 July 2013.

However, these announcements failed to appease Morsi's supporters, who rejected the timetable for the elections and continued to demonstrate in support of him. The head of the country's Armed Forces, Al Sisi, called for rallies across the country on 26 July 2013 to support the military's actions to confront terrorism and violence, to which the Muslim Brotherhood responded with a call for counter-rallies. The possibility that these actions might lead to a civil war prompted the military to set the Muslim Brotherhood a date of 27 July 2013 to sign up to the political reconciliation process. On 26 July, the government ordered the detention of former President Morsi for 15 days on the grounds that he had conspired with Hamas in prison break-outs that took place in 2011. In November 2013, he was placed on trial for inciting violence and complicity in the deaths of protesters following his ousting as President.

These actions failed to halt the violence between pro- and anti-Morsi demonstrators or between the Muslim Brotherhood and the state. Pro-Morsi supporters (who organised themselves into a National Coalition for Supporting Legitimacy) embarked upon the use of sit-in tactics (or protest vigils) in places that included the Rabaa al-Adawiya Mosque in Cairo. Attempts by the security forces to prevent protesters from expanding the site of their protest at this location resulted in over 70 protesters being shot dead on 27 July.

Violence further escalated in early August 2013 in which 'at least 278 people were killed nationwide, many of them in the assaults on the protest vigils' (Hendawi and Michael, 2013). Following the operation by the security forces on 17 August to clear the site of the al-Fath Mosque in Cairo from demonstrators who were sitting in support of President Morsi, thousands of Muslim Brotherhood supporters took to the streets across Egypt, defying a curfew that had been imposed as an aspect of the state of emergency that had been declared in the country. These protests continued, including calls (in defiance of the curfew) on 18 August by the Muslim Brotherhood for a week of nationwide marches and for a 'Friday of Martyrs' protest on 23 August to protest against the military intervention.

Violence has also been directed against Christian communities in

Egypt (the Copts or Coptic Church) during this violence: 'Human rights organizations have linked some attacks against Copts to partisans of the Muslim Brotherhood and other Islamist organizations. They have also reported that the military and police have often made a bad situation worse, by ignoring calls for help and letting the perpetrators rampage freely' (Brownlee, 2013). One example of this was the capture of the town of Dalga by Islamist hardliners in July 2013 following the ousting of President Morsi.

In addition to the use of coercive tactics against pro-Morsi supporters, the government also initiated actions against its leadership. This included the arrest of the Muslim Brotherhood's spiritual leader (Supreme Guide) in late August 2013 and also of a leading figure in the movement, Mohamed El-Beltagy. In early September, the government announced its intention to dissolve the Muslim Brotherhood as a non-governmental organisation. This action had been underpinned by the use of rhetoric by the government that associated the Muslim Brotherhood with extremism and terrorism. However, this failed to prevent demonstrations by Muslim Brotherhood supporters, including demonstrations across Egypt on 14 October 2013, where tear gas was deployed against students who were protesting against the military intervention at Cairo's al-Azhar University (the country's chief Islamic institution). Tear gas was also used against demonstrators at Cairo's Rebaca Mosque in November 2013.

Other countries became involved in the conflict within Egypt. In August, the Egyptian Consulate building in Bengazi, Libya was subject to a bomb attack and later that month Israel launched an attack on a military site in Lebanon following a cross-border exchange of fire. In late November, 2013, the Egyptian authorities expelled the Turkish Ambassador because of that country's opposition to the overthrow of President Morsi.

Despite the violence, the task of drawing up a new constitution proceeded. This task was completed towards the end of December 2013 and was placed before a referendum held on 14–15 January 2014. It was approved by 98.1 per cent of voters, although the turnout was below 40 per cent, the Muslim Brotherhood urging a boycott of the vote. However, violence still occurred, including four bomb blasts in Cairo on 24 January that were carried out by an al-Qaeda-inspired group.

In June 2014, the former Army chief who had overthrown Morsi in 2013, Field Marshall Abdel Fattah el-Sisi, was elected as President.

Libya

Following the fall of Colonel Gaddafi in 2011, the National Transition Council governed Libya. It has headed by Mahmoud Jibril and organised elections for the General National Congress, which was elected in July 2012. The transitional government handed over power to Congress in August 2012, which became the country's new Parliament. In October 2012, Congress elected Ali Zeidan as Prime Minister following the failure of its previous choice, Mustafa Abu Shagur, to form a government. He and his Cabinet took office in November 2012.

A key function of the General National Congress was to draft a new constitution. However, decisions relating to the composition of constitutional panels were only resolved in February 2013, thus delaying this task. One contentious key issue that required resolution was the role of Sharia law in the new governing arrangements of the country, an issue that had particular implications for the place of women in the new Libya. An additional issue was the balance of power in the new country, highlighting an East–West division between the oil-rich East, centred on Benghazi (from where the revolution began) and the traditional and the centre of power traditionally wielded by Tripoli in the west of the country: 'This means that many people in Benghazi want more rights and more power, and that the people in Tripoli are reluctant to accept decentralized government – causing tension within the country' (Momani, 2013).

Following the fall of Gaddafi, armed militias occupied an important place in Libyan affairs. Although some of these comprised radical Islamists who had links with al-Qaeda, they also had their own agendas, which included criminal motivations, and many members had been rebels who had fought in the civil war that toppled Gaddafi. The existence of these militia groups produced a significant degree of lawlessness in the country, including in the key cities of Tripoli and Benghazi, to which security forces were not able to effectively respond. This development was often underpinned by traditional tribal rivalries, which entailed attempts to secure control over the country's oil and gas industries.

It was thus observed that 'there are hundreds of local militias who use force to intimidate foreigners, citizens and government officials alike. These groups want to impose their ideology as well as control the economy and security' (Bitar, quoted in Mouterde, 2013). They were responsible for a number of violent acts.

The attack on the French Embassy in Tripoli in April 2013 was blamed on either militia loyal to Gaddafi or on Islamist forces that were angered by the French President François Hollande's decision to launch a military operation in Mali (Bitar, quoted in Mouterde, 2013). In May 2013, militias besieged the Libyan Ministries of Justice and Foreign Affairs to force Parliament to pass a law that banned officials from the Gaddafi era from holding political office. This situation has led to the conclusion that 'if Colonel Gaddafi had suppressed the opposition in March 2011, possibly hundreds of people would have died. Perhaps as many as 30,000 have died since, and the country is in a deep state of disorder and uncertainty' (Almond, 2013).

Further violence associated with militias included a wave of killings in July 2013, which included the assassination of a leading political figure, Abdul-Salam al-Mismari, in Benghazi, who was an outspoken critic of the Muslim Brotherhood. His death prompted counter-reactions that included an attack on the offices of the Muslim Brotherhood in Benghazi. Protesters who took to the streets demanded the dissolution of Muslim political parties.

A mass jail-break took place in Benghazi in July 2013 in which over 1,000 prisoners escaped. Although the precise cause of this event was uncertain, it was linked to similar jail-breaks in Iraq and Pakistan in which al-Qaeda had been involved and prompted Interpol to issue a global alert.

The death of soldiers at a checkpoint in Libya in October 2013 resulted in US Special Forces mounting an operation in Tripoli, which resulted in the capture of an al-Qaeda leader in Tripoli, Nazih Abdul-Hamed al-Ruqai (known as Anas al-Liby). He was linked to the 1998 bombings of American embassies in East Africa.

Subsequent violence in Tripoli that killed 40 people and injured 400 led to a state of emergency in the city being declared by the government on 17 November 2013. On 22 November, thousands of protesters took to the streets of Tripoli to demand that all militias left the city. Later in November, clashes occurred in Benghazi between the army and Salafists which led to a state of emergency being declared in the city. In January 2014, six Egyptians, including two diplomats, were kidnapped in Tripoli. They were released in return for Egypt releasing the Islamic militia commander, Shaaban Hadiya, who was the head of a militia called the Revolutionaries Operation Room.

The security situation led a senior military figure, Major General Khalifa Hafta, in February 2014 to call for the suspension of the General National Congress and the government of Prime Minister Ali Zeidan. He proposed the formation of a Presidential Commission to govern the country until new elections were held. This development entailed using the military to rescue the country from the chaos that it was facing.

Yemen

Since Abd Rabbuh Mansur Hadi took office, a number of problems hindered the pace of reform, giving rise of a perception of 'political stalemate' in the country (Alsarras, 2013). One of these was that the civil war gave al-Qaeda the opportunity to establish a number of strongholds in the Abyan province, which led to clashes between government forces and al-Qaeda for the control of towns in the region. The independence movement in the south of the country has also influenced events, causing the delay in the meeting of the National Dialogue assembly, which was originally planned for November 2012.

Much of the violence that has taken place has been associated with the Yemen-based AQAP (al-Qaeda in the Arabian Peninsula), whose strength substantially increased in the wake of the Arab Spring. A key concern in its quest for securing an increased degree of control in Yemen is to consolidate its strength amongst the tribes which are located in the peripheral areas of the country. Here the control wielded by the central government is weak and attempts to extend it by courting the favour of the sheikhs served to distance them from their tribes. By 'selectively delivering wealth to Yemen's sheikhs at the expense of their tribes' (Phillips, 2010: 5), sheikhs now often 'derive their wealth and status from the political center, rather than their traditional constituency in their local area' (Phillips, 2010: 7). This caused a power vacuum that AQAP has sought to exploit to its advantage.

One example of this new-found strength of AQAP was the seizure of the strategic town of Radaa in January 2012. Although the Yemeni Army launched a counter-offensive in May 2012, when it initiated a major offensive to regain control of Abyan, AQAP responded with actions of its own. This included one in early August 2013 which resulted in the country's security forces being placed on a state of high alert. America used drone flights in an attempt to attack and kill al-Qaeda militants. Although actions of this nature did succeed in killing such combatants, they continued mounting attacks, one of which (on 31 August 2013) targeted a convoy carrying Prime Minister Mohammed Salem Bassindwa (who survived the attack) in the Yemeni capital, Sana'a.

The violence associated with AQAP has been aggravated by attacks involving tribesmen with their own agendas that include the quest for compensation from central government. Attacks of this nature have included attacks on oil pipelines, such as an attack mounted on the country's main export pipeline east of Sana'a on 30 November 2013, which is a key source of its revenue. Intertribal rivalries have also formed the basis of violent conflicts, including the clash in February 2014 between Shi'ite and Sunni tribesman over land in northwest Yemen, which killed over 60 people.

Syria

The war in Syria exhibited the tensions between Shi'ite and Sunni Muslims, and the involvement of groups associated with both factions in the war in Syria could have repercussions in a number of other countries in the region in which similar sectarian divisions were exhibited. The Sunni-led Syrian opposition was aided by the al-Qaeda-linked Nusra Front (Jabhat al-Nusra), whose aim is the creation of an Islamic state in Syria and whose activities included suicide bombing attacks in Damascus in 2011–12. The Shi'a Islamic militant organisation, Hezbollah, entered the war on the side of the Syrian government. This organisation (which had been founded following the Israeli invasion of Lebanon in 1982) was funded by Syria and Iran, and its anti-Israeli stance posed a further threat to stability in the region.

This issue became acute when, on 30 January 2013, air strikes by the Israeli Army took place inside Syria, targeting weapons convoys that were believed by the Israelis to be carrying sophisticated anti-aircraft missiles from Syria to Lebanon, where they could be deployed against Israel. Further air strikes by Israel against Syria took place in early May, targeting weapons and a military research centre in Damascus.

In May, the United Nations (UN) General Assembly supported a declaration that condemned the Syrian government's escalation of the war and supported the involvement of the opposition Syrian National Council in transition talks (General Assembly of the United Nations, 2013). A key issue was the use of chemical weapons by the Syrian regime against opposition forces and international concern was provoked by their alleged use near Damascus on 20 August 2013, in which a large number of people (perhaps as many as 1500, although the figure is disputed) were killed. This incident raised the possibility of an invasion involving Member States of the European Union and America, although on 29 August 2013, the House of Commons in the UK voted against this course of action, despite the government favouring it.

Ultimately a deal between America and Russia (the latter supporting the Syrian regime and insisting that if chemical weapons were used, it was by opposition forces) was concluded that avoided invasion. This entailed Syria agreeing to hand over all of its chemical weapons and to engage in peace talks (termed Geneva II) with rebel forces. Russia warned President Assad in September 2013 that he might lose their support if he reneged on the commitments he had agreed to.

However, negotiating a ceasefire proved hard to accomplish and in the absence of this, the refugee crisis worsened, the UN Refugee Agency stating in early September 2013 that around two million people from Syria were refugees and many more had been displaced because of the fighting; moreover, as the violence continued, it became more complex than a simple rebel versus government conflict. Both sides to the conflict were supported by jihadist militias. In addition to contributing towards the scale of existing violence, these groups had their own agendas, which served to further escalate the level of violence.

Clashes occurred between opposition forces and jihadist group fighters who supported the Syrian government, one example of this being in September 2013 around the town of Azaz. In January 2014, pro-government jihadist groups were accused of executing rebel fighters. However, opposition forces were also supported by jihadist groups whose violence extended beyond the attacking government forces to attacking Christian communities. One example of this was the capture of the Christian town of Maaloula in December 2013 by opposition forces, which included the jihadist al-Nusra Front. Their antagonism towards Christians derived from their belief that they were sympathetic to the Assad regime. Further, the involvement of Israel added to the complexity of the situation, one example of this being an air strike that was launched inside Syria on 1 November 2013 that targeted missiles destined for Hezbollah.

Against the background of this violence, progress in arranging the peace talks stalled, opposition groups being concerned that their involvement might result in the undoing of the revolution. Thus, initially, key opposition groups insisted that their participation was dependent on a timeframe being drawn up for Assad's departure from office, a demand that was subsequently endorsed by the Syrian National Coalition in November 2013, which insisted that Assad had to step down before talks could commence. These were demands that the Assad regime would not contemplate and in the meantime it continued its military campaign against areas occupied by opposition forces, allegedly using barrel bombs in Aleppo towards the end of December 2013.

The Geneva II peace talks eventually began on 24 January 2014, but the inability to find a compromise between the demands of the Syrian National Coalition for the formation of a transitional government without Assad and the government's unwillingness to accept such as pre-condition for talks meant that virtually no progress had been made by the end of February 2014. In the meantime, violence in Syria continued and the regime missed deadlines that had been set for the removal of its store of chemical weapons.

In June 2014, President Assad was elected for a third term in office. His victory was dismissed by US Secretary of State John Kerry as 'a great big zero' (Kerry, 2014).

Algeria

Algeria did not experience a regime change in connection with the Arab Spring protests elsewhere in the region. However, political stability in Algeria is threatened by unemployment. Unemployment affects around 22 per cent of those aged under 35 and gave rise to protests in 2013 in Ouargla, where the unemployed demanded jobs and the end to lawsuits against them (*Middle East Online*, 2013). Demonstrations and strikes for better working conditions by teachers, doctors, students and postal workers have also taken place, with political corruption being raised as a key concern (Cunningham, 2013).

Nonetheless, it has been argued that 'it is hard to see any future for the Islamist parties in Algeria after the decade of violence that followed the 1992 elections. For most Algerians, Islamists are associated with violence and radicalism. The tensions between Islamists and other political groups in Tunisia and Egypt are reinforcing that view' (Archy, 2012).

However, some disorder did take place, including ethnic clashes between Arabs and Tuaregs in Bordj Badji-Mokhtar (situated on Algeria's border with Mali) in August 2013. The former group is Islamist and the latter is separatist. These events were associated with al-Qaeda-inspired unrest in the Sahel region.

In November 2013, the National Liberation Front nominated the incumbent President, Abdelaziz Bouteflika, as its candidate for the presidency in the elections to be held in April 2014. The Islamist Movement of Society for Peace and Islamic Renaissance Movement boycotted the election, in which President Bouteflika was returned for a fourth term in office.

See also: Arab Spring, Islamist terrorist groups, terrorism

Sources and further reading

Almond, M. (2013) 'Life for Most Libyans is Worse than it was Under Gaddafi', *Russia Today*, 11 May, http://rt.com/op-edge/withdraw-staff-libya-gaddafi-158 (date accessed 6 May 2014).

Alsarras, N. (2013) 'Yemen and the Arab Spring: Revolution on Hold', *Qantarra. de*, 26 February, http://en.qantara.de/Revolution-on-Hold/20726c502/index.html (date accessed 6 May 2014).

Archy, L. (2012) 'Algeria Avoids the Arab Spring?', *Carnegie Endowment*, http://carnegieendowment.org/2012/05/31/algeria-avoids-arab-spring/b0xu (date accessed 6 May 2014).

BBC News (2013) 'Tunisia Holds Four over Chokri Belaid Killing', 26 February, www.bbc.co.uk/news/world-middle-east-21592419 (date accessed 6 May 2014).

Brownlee, J. (2013) 'Violence Against Copts in Egypt', *Carnegie Endowment for International Peace*, http://egyptelections.carnegieendowment.org/2013/11/14/violence-against-copts-in-egypt (date accessed 6 May 2014).

Cunningham, E. (2013) 'Protests Mount in Algeria', *Global Post*, www.globalpost.com/dispatch/news/regions/africa/130313/algeria-protests-arab-spring-strikes (date accessed 6 May 2014).

FIDH (2012) *Women and the Arab Spring: Taking their Place?*, www.europarl.europa.eu/document/activities/cont/201206/20120608ATT46510/20120608ATT46510EN.pdf (date accessed 6 May 2014).

General Assembly of the United Nations (2013) 'General Assembly Adopts Text Condemning Violence in Syria, Demanding that All Sides End hostilities', General Assembly GA/11372, www.un.org/News/Press/docs//2013/ga11372.doc.htm (date accessed 6 May 2014).

Hendawi, H. and Michael, M. (2013) 'Egypt Declares Month-Long State of Emergency, Puts Curfew on Cairo', *Global News*, http://globalnews.ca/news/779203/egypt-declares-month-long-state-of-emergency-amid-clashes (date accessed 6 May 2014).

Kerry, J. (2014) 'Bashar Assad Claims Landslide Election Win in Syria', CTV News, www.ctvnews.ca/world/bashar-assad-claims-landslide-election-win-in-syria-1.1852856 (date accessed 6 June 2014).

Middle East Online (2013) '"Arab Spring" Winds Blow on Algeria from Desert', www.middle-east-online.com/english/?id=57536 (date accessed 6 May 2014).

Momani, B. (2013) 'Libya Since Gaddafi – Where Has it Been, Where Will it Go?', *CIGI*, 13 March, www.cigionline.org/articles/2013/03/libya-gaddafi-% (date accessed 6 May 2014).

Mouterde, P. (2013) 'France Seeks Answers after Libya Embassy Attack', *France 24*

International News, 24 April, www.france 24.com/en/20130424-france-tripoli-embassy-bombing-islamists-militia (date accessed 6 May 2014).

Phillips, S. (2010) 'What Comes Next in Yemen? Al-Qaeda, the Tribes and State Building', *Carnegie Endowment for International Peace*, Carnegie Paper 107, http://carnegieendowment.org/files/yemen_tribes.pdf (date accessed 6 May 2014).

PROTEST LIAISON OFFICERS (ENGLAND AND WALES)

In 2009, two reports by Her Majesty's Inspectorate of Constabulary into the G20 protests in London highlighted the need for police commanders and those engaged in policing protest to engage in more effective communication with the protestors, the public and the media. The second of these reports gave two case studies of how police agencies from Sweden and Northern Ireland had adopted different models of communication.

The Irish model involves constant dialogue by the Police Service of Northern Ireland (PSNI) with parade organisers from the earliest stages through to the conclusion of the event and is described as a 'no surprises' approach. The report suggested that the PSNI now puts great emphasis upon individual officers' understanding of their own behaviour and actions upon crowd behaviour during marches and protests. The Swedish approach, known as 'Dialogue Police', also focuses upon improving communication between individual police officers and protest groups, and grew out of concerns raised by the public after the protests at the European Union (EU) summit in Gothenburg in 2001.

The Dialogue Police tactic is unusual as it involves deploying police officers into the actual crowd as opposed to being behind a cordon and separate from the demonstrators. These officers, who are deployed in standard day uniform without riot equipment, are there to undertake a 'community policing' role within the crowd. They act as a direct communication link between those in the crowd and the police commander, facilitating legitimate requests but also trying to avoid over-zealous police reactions to events. The dialogue officers' core functions are defined as: negotiation, mediation, initiation, communication and sensing. The function of 'initiation' is about problem solving and seeking to avoid confrontation, whilst 'sensing' is about assessing the threat from a crowd, but also reading the mood of the crowd and how it changes.

The approach has been deployed at a number of events in Sweden since 2001, including animal rights protests, right-wing demonstrations and football matches, and has been seen as a major reason why conflict between police and demonstrators has reduced. However, it is a somewhat controversial tactic as it is treated with suspicion by some police colleagues, who saw the officers as being soft or going native, and the protestors, who saw such officers as sneaky intelligence gatherers. Regular officers and commanders are also nervous about being deployed into large crowds in ones and twos without the usual protective riot equipment.

This approach has now been adopted in the UK through the deployment at many events of Protest Liaison Officers, who seek to engage with organisers, understand the mood of the crowd and, much like their Swedish colleagues, attempt to provide a direct means of communication. Understanding groups and changes within the crowd was not something that was within UK police training until recent years; up until 2008, the public order training curriculum for officers in England and Wales was based upon a classical view of the crowd as espoused by Gustave Le Bon in 1895. This approach suggested that members of a crowd lost their individuality once in a crowd and were affected by a group mindset, in effect becoming a 'mad mob'. It was suggested that this approach led directly to the police using indiscriminate tactics against protestors – in particular, where small pockets of violence had occurred, the police would react without discriminating, treating all those present as the same. One example of this would have been the containment or 'kettling' of protestors at the 2001 May Day protests. It is argued that such an approach not only risks civil action against the police but also undermines their legitimacy both at and after the event. It can also draw people into conflict with the police who had no prior intention of engaging in disorder.

Understanding crowd psychology and the utilisation of academic models such as the Elaborated Social Identity Model (Reicher et al., 2004; Stott, 2009) is now more commonplace in UK policing. These approaches encourage the police to take a more graded, flexible and preventative approach to dealing with public order and protests, and advocate a move away from the reactive riot control response. These approaches have now been incorporated into the UK police public order manual *Keeping the Peace* (National Police Improvement Agency, 2010), with a section on crowd behaviour and the factors that should be considered in developing a crowd engagement plan. Whilst there is no specific instruction on the development of Protest Liaison Officers, many forces have now adopted this approach. The role was first successfully used in the policing of the Liberal Democrat Conference in March 2011. Police and organisers had concerns over the scale and intention of demonstrations scheduled to take place over tuition fee rises and educational maintenance grant cuts that had been agreed by the Coalition government. There were specific concerns over the security of the Party leader and Deputy Prime Minister, Nick Clegg, who was the focus of many of the protests and in whose constituency the conference was taking place. South Yorkshire Police employed Protest Liaison Officers for the first time, deploying police officers in normal day uniform with blue tabards emblazoned with the words 'Liaison Officer'. On a number of occasions, the Officers were able to feed back information from the crowd that might otherwise have resulted in over-zealous police action, so they were able to much better interpret the actions and motive of the crowd and correct police assumptions about crowd intentions. Both police commanders and organisers hailed the approach as a success.

The development of Protest Liaison Officers is part of a wider attempt by UK policing to engage more with crowds and protesters, and is part of other innovative attempts to communicate and facilitate democratic policing not just during the event but throughout the year. Whether they will be accepted by protestors or the police themselves is yet to be seen: of the 30 approved tactics contained within the police public order manual, there is no mention of the use of Protest Liaison Officers.

See also: English Defence League, G20 protests (London) 2011, kettling, public order policing (England and Wales), riots

Sources and further reading

Her Majesty's Inspectorate of Constabulary. (2009a) *Adapting to Protest*. London: HMIC. Available at: www.hmic.gov.uk/media/adapting-to-protest-20090705.pdf (date accessed 6 May 2014).

——. (2009b) *Adapting to Protest: Nuturing the British Model of Policing*. London: HMIC. Available at: www.hmic.gov.uk/media/adapting-to-protest-nurturing-the-british-model-of-policing-20091125.pdf (date accessed 6 May 2014).

Le Bon, G. (1926 [1895]) *The Crowd: A Study of the Popular Mind*. London. Unwin.

National Police Improvement Agency. (2010) *Keeping the Peace*. London NPIA.

Reicher, S., Stott, C., Cronin, P. and Adang, O. (2004) 'An Integrated Approach to Crowd Psychology and Public Order Policing'. *Policing*, 27(4): 558–72.

Stott, C. (2009) 'Crowd Psychology and Public Order Policing: An Overview of Scientific Theory and Evidence'. Unpublished, University of Liverpool, http://content.yudu.com/Library/A1vpaw/HMCICSubmissionCrowd/resources/index.htm?referrerUrl= (date accessed 7 June 2014).

PROTEST SONGS

A protest song is a form of counter-culture protest that seeks to promote a cause or to highlight a social injustice and act as a mechanism for change. It may be defined as 'songs whose lyrics convey a message which is opposed to a policy or course of action adopted by an authority or by society as an institution (e.g. discrimination)' (Haynes, 2008).

Protest songs are not associated with any particular type of music and have embraced genres including folk, blues, soul, punk rock and reggae. A particular advantage of using the medium of music to deliver a message of protest is that it will reach audiences who may not otherwise be politically informed, especially young people. Its advantage over other forms of political protest has been stated to be that: 'A pamphlet, no matter how good, is never read more than once. But a song is learned by heart and repeated over and over' (Hill, quoted in Cousins, 2007).

A wide range of concerns have formed the basis of protest songs. In America the civil rights cause used music as a form of protest in the 1960s. Bob Dylan was a key figure in the protest music of this period and he and Joan Baez were prominent civil rights activists who often sang together at rallies.

Protest music was also associated with the anti-Vietnam War movement. Songs associated with this protest included 'The Unknown Soldier' by the Doors in 1968 and Arlo Guthrie's satirical criticism of the draft in 'Alice's Restaurant Massacree' released in 1967. This recounts the tale of a young man with a conviction for littering (and creating a nuisance) being asked whether he had been rehabilitated, which brought the response: '"Sargeant, you got a lot a damn gall to ask me if I've rehabilitated myself ... Cause you want to know if I'm moral enough join the army, burn women, kids, houses and villages after being a litterbug." He looked at me and said, "Kid, we don't like your kind..."' (Guthrie, 1967).

Edwin Starr's version of 'War' ('What is it good for? Absolutely nothing'), released in 1970, also expressed opposition to the war in Vietnam. The escalation of the Vietnam War in the 1970s produced further protest songs that included 'It Better End Soon' by Chicago in 1970 and 'Ohio' by Crosby, Stills, Nash and Young in 1970. This held President Richard Nixon to be responsible for the fatal shootings of four students involved in an anti-Vietnam War protest at Kent University by the National Guard in 1970.

Pete Seeger was also involved in civil rights and anti-Vietnam War protests: his adaption of 'We Shall Overcome' in 1963 (which was also sung by other singers' including Joan Baez) subsequently became an anthem for civil rights movements across the world.

In more recent years in America, protest songs have been performed to raise awareness of a very wide range of issues such as feminism, Helen Reddy's 'I am Woman' in 1972 being an important example of this. Women's issues also formed the agenda of protest songs later and included Ani DiFranco's 'Lost Woman Song' in 1990, which argued that abortion was a woman's right to choose. The wars waged by America in Afghanistan and Iraq in more recent years have also inspired protest songs such as Neil Young's 'Let's Impeach the President' in 2006.

Outside of America, protest songs have been used to raise awareness of a range of issues, both internal and domestic. Opposition to the apartheid regime in South Africa and the call to free the political prisoner Nelson Mandela were voiced in protest songs that included the Special AKA's 'Nelson Mandela' in 1984. This cause was also endorsed by the popular British television programme

Spitting Image in a song released in 1986 entitled '(I've Never Met) A Nice South African', the chorus of which proclaimed 'he's never met a nice South African, and that's not bloody surprising, man. 'Cos we're a bunch of ignorant bastards who hate black people' (Lloyd, 1986). Although this was unfair to those white South Africans who opposed apartheid in their own country, it did reflect the negative views felt throughout much of the world to this form of state-sponsored injustice and oppression.

The Cold War and the dangers posed to the planet by the threat of nuclear war were raised by the British group Frankie Goes to Hollywood in their song 'Two Tribes', which was released in 1984. Although not intended for this purpose, this song was also appropriate to describe the battles between the police and miners during the 1984/5 miners' dispute. The oppression of black people was raised in protest songs performed worldwide by the Jamaican group Bob Marley and the Wailers. One of these included 'Get Up, Stand Up' in 1973, whose inclusion in the group's Exodus Tour of Britain in 1977 contributed to the radicalising of black youth and to the outbreak of riots in Brixton in 1981. The British monarchy was also the subject of a protest song, 'God Save the Queen', by the Sex Pistols, which was released to coincide with the Silver Jubilee celebrations in 1977. Gay rights were also the subject of protest songs, including 'Glad to Be Gay' by the Tom Robinson Band in 1978, which was fiercely critical of the negative attitudes society displayed towards gay people even though homosexual acts had been decriminalised by the Sexual Offences Acts 1967.

The wide range of technology (especially the Internet) that has become available to disseminate protest songs may overcome state censorship of the reporting of other forms of protest. However, the ability of protest songs to influence public opinion and stimulate debate about the issues they raise can be thwarted by various forms of state intervention.

In connection with the Sex Pistols 1977 song: 'It was widely rumoured (with no supporting evidence) that the BBC tampered with the charts, so that the Pistols protest stalled at number 2, and Rod Stewart was allowed to soundtrack the Queen's celebrations with ... I Don't Want To Talk About It' (McCormick, 2013). Similarly, the BBC's Top 40 programme banned the Tom Robinson Band's 'Glad to Be Gay' in 1978 and in 2013 also refused to play the full version of a clip from a song 'Ding-Dong! The Witch is Dead'. This was taken from the 1930s version of the film *The Wizard of Oz* and was propelled into the charts by a campaign mounted on Facebook, which wished to use it as a protest song following the death of the former Conservative Prime Minister, Margaret Thatcher.

In other countries, protest delivered through the medium of music is treated harshly. Some members of the Russian punk rock group Pussy

Riot received prison sentences for their attack on the government of President Vladimir Putin and the links between the Russian Orthodox Church and the state, which was delivered in a protest at Moscow's Christ the Saviour Cathedral in 2012.

See also: counterculture protest, Pussy Riot protest (Moscow) 2012

Sources and further reading

Cousins, A. (2007) 'Can Protest Music Influence Social Change?' *Inside Time*, www.insidetime.org/articleview.asp?a=87 (date accessed 6 May 2014).

Guthrie, A. (1967) 'Alice's Restaurant' Massacree. Released on the Reprise Label, produced by F. Hellerman.

Haynes, L. (2008) 'From Vietnam to Iraq: A Content Analysis of Protest Music', www.academia.edu/218303/From_Vietnam_to_Iraq_A_Content_Analysis_of_Protest_Music (date accessed 6 May 2014).

Kutschke, B. and Norton, B. (2013) *Music and Protest in 1968*. Cambridge University Press.

Lloyd, J. (1986) Writer of the lyrics to '(I've Never Met) A Nice South African'. Released on the Virgin Label, produced by P. Brewis.

McCormick, N. (2013) 'Ding Dong The Witch is Dead: Why the BBC Shouldn't Play it', *Daily Telegraph*, 11 April, www.telegraph.co.uk/culture/music/rockandpopmusic/9986928/Ding-Dong-The-Witch-Is-Dead-why-the-BBC-shouldnt-play-it.html (date accessed 6 May 2014).

PROVISIONAL IRA

The Provisional Irish Republican Army (PIRA) waged campaigns of violence in Northern Ireland, mainland Britain and sometimes elsewhere in Europe in order to advance its aims of the reunification of Ireland, which had been partitioned in 1921 following a war of independence that had been waged by this group.

Partition provided 26 of Ireland's counties with self-government in a state initially named the Irish Free State and now called the Irish Republic. The remaining six counties constituted the state of Northern Ireland (sometimes referred to as Ulster), which was given considerable powers of self-government, but retained its link with the UK government and sent Members of Parliament to the UK House of Commons.

The rationale for partition was that a large number of people living in these six counties did not want to be part of an independent Ireland. These were derived from settlers who had left England and Scotland during what was termed the 'Plantation Period' in the sixteenth and seventeenth centuries. Their political stance was that of Loyalism and their religion was Protestantism. Their culture and religion sharply differentiated them from the remainder of the population of Ireland, who were Nationalist in politics (the term 'Republican' is applied to those Nationalists who wished to use violence to free their country from British rule) and Catholic in religion.

In 1913, the Loyalists established a paramilitary army, the Ulster Volunteer Force, to resist by the use of force the imposition of home rule upon them. The desire to avoid a civil war led the UK government to abandon the grant of home rule that was contained in the Government of Ireland Act 1914. However, prompted by the 1919–21 War of Independence waged against the British presence in Ireland by the Irish Republican Army (IRA), the British government introduced partition in the Government of Ireland Act 1920. This came into force in 1921 after being confirmed by the 1921 Anglo-Irish Treaty signed between the British government and the lower House of the Irish Free State Parliament, the Dáil Éireann.

The partition of Ireland was never accepted by Nationalists, who wished to scrap this arrangement and replace it with a totally free and independent nation embracing all 32 of Ireland's counties. One way in which they sought to achieve this objective was through violence. As the 1916 Easter Rising had demonstrated to Nationalists the futility of seeking to wage a conventional war to achieve their objectives, the violence subsequently carried out by the IRA embraced tactics associated with terrorism. These included the border campaigns of the 1950s, consisting of raids on customs posts and British military barracks in Northern Ireland to acquire arms.

During the course of the 1960s, divisions appeared within the IRA over the tactics that should be used to secure the goal of a reunified Ireland. The Dublin-based leadership of the IRA moved towards a more conventional political route that was underpinned by Marxism and that viewed the unification of the working class throughout Ireland as a key objective. This led it to spurn the use of violence, which was officially abandoned on 26 February 1962 (Kennedy-Pipe, 1997: 43).

The main rationale of the Northern Irish state was to serve the interests of the Loyalist/Protestant population. This led to the adoption of discriminatory practices towards the Nationalist/Catholic population in key areas such as employment, housing, education and politics, where the practice of gerrymandering served to marginalise the Nationalist population even in areas such as Derry where they were in the majority. However, the American civil rights movement inspired a campaign for equal rights to be mounted. Episodes associated with this campaign (such as Burntollet Bridge in 1969) led to severe disorder from Loyalists unwilling to cede any ground to Nationalists. The tensions that these disturbances created resulted in spontaneous outbreaks of sectarian violence across Northern Ireland, and the inability of the police (the Royal Ulster Constabulary (RUC)) to contain the disorders led the British government to deploy troops in a policing role in 1969.

The events that had taken place in the 1960s had largely bypassed the IRA, whose swing towards conventional politics meant that the military line associated with Republicanism had been neglected. It was a cause of extreme embarrassment to many of its members that they were unable to protect Nationalist communities subjected to sectarian violence by Protestant mobs and that the only meaningful form of protection was afforded by soldiers of the British Army in 1969.

This resulted in the IRA splitting into the official and provisional wings, an initiative that began in Belfast in August 1969 and was completed by the end of the year with the formation of the Provisional Army Council in December 1969 following the IRA Army Convention in Boyle, County Roscommon. The political wing of the IRA, Sinn Féin, split along similar lines in January 1970. In 1972, the official IRA declared a ceasefire, following which the PIRA tended to abandon the prefix 'provisional' and referred to itself simply as the IRA.

The PIRA endorsed the use of violence to attain its objective of the reunification of Ireland, although it viewed itself as a guerrilla movement and not as a terrorist organisation. The initial objective of its actions was defensive: to protect Nationalist communities from Loyalist attack during the Protestant 'marching season'. The first main armed action conducted by the PIRA was carried in June 1970 to defend the Nationalist minority living in the Short Strand district of Belfast. This resulted in the deaths of three people and the action was known as the Battle of St Matthews.

This event brought them in conflict with the Loyalist government, the RUC and ultimately with the British Army (whose actions were controlled by Northern Ireland's Minister of Home Affairs). A key turning point in the relationship between the British Army and Nationalist communities was the curfew imposed on the Lower Falls area of Belfast in July 1970 by the Army, which included house-to-house searches looking for weapons. By the early 1970s, the British Army was no longer viewed as the defender of Nationalist communities and was instead viewed as an occupying army whose presence needed to be removed in order to achieve Irish reunification. Actions with which the Army was involved (especially Bloody Sunday in 1972) helped to popularise within Nationalist communities the PIRA's campaign of violence, which now assumed an offensive direction. The period of violence lasted from 1969 until 1998 and is usually referred to as 'the Troubles'.

The PIRA had a hierarchical structure. It was headed by the IRA Army Council and key decisions were made by the IRA General Army Conventions. However, these met very infrequently during the Troubles. The movement was divided into a Northern and Southern Command, the latter based in the Irish Republic. Below these were battalions, brigades and companies into which members, termed 'volunteers' (or óglaigh), were recruited. During the course of the Troubles, organisational changes occurred within the PIRA, the main one being the abandonment of battalions in most areas and the introduction of active service units (ASUs) organised around a cell structure that was responsible for the majority of attacks. Volunteers (at company level) who were not active in ASUs were primarily involved in other tasks, including the policing of Nationalist areas. This latter activity led to the PIRA being associated with various forms of vigilante action that included punishment beatings, knee-capping and executions. The PIRA was also accused of involvement in various forms of criminal activity, including the 2004 raid at the Northern Bank in Belfast.

The campaign of the PIRA was that of a war of attrition (sometimes referred to as the 'Long War'). It consisted of acts of violence that took numerous forms, including the terrorist tactics of indiscriminate and selective violence, the latter directed at targets such as soldiers, police officers and politicians. This violence was sporadic, although was sometimes (as in 1992) conducted intensively.

In Northern Ireland, indiscriminate attacks included a bomb attack on the Abercorn Restaurant in Belfast in March 1972 (which killed two people and injured around 130) and what was termed 'Bloody Friday' on 21 July 1972, when over 20 bombs were exploded across Belfast, killing three people and injuring 130. In 1978, an incendiary bomb planted at the La Mon restaurant killed 12 people and in November almost 40 were injured in a series of bomb attacks that were detonated in a number of cities, including Belfast, Derry, Cookstown and Enniskillen. A further series of attacks of this nature occurred in March 1979 and April 1980. A bomb planted at a Remembrance Day service at Enniskillen, County Fermanagh, in November 1987 resulted in the deaths of 11 people and injured over 60. In July 1993, a bomb caused widespread damage to the centre of Newtownards, County Down.

Selective violence included attacks directed at members of the security forces. These included the killing of five soldiers at Omagh in May 1973 and four near Forkhill, County Armagh in July 1975. On 27 August 1979, 18 soldiers were killed (and six were seriously injured) by two roadside bombs at Warrenpoint (an event also termed the Narrow Water ambush). A landmine was used in December 1979 that killed a further four soldiers. In June 1988, six soldiers were killed by a bomb that had been planted on their minibus and a further eight soldiers were killed and 28 injured by an IRA roadside bomb near Ballygawley, County Tyrone.

In October 1990, a new tactic was introduced in selective violence against the Army – that of proxy bombing. This involved kidnapping civilians who were forced to drive through army checkpoints in cars loaded with explosives, which were detonated by remote control. In October 1990, the driver and five soldiers were killed at Coshquin and another soldier was killed in a similar attack at Killean. This tactic was repeated in February 1991 in an attack launched at the Ulster Defence Regiment (UDR) base at Magherafelt, which caused extensive damage to the base and adjacent properties. A UDR target (Glenanne Barracks) was also attacked in May 1991, killing three soldiers and injuring a further ten.

Attacks were also mounted against individuals working on military installations. One example of this occurred in January 1992 when a roadside bomb planted at Teebane targeted construction workers (one of whom was a soldier) returning from Lisanelly Barracks in Omagh, County Tyrone. Eight people were killed in this attack. In May 1992, a bomb attack on an Army checkpoint in South Armagh killed one soldier and injured 23. The bomb was placed in a van that had been modified to run on railway tracks. In October 1996, two car bombs exploded outside the British Army headquarters in Thiepval Barracks, Lisburn. One soldier was killed and 31 were injured in this attack.

Attacks against members of the RUC included the killing of four officers at Bessbrook, County Armagh by a van bomb in April 1979. In 1985, a number of attacks were mounted against the RUC, including a mortar attack on Newry Police Station, Armagh, which killed nine officers and injured 37, and an assault on the RUC barracks at Ballygawley, County Tyrone, which killed two officers and destroyed the barracks. Other selective targets included the bombing of the Northern Ireland Forensic Science Laboratory in South Belfast in September 1992, which completely destroyed the facility.

Targeted violence was also directed at non-military personnel. These attacks included the car-bomb assassination of the British Ambassador to Ireland, Christopher Ewart-Biggs, and his secretary in Dublin in July 1976. Some targeted attacks were also sectarian in nature, directed at members of the Loyalist community. This included a bomb planted in Coleraine in June 1973 that killed six Loyalist civilians.

The IRA was not the only Republican group using selective violence. Another was the Irish National Liberation Army (INLA), which has been described as 'probably the most ruthless of all paramilitary organisations in the province' (Wichert, 1991: 171). Its actions included the assassinations in 1979 of Earl Mountbatten of Burma off the coast of Sligo, Ireland, in 1979 and the Conservative MP and the Party's Northern Ireland spokesman, Airey Neave, at the House of Commons. In December 1982, a bomb planted in the Droppin Well Bar, Ballykelly, County Londonderry killed 11 soldiers and six civilians.

In addition, Loyalist paramilitary groups such as the Ulster Protestant Volunteers and the Ulster Volunteer Force also carried out acts of violence in Northern Ireland. These included the bombings in Dublin and Monaghan in the Irish Republic in May 1974, which killed 33 people including a pregnant woman. In March 1999, a booby-trap car bomb planted by the Loyalist group the Red Hand Defenders killed the solicitor Rosemary Nelson, who had represented Nationalist residents engaged in the dispute related to the Orange Order's desire to parade at Drumcree.

One difficulty faced by the IRA was that a campaign of violence waged solely in Northern Ireland might be disregarded by British politicians as it was not on their 'doorstep'. It was reported that in 1972, the Home Secretary William Whitelaw informed a meeting of ministers and a delegation from the PIRA that 'we can accept the casualties ... we probably lose as many soldiers in accidents in Germany'. This attitude was asserted to have been 'a major factor in the IRA's decision to have a bombing campaign in England – where casualties would not be "acceptable"' (Coogan, 1980: 492).

The mainland campaign began in February 1972 when a bomb was planted at Aldershot, and the following month a car bomb exploded outside the Old Bailey in London, causing extensive damage. Such attacks were carried out intermittently in subsequent years. A wide range of tactics were subsequently used, which included indiscriminate and selective violence, targeting prestige and 'soft' targets, that were carried out using a variety of weapons such as car bombs and incendiary devices.

Selective terrorism was directed at members of the security forces and leading politicians. These attacks included the M62 coach bombing in February 1974 (which killed nine soldiers, a mother and her two children) and bombs in London's Hyde Park and Regent's Park in July 1982, which killed 11 soldiers, seven horses and injured a large number of spectators. A further attack at the Royal Marine School of Music at Deal Barracks, Kent in September 1989 resulted in the deaths of ten Royal Marine Bandsmen and injured over 30.

Attacks on politicians and others who were supportive of government policy in Northern Ireland included the assassinations of Ross McWhirter in 1974 (who had sponsored a reward scheme for the apprehension of those involved in terrorism). An attack was also directed at the Grand Hotel in Brighton, which was housing a number of leading Conservative politicians, including the Prime Minister Margaret Thatcher, who were attending the October 1984 Party Conference. This resulted in the deaths of five people. In 1990, another Conservative MP, Ian Gow, was killed by an act of selective violence arising from a bomb planted under his car.

Indiscriminate violence carried out on mainland Britain included the attacks on the Houses of Parliament in June 1974, the planting of a bomb at the Tower of London in July 1974 (which injured 41 children and killed one person) and the bombings of public houses in Guildford in October and Birmingham in November, which caused extensive damage and loss of life. In Birmingham, 21 people were killed and 182 were injured and this prompted the government to introduce the Prevention of Terrorism (Temporary Provisions) Act 1974, which gave the security forces enhanced powers with which to deal with terrorism.

This measure did not, however, succeed in preventing terrorist attacks, one occurring the following year at London's Hilton Hotel, which killed two people and injured over 60. In December 1983, three police officers and three members of the public were killed by a car bomb outside the Harrods store in London and 90 others were injured. Attacks occurred in 1992 at the *Sussex* public house in London, in a shopping centre at Wood Green, London and also in Manchester, where two bombs injured over 60 people. In February 1993, two bombs were placed at a London Underground station and on a train in Kent, and in March 1993, explosions in Warrington city centre killed two children and injured 56 other people.

Part of the IRA's mainland bombing campaign was directed at disrupting the commercial and social life of major cities, and included attacks mounted in the West End of London in 1974–5 and the City of London in the 1990s. This began with the bombing of the Stock Exchange in 1990 and included attacks on the Baltic Exchange (which killed three people and caused over £800 million of damage) in April 1992 and the Hong Kong and Shanghai Bank in Bishopsgate, London in 1993. A 17-month ceasefire to enable political initiatives to be considered was broken on 9 February 1996 when a bomb was exploded in London's Docklands, killing two people. In June 1996, Manchester city centre was bombed, causing widespread devastation and damage that was estimated to amount to £1 billion. Over 200 people were injured in this attack.

Some of the attacks on mainland Britain that were mounted by Northern Irish Republican groups were primarily in the nature of public relations exercises that sought to demonstrate their capacity to strike when and where they wished and to highlight that, despite innovations in security policy, the public remained vulnerable to acts of violence. Examples of such attacks included the shelling by a homemade mortar into the garden of the Prime Minister's residence at 10 Downing Street in 1991, the planting of a bomb near Downing Street in January 1992 and a series of attacks directed at London's Heathrow Airport in March 1994.

The campaigns of violence waged by the PIRA sought to bomb its way onto the conference table and to achieve this end, these were punctuated by ceasefires (such as that in 1975–6, 1994–6 and 1997–8) to enable political dialogue to take place.

Furthermore, the PIRA had a political wing, Sinn Féin, that operated openly and contested elections through which the support for the

PIRA might be gauged as an added weight on advancing its political objectives. Conventional electoral politics assumed a greater role in Republican circles following the election of the hunger striker Bobby Sands as MP for Fermanagh and South Tyrone in April 1981 and led to the adoption of an approach that was termed 'the armalite and the ballot box' (also referred to as the 'Tactical Use of Armed Struggle' (TUAS)). This term was coined by Sinn Féin organiser Danny Morrison at the 1981 *Ard Fheis* (English, 2005: 224-5): the armalite was the AR-18 assault rifle favoured by members of the PIRA.

Although tensions within the Republican movement and political pressures resulted in the emphasis on one or other of these approaches shifting during the 1980s and 1990s, the campaign of violence by the PIRA came to an end with a constitutional settlement known as the Good Friday Peace Accord, which was agreed to on 10 April 1998 by the key political parties in Northern Ireland. Following this, Sinn Féin contested elections to the newly established Northern Ireland Assembly (the first of which were held in June 1998) and has subsequently participated in the governance of Northern Ireland. On 28 July 2005, the IRA Army Council formally announced an end of its armed campaign and pledged henceforth to achieve its aims by 'purely political and democratic programmes through exclusively peaceful means' (IRA Army Council, 2008).

This did not, however, totally eliminate further acts of violence by Republican groups and following the Good Friday Peace Agreement, other dissident Republican groups that opposed the Agreement mounted terrorist attacks. These included the bombing at Markethill, County Armagh in September 1997, which was directed at an RUC police station by the Continuity IRA (which had been formed in 1996) and the bombing at Omagh, County Tyrone by the Real IRA (set up in 1997), which killed 29 civilians, the largest number of civilians killed in any incident during the Troubles. The Real IRA also mounted a campaign on mainland Britain, which included explosions outside the BBC Television Centre in March 2001 and at Ealing in August 2001.

See also: Battle of the Bogside (Derry, Northern Ireland), 1969, Bloody Sunday (or the Bogside Massacre) (Derry, Northern Ireland) 1972, Burntollet Bridge (Derry, Northern Ireland) 1969, counter-terrorism, 'dirty protest' (Northern Ireland) 1978-81, nationalist terrorist groups, Northern Ireland: security policy during the 'Troubles', terrorism

Sources and further reading

Adams, G. (1995) *Free Ireland: Towards a Lasting Peace*, revised edn. Dingle, County Kerry: Brandon Books.

Coogan, T. (1980) *The IRA*. London: Fontana.

English, R. (2005) *Armed Struggle: The History of the IRA*. Oxford University Press.

IRA Army Council (2005) Quoted in 'Full Text: IRA Statement', *The Guardian*, 28 July, www.theguardian.com/politics/2005/jul/28/northernireland.devolution (date accessed 6 May 2014).

Kennedy-Pipe, C. (1997) *The Origins of the Present Troubles in Northern Ireland*. Harlow: Longman.

Taylor, P. (1998) *The Provos: The IRA and Sinn Fein*. London: Bloomsbury.

Wichert, S. (1991) *Northern Ireland since 1945*. Harlow: Longman.

PUBLIC DISORDER THEORIES AND MODELS

A number of theories have been put forward to explain the outbreak of public disorder. These are based on the academic disciplines of psychology, sociology and history.

In the late nineteenth century, Le Bon put forward a psychological explanation of crowd behaviour. He argued that when 'a certain number of ... individuals are gathered together in a crowd for purposes of action, observation proves that, from the mere fact of their being assembled, there result certain new psychological characteristics' (Le Bon, 1926 [1895]).

Le Bon asserted that disorder was an irrational action that he attributed to the 'mind of the crowd':

> Under certain given circumstances ... an agglomeration of men presents new characteristics very different from those of the individuals composing it. The sentiments and ideas of all the persons in the gathering take one and the same direction, and their conscious personality vanishes. A collective mind is formed, doubtless transitory, but presenting very clearly defined characteristics. (Le Bon, 1926 [1895])

Le Bon put forward the contagion theory to explain this – crowds exert an influence over the minds of those who compose them. This held that individuals in crowds became 'de-individualised' and thus exhibited a lower standard of behaviour than that exhibited by individuals: 'the individual forming part of a crowd acquires, solely from numerical considerations, a sentiment of invincible power which allows him to yield to instincts which, had he been alone, he would perforce have kept under restraint' (Le Bon, 1926 [1895]).

Twentieth-century psychological explanations for crowd behaviour have developed the ideas of Le Bon as to what causes crowds to behave in a disorderly manner. Key ideas have included de-individuation theory, a concept that was initially put forward in 1952. This entailed the loss of self-awareness and of individual accountability that arises when an individual becomes part of a group: 'individual restraints are lost when individuals are not seen or paid attention to as individuals' (Festinger *et al.*, 1952: 382).

This theory when applied to crowd behaviour asserts that personal inhibitions are weakened by factors such as anonymity and arousal that occur when an individual becomes part of a crowd and give rise to behaviour that is not constrained by factors such as shame or guilt.

However, this view is challenged by convergence theory, which argues that crowds arise from a coming together of like-minded individuals. Thus, if violence arises, it derives from the attitude of individuals who make up the crowd, although their actions may be reinforced and intensified by associating with others who are like-minded (see, for example, Allport, 1924). Convergence theory also asserts the rational nature of crowd behaviour whereby violence is viewed as a calculated act designed to raise a grievance or right a wrong.

The view that crowds are composed of like-minded individuals has itself been challenged by emergent norm theory, which asserts that a crowd is composed of individuals with a variety of motives for gathering together. Their behaviour is shaped in response to events that arise once the crowd has formed, but will not exhibit any uniformity of purpose (Turner and Killian, 1957).

An alternative approach to studying crowd behaviour derives from the academic discipline of sociology. One of the fullest sociological accounts of collective behaviour was provided by Neil Smelser (1962), who included riots and revolutions in his definition of collective behaviour. Smelser turned away from previous psychological approaches that had analysed crowd behaviour by examining the minds of the participants and instead linked the growth of collective behaviour to the operations of the social system, viewing it as the product of tension or strain. Strain caused the entire social system to malfunction and the resultant forms of collective behaviour were thus the manifestation of a pathological society. Smelser's view that the development of collective forms of behaviour proceeded in a number of stages is referred to as the value-added theory of crowd behaviour.

Smelser argued that there were six determinants that governed the emergence of collective behaviour. All of these were essential prerequisites to the emergence of collective behaviour. These were identified as being as follows:

- Structural conduciveness: the existence of factors in the social environment that make collective behaviour possible. This may include a large gathering of people at an event such as a protest meeting or the demographics of a location such as a housing estate. Physical factors have latterly been linked to conduciveness, including the layout or design of an area or the weather.
- Structural strain: a feeling that operations of the existing social system results in grievances being neglected. These grievances may include factors such as poverty, unemployment and discrimination, which prevent an individual from attaining the goals which she or he aspired to achieve.
- Growth and spread of a generalised hostile belief: a situation

whereby the root cause of the problem becomes identified in a manner that makes sense to those with concerns regarding the legitimacy of the existing social order. This analysis is subjective rather than objective and may be based on falsehoods disseminated by the spread of rumours.

These three factors created the underlying conditions for the emergence of collective behaviour. However, whether this actually arose was dependent on two further conditions:

- Precipitating factors: an incident that epitomises the perceived injustices of the social system and that provides substance to the generalised hostile belief. Bungled police arrests in public spaces may often trigger collective behaviour (such as a riot) as it serves to illustrate the unfair operations of the existing social order.
- Mobilisation of participants for action: this requires the emergence of leadership to galvanise crowd action and organise their presence at a specific location. Existing networks or organisations may also secure this end and in the contemporary period, the social media may be an important tool for mobilising participants.

The extent to which the collective forms of behaviour spiralled out of control was then dependent on a sixth condition – that of social control. This referred to the actions undertaken by the state and agencies such as the police to counter the growth of collective behaviour either by nipping such behaviour in the bud before it can get started or by successfully countering it when it has already occurred. Such interventions may include measures that are designed to relieve structural conduciveness or structural strain. The inability or unwillingness of the state to do this promotes the spread of collective behaviour.

This account implied that collective action would take some time to mobilise. Often, however, violence of this nature occurs spontaneously. In addition, there is no focus on the political or historical contexts in which collective behaviour arises.

This latter deficiency is remedied in a further approach to the study of collective behaviour, which is provided through historical analysis of episodes of such action as riots. Historical accounts frequently seek to locate contemporary manifestations of collective behaviour in an historical context, thereby suggesting a common historical thread of purpose (such as the perennial struggle of the working class against bourgeois exploitation). An important aspect of many of these studies is the insistence that disorder is a rational and also a legitimate reaction to social injustice.

The theoretical perspectives that seek to explain the occurrence of collective behaviour form the underpinnings for models that seek to provide a 'time and place' scenario as to when disorder occurs. Two of these models are considered below.

The J-Curve was associated with James Davies (1962) and was adopted from the ideas of the nineteenth-century political philosopher Alexis de Tocqueville. This model is based on a psychological explanation which asserts that frustration results in aggression. The model seeks to provide an understanding as to when and why revolutions occur, but can also be applied to other forms of social unrest. More specifically, it is argued that:

> Revolution is most likely to take place when a prolonged period of rising expectations and rising gratifications is followed by a short period of sharp reversal, during which the gap between expectations and gratifications quickly widens and becomes intolerable. The frustration which develops, which is intense and widespread in society, seeks outlets in violent action ... If the frustration is sufficiently widespread, intense and focused on government, the violence will then become a revolution that displaces irrevocably the ruling government and changes markedly the power structure of society. Or the violence will be contained within the system, which it modifies but does not displace. The latter case is rebellion. (Davies, 1969: 690)

This argument suggests that:

- revolutions tend to occur when a bad situation has begun to improve, but the improvements are abruptly brought to a halt (which may occur because of financial considerations related to the cost of reform);
- this situation results in the emergence of an intolerable gap between what the public want and what the government can deliver. The appetite of the public becomes whetted by reform, which results in frustration when the reform programme tails off;
- for revolutions to take place, there needs to be a common enemy that galvanises the public behind a common cause. One form that this may take is perceived police misbehaviour, which epitomises the injustices within society and may promote a widespread movement to overthrow the government.

This view was applied to events that included race riots in America during the 1960s and also to Northern Ireland in the same decade. The main criticism of the account is its heavy reliance on psychology, which suggests that frustration will always result in aggressive forms of behaviour. It does, however, suggest that social unrest may be avoided if governments that abandon a programme of reform are able to depress the expectations of the people in line with the changed economic circumstances. This approach was compatible with the 'overload thesis' (King, 1975) and a call for elections not to be based on 'the politics of promising'.

An alternative model to explain a wide range of public disorder was the flashpoint model, which was initially developed by an analysis of events that occurred during the 1984/5 miners' dispute in the UK.

This approach sought to provide a multi-dimensional approach to the study of disorder by asserting that there were six levels of influence that related to the outbreak of public disorder. These derived from different academic disciplines (psychology, sociology and history). They were identified as follows:

- Structural: a perception by a group that it is marginalised and its needs are thus being neglected by the state. This perception gives rise to attitudes that the group is 'not wanted', its views 'count for nothing' or that it has 'no prospects' in the way in which society is currently constituted.
- Political/ideological: this relates to the way in which the state reacts to the group, which believes that its needs cannot be met within the existing social structure. These views may be voiced by a variety of actors, including government ministers, the judiciary or senior police officers. This may give rise to attitudes that include sympathy or vilification.
- Cultural: the development of group values/attitudes which enable the group to understand the social world and the position they occupy within it, but which may be at variance with 'official' values and attitudes.
- Contextual: the immediate background to crowd mobilisation. This may be based on a rumour or involve a police intervention, but is seen by the disaffected group within a broader historical context, epitomising the negative views that mainstream society feels towards them.
- Situational: a specific geographical location in which the state and the dissenting group will play out their differences. This 'space' may have symbolic importance, such as a picket line or a 'no go' area that the police intend to occupy. The intention of the police in Brixton in April 1981 to occupy the area that was viewed as a haven by African-Caribbean youths (Railton Road, normally known as the 'Front Line') was a significant cause of the disorders that occurred.
- Interactional: two sets of protagonists (the dissenting group and the police) physically confront each other. Disorder is not inevitable, but will arise through the perception by one group of unreasonable behaviour on the part of the other. This creates a flashpoint that will lead to the outbreak of disorder.

According to the flashpoint model, the interactional level is the key determinant of the outbreak of disorder, which might not occur even when predisposing factors suggested that this was a likely outcome. Alternatively, 'incidents trivial in themselves can ... evoke a response which seems out of all proportion to their objective characteristics. They set in motion a chain of response and counter response, a spiral of mutual recrimination. They have become flashpoints' (Waddington et al., 1989: 166–7).

A particular benefit of this model is that it explains why very similar events may have totally different outcomes regarding the outbreak of public disorder – violence was not, for example, a constant feature on picket lines during the 1984/5 miners' dispute in the UK. It also helps to explain why actions that are viewed negatively at one period in time may be regarded more sympathetically when repeated subsequently – different opinions of similar events may derive from changes, affecting the mood of the public that is influenced by the political/ideological level.

However, there are some criticisms that have been made of the flashpoint model. It implies that crowds are like-minded in their views and attitudes, whereas in reality an event may draw people onto the streets for a wide variety of motives. It also assumes that disorders are triggered by one specific flashpoint – this may not be the case and sometimes there are no discernible flashpoints at all. This was argued to be the case in most of the disorders in England in 2011. In addition, the flashpoint may not result in an immediate breakdown of order as the model suggests – there may be a time lull before this occurs.

See also: August riots (England) 2011, copycat riots (England) 1981, demonstrations, miners' dispute (Britain) 1984–5, public order policing (England and Wales), riots

Sources and further reading

Allport, F. (1924) *Social Psychology*. Boston: Houghton Mifflin.
Davies, J. (1962) 'Towards a Theory of Revolution'. *American Sociological Review*, 27(1): 5–19.
——. (1969) 'The J-Curve of Rising and Declining Satisfactions as a Cause of Some Great Revolutions and a Contained Rebellion' in H. David Graham and T. Kerr (eds), *Violence in America*. New York Times Company.
Festinger, L., Pepitone, A. and Newcomb, T. (1952) 'Some Consequences of Deindividuation in a Group'. *Journal of Social Psychology*, 47: 382–9.
King, A. (1975) 'Overload: Problems of Governing in the 1970s'. *Political Studies*, 23(203): 284–96.
Le Bon, G. (1926 [1895]) *The Crowd: A Study of the Popular Mind*. London. Unwin.
Smelser, N. (1962) *Theory of Collective Behaviour*. New York: Free Press.
Turner, R. and Killian, L. (1957) *Collective Behavior*. Englewood Cliffs, NJ: Prentice Hall.
Waddington, D. (2007) *Policing Public Order: Theory and Practice*. Cullompton: Willan Publishing.
Waddington, D., Jobard, F. and King, M. (eds) (2009) *Rioting in the UK and France: A Comparative Analysis*. Cullompton: Willan Publishing.
Waddington, D., Jones, K. and Critcher, C. (1989) *Flashpoints: A Comparative and Historical Approach*. London: Routledge.

PUBLIC ORDER LEGISLATION (ENGLAND AND WALES)

The law relating to protest in England and Wales is embraced by common law and statute law. The latter is especially significant for the policing of protest since the response by governments has included the utilisation of criminalisation as a mechanism to regulate various aspects of protest under the pretext of maintaining public order.

For many years in the twentieth century, the key legislation providing the police with powers to deal with anticipated or actual occurrences of public disorder was the Public Order Act 1936.

This legislation was enacted against the background of violent confrontations between the British Union of Fascists and its opponents (organised in groups that included the Coordinating Committee against Anti-fascist Activities). The state was concerned that widespread disorder, especially on the streets, could lead to a total breakdown of law and order with potentially revolutionary potential. The action that led to the passage of the 1936 Act was the 'Battle of Cable Street' in London's East End in 1936. Protesters and residents (who were then primarily Jewish) set up barricades in an attempt to prevent a march by the British Union of Fascists from progressing through the area. Their slogan, adopted from the First World War, was 'they shall not pass'.

The resultant legislation contained a number of provisions: it prohibited the wearing in a public place of a uniform signifying attachment to a political organisation; it banned the organisation, training or equipping of quasi-military organisations; and it authorised the police to re-route a procession in order to prevent serious public disorder or to ban a procession if they anticipated would result in *serious* public disorder which could not be resolved by re-routing (a decision that required the agreement of a local authority outside of London and the Home Secretary for events within the Metropolitan Police area). If an event was banned, this took the form of a 'blanket' ban, which applied to every procession of a political nature in the area for the period of time specified in the ban.

Section 5 of the 1936 Act made it an offence to use words or exhibit behaviour in a public place (for example, by publishing or distributing written material) that might be deemed as threatening, abusive or insulting and that thus might result in a breach of the peace. This section was subsequently amended by the Race Relations Act 1976 to embrace actions of this nature that incited racial hatred. The 1936 Act also made it illegal to carry an offensive weapon at public meetings or processions, and it amended the Public Meetings Act 1908 to make it unlawful to disrupt a legally convened meeting.

Although many of these provisions had a direct impact on the British Union of Fascists, whose leading members wore a uniform in public and whose activists were organised into what might appear to be a quasi-military body, the Blackshirts (Benewick, 1969: 235–62), its provisions were applicable to a wider range of organisations and significantly increased the scope of police powers in connection with assemblies. However, the legislation was primarily directed at events that occurred in the 1930s and was not widely used in the post-war period. The 1936 Act was thus dubbed 'an ill-considered response to the street battles of the times' (Cox, 1975: 34).

However, after 1970, protest was often conducted in ways which were not precisely catered for by the 1936 legislation. One major difficulty was that the power to ban or re-route events applied only to 'processions' (Home Office, 1980: 9) in which the key feature was that of crowd mobility. Static demonstrations were not catered for in the legislation. 'Counter-demonstrations' were a feature of the activities of those opposed to the National Front in the 1960s and 1970s and also arose in some industrial disputes. The pickets involved the Grunwick industrial dispute in 1976–8, for example, were sometimes supported by a large force of sympathetic demonstrators numbering many thousands whose purpose, according to the government, was 'deliberately to obstruct the passage of those going to work' (Home Office, 1985: 33).

A further difficulty concerned the definition of 'procession'. In 1977, Greater Manchester's Chief Constable, James Anderton, banned a National Front march in Hyde. In response, Martin Webster (the activities organiser of the National Front) decided to 'walk' through the town. On this occasion, a large police presence ensured that he was able to conduct this activity without physical opposition from his party's opponents. However, he was threatened with arrest when he attempted to repeat this exercise in 1980 in the West Midlands.

In addition, the 1936 Act did not require the police to be given advance notice by an organisation of its intention to hold a procession, although this requirement was included in a number of local Acts covering 107 local authority areas in England and Wales and three in Scotland (Home Office, 1980: 19). There was also no power of arrest for failing to comply with a police direction concerning the banning or re-routing of such an event, save the common law power to arrest where a breach of the peace seemed likely (Home Office, 1980: 17). This meant that the police tended to rely on groups wishing to organise a procession to voluntarily give warning of their intentions and to heed any advice which might be given.

Further, section 5 of the 1936 Act was difficult to enforce. It had been copied from the Metropolitan Police Act 1839, which had totally failed to prevent anti-semitic utterances by the British Union of Fascists before the 1936 Act was passed. A particular problem concerned provocation of violence. If a melee developed arising from remarks made in a political speech, for example, the police tended to take action against those who were unambiguously breaking the law as opposed to the person who had provoked the problem. There were exceptions to this, however. Colin Jordan was arrested for making anti-semitic comments in a speech in Trafalgar Square which led to disorder. In the subsequent trial in 1963 (*Jordan v Burgoyne*), Lord Chief Justice Parker ruled that a speaker had to 'take his audience as he found it', which meant that a speaker who knowingly incited an audience to violence was legally responsible for subsequent events. But this view did not consistently influence police interventions in public order situations after 1970, thus illustrating the discretionary nature of the powers at their disposal.

There were other laws that could be used in connection with protest. Legislation that related to the obstruction of the highway (the Highways Act 1980) or to obstructing or assaulting a constable in the execution of his or her duties (the Police Act 1964) was frequently utilised against protesters since 1970 and, in conjunction with the 1936 legislation, provided the police with a wide range of powers with which to deal with disorderly protests: 'of some 10,000 charges brought in England and Wales for offences committed in connection with the miners' dispute in 1984–85 ... 4,000 were brought under section 5 of the 1936 Act: over 1,500 for obstructing the police; just over 1,000 for criminal damage; 640 for obstructing the highway and 360 for assaulting a police constable' (Home Office, 1980: 9).

The ability of individuals to engage in protest could also be adversely affected by the application of binding over provisions to those arrested in connection with a protest. These powers derived from the Justices of the Peace Act 1361 and were subsequently developed by the Magistrates' Courts Act 1952. They sought to prevent a person's further involvement in the protest by requiring him or her subsequently to either keep the peace or to be of good behaviour. It was argued that this power could be used by the police as a substitute for a prosecution for a more specific offence when they knew that this course of action would not be successful (Christian, 1985: 133). Unwillingness to accept such provisions (which effectively meant that those affected were signing away their right to protest: Cox, 1975: 65) or failure to abide by the conditions that were imposed could result in a term of imprisonment.

In addition, common law powers, the most important of which was breach of the peace, could be used in connection with protest. A benefit of common law powers was that they were vague in content and could be further developed by judicial interpretation to apply to new aspects of public order situations experienced by the police. Examples of this included the use of conspiracy to trespass (effectively transforming a civil law offence into a criminal one), which was successfully applied against the occupation of the Sierra Leonese Embassy in 1972 by a group of students (the Kamara case). However, this was unsuccessful when applied to the 1972 building workers' strike, which led to the use of the charge of conspiracy to intimidate under the antique provisions of the Conspiracy and Protection of Property Act 1875 against others involved in that dispute. Further examples of the development of common law powers to deal with protest related to breach of the peace powers during the 1984/5 miners' dispute, whereby this charge was applied to potential as opposed to imminent situations where a breach of the peace might arise. It was utilised to limit the numbers of those converging on locations where they intended to picket. However, a further court judgment in 2007 (*R (Laporte) v Chief Constable of Gloucestershire*) ruled that a breach of the peace had to be imminent in order to invoke breach of the peace powers and thus made the pre-emptive use of this power less likely in future.

The civil law could also be applied to protest, in particular industrial disputes. Conservative industrial relations legislation that was enacted during the 1980s contained a number of civil remedies for those threatened with industrial action. This included the Employment Acts 1980 and 1982 (which narrowed the definition of a trade dispute to an action between an employer and his or her direct workforce and introduced penalties to prevent pickets or trade unions engaging in activity of this nature), the Trade Union Act 1984 (which required compulsory ballots before strike action could occur) and the Employment Act 1988 (which – in conjunction with the 1984 Act – was concerned with the election of trade union executives and general secretaries). In addition, civil injunctions obtained under the Protection from Harassment Act 1997 could be used to restrict protest outside company premises. A key difficulty with civil law is that remedies might take time to be implemented.

In the late 1970s, a number of protests placed the reform of police public order powers onto the political agenda. These events included serious disturbances in Lewisham and Ladywood in 1977, Digbeth in 1978 and Leicester and Southall in 1979. At the latter event, 2,756 officers were deployed, 345 people were arrested, 97 police officers and 63 members of the public were injured, one of whom died. Accordingly, in 1980 a Green Paper put forward suggestions regarding reform.

This asserted that 'the rights of peaceful protest and assembly are amongst our fundamental freedoms', which were 'numbered among the touchstones which distinguish a free society from a totalitarian one' (Home Office, 1985: 2). The intention of the new legislation was 'to balance the freedom to demonstrate with the sometimes conflicting interests of those who do not wish to do so' (Home Office, 1980: iii). Concern was also voiced by the government regarding the cost of policing demonstrations (Home Office, 1985: 42).

The Public Order Act 1986 created or re-defined a wide range of public order offences (riot, violent disorder, affray, fear or provocation of violence and harassment, alarm or distress). The main impact of the 1986 legislation was to criminalise a range of activities from orchestrated civil disorder to boisterous behaviour in a public place. Approximately 40 criminal charges could be brought against those who transgressed the new legislation.

A number of aspects of the 1986 Act specifically related to protest and provided the police with new powers with which to deal with it. Advance notice to the police of processions (but not assemblies) became a universal requirement and a new offence of participating in a banned event was introduced. The ability of the police to intervene in processions and demonstrations was also re-defined. If the police believed that a procession would result in serious public disorder, they could apply to the relevant local authority to ban it.

The police were also empowered to unilaterally impose conditions both on processions and also on static demonstrations (termed 'assemblies' by the legislation) consisting of 20 or more individuals held in the open air. The criteria used to justify the imposition of conditions were broader than those governing banning an event. They enabled the police to intervene if they believed that an event would cause serious disorder or that it might result in serious damage to property or serious disruption to the life of a community, or if they believed that the purpose of organising the event was the intimidation of others with a view to compelling them not to do an act they had the right to do, or to do an act which they had not the right to do.

Powers were also provided to enable the police to prohibit trespassory assemblies of 20 or more individuals on private land and also to prevent individuals from travelling to such an event.

These new provisions provided the police with increased abilities to intervene in a wide range of extra-parliamentary political activities, including picketing at industrial disputes. The manner in which the Public Order Act could be used to stifle protest was illustrated in April 1995, when the Assistant Chief Constable of Essex wrote to every householder in Brightlingsea advising them to desist from demonstrating in connection with live animal exports and threatening them with arrest and imprisonment if they continued to participate.

Further police powers related to public order were provided in the Criminal Justice and Public Order Act 1994. This measure was enacted against the background of a number of events which were associated with counterculture protest and the actions of 'disorderly youths' in the 1990s, and reflected the changing nature of protest in this period in which demonstrations and mass picketing (King and Brearley, 1996: 104) gave way to alternative tactics. Key events included the hippie convoys at Stonehenge, gatherings of New Age travellers at Castlemorton in 1993, the activities of hunt saboteurs, environmental protesters and the emergence of a rave culture.

The Public Order and Criminal Justice Act was thus particularly directed at youth subcultures and counterculture protest embraced by a diverse range of organisations and performed by a wide array of methods. Part V of the Act created a variety of new offences under the heading of 'collective trespass or nuisance on land', which the police could utilise against these groups. These included aggravated trespass, trespass on land and trespassory assembly. Further, the police were also provided with powers to regulate raves.

The 1994 legislation empowered the police to terminate raves if they believed the loudness of the music caused 'serious distress' to the people living nearby and authorised preemptive action to prevent people within a five-mile radius from travelling to these events. New powers related to trespass applied to common and privately owned land, and further provided for the removal of travellers from places that included scheduled monuments.

The new offence of aggravated trespass related to the activities of a person who trespassed on land and sought to prevent a lawful activity from taking place by intimidating, obstructing or disrupting that event. This was particularly directed at anti-hunt saboteurs and environmental protesters. In addition, the police could apply to the relevant local authority for an order to prohibit trespassory assemblies for a period of up to four days (provided the local authority agreed) and could direct individuals 'reasonably believed' to be on the way to such an assembly not to continue. This restriction was aimed at a wide range of direct action groups and could effectively prevent any demonstration, lobby, picket or vigil from taking place. Further powers were provided to make it easier for squatters to be removed by authorising a displaced or intended occupier or that person's agent to use violence to secure entry to premises once an order for possession had been given.

A number of criticisms were voiced against the legislation passed in 1986 and 1994. In particular, the 1994 Act prompted a wide degree of protest organised by groups such as the Freedom Network and the Coalition Against the Criminal Justice Bill.

It was argued that the 1986 and 1994 Acts extended the scope of police discretion to deal with extra-parliamentary activities. These included the powers to decide whether to impose conditions on a procession or static demonstration under the 1986 Act, to determine the nature of these conditions if they were imposed, to enable them to be the sole power to determine whether activities constituted 'raves', 'trespass' or 'disruptive trespass' and then to take action provided for in the 1994 legislation.

The requirement of the 1986 Act that organisers of demonstrations needed to give the police advance notice of their intentions and the ability of the police to ban or impose conditions on these events has led to organisers having to negotiate with the police. It has been observed that while negotiation of this type might epitomise the principle of 'policing by consent' and underpin the move towards the negotiated management style of policing public order situations, the extent to which genuinely two-sided dialogue actually occurred was debatable: 'the balance of power lay firmly in favour of the police. Negotiation was less a process of "give and take" and more that of the organiser giving and the police taking' (Waddington, 1994a: 101).

However, liaison between the police and protesters is not necessarily confrontational. Organisers of protests know they require the cooperation of the police to direct events such as demonstrations through traffic and will often voluntarily agree to police suggestions. Opposition to police involvement in organising protests is most likely to come from groups that do not accept the authority of the state and that thus refuse to comply with the established rules of the game that are underpinned by the concept of 'give and take' by police and protesters.

It was also alleged that the main purpose of these Acts was to stifle protest. This argument especially related to the requirement to give advance notice of processions and demonstrations, and the ability to use conditions such as 'disruption to the life of the community' contained in the 1986 Act in a restrictive manner either to prevent these activities completely or to permit them in a form designed to minimise their ability to influence public opinion. In addition, the 1994 Act introduced a wide range of pre-emptive powers that effectively provided the police with the ability to place major restrictions on the freedom of movement through their ability to define a peaceful, non-obstructive gathering on the highway as a trespassory assembly. The offence of aggravated trespass was widely used against those who objected to the construction of the Newbury bypass, which began in 1996. During the police operation, 356 arrests were made for this offence (Bucke and James, 1998: 49).

Both the 1986 and 1994 Acts blurred the distinction between public and private, enabling the private interest to commandeer police resources (Waddington, 1996: 128). The civil liberties of those charged with offences under either Act were also adversely affected by both pieces of legislation. In a number of cases, the 1986 Act reversed the burden of proof in a criminal trial. The 1994 Act eroded an accused's right to silence, thus undermining the presumption of innocence that had formerly been at the heart of the criminal justice system.

The 1994 Act was criticised by some senior police officers for seeking to solve social problems such as homelessness through coercive means (Wilmot, 1994) and for enhancing the emphasis on the police enforcement role to the detriment of community-led priorities and ancillary tasks (Smith, 1994). It effectively outlawed collective activities practised by minority groups such as squatters, but failed to offer any solution or alternative to the issue that initially encourage – or forced – them to embark upon these activities or lifestyles. The 1994 Act also provided a good example of how a moral panic directed at particular scapegoats can have a far broader application: thus, powers initially justified by the need to regulate the activities of a broadly defined group of 'New Age travellers' were also applied to gypsies. One study likened its potential effect on this population to ethnic cleansing (Hawes and Perez, 1995).

No legislation can ever be watertight and groups who wish to find ways to avoid the restrictions that it imposes on their ability to protest have frequently been able to do so. This is the case with the statutory requirement of advance notice for holding a demonstration. Groups on the far right instigated disorders in a number of towns in northern England in 2001 by holding, or threatening to hold, political meetings. This had the effect of inciting Muslim youths to commit violent acts. In an attempt to prevent re-occurrences of this tactic, police forces began to ban events planned by these groups. This led extreme right-wing groups to seek ways to circumvent the prohibitions on their activities. These included transforming a demonstration into an assembly or series of assemblies, which were outside the scope of the 1986 legislation. This tactic was used by extreme right-wing groups in Oldham in 2001 following a ban being placed on their intended march. Latterly, an organisation which called itself the National Front Social Club was formed. This planned to hold what it described as 'cultural tours' for its members of racially sensitive towns. This was planned to have the same effect on Muslim youths as a political meeting, but required no advance warning to be given to the police of an intended event taking place (Harris, 2001).

Police public order powers were provided by subsequent legislation. Stop and search powers contained in the Police and Criminal Evidence Act 1984 and section 44 of the Terrorism Act 2000 may be used in connection with a wide range of protests. The Serious Organised Crime and Police Act 2005 criminalised protests, whether static or moving, that took place within the vicinity of Parliament or other designated areas without prior notification to, and authorisation by, the police. The measure also made it an offence to trespass on certain designated sites (such as nuclear facilities) where the Home Secretary felt that this action would threaten national security.

It has been argued that the police service has made only limited use of the new public orders provided to it in the 1986 and 1994 public order legislation. In particular, marches are rarely banned and conditions on assemblies and marches are imposed infrequently. There are various explanations for this. The first concerns the practical effect of using powers such as banning marches. Since the enactment of the Human Rights Act 1998, there are doubts as to whether the requirement to inform the police in advance of a desire to hold a parade is compatible with the European Convention on Human Rights' guarantee of freedom of assembly and this may induce the police to use this power sparingly.

However, even before the 1998 Act was passed, the police were reluctant to use powers bestowed on them in the 1986 and 1994 legislation. This was so for a number of reasons. A group may decide to flout the law and ignore a ban, thus necessitating a large and costly police operation to enforce it. Violence is highly likely to occur in such a charged atmosphere. Accordingly, the police reaction to protest is typically to let events proceed, but to seek to ensure that trouble is avoided through adequate advance preparation, including the processes of negotiation and accommodation that take place with an event's organisers (Waddington: 1994b: 379). The paramount desire to avoid trouble in the form of public disorder or adverse reactions to police actions (Waddington, 1998: 127) may also induce the police service to permit events to proceed even when no prior authorisation has been obtained (an example of this being a march in London in January 1991 to express opposition to the war with Iraq) and to use all powers (including those of arrest) sparingly (Waddington, 1998: 118–19).

A second explanation for the reluctance by police to use their public order powers to the full is that groups which find themselves on the receiving end of restrictive legislation may feel threatened and this may radicalise their activities. Protest may act as a form of 'safety valve' at which advocates of minority causes can take to the streets and 'let off steam'. Those denied the ability to do this may embark upon actions which have a more adverse impact on public order. Thus, protest (including industrial disputes) may be tolerated in the belief that actions of this nature are more preferable to an all-out class war (Reiner, 1998: 43).

Calculations related to the availability of police time and resources may also influence the use made of powers provided in public order legislation. This was one factor governing the use by police forces of powers available to them under the 1994 Act to direct trespassers illegally residing on a piece of land to leave the site. In particular, the police were wary regarding the use of their power to seize vehicles under the provisions of the 1994 Act because of the high level of organisation and expense involved (Bucke and James, 1998: viii).

Finally, the police may often seek to respond to public order situations by using their discretion as opposed to legislation. This entails the use of pragmatic responses to matters which arise. This is referred to as employing the 'Ways and Means Act', a mythical piece of legislation that is invoked to justify a police action which may not be founded on any real legislation and may conceivably be illegal. The use by the police of tactics based on guile as opposed to force (Waddington, 1996: 234) is especially motivated by the desire to avoid confrontation and disorder, since this may have an adverse impact on the image of the police service and, ultimately, its legitimacy.

See also: anti-globalisation/anti-capitalist protests (UK), building workers' strike (England and Wales) 1972, counterculture protest, kettling, Lewisham disorders (Lewisham, London) 1977, live animal exports (England), peace movement, public order policing (England and Wales), Red Lion Square (London) 1974, Southall disorders (Southall, London) 1979, walking (with a political purpose)

Sources and further reading

Benewick, R. (1969) *Political Violence and Public Order: A Study of British Fascism*. London: Allen Lane.
Bucke, T. and James, Z. (1998) *Trespass and Protest: Policing under the Criminal Justice and Public Order Act 1994*. London: Home Office Research, Development and Statistics Directorate, Research Study 190.
Christian, L. (1985) 'Restrictions without Convictions: The Role of the Courts in Legitimising Police Control in Nottinghamshire' in B. Fine and R. Millar (eds), *Policing the Miners' Dispute*. London: Lawrence & Wishart.
Cox, B. (1975) *Civil Liberties in Britain*. Harmondsworth: Penguin.
Harris, P. (2001) 'Exposed: Secret Plot to Start Race Riots', *The Observer*, 2 September.
Hawes. D. and Perez, B. (1995) *The Gypsy and the State: The Ethnic Cleansing of British Society*. Bristol University School for Advanced Urban Studies.
Home Office (1980) *Review of the Public Order Act 1936 and Related Legislation*. London: HMSO, Cmnd. 7891.
——. (1985) *Review of Public Order Law*. London: HMSO, Cmnd. 9510.
King, M. and Brearley, N. (1996) *Public Order Policing: Contemporary Perspectives on Strategy and Tactics*. Leicester: Perpetuity Press.
Reiner, R. (1998) 'Policing Protest and Disorder in Britain' in D. Della Porta and H. Reiter (eds), *The Control of Mass Demonstrations in Western Democracies*. Minneapolis: University of Minnesota Press.
Smith, Sir J. (1994) Quoted in *The Guardian*, 16 October.
Waddington, D. (1996) 'Key Issues and Controversies' in C. Critcher and D. Waddington (eds), *Policing Public Order: Theoretical and Practical Issues*. Aldershot: Avebury.
Waddington, P. (1994a) *Liberty and Order: Public Order Policing in a Capital City*. London: UCL Press.
——. (1994b) 'Coercion and Accommodation: Public Order Policing after the Public Order Act'. *British Journal of Sociology*, 45(3): 367–85.
——. (1998) 'Controlling Protest in Contemporary, Historical and Comparative Perspective' in D. Della Porta and

H. Reiter (eds), *The Control of Mass Demonstrations in Western Democracies.* Minneapolis: University of Minnesota Press.

Wilmot, D. (1994) 'Freedom under the Law', *Police Review*, 18 November, pp. 18–20.

PUBLIC ORDER POLICING (ENGLAND AND WALES)

Public order policing is a specialist area of police work and although concerned with all aspects of crowd situations is especially associated with dealing with a wide range of actions relating to protest. These include industrial disputes, riots, demonstrations, civil disobedience and direct action or what has been referred to as 'the politics of contention' (Waddington, 2003: 415). In order to deal with these situations, major developments have taken place that are discussed under a number of headings below.

Equipment and weaponry

Initially police forces were ill-equipped to handle the public order problems that surfaced after 1968. The anti-statist stance that was displayed by demonstrators at the 1968 Grosvenor Square demonstration was replicated in future episodes of protest during the 1970s and 1980s, when the police frequently found themselves under attack from demonstrators and rioters. This deficiency was publicly demonstrated at Notting Hill in 1976, when officers under attack were forced to improvise their own defence from items such as dustbin lids and traffic cones in order to fend off missiles being thrown by a hostile crowd. This resulted in injuries to 325 police officers (Thackrah, 1985: 149). Following this event, riot shields were issued and were first used in a demonstration against a National Front procession in Lewisham the following year (Waddington, 1987: 39).

The 1981 riots prompted developments affecting protective helmets and the use of petrol bombs by rioters in 1981, and also resulted in the future provision of flameproof overalls to police officers following pressure from the Association of Chief Police Officers (ACPO) and the Police Federation (Reiner, 1991: 171). Other developments affecting equipment during the 1980s included the provision of shinguards and longer truncheons that could be used in connection with short shields. The 1983 ACPO Training Manual listed nine items of protective clothing that officers should wear when dealing with serious disorders. These included riot helmet and visor, fire-resistant overalls and any additional body protection that forces considered necessary. The murder of PC Keith Blakelock in the 1985 Broadwater Farm Estate riot also prompted a consideration of issuing body armour to the police for protection against knife attacks, although this was not adopted at that time.

In addition to developments relating to equipment, major developments have also taken place in connection with the weaponry at the disposal of the police.

Key developments affecting weaponry included the use of CS gas against rioters in Toxteth in 1981. This had not been used on mainland Britain before and required the consent of the Home Secretary to be given before it was deployed. Other events witnessed the use of more time-honoured methods, such as the deployment of police baton charges (for example, at the NGA-Warrington Messenger dispute in 1983) and police horses (at Orgreave, 1984). At Warrington, equipment that was issued for protective reasons became a weapon that was used offensively in order to break up crowds. In 1985, following the Broadwater Farm Estate riot, baton rounds were also made available to the police (Waddington, 1987: 39).

An important issue with both weaponry and equipment relate to when the decision is taken to use them. The availability of both may prompt a premature decision to deploy them before an incident occurs that justifies their use. This may result in the delivery of a more confrontational police response than was warranted, which may in turn increase the violence of the crowd and prompt disorder.

However, judgements as to whether police actions at a particular event were proportionate to the violence that occurred are frequently based upon hindsight analysis rather than an evaluation of circumstances as they were unfolding. Police commanders at public order events are fully aware that health and safety legislation applies to their own officers as well as to members of the general public and this may influence decisions regarding equipment, weaponry and tactics, which may later be regarded as unwarranted and depicted as measures designed to deter protest.

Tactics

Changes affecting weaponry and equipment had implications for the tactics used by the police at crowd situations. Initially the tactics deployed by the police at public order events were relatively non-confrontational. The post-war period was epitomised by a style of public order policing of 'winning by appearing to lose' (a policy that sought to secure public sympathy for the police) and entailed activities such as gently picking up demonstrators who had mounted a 'sit-down' protest or using the time-honoured tactic of 'push and shove' (especially at industrial disputes) in which officers were linked together (in either a straight line or a wedge formation) by the 'butcher's grip'.

The mounting violence that occurred at public order events in the late 1960s and onwards prompted significant changes to the ways in which the police responded to crowd situations. The key deficiency was the absence of any defined police strategy to deal with disorder, especially if this was spontaneous. This was apparent during the 1981 riots, when different forces adopted different methods to deal with them, especially in connection with holding ground and consulting community leaders in an attempt to defuse a tense situation. Officers on the scene were often required to improvise and formulate tactics without any master plan to guide their conduct. One difficulty with this situation was that officers under attack might resort to violence in the absence of instructions on alternative ways to act.

This deficiency was tackled with the publication in 1983 of ACPO's *Public Order Manual of Tactical Operations and Related Matters*. Each force was issued with a binder that contained 'a detailed analysis of the stages of a riot and the police responses appropriate to them'. A total of 238 tactics and manoeuvres were set out in its 30 sections, 'arranged in order of escalating force, from normal policing up to plastic bullets, CS gas and live firearms' (Northam, 1989: 42). This was designed to ensure that the response by the police in public order situations would become standardised.

The new tactics that were evolved in the early 1980s included static lines of officers behind large shields (5'5" high and 24" wide) and snatch squads composed of officers carrying smaller shields who would go into crowds to arrest offenders.

The publication of the *Public Order Manual* in 1983 was preceded by the formation of an ACPO body, the Public Order Forward Planning Group, to review all new developments and emerging tactics. Other centralised developments followed this ACPO initiative, including the formation of a Central Intelligence Unit during the miners' dispute (1984–5) to analyse intelligence gathered by officers on the ground. The ACPO *Manual* was subsequently replaced by the 2007 ACPO *Manual of Guidance on Keeping the Peace*.

Following the 2011 riots, the 2007 *Manual* became part of the Authorised Professional Practice drawn up by the College of Policing (College of Policing, 2013). This embraced guidance regarding issues that included intelligence gathering related to public order, the role of sub-Bronze commanders at public order events and additional and amended tactical options such as the introduction of Police Liaison Teams. It also addressed core questions relating to the use of force.

Management of crowd situations

An important tactic relating to public order policing is that of managing an event. One problem associated with public order events during the early part of the 1980s was that senior commanders lacked training in managing large numbers of police officers that they found under their command during public order events. This resulted in a number of problems, one of which was how police commanders could relay instructions to their officers and enforce these directions.

One key development affecting managerial control over public order events was the introduction (in the wake of the 1984 Libyan Embassy siege) of the Gold/Silver/Bronze hierarchy of command, which sought to provide for an effective chain of command and improved control and coordination of police resources at public order events.

The Gold commander was responsible for setting the overall policing strategy for the event, the Silver commander was charged with implementing this strategy on the ground and the Bronze commanders exercised responsibility for specific territorial areas and over the officers who were allocated to policing them. One aim of this system was to exert more effective supervision over police officers and guard against undisciplined actions at these events. Technology such as closed-circuit television has also been increasingly used to police public order events, enabling commanders to secure an overall view of an event and respond to problems as and when these arise. Improved organisation underpinned by technology has greatly improved the ability of police commanders to control crowd situations.

Pre-emptive tactics

Further initiatives have been undertaken that seek to pre-empt problems before they erupt into disorder. These include the use of tension indicators.

The 1983 *ACPO Public Order Manual* listed eight tension indicators, which included the increase in disturbances between groups or gangs and racial attacks, and enjoined officers to keep their ears to the ground to gather intelligence relating to public order situations. Observations regarding heightened tensions would form the basis for pre-emptive police action in the form of what was termed 'saturation policing', which involved techniques to ensure that the police enjoyed numerical and physical supremacy in the affected area. It was hoped that the spectre of well-trained, disciplined police officers would exert a profound psychological impact to prevent disorder.

However, their presence might have the opposite effect and could be seen as a form of harassment or provocation, leading to a violent response. Saturation policing might be accompanied by a range of tactics that include the use of cordons and interception tactics to prevent crowds from converging on a hot spot.

More recent developments include the use of rumour management and various forms of community engagement. False rumours can fuel disorder, as was evidenced at Brixton in April 1981 in connection with a claim that a stabbed youth had subsequently died as a result of a police intervention. In reality, the youth did not die from this intervention, which was designed to help him get to hospital. Rumour management and community engagement (especially with community leaders) provide the police with tools through which false allegations can be nipped in the bud, thus defusing tensions that have in the past resulted in violent confrontations between the police and members of the public.

Public order specialisation within the police service

In addition to the developments that have been discussed above, the policing of public disorder has also required the police to devote resources into this area of activity. These have taken various forms.

Since the 1960s, a number of police forces developed units which are not tied to a specific division or concerned with implementing routine police functions, but which operate anywhere within a force's boundaries. These units have been extensively utilised in public order situations in addition to dealing with crime-related matters. An early example of this was the Metropolitan Police's Special Patrol Group (SPG). This was initially established as the Special Patrol Group Unit in 1961 and was re-named the SPG in 1965. It played a leading role in policing crowd events during the 1970s (for example, at Red Lion Square in 1974 and Southall in 1979).

These units pose a number of difficulties – they lack local knowledge and sensitivity to the people of an area in which they are deployed, they often regarded themselves as an elite squad, they were frequently associated with heavy-handed and aggressive policing and they may also operate independently of the main policing operation that is being conducted, resulting in a confused situation.

Criticisms of this nature brought about the replacement of the Metropolitan Police's SPG following events in Southall in 1979 (in which allegations of racism were also directed at this unit, perhaps most famously in a sketch on the television programme *Not the Nine O'Clock News* in 1980). It was replaced with District Support Units and later by Territorial Support Groups. These were located within each of the Metropolitan Police districts and were thus more locally oriented than their predecessors. Other forces, however, have retained a centralised specialist unit such as the Tactical Aid Unit of the Greater Manchester Police.

In addition, some forces have specialist squads used in connection with direct action. The Greater Manchester Police unit that performs this work is known as the Protestor Removal Squad, which was used in connection with the fracking protests at Barton Moss in 2014. The Squad has equipment that can be employed to detach protesters from objects to which they have chained or otherwise attached themselves. The British Transport Police has a Policing at Heights Team, whose role also includes protester removal.

One further difficulty with specialist public order units is that they are inevitably composed of a relatively few number of police officers who may be insufficient to handle large-scale public order problems. Accordingly, public order training has been more widely provided within police forces through the mechanism of Police Support Units (PSUs).

In England and Wales, PSUs consist of uniformed police officers whose main role is to perform routine police duties, but who receive a regular degree of public order training on a regular basis. PSUs (termed District Support Units in the Metropolitan Police Service) are organised at divisional (or Basic Command Unit (BCU)) level and are composed of one inspector, three sergeants, 18 constables, three drivers (also constables), two operation support medics and three protected personnel carriers (ACPO, 2004: 20). They train together as a unit and are available to be deployed to public order situations within or outside their police force when the need arises.

PSUs originated in the Cold War era. During the 1960s, police mobile columns were organised at a regional level, consisting of around 100 officers (divided into sections) who in the event of nuclear war would withdraw to places of safety and would subsequently return to provide police services to the areas affected by a nuclear attack.

This idea was further developed during the 1970s (Home Office, 1974), which suggested that some police officers should be organised into a unit now termed PSUs to enable them to perform duties including crowd control, guarding key points and protected areas, and controlling essential services in the event of a nuclear attack. Initially, no special training needs were identified, but this were given when the main operational use of PSUs shifted to providing a police response to public disorder.

Currently police officers are trained to three levels of capability: level 3 (basic), level 2 (enhanced) and level 1 (specialist). Level 3 is typically provided to officers in the early stages of their careers who may be deployed to the least complex public order situations. They are not members of PSUs. Officers in PSUs receive training at either level 2 or 1 (although level 1 is usually used to train officers working in specialist public order units on a full-time basis). Training is conducted in accordance with national standards (ACPO, 2004), termed Mutual Aid Standard Training (MAST). In addition to providing PSU training to a sufficient number of officers to meet its own requirements, each force is required to have a number of PSUs available to meet the force's national mutual aid commitment.

Mutual aid

The nature or scale of some events may be beyond the capacity of individual police forces to handle and in the absence of a national riot police (or 'third force') in the UK, help is required from other forces. The procedure through which this is arranged is known as mutual aid. Requests for help of this nature are commonly associated with various forms of protest that attracts large numbers of people and at which disorder and violence may occur.

Historically, arrangements of this nature were made by informal requests for assistance that one chief constable made to his counterparts in neighbouring forces. The Police Act 1890 formalised the procedure whereby arrangements of this nature could be voluntarily entered into in advance and activated when necessary, and a national structure was developed in 1925 in the wake of the 1919 Desborough Committee. This was designed to remove the need for military involvement in handling public disorder (Geary, 1985: 16–17). The Police Act 1964 effectively made it compulsory for forces to comply with requests for assistance by a force facing a significant strain on its resources and the procedure is currently governed by the Police Act 1996, which also includes police forces in Scotland and Northern Ireland in mutual aid arrangements. The police authority that receives aid from other forces is required to reimburse the police authority that provides this assistance, although the Home Secretary adjudicates in the event of a dispute regarding the sum to be paid (Brown, 1998: 8–9).

Requests for mutual aid were initially made locally by the chief constable whose force was faced with a public order problem. However, the development of the National Reporting Centre during the 1970s enabled the deployment of officers (who were organised in PSUs) to a hot spot to be coordinated centrally. Currently, the Police National Information and Coordination Centre (PNICC) deals with such issues and was responsible for the deployment of police officers from across England and Wales to deal with the 2011 riots in London.

A significant consequence of the use of mutual aid is the need for the standardisation of police weaponry and tactics (including the use of consistent command and control systems) and the training that underpins their utilisation in order that officers from different police forces who are deployed at a specific event are able to function effectively as one unit. The term 'interoperability' is used to describe the ability of forces to work together effectively. A key initiative in securing such standardisation was ACPO's *Public Order Manual of Tactical Operations and Related Matters*, which was first issued in 1983, and in more recent years joint training exercises involving officers from different forces have also been undertaken to pursue this objective. As is referred to above, this Manual has been subsequently superseded by the ACPO *Manual of Guidance on Keeping the Peace* that was published in 2007.

However, progress in securing standardisation was hesitant. A report by Her Majesty's Inspectorate of Constabulary (HMIC) identified a number of problems relating to the effectiveness of mutual aid arrangements that included inconsistencies in the approaches and tactics used by individual forces in public order training programmes (some forces, for example, training officers to use shields in an offensive as well as a defensive manner) and variations in the equipment made available by forces to their officers engaged in public order situations, a problem partly explained by the existence of two separate procurement processes for the purchase of body armour (HMIC, 2009: 6). To address problems of this nature, in July 2010 ACPO devised a new formula for the provision of mutual aid by forces.

Escalated force versus negotiated management

Changes to public order policing affecting training, weaponry and tactics have enabled the police to deliver a more professional service in relation to the policing of public order situations. These changes are often dubbed 'paramilitary policing', which has the potential to give rise to an aggressive and confrontational style of policing. However, the extent to which this happens is subject to variation.

The 1980s have been depicted as the 'decade of disorder' (Joyce, 1992: 232) and witnessed several important manifestations of protest, including demonstrations, riots and industrial disputes. The key changes that were introduced into the policing of protests in this period occurred within a political context that was favourable towards a more aggressive response, to which the term 'escalated force' has been applied (Waddington, 2007: 10).

The Thatcher years (1979–90) gave rise to what has been described as the 'strong state'. This was depicted as the inevitable consequence of the Thatcherite free market policies in which the state and its agencies developed the capacity to be able to counter effectively the opposition of those who were adversely affected by these economic policies or who sought to orchestrate challenges to them (Gamble, 1988; Hall, 1980). These were identified as the working class, who had borne the brunt of the fall in living standards through inflation and who were the first to experience unemployment (Bunyan, 1977: 277). These became viewed as the 'enemy within', a term used by the Prime Minister in connection with the miners during their 1984/5 strike.

The notion of 'escalated force' suggests that the new powers that were given to the police and the development of more robust tactics to deal with crowd situations enabled them to intervene aggressively on behalf of the state, whose legitimacy was threatened by 'a whole panoply of public order challenges' (Brewer *at al.,* 1996: xiv). The use of CS gas in connection with the riots in Toxteth in 1981 event epitomised the aggressive response to protest and dissent and prompted one chief constable to argue that a more appropriate response by the police to inner-city disorders was to 'talk hearts and minds, not CS gas and plastic bullets' (Alderson, 1981). However, escalated force continued to be used and was employed on several occasions during the 1984/5 miners' dispute.

The depiction by the government of protesters as 'enemies' of the state meant that the use by the police of aggressive tactics to quell dissent would be supported by the government – a situation that was starkly evidenced by Margaret

Thatcher's support of controversial police actions at Orgreave during the 1984/5 miners' dispute. The knowledge by the police that methods entailing the use of violence against protesters would not be condemned by the government was an important underpinning of the use of escalated force during the Thatcher years.

Actions associated with escalated force were also pursued in other countries that included Germany, Spain, Canada and the USA. These adopted the practice of 'strategic incapacitation', which sought to create physical obstacles to participation in demonstrations (O'Connor, 2009: 30).

One difficulty with the use of escalated force as an approach to policing public order situations was that robust policing at events of this nature made for poor public relations by presenting an image of policing that was at variance with the historic principle of policing by consent and ultimately exerted an adverse effect on the legitimacy of the police. Accordingly, changes were introduced during the 1990s that were characterised as 'negotiated management'. This embraced a more sensitive form of policing protest, which involved 'a greater respect for the 'rights' of protesters, a more tolerant approach to community disruption, closer communication and cooperation with the public, a reduced tendency to make arrests (particularly as a tactic of first resort) and application of only the minimum force required in order to control a situation. (Waddington, 2007: 10). Changes to public order legislation (especially the advance notice requirement that was contained in the Public Order Act 1986) tended to encourage police and protesters to meet and negotiate issues such as the route of an event, which had previously resulted in disorder.

However, although negotiated management characterised the police response to protest during and after the 1990s, there were variations to this approach. This led to the conclusion that the 'nature of contemporary public order policing is too variable and complicated to lend itself to trite or superficial analysis' (Waddington, 2007: 5). The stance of the police towards protest is influenced by a range of factors that may result in a positive or negative view being taken towards specific events. These include the willingness of protesters to abide by police instructions or requests and the track record of an organisation involved in previous protests. In this respect, a distinction has been drawn between contained and transgressive protests (Noakes, Klocke and Gillham, 2005: 247–8). The former embraces groups willing to abide by the rules of the game and who are likely to be treated differently from those protesters whose attitudes are perceived as less cooperative and antagonistic towards the police and who are unwilling to enter into a dialogue with them regarding a specific event.

Episodes that included the inability of the police to control the 1999 Stop the City demonstration in London exerted an important influence on the policing of subsequent events associated with the anti-capitalist/anti-globalisation movement, which remained on the receiving end of aggressive forms of policing that entailed the use of tactics such as 'kettling' or corralling (whereby crowds were cordoned off into confined spaces and retained there for long periods of time, with attempts sometimes being made by the police to collect the names and addresses of those contained) and the use of batons and snatch squads (Waddington, 2007: 3).

Other factors may also influence the way in which protest is policed (Waddington, 2007: 15). These include the influence exerted over police actions by politicians and by public opinion.

The interpretation placed by the media on an event may be an important source of information that influences subsequent police actions. Media reporting that the fuel protesters in 2000 were widely supported, coupled with the absence of pressure being placed upon the police by the government in the early days of this event, were important factors in explaining the laid-back nature of the initial police response. Conversely, later media arguments that this protest posed a threat to the operations of the NHS and government pressure on the petrol companies to commence the delivery of fuel contributed to a more robust police action, which included escorting tankers to forecourt points of delivery.

See also: anti-globalisation/anti-capitalism protests (UK), Broadwater Farm Estate riot (Haringey, London) 1985, fracking protests, fuel crisis (Britain) 2000, G20 protests (London) 2009, Grosvenor Square (London) 1968, kettling, Lewisham disorders (Lewisham, London) 1976, miners' dispute (Britain) 1984–5, Notting Hill Carnival riot (Notting Hill, London) 1976, paramilitary policing, political policing, Red Lion Square (London) 1974, riot police subversion, third force

Sources and further reading

ACPO (2004) *ACPO Manual of Guidance Public Order Standards, Tactics and Training.* London: CENTREX.

Alderson, J. (1981) Evidence submitted to Lord Scarman's Inquiry into the Brixton Disorders, 2 September, quoted in Northam, G. (1989) *Shooting in the Dark: Riot Police in Britain.* London: Faber & Faber.

Brewer, J., Guelke, A., Hume, I., Moxon-Browne, E. and Wilford, R. (1996) *The Police, Public Order and the State*, 2nd edn. London: Macmillan.

Brown, A. (1998) *Police Governance.* London: Cavendish Publishing.

Bunyan, T. (1977) *The History and Practice of the Political Police in Britain.* London: Quartet Books.

——. (1985) 'From Saltley to Orgreave via Brixton'. *Journal of Law and Society*, 12(3): 293–303.

College of Policing (2013) *Authorised Professional Practice.* www.app.college.police.uk/app-content/public-order/?s= (date accessed 10 May 2014).

Devlin, J. (1966) *Police Procedure, Administration and Organisation.* London: Butterworths.

Fine, B. and Millar, R. (eds) (1985) *Policing the Miners' Strike.* London: Lawrence & Wishart.

Gamble, T. (1988) *The Free Market and the Strong State.* London: Macmillan.

Geary, R. (1985) *Policing Industrial Disputes 1893–1985.* London: Methuen.

Hall, S. (1980) *Drifting into a Law and Order Society*. London: Cobden Trust.

HMIC (2009a) *Adapting to Protest*. London: HMIC. Available at: www.hmic.gov.uk/media/adapting-to-protest-20090705.pdf (date accessed 10 May 2014).

———. (2009b) *Adapting to Protest: Nurturing the British Model of Policing*. London: HMIC. Available at: www.hmic.gov.uk/media/adapting-to-protest-nurturing-the-british-model-of-policing-20091125.pdf (date accessed 10 May 2014).

Home Office (1974) *Police Manual of Home Defence*. London: HMSO.

Joyce, P. (1992) 'Decade of Disorder'. *Policing*, 8(3): 232–48.

Noakes, J., Klocke, B. and Gillham, P. (2005) 'Whose Streets? Police and Protester Struggles over Space in Washington DC, September 2001'. *Police and Society*, 15(3): 235–54.

Northam, G. (1989) *Shooting in the Dark: Riot Police in Britain*. London: Faber & Faber.

O'Connor, D. (2009) *Adapting to Protest: Nurturing the British Model of Policing*. London: HMIC.

Reiner, R. (1991) *Chief Constables: Bobbies, Bosses or Bureaucrats?* Oxford University Press.

Thackrah, J. (ed.) (1985) *Contemporary Policing: An Examination of Society in the 1980s*. London: Sphere.

Waddington, D. (2007) *Policing Public Order: Theory and Practice*. Cullompton: Willan Publishing.

Waddington, P. (1987) 'Towards Paramilitarism? Dilemmas in the Policing of Public Disorder'. *British Journal of Criminology*, 27: 37–46.

———. (2003) 'Policing Public Order and Political Contention' in T. Newburn (ed.), *Handbook of Policing*. Cullompton: Willan Publishing, pp. 394–421.

PUBLIC ORDER POLICING (FRANCE)

In France, like the dual policing system that is in operation across the country, there are two main bodies responsible for riot control. Both the two main organisations in the French policing system have specific units designed to react to disorder and civil unrest. The older military force, the *Gendarmerie Nationale*, has around 17,000 *Gendarmes mobile*, whilst the newer civilian force, the *Police Nationale*, is supported by 14,000 officers of the Republican Security Companies (*Compagnies Républicaines de Sécurité* or CRS).

The *Police Nationale* operate at the local level, reporting to the Minister of the Interior, whilst the Gendarmerie, also a civilian police, originally reported direct to the Minister of Defence, but now report to the Minister of Interior as well. Whilst this fragmented structure is a result of their historical development, it is seen as a strength, particularly in terms of accountability and state power (Stead, 1983). However, at ground level, there is a deep mistrust between the two organisations entrusted with riot control.

The CRS was initially formed from Mobile Reserve Groups formed for the maintenance of order during the war years by the pro-Nazi Vichy government. On the other hand, the Gendarmerie saw themselves as the supporters of the free French by supporting the Resistance, although this was not always the case, with many choosing to collaborate. Since 2009, the French state has legislated to bring the workings of the two organisations together (Faure et al., 2008); however, so far, this does not appear to have had much impact on the units responsible for the maintenance of order.

In 1981, both the *Gendarmes mobile* and the CRS were deployed in the suburbs, or banlieues, of Paris where disaffected migrants from France's former colonies engaged in disorder. The French government's response to these riots was to instigate a programme of reintegration via youth strategies such as the *étés jeunes* (youth summer) programme. This approach took under-privileged, mainly North African, youths out of the banlieues into structured holiday camps over the summer months. A new type of social worker, the *animateur*, was developed to lead these camps, and those undertaking this post were drawn from the same communities.

There were also local crime prevention panels (*conseils départmentaux de prevention de la délinquance* (CDPDs)), which were chaired by locally elected mayors (De Maillard, 2005). However, the police were not involved and stood outside these partnerships, and relationships between them and the minority communities in the banlieues continued to deteriorate (Crawford, 2002). This social approach to crime prevention has been questioned; French commentators have stated prior to the most recent disturbances that these responses have proved to be ineffective and that 'prevention has supported urban rioters rather than preventing them from acting' (De Maillard and Roché, 2004: 141).

In addition, French police officers rarely originate from the areas they police. Young Gendarmes have no say in their deployment and are often placed in areas which are the most violent and deprived, often where more senior or experienced officers do not want to go.

As a result, protest and disorder in France in the last decade has continued to focus upon communities with high minority populations, particularly young ethnic people from North Africa. The colonial past and in particular the Algerian independence struggle (from 1954 to 1962) have played a significant part in the historically tense relationships between the French police and minorities. In the worst outbreak of disorder in France in 2005, laws dating back to the colonial days were enacted to try to stem the level of disorder, including house searches at night and curfews.

The disorders in 2005 that affected the suburbs of Paris and many major French cities were triggered when French police pursued a group of youths of North African descent into a power station in Clichy-sous-Bois, where two were killed by electrocution. These large-scale riots were almost repeated in 2007, when two youths from a minority community north of Paris were killed when a French police vehicle collided with their vehicle. In both instances, the French riot police were criticised for a lack of preparation and, once deployed in the affected communities, these specialised public order squads lacked local knowledge, so often got lost (De Maillard and Roché, 2009). The lack of inter-force training and coordination also impacted upon the response to these disorders, with the CRS and *Gendarmes mobile* responding to the same location. At the time of writing, a commander at the *Gendarmerie Nationale*'s state-of-the-art riot training school at St Astier revealed that no joint training with the CRS has been arranged – nor, due to the deep-seated rivalry and dislike of the other force, was this likely.

In recent years, the same forces have been deployed to clear illegal immigrants' camps belonging to the Roma community (*Daily Mail*, 2013) as well as enforce the ban on Muslim women wearing the burqa (Gatestone Institute, 2013). In 2010 a riot was triggered in Saint-Aignan when a Roma boy was shot and killed by a Gendarme at a checkpoint (*BBC News*, 2010). Tension between the French police and minority communities remains high, despite efforts by the government to introduce new codes of conduct for officers (*Daily Telegraph*, 2013). A recent report by a human rights organisation suggests that black and Arab youths are singled out by the patrolling CRS officers in the banlieues are and subjected to unwarranted identity checks, searches and provocation (Human Rights Watch, 2012).

Unlike the riots in the USA or the UK, which resulted in the Kerner Commission and the Scarman Commission respectively, the major rioting in France in 2005 and 2007 has not led to any major inquiry. The issues of relationships with minority communities, the response to civil unrest and the management of the police have not been subject to any real scrutiny. Whether this will come back to haunt the nation in the wake of its burqa ban and treatment of Roma communities remains to be seen.

See also: banlieue riots (Paris) 2005, riot police, third force

Sources and further reading

BBC News (2010) 'Troops Patrol French Village of Saint-Aignan after Riot', 19 July, www.bbc.co.uk/news/world-europe-10681796 (date accessed 10 May 2014).

Body-Gendrot, S. (2013) 'Urban Violence in France and England: Comparing Paris (2005) and London (2011)'. *Policing and Society: An International Journal of Research and Policy*, 23(1): 6–25.

Crawford, A. (2002) 'The Growth of Crime Prevention in France as Contrasted with the English Experience' in G. Hughes, E. McLaughlin, and J. Muncie (eds), *Crime Prevention and Community Safety: New Directions*. London: Sage, pp. 214–39.

Daily Mail (2013) 'French Police Clear Gypsy Camp in New Crackdown on Illegal Immigrants', 5 June, www.dailymail.co.uk/news/article-2336311/French-police-clear-gypsy-camp-new-crackdown-illegal-immigrants.html (date accessed 10 May 2014).

Daily Telegraph (2013) 'French Police Told to Be More Polite and Less Racist', 4 March, www.telegraph.co.uk/news/worldnews/europe/france/9907016/French-police-told-to-be-more-polite-and-less-racist.html (date accessed 10 May 2014).

De Maillard, J. (2005) 'The Governance of Safety in France: Is There Anybody

in Charge?' *Theoretical Criminology*, 9(3): 325–43.
De Maillard, J. and Roché, S. (2004) 'Crime and Justice in France: Time Trends, Policies and Political Debate'. *European Journal of Criminology*, 1(1): 111–51.
——. (2009) 'Crisis in Policing: The French Rioting of 2005'. *Policing: A Journal of Policy and Practice*, 3(1): 34–40.
Faure, J., Demessine, M., Haenel, H., Madrelle, P., Pasqua, C., Pozzo di Borgo, Y. and Rouviere, A. (2008) 'Quel avenir pour la gendarmerie?' *Report of the Committee on Foreign Affairs*, No. 171, www.senat.fr/rap/r07-271/r07-271.html (date accessed 10 May 2014).
Gatestone Institute (2013) 'France: Muslims Attack Police for Enforcing Burqa Ban', 25 July, www.gatestoneinstitute.org/3877/france-muslim-attack-burqa-ban (date accessed 10 May 2014).
Human Rights Watch (2012) 'The Root of Humiliation: Abusive Identity Checks in France', www.hrw.org/sites/default/files/reports/france0112ForUpload.pdf (date accessed 10 May 2014).
Stead, P.J. (1983) *The Police of France*. New York: Macmillan.

PUSSY RIOT PROTEST (MOSCOW) 2012

On 21 February 2012, members of a Russian punk-rock group, Pussy Riot, staged a protest against President Vladimir Putin in Moscow's Christ the Saviour Cathedral. This took the form of performing a political song in the form of a prayer, which began with the words 'Virgin birth-giver of God, drive away Putin! Drive away Putin' (in the sense of throwing him out of office) (Pussy Riot, quoted in Tayler, 2012). This was performed for less than two minutes before church security stopped them, although the entire event was videotaped by other Pussy Riot members, who escaped.

This protest occurred against the background of Putin's presidential election victory. Although Putin secured around 66 per cent of the vote in the 2012 election, the contest was marked by a series of demonstrations that drew crowds of several tens of thousands.

The protest was also designed to highlight the close ties that existed between the hierarchy in the Russian Orthodox Church and the state's political leadership. The 'prayer' attacked the Church's praise of 'rotten leaders' and included an attack on the Patriarch of Moscow and all Russia with the words 'Patriarch Gundyaev believes in Putin. Would be better, the bastard, if he believed in God!' (Pussy Riot, quoted in Tayler, 2012).

In August 2012, three of the women involved in the protest, Nadezhda Tolokonnikova, Marina Alyokhina and Yekaterina Samutsevich, were given two-year sentences to be served in a penal colony for the offence of hooliganism motivated by religious hatred. Yekaterina Samutsevich was later granted conditional release on appeal and the other two members of group were released under the terms of a general amnesty in December 2012.

Since then, Russia's Parliament adopted several new laws targeting activists and those critical of the authorities whereby 'the rights to freedom of expression, association and assembly have come under increasing attack, despite the fact that these rights are explicitly guaranteed by the Russian Constitution and international human rights treaties to which Russia is party' (Amnesty International, 2013: 5). These included restrictive rules on conducting public protests, which carried high penalties of up to US$32,000, re-criminalising the offence of libel, requiring non-governmental organisations receiving overseas funding to register as 'foreign agents' and the introduction of a broad new legal definition of 'treason', which could potentially criminalise human rights and political activism.

See also: counterculture protest, Tiananmen Square protests (Beijing) 1976 and 1989

Sources and further reading

Amnesty International (2013) *Freedom under Threat: Clampdown on Freedoms of Expression, Association and Assembly in Russia.* London: Amnesty International.

Tayler, J. (2012) 'What Pussy Riot's "Punk Prayer" Really Said', *The Atlantic*, 8 November, www.theatlantic.com/international/archive/2012/11/what-pussy-riots-punk-prayer-really-said/264562 (date accessed 5 June 2014).

R

RED LION SQUARE (LONDON) 1974

On 15 June 1974, the National Front held a march through the West End of London to protest against the government's amnesty for illegal immigrants. The march culminated in a meeting in Conway Hall, situated in Red Lion Square, London.

Opponents of the National Front held a counter-demonstration and open-air meeting in Red Lion Square. A room for a small meeting was also booked in Conway Hall, which could be entered by a separate door from that used by the National Front. These activities were preceded by a march, which began at the Embankment. This event was organised by the London Area Council of Liberation, although it attracted support from other groups such as the International Marxist Group, the International Socialists and the Communist Party of England (Marxist-Leninist). The numbers involved were small – approximately 900 members of the National Front and 1,000 of Liberation. Around 900 police were deployed (Clutterbuck, 1980: 158, 162 and 165).

A police cordon had been set up in Red Lion Square to keep the two demonstrations apart. However, when the Liberation march entered the Square, the police cordon was charged by some of its participants from the International Marxist Group, who had held back from the main body of the march and whose aim was to block the entrance to the hall. The senior police commander (Deputy Assistant Commissioner J. Gerrard) viewed this action as constituting a riot (Gilbert, 1975: 5). This flavoured subsequent police interventions, since 'it was the duty of the police to suppress [it] by force, if necessary' (Scarman, 1975: 8). The police cordon was reinforced by mounted police and the Special Patrol Group, which succeeded in forcing the demonstrators back. Some were forced out of the Square and others remained in it. The situation in the Square was confused by a perception that the police had made a-last minute decision to vary the route into the Square that had been previously agreed with the Liberation organisers, an issue that may have arisen as the result of a misunderstanding between Liberation and the police. Friction between the police and demonstrators was also aggravated by a further view that police actions sought to prevent the open-air meeting in the Square from taking place (Gilbert, 1975: 67), although this did go ahead.

At this stage, the National Front march was approaching the Square. Liberation demonstrators expelled from Red Lion Square re-grouped in the vicinity of Southampton Row, where police cordons separated them from the National Front march. Some friction occurred between the two sets of opponents, which led the police to fear that they might come into direct contact with each other. To prevent this from happening, mounted police from Red Lion Square charged the Liberation demonstrators. Police officers with truncheons drawn joined this attack, which witnessed indiscriminate attacks being carried out on demonstrators. Their means of dispersal were hampered by the existence of a further police cordon that had been formed in Theobald's Road. Accusations were made of the use of excessive force by the police, who were accused of mounting 'an ill-advised assault upon a crowd ... which ... was trapped at the time and which created panic and quite unnecessary disorder and injury, and brought about arrests which never need have taken place' (Gilbert, 1975: 18). Further attacks on the International Marxist Group contingent were later made by the police in an attempt to arrest one of its leaders in Boswell Street.

While the confrontation between the police and Liberation demonstrators took place, the National Front march was escorted by the police into Red Lion Square and into Conway Hall.

In total, 51 demonstrators were arrested and 54 individuals were injured, including 46 police officers (Clutterbuck, 1980: 165). The demonstration in Red Lion Square became infamous as it witnessed the death of a demonstrator, Kevin Gately, the first person to be killed at a political demonstration in Britain since 1919. The subsequent coroner's inquest attributed his death to misadventure, concluding that he had died as the result of a blow to the head from a blunt instrument. Critics of the police actions argued that he had died 'because the police launched an onslaught against the demonstrators' (Rollo, 1980: 180).

A number of key issues arose from the events that occurred on 15 June. Accusations were made of police violence, often of an indiscriminate nature, towards those opposed to the National Front. It was also questioned whether the police should have banned the National Front march under the provisions of the Race Relations Act 1965, whether it was wise for the police to have permitted the two demonstrations to occur within the same vicinity and whether the decision by Liberation to also book a room in Conway Hall was sensible, given its almost inevitable public order implications. Police tactics were also questioned, especially in connection with failing to prevent those involved in the violence in Red Lion Square from advancing towards Southampton Row to confront the National Front march and subsequently trapping demonstrators at Southampton Row following the re-positioning of a police cordon.

These and other issues were considered by a public inquiry conducted by Lord Scarman under the provisions of the Police Act 1964. Its remit was to 'review the events and actions which led to disorder in Red Lion Square on 15 June and to consider whether any lessons may be learned for the better maintenance of public order when demonstrations take place' (Scarman, 1975: 2).

The report recognised that: 'Amongst our fundamental human rights there are without doubt the rights of peaceful assembly and public protest and the right to public order and tranquillity. Civilized living collapses – it is obvious – if public protest becomes violent protest or public order degenerates into the quietism imposed by successful oppression.' He argued that the task of the law in a liberal state is to strike a balance between the two poles in order to accommodate the collective voices of protest within the framework of public order (Scarman, 1975: 5).

Lord Scarman stated that the police were correct not to ban the National Front march, although he suggested that section 6 of the Race Relations Act was 'an embarrassment to the police' and was 'useless to a policeman on the street'. It required 'radical amendment' to make it a more effective sanction (Scarman, 1975: 44–6). He argued that the International Marxist Group's 'inexcusable assault' on the police cordon in Red Lion Square initiated the violence that occurred on that day (Scarman, 1975: 43–4) Nonetheless, he argued that while 'the hostility and aggression of those arrested ... made force unavoidable', he concluded that 'in all probability there were arrests in which excessive force was used' (Scarman, 1975: 45). He also suggested that 'the major party in controlling and managing demonstrations should continue to be played by the ordinary divisional policeman' as opposed to the Special Patrol Group (Scarman, 1975: 46). In addition, he rejected police proposals that were put to him, including an advance notice requirement for processions.

See also: demonstrations, Lewisham disorders (Lewisham, London) 1976, paramilitary policing, public order legislation (England and Wales), public order policing (England and Wales), Southall disorders (Southall, London) 1979

Sources and further reading

Clutterbuck, R. (1980) *Britain in Agony: The Growth of Political Violence.* Harmondsworth: Penguin.

Gilbert, T. (1975) *Only One Died: An Investigation into Police Behaviour in Red Lion Square.* London: Kay Beauchamp.

Rollo, J. (1980) 'The Special Patrol Group' in P. Hain (ed.), *Policing the Police, Volume 2.* London: John Calder.

Scarman, Lord L. (1975) *The Red Lion Square Disorders of 15 June 1974*. London: HMSO, Cmnd. 5919.

RIOT POLICE

Riot police are police officers who are trained to deal with any form of crowd disorder. Their training typically includes the use of tactics designed to quell disturbances and the use of specialised weaponry to deal with disorders.

Most European Union countries have units that act in the capacity of riot police. The arrangements in France (the *Compagnies Républicains de Securité* and the *Gendarmerie nationale*) and the UK (Police Support Units and specialist police force public order units) are dealt with in separate entries in this work.

In Germany, the *Bereitschaftspolizei* (*BePo*) serve as riot police. This is centrally coordinated through the Federal Ministry of the Interior, is structured along military lines and consists of a number of rapid response units of the German Federal police (the *Bunderpolizei*), known as *Bundespolizeiabteilung*, which may be called upon to re-inforce the state *Bereitschaftspolizei* units when required to do so. At the state level, officers perform other police duties when they are not involved in crowd control. The training and equipment available to the *Bereitschaftspolizei* is standardised and their weaponry includes armoured cars, water cannons and earth-moving equipment.

In Spain, riot policing is the responsibility of the National Police Force (*Cuerpo Nacional de Policía* (CNP)), which is controlled by the Ministry of the Interior. This force was created in 1986, involving a merger of the existing plainclothes and uniformed branches of the national police. This force is responsible for policing urban areas when it is not involved in crowd control work and includes a Special Operations Group (*Grupo Especial de Operaciones* (GEO)) that deals with terrorism and related matters, including hostage negotiations. It has prominently features in the anti-austerity protests, where it has been accused of using violence against protesters and bystanders (Tremlett, 2012).

In Greece, Units for the Reinstatement of Order (*Monades Apokatastasis Taksis* (MAT)) are responsible for riot control. They are a specialist division of the Hellenic Police and date from 1976, and were designed to remove the responsibility for public order policing from the regular police and the military. The MAT possess specialist equipment when engaged in crowd control, including Plexiglas shields, long and short batons, tear gas and a range of protective clothing such as helmets with visors. MAT officers do not wear any form of identification.

In the Irish Republic, all public order policing is handled by the Garda Public Order Unit. This is a centrally controlled unit of the *Garda Síochána*. It was used, along with regular members of the police force, at the Corrib gas protests (which opposed the extraction of natural gas off the north-west coast of Ireland by the Shell Oil Company). Police tactics used since 2005 at this protest (including a 'no arrest' policy) resulted in a considerable volume of criticism of its actions. The Public Order Unit was also deployed in connection with anti-austerity protests.

Countries outside of Europe also possess specialist riot police. In Russia, this work is performed by OMON units (initially Otryad Militsii Osobogo Naznacheniya or Special Purpose Militia Unit, but re-named in 2012 to Otryad Mobilniy Osobogo Naznacheniya or Special Purpose Mobile Unit). OMON originated in 1979 in preparation for the 1980 Olympic Games, seeking to avoid a repetition of the massacre of Israeli athletes that had occurred in Munich at the 1972 Olympics. Countering terrorism was initially a key purpose of OMON, many of whose members were former soldiers. However, police reorganisation in 1987 resulted in a diversification of the role of OMON units to embrace a wider range of duties associated with the maintenance of public order. This has included their involvement (alongside the military) in Chechnya following its declaration of independence in 1991. OMON units are paramilitary in nature and its members have first to have completed their military service. Their weaponry includes the AK-74 assault rifle and water cannons. When deployed in Chechnya, OMON units have used more sophisticated weaponry similar to that used by the Army.

In Turkey, the riot police consists of the Çevik Kuvvet (Agile Force or Rapid Response Force). This is a full-time riot police that was established in 1982 and is controlled by the Turkish National Police (or General Directorate of Security). Its members are equipped with tear gas, pepper spray and plastic bullets, and the force has water cannons and Scorpion (Akrep) armoured personnel carriers at its disposal. The Turkish riot police have been active in recent protests in Turkey in 2013 and 2014.

In America, riot police are organised at the level of Police Departments, although federal law-enforcement agencies (such as the FBI, the US Capitol Police, the US Mint Police and the US Park Police) may also have units of this nature. They mainly consist of regular police, who when dealing with public order situations are organised into special weapons and tactics (SWAT) teams (although the acronym 'SWAT' is not universally used and units of this nature sometimes have different titles, such as Special Response Teams, Special Operations Teams (in the case of the New York Police Department) and the Emergency Services Unit.

The first of these units was the Special Weapons and Tactics squad of the Philadelphia Police Department that was set up in 1964 and such units have since become widespread: by the 1990s, 90 per cent of police departments in cities with a population over 50,000 had such units, as did 70 per cent of police departments in smaller cities (Bowling, 2010: 44)

They have the use of sophisticated weaponry, which includes submachine guns, assault rifles, sniper rifles, stun grenades, tasers, pepper spray and tear gas. They also have the use of specialised equipment such as armoured vehicles and heavy body armour. They are deployed in a range of situations, including hostage situations, counter-terrorism and serious crimes, and have increasingly been deployed in public order situations.

It has been argued that the involvement of the police in the 'war on drugs' (launched by President Richard Nixon in 1971) and the threats posed by terrorists following 9/11 have 'lent police forces across the country justification to acquire the latest technology, equipment and tactical training for newly created specialized units' (Baker, 2011). This has led to accusations of the militarisation of American policing. Some units of this nature 'have tanks ... often from military surplus, for use in hostage situations or drug raids – not to mention the sort of equipment and training one would need to deter a Mumbai-style guerrilla assault' (Baker, 2011). A key difficulty with this situation is that it influences the manner in which the police deliver their routine law and order roles, thus threatening police–public relationships.

A further body in America that may be called upon to deal with various threats posed to public order is the National Guard. This is a reserve of the US Armed Forces that is organised at the state level. Most members of the National Guard are civilians who serve part time, although there is also a full-time contingent. The State Governor acts as commander-in-chief of the National Guard and may mobilise it to respond to natural disasters such as floods, hurricanes and earthquakes.

The National Guard may, however, be placed under federal control, a process referred to as 'federalising' the National Guard. This action is carried out on the orders of the President and is often used to augment US forces when they are engaged in theatres of war abroad. However, federalising the National Guard may also take place in order to deal with domestic situations. It had been used in Arkansas in 1954 and Alabama in 1963 to enforce the de-segregation of schools in the face of local opposition headed by the state's governors. The procedure was also used to deal with domestic events such as the 1992 Los Angeles riots and in connection with providing security following the 9/11 terrorist attacks.

The power of the President to use troops (including the National Guard) in connection with civil issues derives from the Insurrection Act 1807. This measure applied to situations of lawlessness, insurrection and rebellion. The scope of situations enabling the President to do this without a request being made by a state governor or state legislature was expended in the Defense Authorization Bill 2007 to cover a natural disaster, epidemic, serious public health emergency, terrorist attack or other condition where the President determined that the state authorities were not capable of maintaining public order. This provision was, however, repealed the following year.

See also: anti-austerity protests (worldwide), public order policing (England and Wales), public order policing (France), states of emergency, third force

Sources and further reading

Baker, A. (2011) 'When the Police Go Military', *The New York Times Sunday Review*, www.nytimes.com/2011/12/04/sunday-review/have-american-police-become-militarized.html?pagewanted=all&_r=0 (date accessed 12 May 2014).
Barrington, B. (2010) *Breakdown in Trust: A Report on the Corrib Gas Dispute*. County Dublin: Frontline.
Bowling, B. (2010) *Policing the Caribbean: Transnational Security Cooperation in Practice*. Oxford University Press.
Tremlett, G. (2012) 'Spain Reels at Violent Tactics by Riot Police', *The Observer*, 29 September, www.theguardian.com/world/2012/sep/29/spain-riot-police (date accessed 12 May 2014).

RIOTS

The term 'riot' denotes an episode of civil disorder that entails violence that is directed against targets including public or privately owned property (typically in the form of looting or vandalism) and the civil authorities and security services (who are present at the event in order to preserve order). Members of the general public may also form the target of the rioters' anger, perhaps in disorders such as race riots or sectarian violence.

In England and Wales, the legal definition of a riot is provided in the Public Order Act 1986 and entails an event where 12 or more individuals who are present together use or threaten unlawful violence for a common purpose, and the conduct of them (taken together) is such as would cause a person of reasonable firmness present at the scene to fear for his or her personal safety. The offence carries a maximum penalty of ten years' imprisonment and an unlimited fine.

Title 18 of the US Code defines the federal offence of riot as:

A public disturbance involving (1) an act or acts of violence by one or more persons part of an assemblage of three or more persons, which act or acts shall constitute a clear and present danger of, or shall result in, damage or injury to the property of any other person or to the person of any other individual or (2) a threat or threats of the commission of an act or acts of violence by one or more persons part of an assemblage of three or more persons having, individually or collectively, the ability of immediate execution of such threat or threats, where the performance of the threatened act or acts of violence would constitute a clear and present danger of, or would result in, damage or injury to the property of any other person or to the person of any other individual.

Individual states have their own definitions of such events.

Often, however, the term 'riot' is more subjectively applied by politicians, the police or the media to any crowd of people who disturb the peace and whose behaviour requires police intervention to restore order. This crowd may have a common purpose or may be composed of participants who have a diverse range of motives that underpin their attendance at a riotous gathering. This latter situation was seen to exist in the riots that occurred in England in 2011 (Morrell *et al.*, 2011: para. 3).

It is often common practice in England and Wales that those engaged in riotous behaviour are prosecuted for a lesser offence (such as breach of the peace), which can be heard summarily in a magistrates' court. In England and Wales, individuals or other property owners who suffer from damage caused by disorderly activities that formally or informally constitute a riot are eligible for compensation from the police under the provisions of the Riot (Damages) Act 1886.

A riot may occur spontaneously or may involve some degree of organisation. In addition, riots may arise in connection with another form of protest, which gives rise to violence: the 1990 anti-Poll Tax riot in London is an example of this, which is discussed elsewhere in this book.

Riots are often viewed as acts of 'mindless hooliganism and yobbery' (Patten, quoted in Marwick, 2003), which have no underlying motive other than criminality or greed on the part of participants whose moral standards are below those of the remainder of society. In this case, rioters are depicted as being morally depraved. The scepticism displayed towards crowds by right-wing political thinking (since the presence of large numbers of people on the streets can have revolutionary consequences) can also be adapted towards riots in which participants are viewed as yielding to instincts that they would as individuals have kept under restraint. This situation has been summarised by the argument that 'a crowd being anonymous, and in consequences irresponsible, the sentiment of responsibility which always controls individuals disappears entirely' (Le Bon, 1895).

However, an alternative view of riots sees them as purposeful forms of protest, often associated with those at the bottom end of the social ladder (the underclass) who feel themselves to be marginalised from the operations of the conventional political system and have no means of expressing their dissatisfaction with society and how it treats them or of getting their concerns placed upon the formal political agenda and addressed.

This view of riots sees them as 'the ballot box of the poor' (Bachrach and Baratz, 1979) or the 'language of the unheard' (King, 1968), a legitimate form of protest directed against injustices that policy makers choose to ignore. The spectacular nature of riots is such that policy makers may be forced to undertake actions that they would otherwise choose not to perform so as to neuter the prevailing dissent and avoid a repetition of the disorder. The nature of the injustices complained of by rioters is varied, although high food prices and scarcities have underpinned disorders of this nature both historically (for example, the Women's March on Versailles on 5 October 1789, an event that triggered the French Revolution) and in the contemporary period (being a major factor in the Arab Spring uprisings).

However, the view that locates rioters at the bottom end of the social ladder is not invariably the case – for example, middle-class students were at the forefront of protests against the rise in university tuition fees that took place in England in 2010.

Although riots may occur spontaneously, they often take place following an event that triggers the disorder. The riots that have taken place in England and Wales since 1980 have frequently been set off by some form of police intervention in a community which has a history of poor police–public relations. This intervention often takes the form of an arrest in a public space, the perceived injustice of which serves to mobilise immediate bystanders, who may attempt to secure the release of a person who has been arrested or who become sufficiently enraged by the event to take to the streets to voice their anger.

However, although police actions may trigger disorder, it does not necessarily mean that bad policing practices are the fundamental cause of them. Other forms of injustice such as social and economic deprivation may be the key sources of dissatisfaction and what is seen as unjust police action serves to epitomise the operations of an unjust society, all aspects of which need to be addressed. It is perhaps for this reason that reforms to policing in England and Wales that were proposed in a report by Lord Scarman following the riots in England in 1981 (Scarman, 1981) failed to prevent further occurrences of disorder in the 1980s and beyond.

The nature of the police response to riots is an important aspect of contemporary public order policing. In England and Wales, a number of reforms have been introduced into policing practices that are collectively referred to as paramilitary policing. A key issue is whether to adopt coercive tactics (that may include the use of CS gas and other forms of weaponry) to break up crowds of rioters or whether to adopt an approach that seeks to win the 'hearts and minds' of disaffected communities (Alderson, 1981). This entails constant engagement by the police with those who live in such localities and the development of analytical tools including tension indicators to monitor community attitudes. In addition, the anger that initially drives people onto the streets may be fuelled by rumours (whether delivered by word of mouth or the social media) of further forms of inappropriate police action, which emphasises the importance of rumour management as a contemporary tool to be used by the police to defuse tense situations.

See also: Arab Spring, Broadwater Farm Estate riot (Haringey, London) 1985, copycat riots (England) 1981, paramilitary policing, public order legislation (England and Wales), public order policing (England and Wales)

Sources and further reading

Alderson, J. (1981) 'Evidence to Lord Scarman's Inquiry into the Brixton Riots'. Quoted in G. Northam (1998) *Shooting in the Dark: Riot Police in Britain*. London: Faber & Faber.

Bachrach, P. and Baratz, M. (1970) *Power and Poverty: Theory and Practice*. Oxford University Press.

Bloom, C. (2012) *Riot City*. Basingstoke: Palgrave Macmillan.

King, M.L. (1968) Speech at the Grosse Pointe Historical Society, 14 March, www.gphistorical.org/mlk/mlkspeech/index.htm (date accessed 15 May 2014).

Le Bon, G. (1895) *The Crowd: A Study of the Popular Mind*. Dunwoody, GA: Norman S. Berg. Available at: www.gutenberg.org/dirs/etext96/tcrwd10.txt (date accessed 15 May 2014).

Marwick, A. (2003) *British Society since 1945: The Penguin Social History of Britain*, 4th edn. London: Penguin.

Morrell, G., Scott, S., McNeish, D. and Webster, S. (2011) *The August Riots in England: Understanding the Involvement of Young People*. London: National Centre for Social Research, prepared for the Cabinet Office.

Scarman, Lord L. (1981) *The Brixton Disorders, 1–12 April 1981: Report of an Inquiry by the Rt Hon Lord Scarman OBE*. London: HMSO, Cm. 8427.

S

SELF-IMMOLATION

Self-immolation entails a protester setting himself or herself on fire. It is a form of non-violent direct action, the intention of which is to make public an injustice experienced directly by the protester that is symptomatic of a more general problem experienced within society or to promote a collective cause that the protester supports. The protester becomes a martyr and his or her act is designed to inspire others to protest in support of the issues that inspired the protester to die. It has been argued that: 'As an act of protest, it is intended to be public in at least one of two senses: performed in a public place in view of other people, or accompanied by a written letter addressed to political figures or to the general public' (Biggs, 2005).

The aims of self-immolation are similar to other forms of sacrifice in support of a political cause, such as hunger strikes. However, the dramatic nature of self-immolation gives the protest (and the cause behind it) considerable publicity both where the protest occurred and within the wider international community. Although self-immolation bears some resemblance to suicide attacks in the sense that it 'involves an individual intentionally killing himself or herself (or at least gambling with death) on behalf of a collective cause', it has been argued that: 'Unlike a suicidal attack, an act of self-immolation is not intended to cause physical harm to anyone else or to inflict material damage. The suicidal attack is an extraordinary weapon of war, whereas self-immolation is an extreme form of protest' (Biggs, 2005).

There have been several examples of self-immolation as a form of political protest. In June 1963, the Buddhist monk Quang Duc immolated himself in Saigon in protest against the discriminatory treatment accorded to Buddhists in South Vietnam under the regime headed by President Ngo Dinh Diem, which was seen to be promoting the interests of the country's minority Catholic population. Subsequently, four other Buddhist monks and a nun performed the same act. These actions 'inspired many others' (Biggs, 2005), triggering self-immolation to be used as a form of protest:

> rather suddenly, setting oneself on fire became a political act. As the American presence increased in Vietnam in the mid- to late 1960s, more and more monks committed self-immolation, including thirteen in one week. It even took place in the U.S., right outside the Pentagon, when Norman Morrison, an American Quaker burned himself to death while clinging onto his child as a mark of his rejection of the Vietnam War. (Sanburn, 2011)

Subsequently, self-immolation 'has become an increasingly common statement of protest in East Asia, particularly amongst Buddhist communities ... the predominant offenders are monks. A spate of self-immolations in Burma during 2007 and 2008 brought attention to the "Saffron Revolution" led by the country's monks in non-violent protest against the military junta that governed the country' (*History's Shadow*, 2012). Self-immolation is also used by Tibetans as a protest against China's suppression of their culture and religion and their demand for the Dalai Lama to be able to return to his homeland. It is not, however, confined to this part of the world or to Buddhist communities.

In 1968, protests against the Soviet invasions of Czechoslovakia, which ended the liberalising reforms of Alexander Dubček known as the Prague Spring, included the self-immolation of Ryszard Siwiec and Jan Palach. Self-immolation has also been practised in India since 1990 as a protest against the programme of affirmative action (known as Reservation) that seeks to allocate a percentage of public sector posts to disadvantaged communities drawn from Scheduled Castes, Scheduled Tribes and Other Backward Classes. It was also a feature of uprisings associated with Arab Spring – events that began with the self-immolation of Mohamed Bouazizi in Tunisia in December 2010.

See also: Arab Spring (Arab world) 2010 onwards, 'dirty protest' (Northern Ireland) 1978–81

Sources and further reading

Biggs, M. (2005) 'Dying without Killing: Self-immolations, 1963–2002' in D. Gambetta (ed.), *Making Sense of Suicide Missions*. Oxford University Press. Available at: http://users.ox.ac.uk/~sfos0060/immolation.pdf (date accessed 14 May 2014).

History's Shadow (2012) 'Self-immolation Losing Shock Value', http://historysshadow.wordpress.com/tag/self-immolation (date accessed 14 May 2014).

Sanburn, J. (2011) 'A Brief History of Self-immolation'. *Time World*, 20 January, http://content.time.com/time/world/article/0,8599,2043123,00.html (date accessed 14 May 2014).

SOCIAL MEDIA AND THE POLICING OF PROTEST AND DISORDER (WORLDWIDE)

The use of social media in policing protest and disorder has been an emerging issue that police forces across the world have had to respond to quickly. Since the Arab Spring in 2011, police agencies have been playing catch-up as people use new technology to organise themselves against authorities. The following discussion analyses the use made of police forces of this technology.

One of the earliest reported uses of the police using social media during protests was during the G8/G20 summits in Canada in 2010, where the Toronto Police Department used social media to track the movements of protestors, receive information from the public and monitor other news channels. Sites such as Twitter, Facebook and YouTube were monitored by officers for intelligence and to provide a communication channel to the public.

In the same year, the Metropolitan Police in the UK started to explore its use in the policing of student protests to open a channel of communication with anarchist groups. Whilst in the same year protest groups made good use of technology and the media to conduct protest campaigns. UK Uncut, an anti-tax-dodging protest group, utilised Twitter to organise a successful campaign against high street stores, while student groups at the 2010 protests in London used messaging and Google Maps to organise protestors, setting up their own control room. The latter initiative is designed to get ahead of police tactics and prevent the demonstrators being 'kettled'. It is termed 'Sukey' after the popular nursery rhyme 'Polly put the Kettle on, Sukey take it off again' (Kingsley, 2011). It has now been taken further with the development of a Web 2.0-based App which protestors can download to a smartphone to keep them up to date with current information in a demonstration, including routes, toilets and police deployments.

Whilst most UK forces now use social media (the most up-to-date figures suggest that 40 police forces out of the 43 in England and Wales have corporate Twitter accounts, as do 140 neighbourhood and other local policing teams: NPIA, 2010), there is still no national strategy or policy in relation to this.

The lack of a strategy was exposed in the UK disorders in August 2011, which became known as 'the BlackBerry riots' when the suggestion was made that rioters organised themselves by both the use of 'open' social media and phone-to-phone messaging services such as BlackBerry Messenger. It was not only the use of messaging to undermine police deployments that UK police failed to anticipate, but also the failure to make effective use of 'Open Source' media channels.

Whilst forces tried to monitor these channels to identify those involved or to identify possible targets, the lack of any structure meant that officers were unable to rate the veracity of the information, while the volume of information meant that those tasked with monitoring it were soon overwhelmed. A West Midlands Police messaging site set up three days into the disturbances had 300,000 hits in one day and one officer reported that the volume was such that messages were disappearing from the bottom of the page before anyone had had a chance to read the content (HMIC, 2011). Forces use different approaches to eventually utilise social media channels in order to dispel rumours, provide public information and track down and prosecute those involved.

In terms of the reaction to the riots, the police were much more successful in their use of this media. Innovative campaigns were run to identify those involved, such as 'Shop a looter' by Greater Manchester Police. In the days following the riots, GMP had one million people view the 'Flickr' website that they had set up containing the photographs of those individuals classed as 'most wanted' for their part in the disorder.

Police forces across the world have now started to proactively monitor activists online and lawyers are advising that those involved in protests are cautious about revealing their tactics on social media. This comes after a New York court ordered Twitter to comply with an order to hand over messages posted by a demonstrator who was involved in the Occupy Wall Street protest in October 2011.

One of the major new challenges that the police have had to deal with is the volume of photographs and messages that can spread rapidly by this media. The traditional filters between journalists and the public have now been removed and 'Citizen Journalists' now upload and record their own reports and observations in real time. Mobile phone footage is quickly uploaded onto websites and eventually onto traditional media platforms; the power of this type of reporting was most visibly demonstrated at the G20 protests in London in 2009, when footage of an assault leading to the death of a member of the public, Ian Tomlinson, led directly to the identification and subsequent trial of the Metropolitan Police Officer involved and a major HMIC inquiry into police tactics at public order events.

Misinformation and malicious communications have long been a problem for Police Incident Commanders, and the use of smartphones and social media makes this even more complex as the results cause significant social harm. This had major consequences for the Indian government and the Indian police service in the summer of 2012. In August 2012, some students from the north-east were attacked by Muslims in Pune as retaliation for what happened to Muslim immigrants in Assam. This led directly to photographs of dead Muslims being posted on social network sites and bulk text messages being sent to people from the northeast warning of reprisals. Tens of thousands of Indians fled southern Indian cities, creating major problems for the security services in the country. The Indian government's response was seen as slow and was criticised as being heavy-handed, as they closed down Internet services and limited text messages from all mobile phones to just five. Whilst the Indian government could be criticised for opting not to use the same media to dispel the rumours and selecting for response described as 'censorship', the scale of the challenge was exponential.

In the future, police leaders at demonstrations and large-scale events will have to take more account of the use of social media in the policing of protest, as well as the speed with which such information is passed on and updated.

See also: Arab Spring (Arab world) 2010 onwards, Bradford riots (Manningham, Bradford) 1995, G20 protests (London) 2009, Occupy movement, public order policing (England and Wales)

Sources and further reading

Dasgupta, A. (2012) 'Fleeing Indians', *The Week*, 2 September.
Harris, G. (2012) 'India faces Criticism for Censorship', *International Herald Tribune*, 27 August.
HMIC (2011) *The Rules of Engagement: A Review of the August 2011 Disorders*. London: HMIC.
Kingsley, P. (2011) 'Inside the Anti-kettling HQ', *The Guardian*, 3 February.
Mason, G. (2012) 'Social Media "Remains Under-Exploited"', *Police Oracle*, www.policeoracle.com/news/Local+and+Neighbourhood+Policing/2012/Oct/11/Social-Media-Remains-Under-Exploited_56259.html (date accessed 19 May 2014).
NPIA (2010) *Engage: Digital and Social Media Engagement for the Police Service*, www.acpo.police.uk/documents/LPpartnerships/2010/20110518%20LPPBA%20dm_engage_v61.pdf (date accessed 19 May 2014).
Rawlinson, K. (2012) 'Activists Warned to Watch What They Say as Social Media Monitoring Becomes "Next Big Thing in Law Enforcement"', *The Independent*, 1 October, http://www.independent.co.uk/news/uk/crime/activists-warned-to-watch-what-they-say-as-social-media-monitoring-becomes-next-big-thing-in-law-enforcement-8191977.html (date accessed 19 May 2014).

SOUTHALL DISORDERS (SOUTHALL, LONDON) 1979

In April 1979, the National Front held an election meeting in Southall Town Hall. Southall contained a large Asian (mainly Indian) population which was not likely to support this right-wing extremist party: 'The meeting was evidently intended as a calculated affront to the local black community' (National Council for Civil Liberties, 1980a: 7) whose main objective was to cause 'mischief, racial aggravation, strife or violence' (Winnick, 1979) in the hope that the media would portray the National Front as victims of such actions. As the event was a meeting, the provisions contained in the Public Order Act 1936 relating to banning processions did not apply (Brain, 2010: 39)

This event was thus noteworthy for the level of violence and the actions of the police service in responding to this issue, one aspect of which resulted in the death of a protester, Blair Peach.

Tensions were running high in Southall against right-wing extremist parties. In 1976, an Asian man,

Gurdip Singh Chaggar, was stabled to death. This event prompted the leader of the right-wing National Party, John Kingsley Read, to state 'one down – a million to go'. The killers were never apprehended, which gave the impression that the police were indifferent towards the victims of racial violence. Kingsley Read was subsequently acquitted in 1977 of an offence under the Race Relations Act 1965 for uttering this remark.

The local Council gave permission for the National Front meeting to go ahead. The Council argued that under existing election law, it had no option other than to grant the application, since a National Front candidate was standing in the Southall constituency (National Council for Civil Liberties, 1980a: 14 and 22). On 19 April 1979, local residents informally met with the Home Secretary, Merlyn Rees, to request that he banned the meeting on the grounds that it would not constitute a meeting that was open to all members of the public, but he declined to do so. A number of local shops, offices and industries also agreed to take strike action on the day of the meeting in protest against it taking place. Local residents also decided to hold a peaceful sit-down protest outside the Town Hall before the start of the meeting and the Southall Youth Movement proposed a picket near the Town Hall in the early afternoon. The police were informed of both of these proposed protests (National Council for Civil Liberties, 1980a: 7) at a meeting held on 17 April and no objections were voiced on their part.

On 22 April, a march for 'unity and peace' was organised by a local coordinating committee (in which the India Workers' Association were prominent participants) to protest against the National Front meeting. Accusations were made of over-policing this event (including the use of officers from Scotland Yard's Public Order Division and the presence of mounted police), numbering around 1,200. The march was poorly stewarded, the police regarded the event as 'very unruly' and the march was punctuated by sit-down protests (Deputy Assistant Commissioner 'A' Operations, 1979). The friction between some of the participants and the police (National Council for Civil Liberties, 1980a: 28–30) set the scene for events that occurred on the following day.

The National Front meeting took place on Monday 23 April (St George's Day). Its main speaker was the party's National Activities Organiser, Martin Webster. The policing of the event was controlled by the Public Order Division (A8) of the Metropolitan Police rather than the local police. Arrangements made with the local police (and in particular with the local Police Liaison Officer, Chief Inspector Derek Gosse) regarding protests were overridden on the day (National Council for Civil Liberties, 1980a: 32).

Police tactics were designed to cordon off the town centre to create a 'sterile area' around the Town Hall

(Deputy Assistant Commissioner 'A' Operations, 1979), which meant that the protests organised by local residents against the National Front could not take place. There was thus 'no demonstration ... there were would-be demonstrators, and there were manifestations of their anger and frustration, but there was no demonstration' (National Council for Civil Liberties, 1980a: 8). A token protest of around 30 people was latterly permitted by the police in the early evening prior to the arrival of the National Front at the Town Hall.

The use of police cordons to prevent a demonstration taking place was 'extremely unusual' (National Council for Civil Liberties, 1980a: 151) and had the effect of placing Southall 'under a virtual state of siege' (Rollo, 1980: 156) Police tactics were of a pre-emptive nature, were put into operation before any violence had occurred and gave rise to the accusation that the police were clearing a way for the National Front, who would otherwise 'never have dared hold a meeting in the strong Southall community' (Ransom, 1980: 11). The cordoning-off of the centre of Southall was branded 'unreasonable and unjustified' (National Council for Civil Liberties, 1980a: 135). The cordons further served to break the assembled crowd into different groups and this fragmentation made effective stewarding impossible (National Council for Civil Liberties, 1980a: 155).

In order to erect the cordon, around 2,750 police officers were deployed against a crowd of around 3,000 protesters (Whitelaw, 1979). Police actions effectively hemmed in protesters between two police cordons. Attempts 'by demonstrators to break through police cordons to hold a protest outside the Town Hall were rebuffed by the police who used riot shields and truncheons to disperse the crowds. Mounted police were also deployed. Snatch squads were also used, allegedly against those seen as leaders of the protest' (Ransom, 1980: 63–4). Those on the receiving end of police action fought back with bricks and any other implements that came to hand. In particular, violent incidents involving attacks on demonstrators by the ordinary police, mounted police and the Special Patrol Group (SPG) took place in cul-de-sacs from which demonstrators could not escape, and protesters also damaged property in the area.

All six units of the SPG were on duty in Southall and they were at the forefront of the operation designed to clear the streets around the Town Hall of protesters shortly before the arrival of the National Front (Rollo, 1980: 156). The SPG undertook a number of offensive actions, which included driving their vans at the crowds, and were allegedly 'involved in all the worst violence in Southall' (Ransom, 1980: 67). Some aspects of the SPG actions served to push demonstrators back towards the Town Hall, a situation which was stated to be due to their lack of knowledge of the area, but which critics argued was a deliberate action to drive demonstrators into a trap (Ransom, 1980: 63). Officers from the SPG also raided a building that was used as an organising point by the Anti-Nazi League (the 'Peoples Unite' building) in which considerable damage was caused and many occupants were injured. The police rationale for this action was that officers had been injured by missiles thrown at them by the occupants of this building (Deputy Assistant Commissioner 'A' Operations, 1979).

The fighting between the police and demonstrators became severe in the early evening. Blair Peach, a schoolteacher and a member of the Anti-Nazi League, fled into a side road to avoid the violence, but was hit on the head by a member of the SPG and subsequently died from his injuries. The National Front meeting ended at around 10 pm and members of the Party were escorted from the area by the police.

Initially, the right-wing media sided with the police, condemning the violence meted out by demonstrators towards the police. A contemporaneous police report attributed the violence to the behaviour of Asian youths, especially those associated with the Southall Youth Movement, 'who appeared quite often to lose complete control of their emotions' (Deputy Assistant Commissioner 'A' Operations, 1979). The Police Federation put forward the view that Southall evidenced 'a concerted attack on the police with National Front meetings as an excuse' (Jardine, quoted in Ransom, 1980: 53).

However, the death of Blair Peach highlighted the use of violence on that day by the police, which was seen as a breakdown of police discipline. One account accused the SPG of choosing 'to go beserk' and argued that 'it is surprising ... that others did not die from the injuries inflicted on them in Southall' (Ransom, 1980: 9). The National Council for Civil Liberties Inquiry (which also heard evidence that the SPG were 'out of control') (National Council for Civil Liberties, 1980a: 42) indicated that at least 42 head injuries were inflicted by the police at this event (National Council for Civil Liberties, 1980: 163) and accused the police of using truncheons not for protection or as a last resort to effect an arrest, but 'as an instrument of arbitrary, violent and unlawful punishment' (National Council for Civil Liberties, 1980a: 165).

An inquest into Blair Peach's death was delayed for around eight weeks. It was adjourned on 12 October, when the Divisional Court granted leave for an application to be made for a jury to sit with the Coroner. It re-commenced on 28 April 1980.

At these inquests, a distinguished pathologist, Professor Mant (who was called in by Blair Peach's family to perform a second autopsy on his body) stated that the damage inflicted on his skull was caused by an instrument that had not pierced his skin. He suggested this could have been a lead-weighted rubber cosh or a hosepipe filled with lead shot or a similar weapon – but not a truncheon (National Council for Civil

Liberties, 1980a: 79). This conclusion was significant in the light of a vast array of 'unauthorised' weapons (26 in total) (Ransom, 1980: 32) found in searches of the lockers of members of the SPG who were on duty that day, although there was no evidence that these weapons were carried by officers on duty on 23 April.

Although Professor Mant was subsequently shown these weapons and concluded that none of them could have been responsible for Blair Peach's death, Professor Bowen, a pathologist acting for the Coroner, asserted that a police radio was the most likely cause of this death. However, the inquest recorded a verdict of death by misadventure. It was argued that the Coroner, Dr John Burton, led the jury in this direction (Ransom, 1980: 21). However, the jury also added 'riders' that officers from the SPG should have greater liaison with 'ordinary' police officers, that the police should be equipped with maps before major demonstrations and that regular inspections should be made of police lockers to ensure they contained no unauthorised weapons. The Coroner refused to accept the last of these riders as official, since he argued there was no suggestion that such weapons had been used to kill Blair Peach (Ransom, 1980: 46).

No person was ever prosecuted for the death of Blair Peach, although ten eye-witnesses at the inquest stated that they had seen him hit by a police officer (Ransom, 1980: 27) and internal police inquiries had narrowed the responsibility for his death down to six members of the SPG – four from Number One Unit (a unit known collectively as 'the Cowboys' that allegedly had the habit of arriving on duty to the tune of 'the Dam Busters': Ransom, 1980: 70; National Council for Civil Liberties, 1980a: 80) and two from Number Three Unit (Manwaring-White, 1983: 43–4). An internal report into the incident, prepared by Commander John Cass, devoted around 30,000 police man hours to investigate the incident. This was not published at the time, but was considered by the Director of Public Prosecutions (DPP), who concluded that there was insufficient evidence to mount a prosecution. The government refused requests for a public inquiry into his death, although the Home Secretary placed a Memorandum relating to the incident in the library of the House of Commons on 27 June, which amounted to a 'political endorsement' of the Chief Commissioner's report on the events that took place that day (Ransom, 1980: 62).

A wall of silence prevented the investigation proceeding further: 'it seems never to have been suggested that the "blank wall" being presented by the SPG constituted a serious breach of discipline and grounds for immediate dismissal from the police' (Ransom, 1980: 59). A further issue that was worthy of investigation was whether Blair Peach's death was accidental – police surveillance had identified him as a leading anti-fascist activist and the deliberate targeting of him at Southall 'cannot be discounted altogether' (Ransom, 1980: 65).

Prosecutions did, however, take place of individuals arrested during the Southall protest. Many of these (numbering 260 of the 345 defendants who were charged with offences in connection with incidents at Southall on 23 April) took place at Barnet Magistrates' Court, where the procedures adopted have been criticised for reasons such as convictions being based on unsubstantiated evidence and the use of binding-over procedures against some of those acting as witnesses on the grounds that their presence in Southall that day associated them with committing a criminal offence. It was argued that in many of the courts used for the trials, 'there was ... an evident, and at least on one occasion avowed, bias in favour of police witnesses, whose testimony was presumed to be accurate and truthful in the face of any amount of contrary evidence from ordinary people' (National Council for Civil Liberties, 1980a: 10). These trials were dubbed 'the final stage in a process of victimisation [of the local community] which began with the National Front' (Lewis, 1980).

In 2010, the report by Commander Cass was finally published. This stated that 'it can reasonably be concluded that a police officer struck the fatal blow' and that this officer was drawn from carrier U 11 (Cass, 1979, para. 298), which contained officers from SPG Unit 1 (National Council for Civil Liberties, 1980b: 53). The report also referred to 'the attitude and untruthfulness of some of the officers involved'. It referred to false statements made by three officers and stated that 'a strong inference can be drawn from this that they have conspired together to obstruct police' (Cass, 1979: para. 325). It concluded that 'the conduct of these officers made it more difficult to carry out the investigation and arrive at a proper conclusion. Accordingly, I strongly recommend that proceedings be taken [against these three officers] for obstructing police in the execution of their duty, conspiring to do so, and attempting or conspiracy to pervert the course of justice' (Cass, 1979, para. 326). However, the DPP failed to endorse this suggestion, arguing that there was 'insufficient evidence to justify criminal proceedings against any police officers in respect of the death of Blair Peach and other incidents on the same occasion' (Hetherington, 1979).

See also: Lewisham disorders (Lewisham, London) 1977, paramilitary policing, public order legislation (England and Wales), public order policing (England and Wales), Red Lion Square (London) 1974, riot police

Sources and further reading

Brain, T. (2010) *A History of Policing in England and Wales from 1974: A Turbulent Journey.* Oxford University Press.

Cass, J. (1979) *Complaint against Police.* London: Metropolitan Police Service, C.O. OG1/79/2234. Available at: www.met.police.uk/foi/units/blair_peach.htm (date accessed 19 May 2014).

Deputy Assistant Commissioner 'A' Operations (1979) *Demonstration with Disorder and Death – Southall Monday 23 April 1979*, www.met.police.uk/foi/units/blair_peach.htm (date accessed 19 May 2014).

Hetherington, A. (1979) *Letter to Sir David McNee*, 9 October, D/H.P.60009.79. Available at: www.met.police.uk/foi/units/blair_peach.htm (date accessed 19 May 2014).

Lewis, R. (1980) *'The Real Trouble': A Study of Aspects of the Southall Trials.* London: Runnymede Trust.

Manwaring-White, S. (1983) *The Policing Revolution: Police Technology, Democracy and Liberty in Britain.* Brighton: Harvester Press.

National Council for Civil Liberties (1980a) *Southall 23 April 1979: The Report of the Unofficial Committee of Enquiry.* London: National Council for Civil Liberties.

——. (1980b) *The Death of Blair Peach: The Supplementary Report of the Unofficial Committee of Enquiry.* London: National Council for Civil Liberties.

Ransom, D. (1980) *The Blair Peach Case: Licence to Kill.* London: Friends of the Blair Peach Committee.

Rollo. J. (1980) 'The Special Patrol Group' in P. Hain (ed.), *Policing the Police Volume 2.* London: John Calder.

Winnick, D. (1979) Speech in the House of Commons, 27 June, HC Debs, vol. 969, col. 453.

Whitelaw, W. (1979) Speech in the House of Commons, 27 June, HC Debs, vol. 969, col. 440.

STATES OF EMERGENCY

A state of emergency is issued by a government in response to a range of factors that include a natural disaster (such as the cyclone and extensive flooding in eastern Sardinia in November 2013), a prolonged and/or widespread period of civil unrest which the normal law-enforcement agencies find difficult to cope with (such as rioting), an industrial dispute or episode of direct action which imperils the well-being of the nation and the safety of its citizens (perhaps through the absence of essential services) or following a formal declaration of war. It may also be used to combat insurgency within a country, as occurred in three northern states in Nigeria in 2013, which had witnessed episodes of lethal violence associated with the Islamist militant group Boko Haram.

Typically, a state of emergency enables a government to take whatever measures it sees fit in order to deal with the problem at hand, which may entail issuing decrees without the sanction of the county's legislative body, placing restrictions on civil and political liberties (often in the form of curfews or restrictions on the freedom of association and travel), requisitioning materials that are vital to the nation's welfare (such as energy supplies) or curbing the authority of the judiciary (for example, by introducing internment). Measures of this nature may entail temporarily suspending (or amending) the constitution in those countries that possess a codified document of this nature.

There are few restrictions on the powers that a government can take during a state of emergency. The International Covenant for Civil and Political Rights imposes some requirements on governments taking this course of action, which include the need to publicly declare the state of emergency and to immediately contact the General Secretary of the United Nations. States that are signatories to this Covenant are also required to declare the reason for the state of emergency, the date when it will start and is expected to finish, and the main departures from freedoms that are guaranteed in the Covenant. However, this protocol is not always rigidly adhered to by states that declare a state of emergency.

In some countries, the constitution makes provision for a declaration of a state of emergency. In France, for example, the Constitution permits the President to declare a state of emergency within the Council of Ministers, which must be confirmed by Parliament if it is to last for more than 12 days. A state of emergency enables the authorities to impose curfews, close places of assembly, conduct house-to-house searches without judicial oversight and impose censorship. Exceptionally, the military may be empowered to act in place of the civilian authorities. The Constitution also enables the Council of Ministers to declare a state of siege for a period of 12 days, after which parliamentary approval is required if this situation is to persist. A state of siege covers issues such as foreign invasion or an internal political coups and enables restrictions to be placed on fundamental civil liberties and for the military to assume police powers if they feel that this course of action is required.

The US Constitution contains little by way of emergency provisions, although it does permit Congress to suspend habeas corpus in instances of foreign invasion or internal rebellion. The role given to the President as commander-in-chief of the nation's armed forces also enables him to 'federalise' (that is, press into federal service and assume control over) the national guard in times of emergency.

Localised states of emergency may be declared by a city's mayor or a state's governor, a course of action that is usually a response to some form of natural disaster. In the event of a severe crisis that overwhelms the resources of the local or state authorities, the state governor may request the President to issue a disaster declaration. This request is initially made to the regional office of the Federal Emergency Management Agency (an agency of the Department of Homeland Security), which, since its creation in 1978, assesses the request and coordinates responses to a disaster. This may lead the President to issue either an Emergency Declaration (whereby federal aid is provided to deal with a specific crisis) or a Major Disaster Declaration (which entails a long-term federal recovery programme).

In cases of a national emergency, the President may formally declare a state of emergency under the provisions of the National Emergencies Act 1976. Once declared, the President can then respond to the problem, using a variety of mechanisms, the most important of which are executive orders. This power has been used frequently in recent years – by the end of October 2013, 'President Obama has issued 21 unclassified executive orders declaring a state of national emergency or modifying a previously issued executive order declaring a state of national emergency so that he can invoke extraordinary powers' (Saul, 2013).

The UK lacks a codified constitution and states of emergency are governed by legislation. Three pieces of legislation have been enacted during the twentieth century that governed the UK state's response to emergencies.

The Defence of the Realm Act (DORA) 1914 enabled the government to use troops in a variety of civil capacities, including performing the jobs of striking workers. This measure lapsed following the end of the First World War in 1918 and was replaced by the Emergency Powers Act 1920.

The 1920 legislation was the key enactment governing national emergencies until 2004, when it was replaced by the Civil Contingencies Act. Under the 1920 legislation, the monarch could proclaim a state of emergency in order to respond to actions that threatened to interfere with the 'supply and distribution of food, water, fuel or light, or with the means of locomotion'. This enabled the government (making use of the Royal Prerogative) to take virtually any actions it wished to (including the use of the military) in order to provide for the safety and life of the community, provided that Parliament agreed. This Act was used extremely sparingly, being invoked on only 12 occasions, five of which occurred under the premiership of Edward Heath (June 1970–February 1974) (Bunyan, 1977: 54).

A further piece of legislation governing emergency situations was the Emergency Powers Act 1964, whose main impact was to give legislative approval for the use of soldiers in emergency situations that were not of a military nature.

Events that included the 2000 fuel crisis (when the government appeared to be impotent to prevent the chaos arising from the nation running out of fuel arising from protesters blockading oil refineries and fuel distribution depots), the 2001 outbreak of foot-and-mouth disease and the dangers arising from international terrorism prompted a review of existing arrangements to deal with national emergencies. This review resulted in the enactment of the Civil Contingencies Act 2004. This legislation sought to provide an updated definition of the kind of event that constituted an emergency in twenty-first-century Britain. This situation was defined as:

- an event which threatens serious damage to human welfare;
- an event or situation which threatens serious damage to the environment;
- war or terrorism which threatens serious damage to security.

The Act divided the response to situations of this nature into two parts.

Part 1 of the Act was concerned with relatively localised emergencies that would be responded to by what were termed 'local responders', who were given a clear set or roles and responsibilities by the Act. These local responders included local government and the local emergency services, whose role comprised advance planning and they were expected to act according to partnership principles. The legislation further recognised 'category 2 organisations', such as the Health and Safety Executive and transport companies that might be involved should incidents affect their spheres of responsibility.

Part 2 of the Act provided the authority to make special temporary legislation to deal with the most serious emergencies, replacing powers previously provided for in the Emergency Powers Act 1920. The new legislation was mainly justified on the basis that the incidents catered for by the 1920 Act were out of date. However, the procedure adopted was quite similar to that in the 1920 legislation: the monarch would formally declare a state of emergency to exist (unless unable to do so, in which case a senior minister would act instead) and the special powers would be embodied in regulations in the form of statutory instruments which required parliamentary approval.

A similar distinction exists in Canada under the provisions of the Emergency Management Act 2007, which differentiates between Local States of Emergency (enacted by a municipal government) and a State of Emergency that is declared by the Minister of Public Safety and Emergency Preparedness.

To guard against the possible misuse of power, the UK Civil Contingencies Act 2004 introduced the 'triple lock' to ensure that emergency powers would be available only if:

- the emergency threatened *serious* damage to human welfare, the environment or security;
- it was *necessary* to make provision urgently to resolve the emergency and that existing powers were insufficient to do so;
- emergency regulations would be *proportionate* the aspect or effect of the emergency they were directed at.

In addition, there were limits placed upon what could be provided for by emergency regulations, which:

- could not prohibit or enable the prohibition or participation in activities concerned with industrial action;
- could not instigate any form of military conscription;
- could not alter any aspect of criminal procedures;
- could not create any new offence other than breach of the regulations;
- had to be compatible with the Human Rights Act 1998 and EU law;
- were open to challenge in the courts.

The regulations did not necessarily have to have national jurisdiction and could apply to the area or region affected by the emergency. Each region would appoint a Regional Nominated Coordinator to act as the focal point to coordinate the response to the emergency.

Martial law and the use of the military

A related concept to a state of emergency is that of martial law, which enables the military to take over the government of a country (or of disaffected areas within it) and also empowers the military to assume the functions of civil policing. Martial law may be imposed by a government operating under the provisions of its constitution (usually in the face of threatened or actual civil disorder that threatens the ability of the civil authorities to function effectively) and has been used to suppress political dissent in Poland in 1981 and in China in 1989 following the Tiananmen Square protests. Typically, the imposition of martial law entails the suspension of civil rights (including that of habeas corpus), the imposition of curfews and the use of military law to enable those defying martial law to be tried in military courts. Although many of these measures can accompany a state of emergency, typically martial law lasts for a prolonged period of time.

Martial law may also be deployed following the overthrow of a government by the military (an event termed a 'military coup'), as occurred in Pakistan in 1958, 1977 and 1999, in Thailand in 2006 and in Egypt in 2013. This may arise following a prolonged political crisis that cannot be resolved through the channels of conventional politics or because the government is pursuing policies which the military feel to be divisive and not in the national interest. Military rule can last for lengthy periods of time: in Pakistan, it operated in the periods 1958–71, 1977–88 and 1999–2008.

Liberal democracies may also make use of the military when events arise that require exceptional measures to be pursued, usually as a provision of a response associated with a state of emergency. In America, the Posse Comitatus Act 1878 (as amended in 1956) limited the ability of the President to use troops (including the National Guard) as a civilian police force, although the Insurrection Act 1807 (as amended in 2007) enabled the President to deploy troops to combat lawlessness, insurrection and rebellion. The 2007 amendment was, however, repealed the following year.

In the UK, the military were historically deployed in emergency situations if requested to do so by what was termed the 'civil authority' (defined as a magistrate). During the 1970s, the term 'civil authority' was abandoned and instead troops could be summoned using other procedures that included the application by a chief constable to the Home Office (Peak, 1984: 57–8).

However, the possibility of troops overreacting (especially in the sense of the inappropriate use of their weaponry) had been one of the reasons behind the formation of 'new' or professional police forces in the early decades of the nineteenth century and meant that their use was infrequent.

During the 1970s, the circumstances under which troops could be used in non-military situations were rationalised under three headings that are now collectively referred to as *Military Assistance to the Civilian Authorities* (MACA):

- Military Aid to the Civilian Communities.
- Military Aid to the Civilian Ministries (now referred to as Military Aid to Other Government Departments).
- Military Aid to the Civil Power.

The first of these situations authorised troops to respond to natural disasters (such as military involvement to deal with floods in Somerset in 2014), the second entails activities associated with strike breaking and the third involves the use of troops in a policing role.

In addition to legislation relating to various forms of emergencies, there exists machinery to plan and administer services that may be required to respond to events of this nature. This falls under two headings.

What is termed 'emergency planning' stemmed from the post-war concept of 'civil defence' (re-named 'home defence' in 1968) and entailed a regional system of government in which local authorities administer a range of emergency services. Although justified by the threat of a nuclear attack, the purposes of emergency planning have increasingly assumed a domestic emergency orientation (for example, during the 1977 fire brigade dispute).

A second form of preparation relating to emergencies is that of contingency planning, which covers arrangements to respond to a wide range of domestic problems, including industrial unrest and natural disasters. Advance planning for emergencies of this nature is carried out by the Civil Contingencies Unit (formerly known as the National Security Committee) within the Cabinet Office and, in the event of a crisis occurring, a body referred to as the Cabinet Office Briefing Room (COBRA) meets to coordinate a response to the problem, in particular to determine whether to invoke powers contained in the Civil Contingencies Act 2004 (Helm, 2006). COBRA has a communications network which keeps ministers informed of the situation across the country. This machinery was used, for example, in connection with the 2000 fuel crisis, the 2005 London bombings, anticipated flooding in eastern England in November 2007 and following the murder by Islamist extremists of the soldier Lee Rigby in Woolwich, London, in 2013.

See also: Arab Spring (Arab world) 2010 onwards, 'Bloody Sunday' (Derry, Northern Ireland) 1972, fuel crisis (Britain) 2000, Gdańsk Shipyard protests (Gdańsk, Poland) 1981,

Islamic terrorist groups, post-Arab Spring, Tiananmen Square protests (Beijing) 1976 and 1989, workplace protest

Sources and further reading

Bunyan, T. (1977) *The History and Practice of the Political Police in Britain*. London: Quartet Books.

Helm, T. (2006) 'Cobra Team Can Invoke Emergency Powers', *Daily Telegraph*, 11 August, www.telegraph.co.uk/news/1526096/Cobra-team-can-invoke-emergency-powers.html (date accessed 19 May 2014).

Ministry of Defence (1989) *Military Aid to the Civilian Community*, 3rd edn. London: HMSO.

Peak, S. (1984) *Troops in Strikes: Military Intervention in Industrial Disputes*. London: Cobden Trust.

Saul, S. (2013) 'President Obama Should Issue and Executive Order to Raise the Debt Ceiling', *Fixgov*, 14 October, www.brookings.edu/blogs/fixgov/posts/2013/10/12-debt-ceiling-and-the-power-of-the-president-jackman# (date accessed 19 May 2014).

Vogler, R. (1991) *Reading the Riot Act: The Magistracy, the Police and the Army*. Milton Keynes: Open University Press.

STOCKHOLM RIOTS (SWEDEN) 2013

Riots broke out in the Husby area of Stockholm on 19 May 2013, a district that contains a high proportion of immigrant and Muslim residents. Events were triggered by the shooting and killing by the police of a 69-year-old Portuguese man called Lenine Relvas-Martins on 13 May, who then attempted to cover up the incident. He had been seen on the balcony of his home brandishing a knife following a confrontation with some youths. This police intervention was viewed as an overreaction by many local residents.

A political group called Megafonen used social media in the form of a blog post to call for a demonstration on 15 May against police brutality. Subsequent events turned into riots, which began on 19 May involving a small number of young people whose initial actions included arson (mainly in the form of torching cars) and vandalising a shopping centre in the Husby area. Police who were despatched to restore order were attacked with stones. The riot lasted for a relatively short period, but violence flared up the following day. Again, a relatively small number of people were involved and fire-fighters who responded to arson attacks were attacked with stones along with the police.

Although calm was restored, violence broke out in 21 May in a number of areas of Stockholm with a demographic profile similar to that of Husby, which enabled right-wing social media to depict these events as 'race riots' carried out by a 'marauding Muslim mob' (*Before It's News*, 2013). Violence took the form of torching cars and a shopping centre and police station in Jakobsberg. Calm was restored, but further riots occurred the following day, in which a police station in Ragsved was burned to the ground. On the next day (23 May), rioters targeted a subway station, schools and a police station in addition to torching cars. In total, around a dozen of Stockholm's suburbs were involved in the violence.

The involvement of parents and volunteers who patrolled streets in riot-affected areas helped to prevent further outbreaks of violence in the capital, although small-scale riots did occur elsewhere in Sweden. It was estimated that by 25 May in Stockholm, the violence consisted of 'up to 200 cars set ablaze, fires in schools, police stations and restaurants, and about a dozen police officers injured. Police estimate that more than 300 young people have been directly involved, of whom 30 have been arrested' (Orange, 2013). Many of those who were arrested had criminal records, leading to suggestions that depravation rather than deprivation was the main cause of these events, which, according to the Prime Minister, were inspired by 'hooliganism' (Reinfeldt, cited in Higgins, 2013).

Further violence occurred in a number of areas close to Stockholm on 27 May, following which unrest subsided. Rioting also took place in other towns, including Oerebro and Linkoeping. Calm was restored to the riot-affected areas by 28 May.

The riots were attributed to a number of factors that included 'exclusion, poverty and unemployment', the latter issue aggravated by discrimination and low education levels (Zenou, cited in Magnusson and Carlstrom, 2013). Unemployment especially affected young people in the Husby area, where 'more than 10% of those aged 25 to 55 in Husby are unemployed, compared with 3.5% in Stockholm as a whole. Those that do have jobs earn 40% less than the city average ... More than a quarter of Husby's adult population has only GCSE-equivalent education, compared with a tenth for Stockholm as a whole, and only a third have any further education' (Orange, 2013). This situation was also influenced by a perception of an increasing gap between Sweden's rich and poor, a problem attributed to cuts in welfare spending in order to reduce taxation levels. The frustrations experienced by those who lived in the area were also fuelled by perceptions of discriminatory policing, for example, in connection with identity checks undertaken by the police in Stockholm on subway trains (*The Guardian*, 2013).

Racial segregation and its social consequences were cited as a key factor in causing the disturbances. It was estimated that around 85 per cent of the inhabitants of Husby have their origins outside of Sweden (Orange, 2013) and concerns have been previously expressed in government circles in connection with rising anti-immigrant sentiment, which has been especially directed against refugees from Syria, Afghanistan and Somalia. It was argued that 'the great threat to vulnerable groups is not the extreme groups without the many people ... Work towards more brutal forms of xenophobia must begin with the xenophobia found in everyday life. We must begin with ourselves' (Labour Department of Sweden, 2012: 11). These sentiments may, however, be undermined by the anticipated use of the 2013 riots by the far-right Sweden Democrats party to further fuel anti-immigrant sentiments in the run-up to the country's 2014 general election, which may result in similar outbreaks of violence in the future.

See also: Banlieue riots (Paris) 2005, Bradford riots (Manningham, Bradford) 1995, northern English town riots (Bradford, Burnley and Oldham) 2001

Sources and further reading

Before It's News (2013) 'Muslim "Youths" Burn 100 Cars in North Stockholm Riots", http://beforeitsnews.com/opinion-conservative/2013/05/muslim-youths-burn-100-cars-in-north-stockholm-riots-2646760.html (date accessed 19 May 2014).

The Guardian (2013) 'Swedish Riots Rage for Fourth Night', 23 May, www.guardian.co.uk/world/2013/may/23/swedish-riots-stockholm (date accessed 19 May 2014).

Higgins, A. (2013) 'In Sweden, Riots Put an Identity into Question, New York Times, 26 May, www.nytimes.com/2013/05/27/world/europe/swedens-riots-put-its-identity-in-question.html?pagewanted=all&_r=0 (date accessed 19 May 2014).

Labour Department of Sweden (2012) Alien Enemy Within (Främlingsfienden inom oss). Stockholm: Labour Department, SOU 2012/74.

Magnusson, N. and Carlstrom, J. (2013) 'Sweden Riots Put Faces to Statistics as Stockholm Burns', Bloomberg, 27 May, www.bloomberg.com/news/2013-05-26/sweden-riots-put-faces-to-statistics-as-stockholm-burns.html (date accessed 19 May 2014).

Orange, S. (2013) 'Swedish Riots Spark Surprise and Anger', The Observer, 25 May, http://www.theguardian.com/world/2013/may/25/sweden-europe-news (date accessed 19 May 2014).

STUDENT PROTESTS (ENGLAND) 2010

Student protests that took place in England in 2010 were directed against austerity measures of the Coalition government that affected education, especially higher education.

A particularly controversial measure that figured prominently in these protests was the government's decision to raise the cap on tuition fees paid by students entering higher education from around £3,000 to a maximum of £9,000, a change that was to be introduced in September 2012. This was especially controversial as it entailed the Liberal Democrats abandoning a specific pledge made during the 2010 general election not to raise student fees.

Four major events occurred in 2010. A number of student protests to express opposition to spending cuts and changes to the funding of higher education in England were organised by the National Union of Students (NUS) and the University and College Union (UCU) in November and December 2010. The protests (that were termed 'days of action') included demonstrations, rallies and direct action in the form of the occupation of government and university buildings, which took place across the country. The most significant of these events occurred on 10 November 2010, one aspect of which was the occupation of the

Conservative Party headquarters at Millbank. This aspect of direct action was facilitated by a higher turnout of students (perhaps as many as 50,000) than had been anticipated: 'The Met had just 225 officers stewarding the event. There was only a handful stood at the entrance of Millbank when around 200 students first tried to infiltrate the building' (Lewis, 2010). The deployment of inadequate police numbers to the event resulted in them losing control of the situation.

Further actions occurred in 2010, organised by the National Campaign Against Cuts & Fees (NCACF), the largest of which was a mass walkout of education by students and some schoolchildren on 24 November 2010, the social media playing a key role in the organisation of this event, and a demonstration that occurred in central London. Protests were also held in many other cities, including Birmingham, Manchester and Cambridge.

In response to perceptions of underpolicing at the 10 November event, more than 1,000 police officers were deployed to oversee the protest in London and more robust tactics were used, which included deploying officers dressed in riot gear, using mounted police officers to 'control' the crowd and kettling demonstrators in Whitehall. This tactic was criticised by one MP, who stated that 'many hundreds of students and schoolchildren have been kettled for more than four hours ... Whatever one thinks about the student protest, holding people against their will for no reason is neither proportionate nor effective' (Lucas, 2010).

However, this tactic was deployed at a subsequent student protest in central London on 30 November 2010, one consequence of which was that protesters dispersed down a number of side streets to evade containment. This situation created a protest that was potentially difficult to control and the tendency of police officers to give chase to demonstrators contributed to some lapses of police discipline (Gold, 2010).

Tactics that included kettling, the use of police officers dressed in riot gear and the deployment of mounted police to disperse crowds were also used at two separate student protests held on 9 December 2010 in central London to coincide with the vote in the House of Commons to raise the cap on university tuition fees to an upper limit of £9,000. One was organised by the National Union of Students and the other by the University of London Union and the National Campaign Against Fees and Cuts. In the wake of these protests, government buildings (including those housing the Treasury and Supreme Court), statues in Parliament Square (including that of Sir Winston Churchill) and commercial premises were vandalised. A car carrying the Prince of Wales and the Duchess of Cornwall was surrounded by protesters, one of whom allegedly made contact with the Duchess.

Although the government sought to highlight what they regarded as acts of 'appalling violence' (May,

2010), police behaviour (that included pulling a protester who suffered from cerebral palsy from his wheelchair) was also criticised. Police tactics at these four events in 2010 prompted the formation of an organisation, Defend the Right to Protest, which campaigns 'against police brutality, kettling and the use of violence against those who have a right to protest. We campaign to defend all those protestors who have been arrested, bailed or charged and are fighting to clear their names' (Defend the Right to Protest, 2012).

A number of student protests took place after 2010. Major events included demonstrations in London and Manchester on 29 January 2011, where the rise in student tuition fees, cuts in public services and the abolition of the Education Maintenance Allowance were highlighted. In Manchester, a demonstration followed by a rally ('A Future that Works') was organised by the Trades Union Congress (TUC) in conjunction with the NUS and the UCU, and sought to highlight the impact of government economic policy on young people. Additional student protests occurred on 9 November 2011 (when, in the wake of the August riots, over 4,000 police officers were deployed). On 21 November 2012, a protest in the form of a demonstration and rally against spending cuts affecting education was organised by the NUS (termed 'Demo 2012') took place.

Student opposition to reforms linked to austerity measures have also underpinned protests in other countries. In May 2012, schools and universities across Spain closed in protest against government cuts that raised university tuition fees by up to 25 per cent, forced teachers to work longer hours for the same pay and increased the size of classes. In May 2013, thousands of students demonstrated in Valencia to oppose a proposed reform of the Spanish university system by 2015, which sought to improve efficiency in an era of financial austerity. Students believed that this reform would effectively privatise the universities and would drive up tuition fees.

See also: austerity protests (worldwide) 2010–13, G20 protests (London) 2009, kettling, public order policing (England and Wales), student riots (Paris) 1968

Sources and further reading

Defend the Right to Protest (2012) 'London 2012 Protests: Heavy-Handed Policing is an Affront to Rights', www.defendtherighttoprotest.org/london-2012-protests-heavy-handed-policing-is-an-affront-to-rights (date accessed 19 May 2014).

Gold, T. (2010) 'Student Demonstrations: A Game of Protest Monopoly', *The Guardian*, 1 December.

Lewis, P. (2010) 'Why Did the Police So Badly Misjudge the Student Protest?', *The Guardian*, 11 November.

Lucas, C. (2010) Speech in the House of Commons, 24 November, HC Debs, vol. 519, col. 362.

May, T. (2010) Speech in the House of Commons, 13 December, HC Debs, vol. 520, col. 665.

STUDENT RIOTS (PARIS) 1968

The events that occurred in France in May 1968 took place against the background of a range of protests that included the American Anti-Vietnam War Movement, student protests in a number of countries that included Poland, Italy and Japan, and the events in Czechoslovakia (termed the 'Prague Spring') that challenged the domination exerted by the USSR over that country. Young people, students and workers were at the forefront of these protests, which expressed opposition to the state, to authority, to class exploitation, to gender and racial discrimination, and to the stifling rules and regulations that governed everyday life.

Protests in France were triggered by a series of student protests that took the form of the occupation of universities. These were followed by industrial unrest in the form of factory occupations and strikes, including a general strike. This popular uprising (which transcended class, racial and cultural divisions in French society) caused the government to fear that civil war or revolution was taking place.

The May disorders emerged against the background of an alliance forged in February 1968 between the French Socialists and Communists (the 'February Declaration') that was designed to replace the Gaullist government headed by President Charles de Gaulle with a joint government drawn from these parties on the left. Student protests in 1968 were a continuation of events that had taken place at the University of Strasbourg in 1966.

On 22 March 1968, a small group of students (including Daniel Cohn-Bendit) staged a protest at the University of Paris at Nanterre against the recent arrest of a student from Nanterre who was suspected of being involved in an attack against the American Express Office in Paris during demonstrations against the Vietnam War. This protest involved a meeting in the University, following which some of participants occupied a room in the administrative building.

The police were called and surrounded the building, but the occupiers left without causing trouble. Before leaving, those involved decided to constitute the Movement of 22 March in order to develop the agitation. This was 'an informal movement, composed at the beginning of Trotskyists of the *Ligue Communiste Revolutionaire* (LCR) and some anarchists (including Daniel Cohn-Bendit), joined at the end of April by the Maoists of the *Union des Jeunesses Communistes Marxistes-Leniniste* (UJCML), and which brought together over some weeks, more than 1,200 participants' (*Fabienne*, 2008). This movement would play a leading role in subsequent student protests. It aspired to a classless society based on workers' councils, involving the disappearance of the division of labour between those who gave orders and those who took them.

Situationist ideology made an important contribution to the political inspiration that supported and subsequently justified this (and later) protests in 1968. However, student grievances were an important underpinning to these events. The number of students in France had risen threefold between 1958 and 1968, but state funding had not kept pace with the increase in numbers, resulting in universities becoming overcrowded and the facilities inadequate. In addition, students were subjected to strict rules that forbade political activities on campus and placed restrictions on the way in which the students conducted their personal lives.

Weeks of conflict between students and the University authorities followed, characterised by demonstrations and the occupation of University buildings. This culminated in the closure of Nanterre on 2 May 1968, which resulted in the transfer of student protests to the University of the Sorbonne in Paris. The following day (3 May), students at the Sorbonne met to protest against the closure and threatened expulsion of several students at Nanterre. Police intervention spearheaded by the *Compagnies Républicaines de Sécurité* (CRS) led to the arrests of many students and resulted in pitched battles being fought between the police and students. The Sorbonne was also closed, for only the second time in its 700-year history (the first time being in 1940 when the Nazis entered Paris).

On 6 May, the country's largest student union, the *Union Nationale des Etudiants de France* (UNEF), and the Union of University Teachers (SNESup) held a march (which involved over 20,000 people) to demand the re-opening of the Sorbonne, the withdrawal of the police and the release of those who had been arrested. As the march approached the Sorbonne, the police baton charged the protesters, which led to pitched battles between both sides. Tear gas was subsequently deployed to disperse the crowd. By the end of the day: 'Buses with their tyres slashed and windows broken were slewn across the street. Cars upended with windows smashed marked the spots where the hard core of the students put up fierce resistance to the police who, with nerves shattered after a full day of rioting, clubbed the demonstrators when they caught them and sometimes bystanders with a sickening ferocity' (Carroll, 2011). In response to these events, the Rector closed the Sorbonne and UNEF and the SNESup called for an unlimited nationwide strike to protest against police repression (Carroll, 2011).

These events triggered a further protest on 7 May that involved high school students, teachers and some workers. School students had their own set of grievances that included the highly centralised nature of the French educational system and the teaching methods that were used, which depended heavily on memorisation. Their demands were for the re-opening of Nanterre and the Sorbonne, the removal of the police from these institutions and the dropping of all criminal charges against students who had been arrested in the earlier disorders. The police (who faced Molotov cocktails) used tear gas to disperse the protesters.

Events of this nature served to radicalise the student population and on 10 May, a large crowd congregated on the *Rive Gauche* (Left Bank). Their passage across the River Seine was blocked by the police, which led to the erection of barricades. In the early hours of 11 May, the Minister of the Interior ordered the police to storm the student barricades in order to clear the streets for the morning traffic: 'It took three hours of brutal fighting to do that: clouds of tear gas, Molotov cocktails, exploding automobile gas tanks, cobblestones hurled at the police, students chased down and beaten, more than 300 people injured' (Steinfels, 2008).

The actions carried out by the police (which were shown on television) were regarded as overly heavy-handed and led to an escalation of protest. The police were driven from the Latin Quarter in Paris, and occupations and demonstrations spread across France. The scale of the protest prompted the Communist Party, which had initially condemned the Nanterre student activists, to support (albeit with considerable reluctance) the student protests, and the major left-wing union federations, the *Confédération Générale du Travail* (CGT) and the *Force Ouvrière*, called a one-day general strike and demonstration, which was held on 13 May. Around one million people (consisting mainly of students, teachers and workers) marched through Paris calling for the resignation of de Gaulle's government and protesting against the police brutality that had been displayed in the May riots. One of their chants was 'CRS-SS', comparing the actions taken by the French police to the German SS. The police kept a low profile, although they blocked off access to bridges across the Seine, seeking to confine the demonstrators to the Left Bank.

This resulted in the Prime Minister, George Pompidou, making concessions that included the release of student leaders who had been arrested during the earlier riots and the re-opening of the Sorbonne (which was immediately occupied and declared to the an autonomous 'People's University'). However, this tended to embolden the protesters. Strike action escalated and a number of popular action committees were set up in Paris and other cities to articulate grievances against the government and French society in general.

The focus of protest then moved to the factories and a series of occupations occurred, which started with a sit-down strike at the Sud Aviation plant outside Nantes on 14 May. Like the students, the workers also had deep-rooted grievances that included poor public sector salaries, the demand for the decentralisation of economic and political power, and an end to discrimination. This action spread to other manufacturing complexes. Around 200,000 workers were on strike on 17 May, a figure that rose to two million the following day. The following week, around ten million workers were on strike, which was around two-thirds of the French workforce. These strikes were not supported by the Communist Party, nor were they orchestrated by the trade union movement. Many of the strikers were not members of trade unions and the protests were primarily spontaneous with political demands that included the removal of de Gaulle's government. Demands were also sometimes voiced for worker control of the factories. The bypassing of the Communist Party and the trade unions also suggested that these organisations were viewed by protesters as part of the social order ('the Establishment') that students and workers were seeking to challenge.

This industrial action prompted the trade unions to attempt to assert their control over events. Support was given to the workplace actions that had already occurred. In addition, they attempted to divert the protests to the narrower agenda of 'bread and butter' issues affecting pay and conditions of employment. They negotiated with the major employers' associations a 35 per cent increase in the minimum wage, a pay increase for other workers and half-pay for the period when workers were on strike, but failed to neuter the protests. On 24 May, a major demonstration took place in Paris and the Paris Bourse (Stock Exchange) was set on fire. An assault on key government buildings (which were well-protected by the police) could possibly have tipped the protest into a revolution.

Further concessions were offered by the Ministry of Social Affairs on 25 and 26 May in the form of the Grenelle Agreements, which provided for a 35 per cent increase in the minimum wage and an all-round wage increase of around 10 per cent. But this also failed to stop the violence and strikes continued, prompting Prime Minister Pompidou, fearing a revolution was imminent, to deploy tanks on the outskirts of Paris. On 29 May, between 400,000 and 500,000 protesters led by the CGT marched through Paris chanting 'Adieu de Gaulle'. The police avoided the use of force, although units of the military had been summoned to Paris in case protesters stormed key public buildings.

The impotence of the government to control the May protests effectively meant that the national government had ceased to function and in Nantes, workers effectively took control of the city. Elsewhere, civil affairs were disrupted, with day-to-day actions such as withdrawing money from banks or obtaining fuel for cars becoming difficult or impossible to carry out. On 29 May, de Gaulle postponed a meeting of the Council of Ministers and instead went to visit General Massu, commander of French forces in West Germany, at Baden-Baden. The precise motives of this visit remain unclear and it has subsequently been asserted that 'nothing exists to substantiate the claim, advanced at the time, that de Gaulle sought to obtain the support of the military against the possibility of an insurrection' (Berstein, 1993: 221).

De Gaulle then returned to France and the meeting of the Council of Ministers was re-scheduled for 30 May. Later that afternoon, he made a public broadcast on radio (the national television service being on strike) in which he ruled out his own resignation and ordered workers to return to work, threatening to declare a state of emergency if they failed to do so. He also declared that the National Assembly would be dissolved and that legislative elections would be held. He concluded the speech with an appeal to the French people to come to the defence of the existing political order and this call was heeded by a march of around 300,000–400,000 of his supporters through Paris on the evening of 30 May (Berstein, 1993: 222). The government also set up a military operations headquarters to deal with the unrest.

Subsequently, workers returned to work, urged to do so by the Communist Party (whose agreement to participate in the elections effectively removed the threat of revolution) and the CGT. By 5 June, most of the strikes had ended. This isolated the students, whose protests faded away, and the police re-took the Sorbonne on 6 June.

The legislative elections held on 23 June resulted in a crushing defeat for the socialists and the communists by the Gaullist Party. One explanation for this was that voters used the occasion to register their disapproval of the unrest and the inconvenience of strike action. The new government announced a series of reforms to the education system, such as the creation of over 60 new universities and the formation of a more democratic system of governing councils. Other reforms included the loosening of immigration controls.

De Gaulle resigned from office in April 1969 following his failure to secure popular endorsement in a referendum to approve reforms to the Senate and local governments. He was succeeded as President by Georges Pompidou.

Further demonstrations by students occurred in the Latin Quarter of Paris on Bastille Day (14 July), which were robustly handled by the Paris police and the CRS.

See also: austerity protests (worldwide) 2010–13, Chicago Democratic National Convention riot (Chicago) 1968, G20 protests (London) 2009, Grosvenor Square (London) 1968, student protests (London) 2010, urban guerrilla groups

Sources and further reading

Berstein, S. (1993) *The Republic of de Gaulle, 1958–1969*. Cambridge University Press.

Brown, B. (1974) *The Events of May. Protest in Paris: Anatomy of a Revolt*. Morristown, NJ: General Learning Press.

Carroll, J. (2011) 'From the Archive, 7 May 1968: Paris Students in Savage Battles', *The Guardian*, 7 May (originally published 7 May 1968), www.theguardian.com/theguardian/2011/may/09/may-1968-paris-student-riots (date accessed 19 May 2014).

Fabienne, (2008) 'May 68: The Student Movement in France and the World',

International Communist Current, http://en.internationalism.org/wr/313/may-68 (date accessed 19 May 2014).
Steinfels, P. (2008) 'Paris, May 1968: The Revolution that Never Was', *New York Times* (Europe Edition), 11 May, www.nytimes.com/2008/05/11/world/europe/11iht-paris.4.12777919.html?_r=0 (date accessed 19 May 2014).

SUBVERSION

The term 'subversion' has no fixed definition and, like terrorism, is frequently used in a pejorative way. The concept is used to justify the exercise of surveillance by state agencies on individuals and organisations whose ideologies and/or tactics used to advance their ideals is viewed as harmful to the state or its citizens. This function is known as political policing.

In the UK, the activities of the Communist Party were especially targeted by the security services during the 'Cold War' years and attention was also devoted to groups such as the Campaign for Nuclear Disarmament (CND), which was viewed as a 'communist-dominated' or 'communist-penetrated' organisation. In the latter decades of the twentieth century, the new focus of agencies tasked with combatting subversion became directed at terrorism. In 1992, the prime responsibility for gathering intelligence about the Provisional IRA on mainland Britain was transferred from the Metropolitan Police Service to the Security Service (MI5), whose director later stated that 'our principal task today is to help counter the threat from terrorism to this country' (Rimington, 1994).

The term 'subversion' can be applied to a wide range of activities associated with protest, which then serves as a justification for subjecting individuals and organisations to surveillance. This can be illustrated with reference to changes in the way in which this term has been defined in the UK:

- Lord Denning (1963) in his report on the Profumo affair defined subversion as 'an act which contemplated the overthrow of the government by unlawful means' (Denning, quoted in Aubrey, 1981: 16).
- Frank Kitson (a Brigadier in the British Army) defined subversion as 'all illegal measures short of the use of armed force taken by one section of the people of a country to overthrow those governing the country at the time, or to force them to do things which they do not want to do. It can involve the use of political and economic pressure, strikes, protest marches, and propaganda, and can also include the use of small scale violence for the purpose of coercing recalcitrant members of the population into giving support' (Kitson, 1971; 3).
- Lord Harris (a Home Office Minister) described subversion as 'activities which threaten the safety of well-being of the state', which were 'intended to undermine or overthrow parliamentary

democracy by political, industrial or violent means' (quoted in Davies *et al.*, 1984: 33–4). The definition put forward by Lord Harris was latterly incorporated into the Security Service Act 1989 as part of the remit of MI5.
- Lord Harris' definition was subsequently adopted by Home Secretary Merlyn Rees when he stated that Special Branch (a police unit responsible for combating subversion) was concerned with collecting information on those 'whom I think cause problems for the state' (quoted in Davies *et al.*, 1984: 34).
- A later Home Secretary, William Whitelaw, indicated that state surveillance of individuals who were active in political movements was justified 'not because of the views they hold but because the activities of the group could be such as to encourage public disorder' (quoted in Reeves and Smith, 1986: 15).
- Stella Rimington (Director of MI5 from 1992 to 1996) stated that 'the intention to undermine democracy is what "subversion" means to us. It does not include political dissent' (Rimington, 1994).

The definitions accorded to subversion in the UK during the twentieth century suggest that the term has become progressively broader, incorporating a wide range of activities that are articulated through various forms of protest even when these activities are legal. This threatens to undermine key liberal democratic freedoms, in particular the freedom of expression and the ability to protest. In addition, the methods used to monitor organisations and individuals labelled as 'subversive' are also likely to intrude on individual privacy.

It has thus been concluded that subversion has been used as the pretext to justify state intervention on a scale that involved re-drawing the boundaries of the liberal democratic tradition 'by declaring to be illegitimate political and industrial activities which had been thought to have distinguished a liberal democracy from an authoritarian or fascist society' (State Research, 1979). John Alderson, the Chief Constable of Devon and Cornwall during the 1970s and 1980s, pointed to the dangers posed to progressive politics through the association of subversion with 'anything which is designed to change society' (quoted in Davies *et al.*, 1984: 34).

In other countries, stricter statutory limits are imposed on agencies that are concerned with tackling subversion. In Australia, the Australian Security Intelligence Organisation Amendment Act 1986 (which replaced the terms 'subversion' and 'terrorism' with that of 'politically motivated violence') specified that the legislation 'shall not limit the right of persons to engage in lawful advocacy, protest or dissent and the exercise of that right shall not, by itself, be regarded as prejudicial to security, and the functions of the Organisation shall be construed accordingly'.

It has been argued that UK agencies whose role is to combat subversion (which historically was Special Branch, MI5 and GCHQ) may find themselves accused of operating in a manner allegedly adopted by their American counterparts, which 'invaded the privacy of countless citizens, have seriously inhibited the freedom of expression, have arrogated to themselves the making of policy decisions in the most sensitive areas and at have been employed by the administration in power for political purposes' (Emerson, 1983: 270). Individuals who support the ideals of targeted organisations may find themselves discriminated against in areas that include employment (for example, through the policy of positive vetting, which was introduced by a Labour government in 1949).

See also: peace movement, political policing, terrorism

Sources and further reading

Aubrey, C. (1981) *Who's Watching You? Britain's Security Services and the Official Secrets Act*. Harmondsworth: Penguin.

Davies, J. Gifford, Lord T. and Richards, T. (1984) *Political Policing in Wales*. Cardiff: Welsh Campaign for Civil and Political Liberties.

Emerson, R. (1982) 'Control of Government Intelligence Agencies: The American Experience'. *Political Quarterly*, 53: 273–91.

Kitson, F. (1971) *Low Intensity Operations: Subversion, Insurgency and Peacekeeping*. London: Faber & Faber.

Reeve, G. and Smith, J. (1986) *Offence of the Realm: How Peace Campaigners Get Bugged*. London: CND Publications.

Rimington, S. (1994) 'Security and Democracy – Is There a Conflict?' Richard Dimbleby Lecture, BBC, 12 June Available at: https://www.mi5.gov.uk/home/about-us/who-we-are/staff-and-management/director-general/speeches-by-the-director-general/director-generals-richard-dimbleby-lecture-1994.html (date accessed 5 June 2014).

State Research (1979) 'Introduction' in E.P. Thompson, *The Secret State*. London: Independent Research Publications, State Research Pamphlet No. 1.

T

TEA PARTY MOVEMENT

The Tea Party movement derives from America and is associated with the Republican Party. It is engaged in conventional political activities in addition to the use of protest to further its aims.

The use of the term 'tea party' refers to the 1773 Boston Tea Party, an episode of direct action by Americans who were opposed to paying a tax on tea to the British government. 'TEA' also is an acronym for Taxed Enough Already. The opposition of the Tea Party movement (TPM) to taxation is underpinned by its opposition to large-scale government spending and it seeks to substitute 'big' government (and the loss of personal freedoms that are claimed to arise from this) for a return to individualist values.

The origins of the TPM date from Tax Day protests in the 1990s. The event that is widely regarded as triggering the establishment of the TPM was a rant by the CNBC on-air editor, Rick Santelli, from the floor of the Chicago Mercantile Exchange on 19 February 2009 in which he attacked government bailouts and launched an impassioned attack on the Obama administration's Homeowners Affordability and Stability Plan, which sought to enable homeowners facing foreclosure to refinance their mortgages.

The growth of the TPM owes much to social media sites. However, its organisational structure is highly decentralised, reflecting a grassroots movement that has been built from the bottom up: 'Tea Party' is an umbrella term that encompasses a wide variety of localised groups. Insofar as there are national Tea Party policies, they are contained in the 2009 Contract from America. This included a reduction of taxes, a simplified taxation system, a balanced federal budget and the identification of the constitutionality of each law (based on a fundamentalist interpretation of this document). Its dislike of 'big government' underpins opposition to a number of policies pursued by the Obama administration such as the stimulus package, bank bailouts and healthcare reform.

Critics, however, have asserted that the TPM has been inspired by elite interests which have succeeded in mobilising grassroots support in an attempt to further their own interests. They have branded it an astroturf campaign, which is defined as 'a fake grassroots movement: it purports to be a spontaneous uprising of concerned citizens, but in reality it is founded and funded by elite interests'. The Tea Party 'is mostly composed of passionate, well-meaning people who think they are fighting elite power, unaware that they have been organised by the very interests they believe they are confronting ... Its members mobilise for freedom, unaware that the freedom they demand is freedom for corporations to trample them into the dirt' (Monbiot, 2010).

In addition to organising tax-day Tea Party rallies and related events, the TPM also involves itself in conventional political activity. This aspect of activities is especially associated with the Tea Party Express, a political action committee within the TPM. Its origins stem from the Our Country Deserves Better Committee, which launched the Tea Party Express in the wake of the rant by Rick Santelli in 2009 (Tea Party Express, 2012).

The Tea Party Express played a prominent role in the 2010 elections, including asking candidates for political office to endorse the Contract from America. A number of Republican candidates did so and following the elections, House and Senate Tea Party Caucuses were formed.

See also: direct action, Occupy movement

Sources and further reading

Foley, E. (2012) *The Tea Party*. Cambridge University Press.
Monbiot, G. (2010) 'The Tea Party Movement: Deluded and Inspired by Billionaires', *The Guardian*, 25 October.
Tea Party Express (2012) www.teapartyexpress.org (date accessed 19 May 2014).

TERRORISM

Terrorism has been defined as 'the use of physical force in order to damage a political adversary' (Della Porta, 1995: 2). However, it is a difficult term to define precisely or to differentiate from other forms of political activity (especially direct action) that utilise some form of physical activity to attain a political objective. Unlike rioting, however, terrorism is usually underpinned by a political ideology that may seek to redress injustices suffered by the communities from which the terrorists derive (Toolis, 1995: 39).

The operational definition used by the American Federal Bureau of Investigation in the 1990s defined terrorism as: 'The use of serious violence against persons or property, or threat to use such violence, to intimidate or coerce a government, the public or any section of the public, in order to promote political, social or ideological objectives' (Lloyd, 1996: para. 5.22).

In the UK, the current definition of terrorism is provided by the Terrorism Act 2000 (which was slightly amended by the Terrorism

Act 2006). This legislation defined terrorism as the use or threat of action which 'involves serious violence against a person, involves serious damage to property, endangers a person's life, other than that of the person committing the action, creates a serious risk to the health or safety of the public or a section of the public, or is designed seriously to interfere with or seriously to disrupt an electronic system'.

However, in order for actions of this nature to be deemed to constitute terrorism, it is also necessary that the use or threat of action 'is designed to influence the government or an international governmental organisation or to intimidate the public or a section of the public' and the use or threat of action 'is made for the purpose of advancing a political, religious or ideological cause'.

Nevertheless, although these official definitions of terrorism emphasise the 'fear factor' (which includes the threat to use violence), conventional warfare often utilises tactics of this nature (for example, the saturation bombing of civilians), which suggests that terrorism may be a subjective term, determined by one's own political perspective – one person's terrorist is another person's freedom fighter. The civil war that has raged in Syria since 2011 epitomises this dilemma – the government regarding the rebels as terrorists while much of the outside world views them as legitimate opponents of a tyrannical regime which has killed large numbers of its own people. Terrorism is also a term that is frequently applied in a pejorative way – 'the label used by the threatened' (Morris and Hoe, 1987: 22).

One important aspect of terrorism (and often a defining feature when the state is on the receiving end of violence) is that terrorists do not seek a head-on confrontation with the police or the army: in this sense especially, terrorism is depicted as a method of warfare 'for disenfranchised and alienated people' (Combs, 2009) who lack the resources to engage in more conventional forms of warfare against their enemies. Instead, they seek to attain their aims by a war of attrition, which may involve tactics that seek to intimidate the public and whose conduct is not constrained by the conventions of war.

Accordingly, it has been argued that the main aim of terrorism is to cause a state of 'disorientation' (Bowden, 1978: 284) in which people are unable to lead normal, everyday lives. It has thus been argued that 'the purpose of terrorism is not military victory, it is to terrorise, to change your behaviour if you're the victim by making you afraid of today, afraid of tomorrow and in diverse societies ... afraid of each other' (Clinton, 2001). This latter phrase thus suggests that attempts to divide society on racial or ethnic lines may be a specific aim of contemporary terrorist campaigns conducted in multi-racial societies.

As with other forms of protest, terrorism empowers those who engage in it and even if their objectives are not met, the violence with which terrorism is associated may temporarily achieve empowerment by allowing participants in violent actions to feel that they have 'got one over' on their enemies. In addition, violence (especially when used by groups seeking the liberation of their country from occupation by a foreign power) may fulfil the purpose of a 'cleansing force', which 'frees the native from his inferiority complex and from his despair and inaction; it makes him fearless and restores his self-respect' (Fanon, 1961: 73–4). This heightened sense of self-esteem may provide the basis for future and bolder revolutionary acts.

Terrorism has been used by groups with a diverse range of objectives. It may be designed to secure a change in the direction of public policy or to alter the practices performed by commercial organisations or individuals who carry out actions that are disapproved of by those who carry out violence. Terrorism may alternatively be designed to advance radical political changes that were historically associated with replacing absolutist monarchies with liberal democratic political structures and (during the twentieth century) overthrowing capitalism in favour of socialism. In the twenty-first century, terrorism has been influenced by religious impulses and carried out by Islamist fundamentalist groups, in particular al-Qaeda. Terrorism has also been carried out by groups who seek the liberation of their country from occupation by foreign powers. However, an important factor that links these diverse groups is that terrorism courts publicity, the level of which is influenced by the spectacular nature of the violence that takes place.

In addition, although states are frequently on the receiving end of terrorist campaigns, they may conduct violence of this nature themselves against their external or internal enemies. Death squads that eliminate internal opposition to a regime are an example of state-sponsored violence. These are usually associated with authoritarian societies, which is one reason why the alleged 'shoot to kill' policy of the Royal Ulster Constabulary against assumed republican terrorists during the early 1980s was a particularly damaging accusation – liberal democracies such as the UK should not engage in acts of this nature.

The violence that is associated with terrorism is diverse and includes selective (or targeted) violence, indiscriminate violence and attacks mounted on economic targets. Terrorism may also entail hostage-taking and hijacking, tactics that may seek to trade the victims of such activities for terrorists who have been imprisoned.

The target of selective violence carried out by terrorists is typically those whose activities are deemed essential to the functioning of the state: politicians, judges, soldiers and police officers are frequently targeted by activities ranging from kidnapping to murder. One example of this was the assassination of two senior members of the Royal Ulster Constabulary (Chief Superintendant Harry Breen and Superintendant Bob Buchanan) by the IRA in South Armagh in 1989. Violence is thus applied directly to the apparatus of the state, those viewed as 'the social and political "adversaries"' (Della Porta, 1995: 12) of the terrorists.

The prime aims of violence of this nature are to incapacitate the operations of the state (so that it cannot govern) and to undermine a government's resolve to continue with a course of action upon which it was embarked, since 'the required outlay becomes so great that the political object is no longer equal in value [and] ... must be given up' (von Clausewitz, 1832). A secondary aim of this violence is to 'stimulate the political will and resolve of those who perpetrate it by demonstrating the extent to which the state and its key personnel are vulnerable to a concerted campaign of violence' (Joyce, 2002: 159–60), thus encouraging further acts of violence against its functionaries.

Selective violence may also be used by groups whose opponents are not associated with the state, but who are responsible for performing actions of which they disapprove. One example of this is the violence displayed towards individuals and organisations that provide abortions, which has taken place since the latter years of the twentieth century in America, Canada, Australia and New Zealand. This has included arson (directed against abortion clinics) and the kidnap, assault, attempted murder and murder of those engaged in delivering abortion services. Groups that are involved in committing or advocating violence of this nature, which has been dubbed 'terrorism' (Wilson and Lynxwiler, 1988) or 'Christian terrorism' (Hoffman, 2006: 116), include the Army of God in America.

Indiscriminate violence is directed against members of the general public in a random fashion and may take the form of bombs being planted in public places or facilities used by the general public or, more recently, being carried by suicide bombers. Modes of transportation have especially been the subject of this form of random violence, examples of which include the Madrid train bombings in 2004 and the London bombings in 2005, both events being associated with Islamic fundamentalist groups.

Indiscriminate violence may entail tremendous loss of life (as occurred in the USA on 11 September 2001, when hijacked aircraft were deliberately crashed into the Twin Towers of New York's World Trade Center and the Pentagon Building in Washington DC). Although weapons such as bombs can be made from material that is readily available (a mix of icing sugar and agricultural fertiliser forming the basic ingredients of some weapons used in Northern Ireland during the 'Troubles'), the ability to cause devastation on a large scale has been aided through what Dobson and Payne (1979) referred to as 'the weapons of terror' (which includes explosives such as semtex) and the ability of terrorists to strike anywhere in the world – what Clinton (2001) referred to as 'universal vulnerability'. In this case violence is indirectly applied to the state – this form of violence 'works' if an intimidated public (whose fear is underpinned by the perception that their government is failing in its prime purpose of safeguarding the lives of its citizens) puts pressure on the government to concede to the terrorists' demands: 'therefore, by definition, a terror campaign cannot succeed unless we become its accomplices and out of fear, give in' (Clinton, 2001).

Terrorists are also associated with acts of violence directed at economic targets. Typically violence of this nature has been directed against property seen as essential to the nation's trading, business or commercial life. One example of this was the 'commercial bombing campaign' waged by the Provisional IRA during the 1970s to discourage investment and destroy jobs in Northern Ireland in order to dissuade moderate nationalists from backing the political status quo there on the grounds that it secured good economic prospects. Similarly, the IRA's bombing campaign on mainland Britain was directed at targets that sought to disrupt the tourist industry (such as the Tower of London bombing in 1976), the commercial life of the City of London (including the bombing of the Baltic Exchange in 1992 and Bishopsgate in 1993) and to cause damage and disruption in shopping centres (such as the bombing of Manchester city centre in 1996). Violence of this nature may be designed to undermine the economic basis of approaches pursued by a government to 'buy' support for itself and its policies or (as with indiscriminate violence) to pressurise a government into making concessions to the demands of the terrorists.

Old versus new terrorism

In recent years, a distinction has been drawn between what is termed 'old' and 'new' terrorism.

Although the term 'new terrorism' has been used since the 1990s, the 9/11 attacks provoked a more intense debate as to whether terrorism was different in nature from that which had existed before, a debate that identified al-Qaeda as the prototype of new terrorism underpinned by religious fanaticism. The key features of new terrorism have been identified as 'structured in loose networks rather than organisational hierarchies', 'transnational, rather than localised, in its reach', 'deliberately targeted at innocent civilians', 'motivated by religious fanaticism rather than political ideology' and 'aimed at causing maximum destruction' (Gofas, 2012: 18). The targets often have symbolic significance to the nation, such as the Twin Towers of New York's World Trade Center. In particular, it has been argued that new terrorism is 'apocalyptic, catastrophic terrorism' (Morgan, 2004: 29) in which extreme violence is viewed as an end in itself rather than as the means to an end (Morgan, 2004: 30).

However, the extent to which terrorism is 'new' has been debated. Religiously motivated terrorism has been in existence since the 1980s and the view that new terrorism is organised differently and is characterised by an international network of loosely connected cells and support networks rather than by a hierarchical command-and-control structure located in a specific country or region has been countered by assertions that 'traditional' terrorist groups like the Provisional IRA accorded a considerable degree of autonomy to their cells (Gofas, 2012: 23) In addition, although religion is a 'core-defining feature of contemporary terrorist activity' (Gofas, 2012: 26), such a motivation is not new and can be traced back to the Zealots of the first century AD. It has also been argued that indiscriminate mass-casualty attacks have characterised terrorism before the 9/11 attacks (Gofas, 2012: 28). It has thus been argued that 'by pointing out that defining religious, jihadist terror as "new" is an effective way of framing the threat so as to mobilize both public and elite support for major policy change' (Gofas, 2012: 19).

See also: counter-terrorism, direct action, Islamic terrorist groups, Northern Ireland: security policy during the 'Troubles', urban guerrilla groups

Sources and further reading

Bowden, T. (1978) *Beyond the Limits of the Law*. Harmondsworth: Penguin.

Clinton, B. (2001) 'The Struggle for the Soul of the Twenty-First Century'. Dimbleby Lecture, BBC Television, 14 December. Available at: http://australianpolitics.com/news/2001/01-12-14.shtml (date accessed 19 May 2014).

Combs, C. (2009) *Terrorism in the Twenty-First Century*, 5th edn. Harlow: Longman.

Della Porta, D. (1995) *Social Movements, Political Violence and the State*. Cambridge University Press.

Dobson, C. and Payne, R. (1979) *The Weapons of Terror: International Terrorism at Work*. Basingstoke: Macmillan.

Fanon, F. (1961) *The Wretched of the Earth*. Harmondsworth: Penguin.

Gofas, A. (2012) '"Old" versus "New" Terrorism: What's in a Name?' *Uluslararası İlişkiler*, 8(32): 17–32. Available at: www.academia.edu/3588549/Old_vs._New_Terrorism_Whats_in_a_Name (date accessed 19 May 2014).

Hoffman, B. (2006) *Inside Terrorism*. New York: Columbia University Press.

Joyce, P. (2002) *The Politics of Protest: Extra-Parliamentary Politics in Britain since 1970*. Basingstoke: Palgrave.

Lloyd, Lord (1996) *Inquiry into Legislation Against Terrorism*. London: TSO, Cmnd. 3420.

Morgan, M. (2004) 'The Origins of the New Terrorism', Institute of Strategic Studies, http://strategicstudiesinstitute.army.mil/pubs/parameters/articles/04spring/morgan.pdf (date accessed 19 May 2014)

Morris, E. and Hoe, A. (1987) *Terrorism: Threat and Response*. Basingstoke: Macmillan.

Toolis, K. (1995) *Rebel Hearts: Journeys within the IRA's Soul*. London: Picador.

Von Clausewitz, C. (1832) *On War*. Translated by J.J. Graham (1873) London: N. Trübner. Available at: www.clausewitz.com/readings/OnWar1873/BK1ch02.html (date accessed 19 May 2014).

Wilson, M. and Lynxwiler, J. (1988) 'Abortion Clinic Violence as Terrorism'. *Studies in Conflict & Terrorism*, 11(4): 263–73.

THIRD FORCE

A third force is used to deal with serious breakdowns of public order and is frequently depicted as a form of riot police.

Riot police may consist of regular police officers who undergo specialist training (as is the case in England and Wales) or (as in France) they may constitute a separate organisation within the police service which, like fire fighters, can be called upon when disturbances arise or are anticipated to occur. The term 'third force' is used to describe the latter arrangement.

A third force is a highly disciplined unit that stands midway between the regular police and the military (Wright, 2002: 68). Its main advantages are that a full-time focus on dealing with riots and other forms of disorder may enhance efficiency in quelling disturbances and it also relieves the regular police from having to perform duties that take them away from their normal crime-fighting roles. In addition, dealing with the public in a confrontational setting may deprive the police of their legitimacy 'that results from violence against the public' (Tupman and Tupman, 1999: 72). Confrontational policing may also breed attitudes that influence the way in which they act when they return to normal police duties.

There are, however, problems with riot police not being drawn from the regular police. The cost of a separate riot police may be queried in times when disorders do not regularly occur, although officers may be deployed to police any form of crowd situation, including crowd control at sporting events. In addition, riot police may use aggressive tactics derived from the knowledge that they have no need to cultivate good relations with those they are policing. Such tactics (especially when members of the public are injured) may have an adverse effect on the overall image of the police service.

The weaponry associated with riot police includes protective clothing ('riot gear'), batons and riot shields, and an array of weapons such as pepper spray, CS spray, tear gas, stun grenades and rubber bullets. Specialist vehicles, including water cannons, may also be available in some countries. Although the availability of such weaponry may be justified by the violence that is displayed towards the police when dealing with crowd disorders, it does pose problems, one of which is that the presence of police officers dressed and equipped for confrontation may actually provoke it. For this reason, riot police are sometimes held in reserve, outside the view of a crowd, and are only deployed if violence breaks out.

An additional issue is that suppressing violence with violence does not address why riots or other forms of disorderly conduct occurred in the first place: 'instead of dealing with problems that have caused public outrage they [politicians] can try to use violence to make those problems go away. This is not good for the democratic system, as it allows politicians to ignore legitimate public demand' (Tupman and Tupman, 1999: 72). It was in this vein that in his evidence to the Scarman Inquiry in 1981, John Alderson, then a serving chief constable, argued that the police should 'talk hearts and minds rather than CS gas and plastic bullets' (Alderson, 1981).

See also: paramilitary policing, public order policing (England and Wales), public order policing (France), riot police

Sources and further reading:
Alderson, J. (1981) 'Evidence to Lord Scarman's Inquiry into the Brixton Riots'. Quoted in G. Northam (1998) *Shooting in the Dark: Riot Police in Britain.* London: Faber & Faber.
Tupman, B. and Tupman, A. (1999) *Policing in Europe: Uniform in Diversity.* Exeter: Intellect.
Wright, A. (2002) *Policing: An Introduction to Concepts and Practice.* Cullompton: Willan Publishing.

TIANANMEN SQUARE PROTESTS (BEIJING) 1976 AND 1989

Tiananmen Square, Beijing, has been the venue for a number of protests in modern China. Two of these events are considered below.

1976

The 1976 protest was triggered by the death of the Chinese Premier, Zhou Enlai, in January. The public mourning that followed this was seen by key figures in the Politburo of the Communist Party of China (especially a number of its senior members, who were dubbed 'the gang of four' and who had been locked in a power struggle with the Premier) as an attack on their authority and on the Cultural Revolution with which they were associated.

The protests in Tiananmen Square, Beijing, on 4 April took the form of laying paper wreaths and white paper chrysanthemums at the foot of the Monument to the People's Heroes in the Square and posting poems which purported to celebrate Chinese history, but in fact constituted a veiled attack on China's contemporary leaders. It was in this sense, especially, that these actions were viewed as protests. At its height, hundreds of thousands of people were involved in these events.

The leaders of the Politburo resolved to remove the wreaths, flowers and poems, and public security forces carried out these actions on the night of 4–5 April. The area around the Monument was also cordoned off by public security forces on 5 April to prevent access to mourners. That night, the few thousand mourners who were in the vicinity were forcibly driven away by the militia, under the control of the Mayor of Beijing.

The state-controlled media blamed these events on Deng Xiaoping, who was performing the duties of the Premier. He had been an ally of Zhou Enlai and the Gang of Four wished to remove him as they were concerned that his political influence constituted a challenge to their authority within the country. He was accordingly placed under house arrest, but following the death of Chairman Mao Zedong and the subsequent fall of the Gang of Four in October 1976, he was restored to power, becoming China's Paramount Leader in 1978.

1989

The 1989 protests were triggered by the death Hu Yaobang, who had held office as General Secretary of the Communist Party between 1980 and 1987. He was a liberal reformer whose views on social and economic reform, his desire to rehabilitate those who had been persecuted during the Cultural Revolution (1966–76) and his tolerance of student protests in 1986 in Beijing brought him into conflict with hardliners in the Communist Party, who wished to make no concessions in these areas. This had led to him being deposed in 1987 and forced to make a humiliating public self-criticism of his allegedly 'bourgeois' ideas.

Following his death, university students marched to the Square on 17 April, which they then occupied. The initial sit-in involved a few thousand students, but in the following days these were joined by larger numbers (who boycotted their classes) and other citizens. Their actions were ostensibly to mourn Hu and to demand a posthumous pardon and a state funeral – the latter demand was conceded by the authorities – but they used the occasion to vent their grievances against a range of issues that included inflation, their limited career prospects and what they viewed as the corrupt practices of the Communist Party elite.

In particular, the protesters voiced support for a range of democratic political reforms that included greater accountability of the government, freedom of speech and of the press, and the restoration of workers' control over industry. For this reason, the protests were dubbed 'pro-democracy' and it was observed that 'the protesters at Tiananmen Square ... were striving for more input in the way their country was run, more individual freedom, the ability to elect their leaders, and the removal of corrupt officials' (Lusted, 2010: 12–13).

Although the protest that took place in the Square was student-inspired, around one million people from all walks of life became involved there as it progressed. A broadcasting tent was set up, a daily newspaper was published and on 30 May a large sculpture (called the 'Goddess of Democracy') modelled on the Statue of Liberty was erected in the Square.

The government initially adopted a conciliatory stance towards the protesters, who were unarmed and whose stance was non-violent. However, it became concerned with the growing strength of the protest, which spread to several hundred towns by mid-May in the wake of a student-led hunger strike which had begun on 13 May. Most of the country's leaders became concerned that this mass movement could lead 'to a breakdown of law and order and threaten the power of the Communist Party' (Langley, 2009: 32). This convinced the government (headed by paramount leader Deng Xiaoping and Premier Li Peng) to use force to crush the protest.

Martial law was declared on 20 May and several hundred thousand troops from the People's Liberation Army were sent to Beijing. Following abortive attempts to induce the protesters to leave the Square, on 3 June the Army entered it to clear it of demonstrators and in the process a number (the precise figures being unknown) were killed or injured on 3 and 4 June in what has since been called the 'Beijing Massacre'. The most famous image of the protest was that of a lone Chinese man blocking a line of tanks in the Square on 5 June. Coercive measures were also pursued against protesters in other cities.

A crackdown then occurred. The main Beijing University campus was raided in an attempt to round up the protest's ringleaders and protesters, and their supporters were arrested. Censorship of the media was pursued by the imposition of strict controls over the Chinese press and the expulsion of foreign journalists. Political reforms were halted and economic reforms were put on hold, not being resumed until the early 1990s under the auspices of Deng's 'socialist market economy'. Officials deemed sympathetic to the protesters were purged from office and the police and internal security forces were strengthened to prevent a repeat of the protests.

In December 2010, the prominent intellectual and key participant in the events of 1989, Liu Xiaobo, was awarded the 2010 Nobel Peace Prize for his long and non-violent struggle for fundamental human rights in China. He was unable to attend the event because he was imprisoned and his absence was symbolised by an empty chair at the ceremony, which took place on 10 December.

See also: civil disobedience, demonstrations, Gdańsk Shipyard protests (Gdańsk, Poland) 1980–9, Pussy Riot protest (Moscow) 2012

Sources and further reading

Hay, J. (2010) *The Tiananmen Square Protests of 1989.* San Diego: Greenhaven Press.
Kelly, B. (2003) *The Tiananmen Square Massacre.* San Diego: Greenhaven Press.
Langley, A. (2009) *Tiananmen Square: Massacre Crushes China's Democracy Movement.* Minneapolis, MN: Compass Point Books.
Lusted, M. (2010) *Tiananmen Square Protests.* Edina, MN: ABDO Publishing Company.

TRAFALGAR SQUARE ANTI-POLL TAX RALLY (LONDON) 1990

A key reform to the system of local government finance introduced by Margaret Thatcher's Conservative government was the replacement of the rates (which were based on the value of a property) system with a new tax, officially known as the Community Charge, but more commonly referred to as the Poll Tax because of its similarity to a tax introduced in 1381 that provoked the Peasants' Revolt. This provoked considerable opposition because it failed to take means into account – all individuals were required to contribute towards the cost of local government regardless of their personal financial circumstances.

In response to this reform, a number of local anti-Poll Tax unions were set up to mobilise community resistance against the imposition of this tax (which was due to come into force in April 1990). Some of these unions were organised into local federations. Their actions included civil disobedience, which took the form of urging non-registration to the register councils compiled to administer the tax and non-payment, using the slogan 'can't pay, won't pay'. These unions also organised protests when councils met to set the Poll Tax level for the locality, some of which resulted in disorder.

In November 1989, the All Britain Anti-Poll Tax Federation was set up by the Trotskyite Militant Tendency (latterly called the Socialist Party) to spearhead opposition to this reform. A large number of anti-Poll Tax unions affiliated under its banner. This organisation organised a major demonstration against the Poll Tax in central London on 31 March 1990, which would take place alongside a similar event to be held in Glasgow (where the Poll Tax had been introduced the previous year throughout Scotland). The Glasgow event passed off peacefully.

A march was planned to take place in Trafalgar Square, where a rally would be addressed by politicians including Tony Benn and George Galloway. At the last minute, the organisers asked the Metropolitan Police Service (MPS) and the Department of the Environment for permission to re-schedule the event in Hyde Park. This request was based on the belief that the projected numbers who would attend the event might exceed the 70,000 capacity of Trafalgar Square. However, permission to do this was denied on the grounds that there was no time to re-plan the policing of this event at another location, although the police did close off much of the immediate vicinity so that more people could be accommodated.

The march to Trafalgar Square commenced from Kennington Park, south London on 31 March 1990. It started at around 1.30 pm and consisted of around 200,000 participants. As the march was slowly processing up Whitehall to Trafalgar Square, it encountered a small group of protesters who were engaged in a sit-down protest near to Downing Street after being refused permission to hand in a petition. Tactics used by the police (which included the arrest of a demonstrator who was confined to a wheelchair) increased the scale of the sit-down protest, which was joined by some of the marchers. It was latterly observed that 'the decision to confront the relatively small group of ... protestors gathered around Downing Street initiated a succession of events over which the police had little control' (Waddington, 1994: 53).

The police responded to this escalated sit-down protest with an operation that was designed to split the protesters, forcing half up Whitehall to Trafalgar Square and the remainder down Whitehall to Parliament Square (Waddington, 1994: 53). This manoeuvre met with stiff resistance and at one stage the police were temporarily forced to withdraw (Burns, 1992: 89) until they were reinforced by mounted police. However, the aggression of the group forced into Trafalgar Square was matched by that of other protesters already there and led to fierce fighting breaking out. This resulted in the deployment of riot police, who used baton charges to disperse the rioters in conjunction with operations conducted by mounted police.

The rally in Trafalgar Square ended at around 4 pm. Although most of the protesters had dispersed, around 3,000 'troublemakers' remained behind who engaged in pitched battles with the police (Waddington, 1990). Police actions to cordon off the exits to Trafalgar Square meant that the demonstrators were penned in – an early example of the use of 'kettling'. Mounted riot police charged into the crowd in Trafalgar Square and police riots vans were driven at protesters in the vicinity of the South African Embassy. These actions produced responses from the demonstrators (who became trapped in Trafalgar Square) that saw police vans attacked and debris from a building site in Trafalgar Square being used to attack the police. Fires also broke out in Trafalgar Square and the neighbouring vicinity.

Between 6 pm and 7 pm, some exits of Trafalgar Square were opened by the police, allowing some demonstrators to access public transport and depart from the area. However, other demonstrators were pushed away from the Square into the West End, which resulted in vandalism, looting and cars being overturned there. Sporadic scuffles between the police and rioters continued into the early hours of the morning, and shops and clubs were also attacked. The then Deputy Assistant Commissioner of the MPS estimated that around £400,000 worth of damage was caused and 113 people were injured (Maynell, cited in Graham, 2010). In total, 502 major crimes and 1,336 other crimes were reported, 408 arrests were made on the day and 542 police officers were injured (Metcalfe, cited in Waddington, 1994: 53). A further 123 arrests followed subsequent raids on known anti-Poll Tax activists in an action termed Operation Carnaby. The MPS paid a total of £9 million in riot damages (Waddington, 1994: 53). Further arrests connected with this event occurred on 20 October, when the police dispersed a Trafalgar Square Defendants Campaign picket outside Brixton Police Station.

Blame for the violence that occurred was directed at anarchists, especially those associated with Class War and the Anarchist 121 bookshop in Brixton. This implied that the riots had been a planned event. However, these groups (and the libertarian left and Socialist Workers' Party) defended these actions as a legitimate response to the violence meted out by the police. Following these events, the Trafalgar Square Defendants Campaign was set up to defend those charged with offences in connection with the disturbances. In total, 491 individuals were charged and the efforts of the Campaign managed to secure a large number of acquittals, implying that the police had either exaggerated charges or had fabricated them.

A number of issues arose in connection with the policing of the event. Police organisation was ineffective – 'senior officers were barely in control of their subordinates as personnel carriers raced around with their sirens blaring despite repeated instructions from the control room not to do so' (Waddington, 1994: 53–4). Criticism was also directed at the Gold/Silver/Bronze hierarchy of command on the day arising from the Silver Commander appearing on the scene and making operational decisions that ought to have been made by the Bronze Commanders (Waddington, 1994: 134). Problems were also perceived with the equipment and communications devices used by the police, and the adequacy of the initial number of officers who were deployed to police the event.

The Community Charge was highly unpopular and its close association with Mrs Thatcher posed a question over her leadership. Support for her nationally was in sharp decline, a situation that was especially caused by a downturn in the economy in 1990–1 (characterised by recession, unemployment, inflation and a rising trade deficit). This ultimately led to a challenge being mounted to her by Conservative MPs in December 1989 and to her replacement by John Major following a further challenge to her leadership in 1990.

The anti-Poll Tax movement, especially the Trafalgar Square riot, was argued to have played some part in the abandonment of the Poll Tax: in addition to the 1990 demonstration, further protests took place in London and Glasgow in March 1991. However, conventional politics also played a part.

The defeat of the Conservative candidate at a by-election in the safe seat of Ribble Valley on 7 March 1991 convinced many Conservative MPs that this tax had become an electoral liability and they were thus willing to abandon this reform (which had been closely associated with Mrs Thatcher) in order to win the next general election. Accordingly, on 21 March 1991, the new Prime Minister, John Major, announced the abandonment of the Community Charge in favour of a new source of local government finance, the Council Tax, which was introduced in 1993.

See also: demonstrations, kettling, paramilitary policing, public order policing (England and Wales), riot

Sources and further reading

Books LLC (2010) *Riots in London*. London: General Books LLC.

Burns, D. (1992) *Poll Tax Rebellion*. Stirling: AK Press.

Graham, D. (2010) 'The Battle for Trafalgar Square: The Poll Tax Riots Revisited', *The Independent*, 25 March, http://www.independent.co.uk/news/uk/politics/the-battle-of-trafalgar-square-the-poll-tax-riots-revisited-1926873.html (date accessed 19 May 2014).

Metcalfe, J. (1991) 'Public Order Debriefing: Trafalgar Square Riot'. London: MPS, unpublished.

Waddington, D. (1990) Speech in the House of Commons, 2 April, HC Debs, vol. 170, col. 893.

Waddington, P. (1994) *Liberty and Order: Public Order Policing in a Capital City*. London: UCL Press.

U

UK UNCUT

UK Uncut is a network of protest groups whose origins date back to October 2010. It was 'born in a shop doorway. On October 27th 2010, just one week after George Osborne announced the deepest cuts to public services since the 1920s, around 70 people ran along Oxford Street, entered Vodafone's flagship store and sat down. We had shut down tax-dodging Vodafone's flagship store' (UK Uncut, 2014).

UK Uncut utilises innovative forms of direct action (including sit-ins, blockades and street parties) to oppose the spending cuts that have been initiated by the 2010 Coalition government. One aspect of its protest were the Great British Street Parties held on 26 May 2012, one of which took place outside the house in London owned by the Deputy Prime Minister, Nick Clegg.

UK Uncut argues that austerity politics are the 'the policy of the powerful'. The movement claims that:

> The brutal cuts to services about to be inflicted by the current Government are unnecessary, unfair and ideologically motivated ... The cuts will dismantle the welfare state, send inequality sky-rocketing and hit the poorest and most vulnerable hardest. A cabinet of millionaires have decided that libraries, healthcare, education funding, voluntary services, sports, the environment, the disabled, the poor and the elderly must pay the price for the recklessness of the rich. (UK Uncut, 2014)

UK Uncut encourages community campaigning and many events associated with the movement (such as the picket of the council in Harrogate in connection with council spending cuts on 16 November 2010) are directed at local issues. However, a central website is used to publicise such events, to promote coordinated local direct action in connection with key protest themes and to organise other forms of protest, such as the petition against legal aid cuts in 2013.

The belief that public spending cuts were driven by big business and the financial sector are compatible views held by other groups that include Occupy London. An important target of UK Uncut's direct action are large businesses and multinational corporations whom they accuse of tax avoidance.

Among the retailers that were initially targeted for tax avoidance were Vodafone, Boots and shops owned by the Arcadia group (that include BHS, Topshop and Burtons). The protests commonly take the form of mass sit-ins that are designed to close the premises. These protests culminated in the legal arm of UK Uncut taking HM Revenue & Customs (HMRC) to court in November 2011 for its failure to provide substantial reasons for not collecting billions of pounds in taxes from retailers who had been targeted by the protests. This led to an investigation by the National Audit Office, which concluded that the settlements that had been reached by HMRC in five cases 'were reasonable ones for the Department to have reached in the circumstances' (National Audit Office, 2012: para. 10). However, HMRC did subsequently alter its procedures to deal with future cases of large tax disputes.

Further protests against tax avoidance were mounted against Starbucks in December 2012, whose non-payment of corporation tax resulted in it agreeing to pay the sum of £20 million in the next two years. This protest took the form of a national day of action directed at the company's retail outlets.

Campaigns by UK Uncut have also been mounted against commercial concerns that it feels are exploiting the public. One example of this was the protest mounted in November 2013 against offices of the energy supplier Npower against the backdrop of a recent announcement that the company would raise its household charges for electricity and gas by 9.3 per cent and 11.1 per cent respectively.

In addition to mounting campaigns of direct action to further the aims of UK Uncut, a separate campaign group, UK Uncut Legal Action, has mounted legal challenges in connection with tax avoidance. One of these challenges was mounted in connection with a deal struck in late 2010 between HMRC and the bank Goldman Sachs, which led to the latter being let off paying £20 million that it owed in interest arising from a tax avoidance scheme that it used during the 1990s. Although this deal was declared lawful by the High Court, it was revealed that the bank had threatened to withdraw from the voluntary Code of Practice on Taxation (which was designed to ensure that banks paid their fair share of taxes) if HMRC pursued it for the money that was owed, which, had this happened, would have been politically embarrassing for the Chancellor of the Exchequer.

High street banks have also been targeted by UK Uncut. Such actions were in part motivated by their role in causing the financial crisis and took the form of 'bail-ins', whereby the banks were turned into services threatened by the cuts initiated in response to the financial crisis. These protests also arose from accusations of tax avoidance and as a protest against bankers' bonuses. One example of this was the protest mounted in July 2013 that sought to close branches of the HSBC bank by organising food banks outside the premises. This protest was designed to highlight the manner in which welfare spending cuts (including the benefit cap and the 'bedroom tax') had increased poverty and enhanced people's reliance on food banks. This bank was chosen because of its use of tax havens as a mechanism of tax avoidance, which resulted in a loss of revenue to the Exchequer.

A number of protests have also been directed against government austerity measures. A sit-down protest on Westminster Bridge on 9 October 2011 was directed at the Health and Social Care Bill and drew support from health workers. The aim of this legislation was to reduce the number of individuals claiming disability benefit and protests were also directed at Atos, an IT company whose healthcare division operates a programme for the Department of Work and Pensions to assess whether people claiming disability benefit are fit for work. Atos was a sponsor for the 2012 Paralympic Games and UK Uncut believed that its activities on behalf of the government department disqualified it from being a supporter of this event. UK Uncut held a week of protests referred to as the 'Atos games' in August 2012 to coincide with the opening of the Paralympic Games, which culminated in a demonstration in conjunction with Disabled People Against Cuts outside the Department for Work and Pensions at the headquarters of Atos on 31 August.

A further campaign was mounted on 5 October 2013 by UK Uncut against changes proposed by the Ministry of Justice to reduce the legal aid bill by £220 million per year by 2018. This took the form of blocking roads near courts and legal buildings in a number of towns and cities, including the Old Bailey in London, where a mock trial was held of the Justice Secretary, Chris Grayling.

Protests undertaken by UK Uncut have frequently met with a robust police response, an approach referred to as total policing (Taylor, 2013). Actions that have been taken include the use of CS spray at protesters outside a branch of Boots in central London on 30 January 2011. The officer who took this action (which he claimed was in self-defence) was subsequently criticised by the Independent Police Complaints Commission (IPCC), which urged that a misconduct meeting should be initiated. The IPCC also criticised police failures in securing medical help for those who had been sprayed with the gas (Taylor, 2013).

Other examples of police intervention at UK Uncut's protests include the mass arrest tactic which led to charging around 150 protesters for the offence of aggravated trespass in connection with a protest at Fortnum & Mason on 26 March 2011. The group accused the company of tax avoidance and this date had been chosen to coincide with a march organised by the Trades Union Congress in London against cuts. The Crown Prosecution Service subsequently dropped the charge of aggravated trespass against over 100 of those who had been arrested.

See also: austerity protests (worldwide) 2010–13, civil disobedience, direct action, Occupy movement, paramilitary policing, public order policing (England and Wales)

Sources and further reading

National Audit Office (2012) *HM Revenue and Customs: Settling Large Tax Disputes. Report by the Comptroller and Auditor General.* London: TSO, House of Commons Paper 188, Session 2011/12.

Taylor, M. (2013) 'Police Watchdog Criticises Met Officer over Use of CS Gas on Protesters', *The Guardian*, 8 August, http://www.theguardian.com/uk-news/2013/aug/08/met-officer-cs-gas-protesters (date accessed 19 May 2014).

UK Uncut (2014) 'False Economy. Why Cuts are the Wrong Cure', http://falseeconomy.org.uk/campaigns/item/uk-uncut (date accessed 19 May 2014).

The UK Uncut website is: www.UKuncut.org.uk.

URBAN GUERRILLA GROUPS

Guerrilla warfare entails the use of military tactics deployed by individuals who are not part of a conventional army and who typically seek to overthrow a government or to rid their country of an occupying power. Their tactics fall short of a conventional 'stand-up' fight with the forces of the government that they wish to defeat and instead take the form of a war of attrition that aims to pick off the enemy when they present themselves to the guerrillas in a position of vulnerability.

Guerrilla warfare is characterised by its mobility. Guerrillas typically operate from bases in inaccessible parts of a country (such as mountainous areas) from which they carry out hit-and-run tactics that are performed in such a manner as to ensure that the guerrillas are constantly on the offensive, seizing the initiative when it presents itself to them. Their actions include raids, ambushes and targeted assassinations in which they utilise the factor of surprise, hitting the enemy when they were not expecting an attack to occur. These attacks may be directed at key targets such as military or police personnel, the barracks that houses them or may involve the sabotage of communications and transport infrastructure that have military purposes. The warfare that is waged may entail the guerrillas being dispersed into small units so that they can direct their attacks at several targets at the same time. A particular aim of violence of this nature is to challenge the idea that the forces of the state are unassailable: 'unassailability cannot be challenged by words but by showing that a soldier and a policeman are no more bulletproof than anyone else' (Debray, 1968: 51).

Traditionally this form of warfare was conducted in a rural terrain – the guerrillas could carry out their military actions and disappear into the countryside before the forces they were fighting had any opportunity to mount a counter-offensive operation. The aim of such warfare is that the guerrillas secure control of the countryside and encircle the towns, enabling food supplies to be cut off and communications severed (Mao Zedong, 1937: 107–8). In conducting actions of this nature, areas of the countryside may become 'no go' areas for the forces of the state and in which the guerrillas establish a de facto government. The growth in the power (political and numerical) wielded by guerrilla armies may lead to them adopting approaches associated with conventional armed warfare, seeking the total military defeat of those they are fighting.

The belief that armed actions initially waged by small groups of rural guerrillas could set in motion the overthrow of the government they were confronting was rationalised in the *foco* theory that was associated with the revolutionary activities of Che Guevera and the writings of Regis Debray. This approach believed that armed actions would provide a focus for popular discontent towards a government or an occupying power, which would eventually result in a popular revolution which swept it from power.

However, the view that the initial focus of guerrilla warfare should be rural areas was challenged towards the end of the 1960s. This challenge came from Latin America, where factors such as the extent of urbanisation in countries like Uruguay, Argentina and Venezuela, the development of successful counter-insurgency techniques against rural guerrilla movements and the potential isolation of rural guerrilla movements from other forms of urban-based political opposition to the incumbent government promoted the development of urban guerrilla movements. The death of Che Guevera in Bolivia in 1967 was an especially important factor in this transition of guerrilla activity to an urban setting.

The movements that arose towards the end of the late 1970s included the Tupamoros (MLN) in Uruguay, the Montoneros and People's Revolutionary Army (ERP) in Argentina and the Action for National Liberation (ALN), the Popular Revolutionary Vanguard (VPR) and the Armed Revolutionary Guard (VAR – Palmares), all in Brazil. It has been argued that '"urban guerrilla" strategy is based on the recognition ... that the political-military-economic centre of power is the great conurbation, that it could and should be attacked there, not from the periphery' (Laqueur, 2009: 344). The main exponent of urban guerrilla warfare was Carlos Marighella, a Brazilian who established the ALN, whose key work was the *Minimanual of the Urban Guerrilla* (1969).

Marighella shared many of the views of Guevera and Debray. The latter had written that urban violence (he used the term 'city terrorism') could play a part in the armed struggle: 'it immobilizes thousands of enemy soldiers, it ties up most of the repressive mechanisms in unrewarding tasks of protection: factories, bridges, electric generators, public buildings, highways, oil pipe lines – these can keep busy as much as three quarters of the army' (Debray, 1968: 74). However, urban actions had to be 'subordinate to the fundamental struggle, the struggle in the countryside' (Debray, 1968: 74).

Marighella did not dissent from this, arguing that the aim of the urban guerrilla was 'to aid the rural guerrillas and to help in the creation of a totally new and revolutionary social and political structure, with the armed population in power'. In addition, he accepted the fundamental idea of the *foco* theory that a successful revolution would be led from 'the top down' rather than from 'the bottom up'. However, he gave prominence to the manner in which urban-based violence would contribute to the success of the revolutionary struggle, indicating the nature of the violence that should be carried out and the intended consequences of such actions.

Marighella described the urban guerrilla as: 'a person who fights the military dictatorship with weapons, using unconventional methods ... The urban guerrilla follows a political goal, and only attacks the government, big businesses, and foreign imperialists'. The tactics of selective violence were directed at government officials and members of law-enforcement agencies and entailed economic warfare in the form of arson, sabotage and bombing that targeted essential installations, services and workplaces. They were designed to aid the cause of the urban guerrilla in two ways.

Although methods of this nature might be associated with terrorism, the key difference between these two forms of action were that urban guerrillas used terrorism as a tactic and not an end in itself – 'the key difference between terrorism and urban guerrilla movements is that the latter use terrorism as a tactic to build support and the first step in the direction of revolution' (Oppenheimer, 1969: 69). It was in this sense that the use of terrorist tactics by urban guerrilla movements was depicted as 'an entering wedge, and it can be effectively used to build a larger movement even by a very small vanguard' (Oppenheimer, 1969: 66)

First, they sought to create panic in governing circles and cause divisions in which 'pacifiers', 'right-wing opportunists' and 'partisans of non-violent struggle' joined together and pressurised the government to make concessions in the form of elections, 'redemocratisation', constitutional reform and other 'tripe' designed to fool the masses and stop the revolutionary rebellion in the cities and urban areas of the country (Marighella, 1969).

Second, the violence sought to provoke the government into a situation whereby it had 'no alternative except to intensify repression. The police networks, house searches, arrests of innocent people and of suspects makes life in the city unbearable. The military dictatorship embark on massive political persecution. Political assassination and political terror becomes routine' (Marighella, 1969).

The government response to the urban guerrillas was thus designed to provoke overreaction, effectively militarising a political conflict whereby the political crisis was transformed into an armed crisis that forced those in power 'to transform the political situation of the country into a military situation' (Marighella, 1969). It was intended that this overreaction would add to the strength of the struggle being waged by the urban guerrillas since it would 'alienate the masses, who, from then on, will revolt against the army and police and blame them for the state of things' (Marighella, 1969). It was thus concluded that 'terrorism and sabotage, especially when combated by a government using repression and counter-terror (for example, taking and shooting hostages), can create a movement where none existed before' (Oppenheimer, 1969: 66).

European urban guerrilla movements

Urban guerrilla movements performed actions in a wide range of countries outside of Latin America. Some of these organisations are briefly discussed below.

The *Rote Armee Fraktion* (Red Army Faction (RAF), but usually known as the Baader-Meinhof Gang) was an urban guerrilla group that operated in the former state of West Germany. It was named after two of its founding members, Andreas Baader and Ulrike Meinhof. The RAF emerged out of the student protests in 1967–8 which, in addition to opposition to the war in Vietnam, were organised in opposition to the visit of the Shah of Iran to West Berlin in 1967. In one of these demonstrations, a student protester was shot dead by a police officer, which added police brutality to the list of student grievances.

The Baader-Meinhof Gang was middle class in social background and its revolutionary aims (derived from a diffuse range of ideologies) were 'to hit the Establishment in the face, to mobilise the masses, and to maintain international solidarity' (Meinhof, quoted in Dobson and Payne, 1979: 153).

The activities of the RAF group included bombings, the first of which comprised attacks on two Frankfurt department stores in 1968. The RAF also performed attacks on US Army installations, police stations and property owned by the Axel Springer media empire, assassinations, arson and bank robbery. They were performed by seasoned members of the RAF operating in cell structures. These actions were viewed as armed resistance directed at a fascist state which was depicted in this way because, despite the process of denazification, former Nazis continued to hold positions of political and economic power and since 1966 the government was controlled by a Grand Coalition of the two major parties, effectively marginalising left-wing and radical opinion.

The widespread series of incidents associated with the RAF during the 1970s forced the West German government to adopt new powers with which to combat terrorism in 1972, based upon changes to the law and constitution. One aspect of this was to provide the Federal Criminal Investigation Bureau with independent executive powers to prosecute offences involving arms, ammunition, explosives and narcotics, and also crimes against the life and liberty of politicians (Cobler, 1978: 53). The security service was empowered to use intelligence methods to observe movements that were hostile to the constitution (Cobler, 1978: 55). These changes led to the conclusion that West Germany was 'on the way to becoming a Big Brother police state' (Cobler, 1978: 143).

Most of the leaders of the RAF were arrested in 1972 and imprisoned. However, a second generation of activists replaced them and performed similar actions that included killing two attachés attached to the German Embassy in Sweden in 1975. However, the main activities of this second RAF generation were to secure the release of the original surviving members of the group (Ulrike Meinhof having committed suicide in prison in 1976).

Attempts to bargain for their release in 1977 entailed kidnapping the businessman Hans-Martin Schleyer and hijacking a Lufthansa plane bound for Frankfurt which was forced to divert to Mogadishu (an act performed by the Lebanon-based Popular Front for the Liberation of Palestine, with whom the RAF had forged links). These acts were unsuccessful in securing the release of the prisoners, although Schleyer was murdered. This led the leading members of the RAF to commit suicide in 1977 whilst in prison. However, activities performed in the name of the RAF continued until the late 1990s.

Other urban guerrilla groups that operated in Europe included the Italian *Brigate Rosse* (Red Brigades), which like the RAF emerged from student-inspired protests in the late 1960s. It was formed in 1970, although the arrest and imprisonment of its founders Renato Curcio and Alberto Franceschini in 1974 resulted in the emergence of a second generation of activists.

The Red Brigades sought the establishment of a communist society through waging an armed struggle. This took the form of arson, bombings, industrial sabotage, bank robbery, kidnappings, ransom demands and murder, and its targets were those associated with right-wing politics and journalism. One prominent victim was the former Christian Democrat Prime Minister, Aldo Moro, who was kidnapped and subsequently murdered in 1978. This event, followed by the murder in 1979 of the prominent trade union organiser Guido Rossa, reduced the potential support that the Red Brigades might have attracted. Nonetheless, it continued its campaign of violence, which included the kidnapping of US Army Brigadier General James Dozier in 1981, the NATO Deputy Chief of Staff at Southern European land forces. He was subsequently freed by Italian anti-terrorist forces.

An urban guerrilla group that operated in America during the 1970s was known as the Weather Underground Organization (initially referred to as the Weathermen). This was formed in 1969 at the University of Michigan, was opposed to the war in Vietnam and advocated Black Power and, more latterly, feminism. Its members were engaged in what they viewed to be an anti-imperialist and anti-racist struggle and, in connection with the latter aim, sought solidarity with the Black Panthers. The group's first main activity was the 'Days of Rage' riot in Chicago in October 1969, a protest against the Vietnam War whose timing was designed to coincide with the start of the trial of the Chicago Seven. It sought to overthrow the American government by performing acts of violence which embraced a bombing campaign (termed 'armed propaganda') during the 1970s that was primarily directed at government buildings (including the United States Capitol Building and the Pentagon) and also banks. The end of the Vietnam War in 1973 significantly contributed to the demise of the group in the late 1970s.

The Japanese Red Army (Sekigun) also emerged out of student protests and opposition to the Vietnam War. It was formed in 1969 and subsequently developed by merging with other like-minded groups during the 1970s. It was a revolutionary socialist organisation which sought to overthrow the Japanese government and monarchy, and was anti-American and pro-Palestinian. Its activities included robberies, kidnappings and hijacking. It initially confined these to Japan, but subsequently expanded its base of operations. Actions with which it was associated included an attack on Lod Airport, Israel in 1972, which resulted in the deaths of 26 people and injury to around 80. It was also responsible for hijacking aircraft (such as the Japan Airlines plane over the Netherlands in 1973), embassy seizures (including the Japanese Embassy in Kuwait and the French Embassy in The Hague, the Netherlands in 1974) and hostage-taking (as occurred following the attack on a Shell facility in Singapore in 1974). The latter sought to obtain money from ransom demands or secure the release of imprisoned Red Brigade members.

Most of these attacks took place during the 1970s, although some occurred in the 1980s, including mortar attacks on the Canadian, US and Japanese Embassies in Jakarta, Indonesia in 1987 and on the US and UK Embassies in Rome in 1987. The Red Army had close connections with the Popular Front for the Liberation of Palestine and following the Lod Airport attack in 1972 sometimes referred to itself as the Arab-Japanese Red Army.

The Angry Brigade was active in Britain between 1970 and 1971. It has been labelled an urban guerrilla group, similar to international groups such as the Red Brigades, the Red Army or the Baader-Meinhof Gang, all of whom were dubbed 'alienated children of the bourgeoisie, seeking to create a new world ... through hard, destructive action' (Green, 2001). Many of its leading members were middle class and university-educated.

The Angry Brigade consisted of a small, loose group of anarchists who formed themselves into a libertarian socialist group. Their perception of the injustices associated with capitalism and the manner in which agencies of the state perpetuated this were influenced by the views of the Guy Debord and the situationists, whose central critique was directed against modern consumer society, which they believed was responsible for transforming people's lives into the meaningless pursuit of commodities and the mechanisms (or 'forms of the spectacle') such as television and advertising that were responsible for manufacturing and conveying a false sense of reality whose purpose was to secure popular acquiescence to the ruling class.

The Angry Brigade mounted bombing attacks on targets that included a police station, government ministers, banks, boutiques and the embassies of regimes deemed to be oppressive, where property rather than individuals was the key target. The timing of the campaign was influenced by the adoption by the Conservative government of the 'Selsdon Man' policies of free market capitalism. In total, 25 bombs were sent between May 1970 and August 1971, resulting in the injury of one person. Those on the receiving end included the Secretary of State for Employment and Productivity, Robert Carr, in January 1971.

In 1971, a total of nine people were arrested and in 1972 eight (dubbed the 'Stoke Newington Eight') were tried for conspiracy to cause explosions. Four were convicted (receiving ten-year prison sentences) and four were acquitted.

See also: Chicago, Democratic National Convention riot (Chicago) 1968, Grosvenor Square (London) 1968, student riots (Paris) 1968, terrorism

Sources and further reading

Carr. G. (1975) *The Angry Brigade: The Cause and the Case*. London: Gollanz.
Clutterbuck, R. (2012) *Terrorism and Guerrilla Warfare. Forecasts and Remedies*. London: Routledge.
Cobler, S. (1978) *Law, Order and Politics in West Germany*. Harmondsworth: Penguin.
Debray, R. (1968) *Revolution in the Revolution?* Harmondsworth: Penguin.
Dobson, C. and Payne, R. (1979) *The Weapons of Terror: International Terrorism at Work*. Basingstoke: Macmillan
Farrell, W. (1990) *Blood and Rage: The Story of the Japanese Red Army*. Lexington Books.
Green, J. (2001) 'The Urban Guerrillas Britain Forgot', *New Statesman*, 27 August, p. 10.
Laqueur W. (2009) *Guerrilla Warfare: A Historical and Critical Study*, 2nd edn. New Brunswick, NJ: Transaction Publishers.
Mao Zedong (1937) *Collected Writings of Chairman Mao: Volume 2 Guerrilla Warfare*. El Paso, TX: El Paso Norte Press. This translated edition was published in 2009.
Marighella C. (1969) *The Minimanual of the Urban Guerrilla*. Available at: www.latinamericanstudies.org/marighella.htm (date accessed 19 May 2014).
Oppenheimer, M. (1969) *Urban Guerrilla*. Harmondsworth: Penguin.

W

WALKING (WITH A POLITICAL PURPOSE) (ENGLAND) 1977 ONWARDS

In the UK, events such as processions and demonstrations are subject to restrictions and can, in extreme circumstances, be prohibited. However, a key issue is what constitutes a demonstration or related event and, in particular, how many participants are required for an event to be labelled as such and become subject to legal considerations. The lack of clarity concerning the definition of a procession or demonstration has led to political activists using walking as a method to secure publicity for their cause.

In 1977, the Chief Constable of Greater Manchester, James Anderton, banned a proposed procession by the National Front through the town centre of Hyde under provisions granted by the Public Order Act 1936. This was due to take place on 8 October. A ban could be invoked if the police felt that the event was likely to cause serious public disorder, a possibility that was likely to be realised arising from the opposition that the Anti-Nazi League would mount to the event, a situation that had arisen in Lewisham on 13 August of that year. However, an important motive for police actions was the difficulty in maintaining order on the route that the Hyde march would take and permission was given for processions to occur elsewhere in the Greater Manchester area at Stockport and Levenshulme.

The National Front obeyed this restriction on its scheduled event in Hyde, but its National Activities Organiser, Martin Webster, turned up to mount a one-man walk through the main street of Hyde. The police took the view that this did not constitute a breach of the ban and allowed him to proceed. He briskly walked down the road carrying a Union Flag over his shoulder and a placard across his chest that read 'Defend Free Speech from Red Terrorism' surrounded by over 2,000 police officers. Although he was proceeded throughout by a member of the Asian Youth Movement who carried a placard stating 'This man is a Nazi', this tactic made a mockery of the ban and also secured valuable media publicity for the National Front.

It was estimated that, overall, around 9,000 police officers had been deployed to deal with these processions across Greater Manchester and complaints were subsequently made regarding police actions that included frisking anti-fascist demonstrators, detaining people without arrest and the removal by police officers of their identity numbers (Renton, undated).

The issue as to whether a set number of individuals was required before an event could be dubbed a procession highlighted the discretionary nature of police powers. When Webster attempted a similar act in the West Midlands in 1980 (following the banning of a National Front march), he was threatened with arrest by officers at the scene for obstructing the police if he attempted to step out of his car. This view was subsequently adopted by the Metropolitan Police Service (MPS) regarding an event associated with the English Defence League (EDL) in 2013.

On 29 June 2013, the police imposed conditions under provisions of the Public Order Act 1986 on an EDL 'sponsored walk' that was timed to coincide with Armed Forces Day. It was ostensibly designed to raise money for the charity Help for Heroes, although it announced in advance that it would not accept donations from the EDL (Press Association, 2013).

The EDL's proposed event entailed a demonstration from Hyde Park to Woolwich, where it was intended to hold an assembly (rally) and lay flowers at the site in Woolwich where the soldier Lee Rigby had been murdered on 22 May. The conditions confined the demonstration and assembly to an area between Hyde Park Corner and Westminster, and also stipulated that the assembly could be no longer than two hours in duration. These actions were undertaken because of concerns that the original route proposed could result in serious public disorder and disruption to the life of the local community, and was influenced by the likely reaction of the organisation Unite Against Fascism to this event.

In conjunction with these restrictions, the government banned Pamela Geller and Robert Spencer (two Americans who had set up the organisation Stop Islamization of America and who operated the website Jihad Watch) from entering the country on the grounds that their presence would not be conducive to the public good. It had been intended that they would address the EDL rally in Woolwich.

These actions resulted in the march and rally not taking place. However, two leading members of the EDL, Tommy Robinson and Kevin Carroll, planned an alternative event (a 'walk of honour') ostensibly to raise funds in connection with the Amelia-Mae Charity (a young girl fighting for her life against neuroblastoma), although the Neuroblastoma Children's Cancer Alliance (NCCA) refused to accept donations from the EDL.

The two men's proposed route took them past the East London Mosque in Tower Hamlets and the MPS took the view that this constituted an attempt to circumvent the conditions imposed on the original demonstration. Accordingly, both men were arrested outside Aldgate East underground station on a charge of obstructing the police. Two other men were arrested on suspicion of assault.

See also: English Defence League, Lewisham disorders (Lewisham, London) 1977, public order legislation (England and Wales), public order policing (England and Wales), Red Lion Square (London) 1974

Sources and further reading

Press Association (2013) 'Help for Heroes Rejects EDL Donation Cash', *The Guardian*, 28 May, www.guardian.co.uk/society/2013/may/27/help-for-heroes-english-defence-league (date accessed 19 May 2014).

Renton, D. (undated) 'Anti-fascism in the Northwest 1976–1981', www.dkrenton.co.uk/anl/northw.htm (date accessed 19 May 2014).

WHISTLEBLOWING (WORLDWIDE)

Whistleblowing refers to an action performed by past or present members of an organisation who disclose their employers' 'illegal, immoral, or illegitimate practices' to persons or organisations 'who may be able to affect action' (Miceli and Near, 1984: 689).

These activities may be carried out by commercial organisations or government bodies and the motives of the person making the disclosure (the whistleblower) are typically driven by a belief that it is in the public interest to reveal the information that is disclosed and that the public's right to know should be given precedence over individual or corporate claims of the need for confidentiality or secrecy in the conduct of their affairs. Although typically, the whistleblower derives their knowledge because of their employment in the organisation whose activities they wish to expose, the term may be extended to those who are the recipient of such information, which they then place into the public domain.

Whistleblowing may be encouraged by the existence of internal mechanisms within organisations through which concerns regarding its operations or the conduct of those employed within it can be articulated. Legislation may also underpin whistleblowing: one example of this was the American False Claims Act 1863 (subsequently revised in 1986), which sought to combat fraud by military suppliers by encouraging whistleblowers to report actions of this nature, which, if substantiated, would lead to the whistleblower receiving a percentage of the money that was recovered (or the damages that were obtained in a court case). This legislation also protected the whistleblower from unlawful dismissal by the organisation whose activities had been made public. Later legislation included the Whistleblower Protection Act 1989, which, as amended, gave individuals who worked for the federal government protection when they reported alleged agency misconduct.

In the UK, the Public Interest Disclosure Act 1998 established a legal framework to protect from retribution from their employers individuals who disclosed certain types of information that exposed malpractice and related issues in the public interest. This legislation encouraged many organisations to set up internal whistleblowing procedures. The charity Public Concern at Work established an independent Whistleblowing Commission in 2013 to examine the effectiveness of existing arrangements for workplace whistleblowing and make recommendations for change.

However, whistleblowing is frequently not officially endorsed. This is especially the case in connection with actions undertaken by governments where it is argued that these activities should be undertaken in private and that to expose them to the public gaze would threaten the national interest. Consequently, legislation such as the UK's Official Secrets Act 1989 may be enacted to deter whistleblowing by providing severe penalties for those seek to expose certain aspects of the way in which governments operate and the decisions that they take.

In these circumstances, a whistleblower takes a conscious decision to break the law and their actions thus constitute protest in the form of civil disobedience which is motivated by the belief that injustice has arisen or will arise if actions undertaken under a cloak of secrecy that are protected by law are not made public. Those who undertake actions of this nature may also claim that legislation that is designed to protect state secrecy conflicts with freedom of speech that underpins the operations of liberal democratic political systems.

There have been several examples of whistleblowing which have sought to expose actions that governments would prefer to remain secret. In America in June 1971, the *New York Times* began publishing of a series of articles relating to America's involvement in the Vietnam War. These were derived from a US Department of Defense report, officially entitled *United States – Vietnam Relations, 1945–1967: A Study Prepared by the Department of Defense*, but which became more popularly known as the *Pentagon Papers*, and the source of the disclosure came from a whistleblower, Daniel Ellsberg, who had access to the material by virtue of his employment at the RAND Corporation think tank.

The papers revealed that a succession of Presidents from Harry Truman through to Lyndon Johnson has misled the public regarding their intentions regarding Vietnam and that, in particular, Johnson had planned to bomb North Vietnam before the 1964 presidential election in which he promised not to expand the war and had accused his Republican opponent, Barry Goldwater, of wishing to undertake such an action. Ellsberg subsequently stated that he sought to publicise through his disclosures 'unconstitutional behavior by a succession of presidents, the violation of their oath and the violation of the oath of every one of their subordinates' (Ellsberg, 2007).

There have been several other examples of whistleblowing in the UK. In 1985, a senior civil servant who had worked in the Ministry of Defence, Clive Ponting, was charged under the Official Secrets Act 1911 for leaking internal Ministry of Defence documents to a senior Labour Member of Parliament, Tam Dalyell, in 1984. These related to the sinking by a Royal Navy submarine of the Argentinean warship, the *General Belgrano*, during the 1982 Falklands War, which resulted in the deaths of over 350 Argentinean sailors. His motives for acting as a whistleblower were to expose as an untruth government claims made in the House of Commons that this act took place because the Argentinean ship posed a threat to the lives of members of the British armed forces, since the document showed it was sailing away from the British-imposed exclusion zone around the Falkland Islands when it was attacked.

The decision to prosecute Ponting shows how governments may seek to use legislation designed to safeguard official secrecy in order to avoid information being made public that may prove embarrassing to them. Although the trial judge asserted that the government was able to define the term 'state interest', the jury did not agree and despite the judge's instruction to convict Ponting, the jury acquitted him of any crime, accepting his defence that his actions were in the public interest. He had also asserted that leaking the information to a Member of Parliament was protected by parliamentary privilege.

A further prominent act of whistleblowing occurred in 1987, when a former senior intelligence officer employed by the UK Security Service (MI5), Peter Wright, published a book, *Spycatcher*, relating to his experiences in working for an organisation which at that time did not officially exist. This book contained a number of interesting allegations regarding the work performed by the intelligence agencies, which included an MI6 plot to assassinate President Nasser of Egypt during the 1956 Suez Crisis, a joint MI5–CIA plot to discredit Harold Wilson's 1974–6 Labour government and the use by MI5 of bugging devices to monitor targets such as Commonwealth Conferences and the headquarters of the Communist Party of Great Britain, where access was obtained through burglary. Wright also claimed that he was charged with unmasking a Soviet mole who had been planted in MI5, whom he named as a formed Director General of that agency, Roger Hollis.

The Conservative government took the view that Wright was bound by a lifelong duty of confidentiality and was in violation of the Official Secrets Act. Publication of the book was thus banned in Britain (but not Scotland) and gagging orders were also served on British newspapers to prevent their publication of revelations contained in the book, which were reinforced by threats to prosecute them for contempt of court if they did so. The government further sought to prevent its publication in Australia (where Wright lived) and attempts were also made to extradite Wright from Australia. All of these efforts proved unsuccessful. The book was published in Australia and America in 1987, and in 1988 the Law Lords overturned a blanket injunction that prevented all media outlets from reporting anything said by former intelligence officers on the grounds that its publication abroad had undermined the objective of protecting official secrecy. Subsequently, in 1991, the European Court of Human Rights ruled that the actions of the UK government in seeking to prevent media publication of excerpts from the book had violated the freedom of speech.

The Clive Ponting and Peter Wright cases resulted in the government tightening up the legislation relating to official secrecy. The Official Secrets Act 1989 asserted the ability of the government to define the national interest. It also made it an offence for a person who was (or had been) a member of the security or intelligence services to disclose without lawful authority any information, document or other article related to security or intelligence which was (or had been) in that person's possession by virtue of their being a member of such services.

Technological advances have further facilitated whistleblowing, whereby information can be published on websites that can be set up (and accessed) anywhere in the world. One important contemporary example of this is WikiLeaks, which had been set up in 2006 with the aim of making public classified documents. Its editor-in-chief was Julian Assange. Examples of its activities included exposing corruption in Kenya in 2007 and publishing footage (known as the *Collateral Murder* video) from an airstrike in July 2007 in Baghdad in which Iraqi journalists were among those killed by an American Apache helicopter. Also in 2007, WikiLeaks released the *Afghan War Diary*, which consisted of over 70,000 documents related to the war in Afghanistan which had not been previously made available to the public.

On 28 November 2010, WikiLeaks commenced publishing a series of US State Department cables. Some of this material was supplied by a whistleblower, Bradley (now Chelsea) Manning. Eventually over 250,000 cables were released, the majority being unclassified, but a significant proportion (around 40 per cent) were classed as confidential and around six per cent as secret. Some of these related to the corruption of the governing regime in Tunisia and their release has been seen as a factor in that country's revolution in December 2010 (Horne, 2011). Others related to the war in Afghanistan, where the release of personal information relating to informants was argued to have put their lives at risk because of possible retaliation by the Taliban.

Although the actions of WikiLeaks might be viewed as an acceptable form of civil disobedience that sought to expose secrecy and injustice in the operations of government, many senior American politicians including the US Vice President viewed Assange as a 'high tech terrorist' (Biden, quoted in MacAskill, 2010). Suggestions were made that he should be prosecuted under the provisions of the Espionage Act 1917, which carried the death penalty.

Later that year, a European Arrest Warrant was issued in connection with a request by the Swedish police to question Assange in connection with an investigation into cases of sexual assault involving two women in August 2010. Assange sought to challenge the enforcement of this warrant through the British courts, arguing that it would result in his extradition to America to face charges in connection with the WikiLeaks disclosures. He was initially placed in prison in December 2010, but was later released on bail. Following the final rejection of this attempt by the Supreme Court of the United Kingdom in June 2012, he entered the Ecuadorian Embassy in London, where he was granted diplomatic asylum. It remains the intention of the UK government to enforce the warrant whenever he leaves the Embassy and a police presence has been placed there with this intention.

One of WikiLeaks' key sources was Bradley Manning, a soldier who served as an intelligence analyst in Iraq and who had access to databases used by the US military to transmit classified information. This provided the opportunity to download material and pass it on to WikiLeaks, which published it (either directly or through its media partners). The material that was leaked included the Baghdad air strike and the Iraq and Afghan war logs. In total, Manning sent WikiLeaks more than 470,000 Iraq and Afghanistan battlefield reports, 250,000 State Department Diplomatic cables and other material that included battlefield video clips (Oddie, 2013).

Manning was arrested in Iraq in May 2010 following revelations made to Army Counterintelligence by a computer hacker, Adrian Lamo. Manning was charged with 22 offences that included violating the Espionage Act 1917 and the Computer Fraud and Abuse Act 1986, stealing government property and disobeying orders. His defence was that he aimed 'to expose war crimes and deceitful diplomacy, that the information was not harmful to the US, and that the vast majority of the material he released was not classified, and was more embarrassing than damaging for the government' (Oddie, 2013). A trial took place in June 2013 and in July, Manning was found guilty of 17 of these charges, but was acquitted of the most serious – that of aiding the enemy. He was sentenced to 35 years' imprisonment,

A similar episode related to Edward Snowden, an American computer specialist who worked for Booz Allen Hamilton, a contractor to the American National Security Administration (NSA). He leaked details of top-secret mass surveillance programmes carried out by the US and UK governments that embraced the American and

European telephone metadata and the PRISM, XKeyscore and Tempora Internet surveillance programmes.

PRISM enables the NSA to access the servers of major Internet organisations such as Facebook, Google, Apple, Microsoft and Yahoo. XKeyscore is an NSA programme that enables scrutiny of all actions undertaken by an individual on the Internet, including emails, browsing history and online conversations. Tempora is operated by the UK's GCHQ and amasses data from online and telephone traffic. Although actions of this nature are justified by the contribution they make to the war against terrorism, they have the potential to undermine the privacy of all members of the general public.

These revelations were published in *The Guardian* in May 2013. Subsequent revelations suggested that intelligence agencies from the US and the UK had broken encryption protocols used to protect the privacy of Internet users' personal data, emails and online transactions, thus potentially compromising the security of the personal data of billions of people (Vincent, 2013).

Snowden defended his actions on the grounds that he sought 'to inform the public as to that which is done in their name and that which is done against them' (Snowden, quoted in Greenwald *et al.*, 2013) and he received some popular backing: in October 2013, protesters supporting Snowden and opposing America's mass surveillance programme gathered at Capitol Hill. Their slogans included 'read the Constitution, not my email'.

However, the US government took a different view and Snowden was charged by the federal authorities with theft of government property, unauthorised communication of national defence information and wilful communication of classified communications intelligence. Each of these charges carries a maximum penalty of ten years' imprisonment. However, he had left the country before his disclosures were published. He initially went to Hong Kong and subsequently received temporary asylum in Russia.

See also: anti-National Security Agency protests (Germany) 2013, Arab Spring (Arab world) 2010 onwards, civil disobedience, hactivism, political policing, subversion

Sources and further reading

Burnet, D. and Thomas, R. (1989). 'Spycatcher: The Commodification of Truth'. *Journal of Law and Society*, 16(2): 210–24.

Ellsberg, D. (2003) *Secrets: A Memoir of Vietnam and the Pentagon Papers*. New York: Penguin.

———. (2007) 'How the Pentagon Papers Came to Be Published by the Beacon Press', *Democracy Now*, www.democracynow.org/2007/7/2/how_the_pentagon_papers_came_to (date accessed 19 May 2014).

Greenwald, G., MacAskill, E. and Poitras, L. (2013) 'Edward Snowden: The Whistleblower Behind the NSA Surveillance Revelations', *The Guardian*, 10 June.

Horne, N. (2011) 'Tunisia: WikiLeaks Had a Part in Ben Ali's Downfall', *The Week*,

15 January, www.theweek.co.uk/africa/wikileaks/8571/tunisia-wikileaks-had-part-ben-ali%E2%80%99s-downfall (date accessed 19 May 2014)

Leigh, D. and Harding, L. (2011) *WikiLeaks: Inside Julian Assange's War on Secrecy.* London: Guardian Books.

MacAskill, E. (2010) 'Julian Assange Like a Hi-tech Terrorist, Says Joe Biden', *The Guardian*, 20 December.

Miceli, M. and Near, J. (1984) 'The Relationships among Beliefs, Organizational Position, and Whistle-blowing Status: A Discriminant Analysis'. *Academy of Management Journal*, 27(4): 687–705.

Oddie, W. (2013) 'Whistleblowing in England is Now Honoured. So it Should Be in the US: Bradley Manning and Edward Snowden are Not Traitors But Patriotic Americans', *Catholic Herald*, 2 August, www.catholicherald.co.uk/commentandblogs/2013/08/02/whistleblowing-in-england-is-now-honoured-so-it-should-be-in-the-us-bradley-manning-and-edward-snowden-are-not-traitors-but-patriotic-americans (date accessed 19 May 2014).

Vincent, J. (2013) 'Encryption Protocols Compromised by NSA and GCHQ, According to Leaked Edward Snowden Documents', *The Independent*, 6 September.

Wright, P. with Greengrass, P. (1987) *Spycatcher: The Candid Autobiography of a Senior Intelligence Officer.* New York: Viking.

WORKPLACE PROTEST

Protest may take place within the workplace. A common form of action is that of a strike which entails a temporary stoppage of work by a group of employees in order to express a grievance or to enforce a demand (Griffin, 1939: 20–2). This constitutes a form of direct action in which the workforce withdraws its labour and refuses to return to work until its demands have been met. The protest is directed against the employer and the demands are typically associated with 'bread and butter' issues that include hours of labour, demarcation disputes, employment and dismissal questions (including redundancy), other personnel questions, other working arrangements, rules and discipline, trade union status and sympathetic action (Department of Employment, quoted in Hyman, 1972: 115–16). However, the most common cause of strikes centres around wages (Hyman, 1972: 117), even if there are other issues at stake (Knowles, 1952: 30).

It has been argued that strikes constitute 'a form of rational social action' as 'they represent an explicit attempt to exert some control over the employment relationship' (Hyman, 1972: 107, 136). Strikes empower those who participate in them by changing the nature of the employer–employee relationship. This alteration may be permanent if the employer is forced to concede to the demands of the workforce. However, if the workforce fails to get its demands acted upon, a temporary form of empowerment may arise from the financial damage that workers inflict on a commercial concern as the consequence of the disruption caused by a strike.

In addition, the solidarity associated with strike action may embolden workers and form the basis of further strikes in the future. It is for this reason that some socialists view factories rather than the ballot box as the means to bring about the downfall of capitalism. Syndicalism is associated with this approach, in which workers seize control of the ownership and control of the means of production and distribution through the tactic of a general strike and capitalism is replaced with a new social order based on workers owning and managing industry.

Some strikes are more overtly political and constitute a protest directed at the government. The 'bread and butter' demands of workers may constitute a challenge to government policy in cases where the government itself is the employer or where wages are controlled by government legislation. This was the case in the UK during the 1970s, when successive governments imposed legislative controls over wages as a weapon with which to combat inflation. Thus, workers seeking a higher wage rise than that permitted by law were seeking to force the government to alter the direction of its economic policy. Examples of this in the UK were the 1972 and 1973/4 miners' disputes.

In extreme cases, strike action may constitute protest that seeks to challenge the authority of the government rather than aspects of its policy. This was the case in the UK in 1973, when a strike by the National Union of Miners led to the Conservative Prime Minister Edward Heath calling a general election in 1974 whose theme was: 'Who runs the country?' The government narrowly lost this election, illustrating the power of strikes to bring about the downfall of governments.

Similarly, the election victory secured by Margaret Thatcher in 1979 was attributed to public dislike of the power wielded by trade unions, which was illustrated by a range of strikes in 1979, collectively dubbed 'the winter of discontent' and which effectively destroyed the Labour government's policy on pay restraint. The robust measures undertaken by the Thatcher government to defeat the miners' strike of 1984/5 were also prompted by a perception that it sought to undermine the authority of the government, whose credibility would have been irreparably damaged had it succeeded.

Governments may be forced to intervene in a strike even if it entails a conflict between workers and management in which the government has no direct involvement. This intervention is prompted by the need to safeguard the national interest, which is threatened by strikes that damage the economy or interfere with the safety and well-being of citizens. In the UK, industrial militancy in the form of strike action was a serious problem – the number of working days lost through industrial action on a yearly average basis was 12.9 million in the 1970s and 7.2 million in the 1980s (Metcalf and Milner, 1993: 1). This situation prompted successive governments to introduce legislation that was designed to curb the power of trade unions, in particular their ability to enforce strike action through tactics that included mass picketing and flying picketing.

The key legislation that was enacted in the UK included the Industrial

Relations Act 1971 (much of which was repealed by the following Labour government's Trade Union and Industrial Relations Act 1974 and the Employment Protection Act 1975) and a number of Acts promoted by Margaret Thatcher's Conservative government in the 1980s that included the Employment Acts 1980 and 1982, the Trade Union Act 1984 and the Employment Act 1988. Legislation of this nature helped to substantially reduce the number of working days lost to strike action in the UK, which in 1991 was the lowest since records were first kept in 1893 (Metcalf and Milner, 1993: 1).

Legislation to regulate trade union activity is frequently in the form of civil legislation, which requires the employer to initiate action against unions that are contravening it. This course of action can be slow, even if ultimately effective, and is one factor that may prompt the involvement of the police in industrial disputes, which in the UK entails using powers such as breach of the peace against those wishing to enforce an industrial dispute.

Strikes are commonly organised by trade unions, although unofficial strikes ('one which is not recognised by the Executive Committee of a Union': Knowles, 1952: 30) also occur. This form of action may be planned by militant members of a workforce or may arise spontaneously as a workforce protest against a perceived injustice such as a dismissal. The term 'wildcat strike' is applied to episodes of this nature. Examples of such actions in England include the seven-week dispute at the Pilkington Glass Works in St Helens in 1970 (Lane and Roberts, 1971) and the 28-month strike of Liverpool dockers between 1995 and 1997.

This latter dispute arose as the consequence of the dismissal of five dockers following an overtime dispute, which led to fellow workers mounting a picket line that others then refused to cross – 'there was no strike ballot – they simply turned around and went home' (Wynne-Jones, 1997). This action led to the dismissal of a further 500 dockers, who were deemed by their employer to be in breach of contract. Although the Transport and General Workers' Union declared the strike to be unofficial, support was obtained from abroad (one feature of which was the use of the Internet to construct networks of support) and in September 1997, 30 ports across the world staged a 24-hour strike in support of the striking Liverpool dockers.

A further form of workplace protest is that of a general strike. This involves coordinated action by a number of trade unions at the same time. Actions of this nature are political in that they seek to challenge the authority of a government and commonly seek to secure its resignation. General strikes have been a feature of anti-austerity protests in a number of countries such as Greece and Portugal. In addition, general strikes may seek to highlight an injustice, an example being the 1 May 2012 protests across America that sought to highlight income inequality and unjust corporate practices. The Occupy movement played an important role in organising this event, which was dubbed a 'general strike' by the media, although labour union leaders refused to be involved in it (Abrahamian and Berg, 2012).

Although strike action is an important form of workplace protest, the latter is associated with other actions. Employers who are faced with a labour dispute may resort to a lockout, which involves preventing a workforce from entering a place of employment during an industrial dispute. One recent example of this in 2011 entailed the Australian company Qantas Airways declaring a lockout of its domestic employees as a response to the industrial action that they were taking.

Conflict by workers with an employer may take the form of 'peaceful bargaining and grievance handling, of sabotage, of absenteeism or of personal turnover' (Kerr, 1964: 171). It may involve a refusal by workers to handle goods related to a dispute between themselves and their employer. This is referred to as 'blacking' and the refusal of dockers (who were concerned about the impact of mechanisation on the long-term future of their industry) to handle lorries delivering goods from container firms to the docks resulted in the imprisonment of five London dockers (the 'Pentonville Five') in 1972 and a subsequent national docks strike.

Work-ins are a further form of protest associated with direct action undertaken in the workplace. These entail workers taking control of the means of production, typically to prevent the scaling-down of an industrial enterprise. An important example of this occurred in Scotland in connection with the work-in staged at the Upper Clyde Shipbuilders (UCS) in 1971–2.

The background to this episode was the recession that affected the shipbuilding industry. In June 1971, the Conservative government allowed UCS to go into liquidation and the government's advisors suggested that a smaller company should be formed, entailing a reduction of the workforce from 8,000 to 2,500 (Collins, 1996: 71). The workforce responded to this news with a work-in and the demand for no redundancies and the maintenance of the four existing shipyards. This lasted for 14 months until Marathon UK, a subsidiary of an American-owned company, announced its intention to take over the yards, which would build oil rigs. Those declared redundant by the liquidator would be re-employed. The Shop Stewards Coordinating Committee urged that the work-in should end following the announcement of these terms. One factor that enabled this action to achieve its objective was the support given throughout Scottish society – small and medium-sized companies that supplied the yards were unhappy with a policy which seemed overwhelmingly geared towards the interests for monopoly capital (Collins, 1996: 72).

See also: austerity protests (worldwide) 2010–13, building workers' strike (England and Wales) 1972, direct action, miners' dispute (Britain) 1972, miners' dispute (Britain) 1973–4, miners' dispute (Britain) 1984–5, News International dispute (Wapping, London) 1986, public order policing (England and Wales), states of emergency

Sources and further reading

Abrahamian, A. and Berg, E. (2012) 'May Day Protests Draw Police But Most are Peaceful', *Reuters*, 1 May, www.reuters.com/article/2012/05/01/us-usa-occupy-may-idUSBRE8400UV20120501 (date accessed 19 May 2014).

Collins, C. (1996) 'To Concede or to Contest? Language and Class Struggle' in C. Barker and P. Kennedy (eds), *To Make Another World: Studies in Protest and Collective Action*. Aldershot: Avebury.

Griffin, J. (1939) *Strikes: A Study in Quantitative Economics*. New York: Columbia University Press.

Hyman, R. (1972) *Strikes*. London: Fontana.

Kerr, C. (1964) *Labour and Management in Industrial Society*. New York: Doubleday.

Knowles, K. (1952) *Strikes: A Study in Industrial Conflict*. Oxford: Blackwell.

Lane, T. and Roberts, K. (1971) *Strike at Pilkingtons*. London: Fontana.

Metcalf, D. and Milner, S. (eds) (1993) *New Perspectives in Industrial Disputes*. London: Routledge.

Wynne-Jones, P. (1997) 'No Going Back at Liverpool Docks', *The Independent*, 21 September.

Index

Act Now to Stop the War and End Racism (ANSWER)   215
Action for National Liberation (ALN)   339
Aggravated trespass   261, 337
al-Hahda   18
al-Shabaab   152
al-Qaeda   22, 23, 89, 93, 150–2, 181, 231–3, 236, 323, 325–6
al-Qaeda in the Arabian Peninsula (AQAP)   233
Anglo-Irish Treaty 1921   243
Angry Brigade   91, 343–4
Animal Enterprise Protection Act 1992 (USA)   5
Animal Liberation Front (ALF)   2–3, 78, 217
Animal Rights Militia (ARM)   3–4
Animal rights movement   9
Animal rights protest groups   1–5
Animal welfare groups   1, 2, 160–2
Anonymous   141
Anti-capitalist movement   5, 217
Anti-capitalist protests (UK)   9–11, 38, 50, 126–9, 274–5
Anti-capitalist protests (worldwide)   12–16
Anti-globalisation   5–7
Anti-globalisation movement   5, 6, 7, 8–9
Anti-globalisation protests
  UK   9–11, 274–5
  worldwide   12–16, 204
Anti-National Security Agency protests (Germany) 2013   16–17
Anti-terrorism, Crime and Security Act 2001 (UK)   89, 90, 94
Anti-terrorist Squad   91
Anti-World Trade Organization protest 1999   10–11
Apprentice Boys (Northern Ireland)   51, 53
Arab Spring   17–28, 204, 289, 292, 293
  Algeria   27
  Egypt   19
  Libya   19–22
  Syria   24–7
  Tunisia   18–19, 141, 351
  Yemen   22–4
Armed Revolutionary Guard (VAR–Palmares)   339
Assad, Bashar al-   24, 25, 26, 234, 235
Assange, Julian   141, 350–1
Association of Chief Police Officers (ACPO)   83, 266, 268
Attenuating Energy Projectiles   32
August riots (England) 2011   28–33, 255, 293–4
Austerity protests
  Greece   34, 355
  Ireland   37–8
  Portugal   34–5, 39, 355
  Spain   36–7, 39, 311
  UK   38–9, 309–11, 337
  worldwide   33–40
Australian Security Intelligence Organisation Amendment Act 1986   318

Baader-Meinhof Gang   341–2, 343
Bail-out loans   33, 34, 35, 36
Band Aid   103
Band of Mercy   2–3
Banlieue riots (Paris)   41–9, 277–8
Battle of Brightlingsea   160–2, 260
Battle of the Beanfield (England)   49
Battle of Cable Street   256
Battle of the Bogside   50–6
Belaid, Chokri   226
Ben Ali, Zine El Abidine   18, 19, 225
Bereitschaftspolizei (BePo)   284
Bin Laden, Osama   150–2
BlackBerry   30
Black Bloc protest tactics   8, 12
Black Panthers   76, 343
Blakelock, Keith   65, 266
'Blanket Protest'   107
Blockades   39, 77, 101, 104, 121, 136, 335
Blockupy movement   39

358

'Bloody Friday' (Northern Ireland)   245
'Bloody Sunday' (Northern Ireland)
   56–8, 244
'Bogside Massacre' (Northern Ireland)
   56–8
Boko Haram   152, 301
Bouazizi, Mohamed   17, 292
Bouteflika, Abdelaziz   236
Bradford riots   58–64, 199–200
Brahmi, Mohamed   226
Breach of the peace   174, 175, 258, 259, 355
Brigate Rosse (Red Brigades)   342, 343
Brixton disorders   80–4, 241, 254, 269
Broadwater Farm Estate riots (England)
   64–6, 267
Building workers' strike (England and Wales)   66–9, 259
Burnley riots   199–202
Burntollet Bridge   52, 70–71, 243

Cabinet office briefing room (COBRA)
   92, 306
Cable Street   111
Campaign Against Household and Water Taxes (Ireland)   38
Campaign for Nuclear Disarmament (CND)   78, 127, 136, 211–13, 215, 317
Carnival Against Capitalism 1999 (London)   10, 12
Cass, John   299–300
Castlemorton   10, 261
Çevik Kuvvet   285
Chicago Democratic National Convention riot   72–6, 214
'Chicago Eight'   76
Civil Authorities (Special Powers) Act 1922 (Northern Ireland)   188
Civil Contingencies Act 2004 (UK)   91, 303–5
Civil Contingencies Unit   168
Civil disobedience   8, 10, 38, 76–80, 105, 140, 214, 266–76, 331, 348, 350
Climate Camp   9
Combat   18, 184
Committee of One Hundred   77–8, 212
Compagnies Républicaines de Sécurité (CRS) (France)   41, 276–8, 284, 313–14, 316

Community engagement   31, 59, 60, 63, 65–6, 165, 202
Compassion in World Farming (CIWF)   160
Conspiracy and Protection of Property Act 1875 (UK)   68, 175, 259
Consumer boycotts   103–4, 178
Contained protests   274–5
CONTEST programme   91–2
Contingency planning   306
Continuity Irish Republican Army   249
Control orders   90, 94
Convergence theory   251
Copycat disorders   28, 80–4, 210, 241, 267–8, 289
Cordon   296–7, 332
Corporate globalisation   8
Counterculture protest   10, 73, 84–6, 239–42, 260–1, 279–80
Counter-globalisation movement   6
Counter-terrorism   86–94
Counter-terrorism units   91
Countering Violent Extremism policy (USA)   87
Creative occupation   78
Criminal Justice Act 2003 (UK)   88
Criminal Justice and Police Act 2001 (UK)   4, 89
Criminal Justice and Public Order Act 1994 (UK)   10, 50, 85, 86, 91, 105, 140, 260–5
Criminal Justice (Temporary Provisions) Act 1970 (Northern Ireland)   188–9
Criminalisation   190–1
Critical Mass   10, 11, 78
CS gas   10, 54, 81, 267, 268, 273, 289, 327, 337
Cuerpo Nacional de Policía (CNP)   284
Cyber-attacks   140

Dale Farm evictions   50, 95–8
Daley, Richard   72, 73–4, 75
Darley Oaks Farm   4, 105–6
Data Protection Act 1984 (UK)   221
Data Protection Act 1998 (UK)   221
Davies, James   253–4
'Day of Rage' (Libya) 2011   20
'Day of Rage' (Yemen) 2011   22
'Days of Rage' (USA)   343
De-individuation theory   250–1

Debray, Regis 339, 340
Deep Ecology 116
Defence of the Realm Act 1914 (UK) 303
Defense Authorization Bill 2007 (USA) 286–7
Demonstrations 9, 10, 34, 35, 36–7, 38, 39, 98–102, 110–12, 132, 137–9, 157–9, 186, 214, 227–8, 235, 237–9, 256–76, 279, 281–4, 297
Denial of Service (DoS) 140
Denning, Lord Alfred 317
Deprivation 28–30, 43–4, 61–2, 65, 81, 82, 143, 144, 164–5, 199, 204, 235, 308
Derry Citizens' Defence Association (DCDA) 52–3, 54
Derry Housing Action Committee 51
Detention without trial 90, 94
'Dialogue police' 237
'Diplock Courts' 89–90, 107, 190–1
Direct action 2, 8, 9, 10, 39, 51, 77, 98, 102–6, 113, 115, 121–5, 126, 266–76, 291, 301, 335, 353
'Dirty protest' 106–9
'Dirty war' (Spain) 183
Dirty war (Northern Ireland) 194–5
Dongas Tribe 104, 105, 116
Doorstepping 4, 89
Duggan, Mark 28

Easter Rising 1916 243
Earth First! 104, 115–16
Ecotage 116
Ellsberg, Daniel 348
Emergency Management Act 2007 (Canada) 303
Emergency powers 122
Emergency Powers Act 1920 (UK) 303, 304
Emergency Powers Act 1964 (UK) 303
Emergency planning 306
Employment Act 1980 (UK) 173, 259, 355
Employment Act 1982 (UK) 173, 259, 355
Employment Act 1988 (UK) 259, 355
Employment Protection Act 1975 (UK) 355
Energy Act 1976 (UK) 122
Energy Act 2004 (UK) 218

English Defence League 110–12, 128, 346–7
Ennahda 18, 226–7
Environmental protest 50, 84, 104–5, 112–17, 118–20, 126–7, 205, 261
Escalated force 273–5
Escalated violence 50
Espionage Act 1917 (USA) 351
European Central Bank (ECB) 33, 38
European Nuclear Disarmament (END) 215
Europol 93
Euskadi Ta Askatasuna (ETA) 93, 181–3
Exclusion zone 49, 50, 85

Facebook 18, 30
Fathers4Justice 79
Federal Bureau of Investigation (FBI) 87–8, 216, 219
Finucane, Patrick 195
'Flash-mobbing' 31
Flashpoint model of public disorder 254–5
Flying pickets 68
Foco theory of revolution 340
'Food democracy' 178
Foreign Intelligence Surveillance Act 1978 (USA) 219–20
Foreign Intelligence Surveillance Amendments Act 2008 (USA) 220
Fracking protests 113, 116, 117, 118–20, 270
Free Syrian Army 25, 26
Free trade 7
Freedom fighters 180
Freedom of Information Act 2000 (UK) 69, 223
'Friday of Anger' (Yemen) 2011 22
'Friday of Martyrs' (Egypt) 229
'Friday of No Return' (Yemen) 2011 22
'Friday of Rage' (Yemen) 2011 22
Friends of the Earth International 116–17
Fuel crisis (Britain) 121–5, 275, 303, 306

G7 summit meetings 8, 12
G8 summit meetings 8, 10, 12, 14, 293
G20 Meltdown Protest 126–9
G20 protest (London) 100, 126–9, 154–5, 237

G20 summit meetings 8, 9, 100, 126–9, 293
Gaddafi, Muammar 19, 20, 21, 22, 230–1
Gangs 29–30, 44
Garda public order unit 284–5
Gardiner, Lord Gerald 106
Gately, Kevin 282
Gdańsk agreement 131–2
Gdańsk Shipyard protests 129–35
Gendarmerie Nationale 276–8
General strike 34, 35, 39, 314, 354, 355–6
Genetically modified crops 78, 117, 177–8
Genetically modified organisms 177–8
Genoa G8 summit protests 2001 14–15
Giuliana, Carlo 15
Global Justice Movement 6
Globalisation 5–6, 7
'God is with us' demonstration (Syria) 2011 25
Gold/Silver/Bronze hierarchy of command 269, 333
Golden Dawn 183–4
Government Communications Headquarters (GCHQ) 174, 218, 221, 222, 223–4, 319, 352
Government of Ireland Act 1914 (UK) 243
Government of Ireland Act 1920 (UK) 243
Greenham Common Peace Camp 101, 135–7, 213
Greenpeace 9, 78, 113–15, 217
Groce, Mrs Cherry 65
Grosvenor Square 137–9, 266
Guerrilla gardening 11, 78–9
Guevera, Che 339

Habitation à loyer modéré (HLM) (France) 42–3, 44
Hactivism 78, 140–2
Hamas 93, 149–50, 229
Harris, Lord John 317–18
Hermon, John 190, 193
Hezbollah 148–9, 233–4, 235
Hoffman, Abbie 73, 76
Holy Terror 146–53
Homeland Security Act 2002 (USA) 91
Housing estate riots (England) 142–5

Human rights 7, 93, 98, 117, 128, 154, 181, 192, 221, 222, 350
Human Rights Act 1998 (UK) 129, 221–2, 264, 304
Hunger strike 108–9
Huntingdon Life Sciences 4

Independent Police Complaints Commission 127, 337
Indignados Movement (Spain) 36, 204–5
Indignant Citizens' Movement (Greece) 34
Industrial Relations Act 1971 (UK) 66–7, 355
Institutional racism 82
Intelligence Services Act 1994 (UK) 221
Interception of Communications Act 1985 (UK) 220–1, 222
International Council of the World Social Forum 8
International Criminal Court 20
International Organization for Migration (IOM) 7
International Monetary Fund (IMF) 6, 8, 12, 13, 33, 34, 35, 37
Internment 56, 90, 190, 191, 301
Interoperability 272
Interrogation 191, 192–3
Irish National Liberation Army (INLA) 246
Islamic Jihad Organisation (IJO) 148–9
Islamic terrorist groups 46, 146–53, 180–1, 226–36, 231–2, 235–6, 301, 323–6
Izz ad-Din al-Qassam Brigades 149

J-curve 253–4
Jabat al–Nusra (Nusra Front) 233
Japanese Red Army 343
Jarrett, Cynthia 65
Jihad 146, 180–1, 234–5, 326
Joint Information Centres 100

Kale borroka 182
Kettling (containment) 9, 10–11, 99, 100, 127–8, 154–6, 205, 238, 275, 293, 310–11, 332
King, Rodney 163–5
Kitson, Frank 317

Le Bon, Gustave   238, 250–1, 288
League Against Cruel Sports   2
Lewisham disorders   157–9, 198, 259, 345
Libyan National Council   20
Live animal export protests   160–3
Lockout   356
Looting   29, 31, 80
Los Angeles riots   163–5
Lump Labour Scheme   67, 68

MacGregor, Sir Ian   172
Manning, Bradley (now Chelsea)   17, 350–1
Manningham riots (Bradford)   58–64
'Mansouron Friday' (Yemen) 2011   23
March 12 Movement (Portugal)   35
'March Against Monsanto'   177, 178
'March for Dignity' (Spain)   37
Marighella, Carlos   339–41
Martial law   132, 133, 305–7, 330
Mass picketing   166–8, 171, 173, 185, 261
May Day protests (UK) 2000   11
May Day protests (UK) 2001   11, 238
Memorandum of Understanding (fuel supplies)   123–4
Military Aid to Other Government Departments   306
Military Aid to the Civil Power   55, 57, 188, 306
Military Aid to the Civilian Communities   306
Military Assistance to the Civil Authorities   305–6
Miners' dispute 1972   166–8
Miners' dispute 1973–4   168–72, 354
Miners' dispute 1984–5   122, 172–7, 210, 218, 219, 241, 254, 255, 258, 259, 267, 273–4, 354
Minimum force   210–11, 274
Monades Apokatastasis Taksis (MAT)   284
Montoneros   339
Monsanto   7, 177–9
Moro Islamic Liberation Front   180–1
Morsi, Mohamed   101, 150, 228–30
Moss Side disorders   81
Mubarak, Hosni   19
Multinational corporations   6, 8, 204, 336

Muslim Brotherhood   149, 228–30, 232
Mutual aid   81, 96, 122, 160–1, 173, 186, 200, 271–3

National Campaign Against Cuts and Fees (NCACF)   310
National Coal Board (NCB)   166, 168–9, 171, 175–6
National Domestic Extremism Unit   217
National Emergencies Act 1976 (USA)   302–3
National Extremism Tactical Coordination Unit (UK)   4, 217
National Front   101, 112, 157–9, 198, 200, 263, 266, 281–3, 295–301
National Graphical Association (NGA)   172, 185–7, 267
National Guard   286–7
National Mobilization Committee to End the War in Vietnam (MOBE)   73, 74
National Nuclear Weapons Freeze Campaign   214
National Public Order Intelligence Unit   217
National Reporting Centre   168, 272
National Risk Assessment (NRA)   91–2
National Security Agency (USA)   16, 17, 87, 216, 218, 219–20, 223–4, 352, 353
National Security Committee   168
National Special Security Events (NSSE) (USA)   90–1
National Union of Miners (NUM)   166–8, 168–76
Nationalist terrorist groups   180–5, 323
Negotiated management   273–5
Neoliberalism   5, 6
New Age travellers   10, 49–50, 84, 85, 261, 263
New terrorism   325–6
Newbury bypass protest   105, 262
News International Dispute   185–7
'No Borders' campaign   7
Non-governmental organisation   114
North Atlantic Treaty Organization (NATO)   21, 135, 212
Northern England towns riots   64, 199–203, 263
Northern Ireland Civil Rights Association   51, 52, 54, 56, 70

Northern Ireland (Emergency Provisions) Act 1973 107, 189
Northern Ireland Police Authority 190
Northern Ireland: security policy during the 'Troubles' 187–97
Notting Hill Carnival riot 197–9, 266

Occupations 39, 132, 309–10, 314
Occupy London protests 10, 39, 206, 335
Occupy movement 39, 137, 204–9, 355–6
Occupy Wall Street 156, 204–9
Official Secrets Act 1911 (UK) 212, 349
Official Secrets Act 1989 (UK) 222–3, 348, 350
Old terrorism 325–6
Oldham riots 199–201, 263
Omnibus Crime Control and Safe Streets Act 1968 (USA) 219
Organisation for Economic Co-operation and Development (OECD) 6
Otryad Mobilniy Osobogo Naznacheniya (OMON) 285
Overreaction 57, 305–6
Oxfam 102, 103

Palestine Liberation Organization (PLO) 148, 149–50
Paramilitary policing 210–11, 273
PATRIOT Act 2001 (USA) 87–8, 89
Peace Action 214–15
Peace Direct 215
Peace Movement 77–8, 211–16
Peach, Blair 298–300
People for the Ethical Treatment of Animals (PETA) 2
People's Fuel Lobby 121
People's Revolutionary Army (ERP) 339
Pentagon Papers 348
Petitions 103
Police Act 1890 (UK) 271–2
Police Act 1964 (UK) 272, 283
Police Act 1996 (UK) 272
Police Act 1997 (UK) 221
Police and Criminal Evidence Act 1984 (UK) 83, 174, 263
Police Complaints Authority (PCA) 60
Police National Information and Cordination Centre (PNICC) 272

Police Nationale 276–8
Police Service of Northern Ireland (PSNI) 237
Police Support Units (PSUs) 270–1, 284
Policing by consent 59, 82, 128–9, 174
Political marginalisation 45, 82, 164, 288
Political policing 216–25
Ponting, Clive 349, 350
Popular Revolutionary Vanguard (VRP) 339
Posse Comitatus Act 1878 (USA) 305
Post-Arab Spring 17, 225–37
 Algeria 235–6
 Egypt 101, 227–30, 305
 Libya 230–2
 Syria 233–5, 322
 Tunisia 225–7
 Yemen 232–3
Prague International Monetary Fund and World Bank summit protests 2000 13–14
Pre-charge detention 88
Prevention of Terrorism (Temporary Provisions) Act 1974 (UK) 88, 89, 189, 248
Politique de la ville 41
PRISM Internet Monitoring programme 17, 224, 352
Privatisation 5, 6, 34
Preventing Violent Extremism Programme (UK) 87
Protect America Act 2007 (USA) 220
Protection of Freedoms Act 2012 (UK) 88
Protest Liaison Officers 100, 128, 237–9
Protest songs 239–42
Protestor Removal Squad 270
Provisional Irish Republican Army 56, 57, 71, 91, 93, 106, 107, 108, 180, 183, 188–97, 242–50, 317, 324–5, 326
Public disorder theories and models 250–5
Public Interest Disclosure Act 1998 (UK) 347–8
Public Order Act 1936 (UK) 112, 157–9, 256–8, 295, 345
Public Order Act 1986 (UK) 111, 127, 142, 159, 161–2, 259–65, 274, 287, 346

Public order legislation (England and Wales)   256–6
Public order policing (England and Wales)   266–76
Public order policing (France)   276–9
Punk rock   85
'Push and shove'   267
Pussy Riot protest   85, 241–2, 279–80

Quang Duc   291

Race Relations Act 1965 (UK)   282, 283, 296
Race Relations Act 1976 (UK)   256
Rally   38, 39, 100–1, 126, 138
Raves   10, 50, 86, 261, 262
Real Irish Republican Army   249
Reclaim the Streets   78, 116, 217
Red Lion Square   270, 281–4
Rees, Merlyn   296, 318
Regulation of Investigatory Powers Act 2000 (UK)   221–2
Rimington, Stella   318
Riot Damages Act 1886 (UK)   58
Riot police   287, 327–8, 332
Riots   8, 28–33, 41–9, 58–64, 64–6, 72–6, 80–4, 111, 142–5, 163–5, 182, 195–7, 199–203, 260, 266–76, 281, 287–90, 293–4, 301, 307–9, 312–17, 330–4
Roadblocks   49, 173–4, 186
Rote Armee Fraktion (Red Army Faction)   341–2
Roundtable Agreement (*Contract Sejm*) (Poland)   134
Royal Society for the Prevention of Cruelty to Animals (RSPCA)   2, 160
Royal Ulster Constabulary   52, 53, 54, 55, 57, 70–1, 188–97, 243, 244, 323–4
Rubin, Jerry   73, 74, 76
Rubber bullets   12
Rumour management   31, 59, 80, 269

Sadat, Anwar   147
'Saffron revolution'   292
Salafists   226, 232
Saleh, Ali Abdullah   22, 23
Saltley Marsh Coal Depot   69, 166–8, 171
Saturation policing   269
Saville, Lord Mark   57

Scargill, Arthur,   166–8, 172–5
Scarman, Lord Leslie   52–5, 71, 80–3, 283, 289
Scheduled offences   189, 190–1
'Screw the Troika' (Portugal)   35
Seale, Bobby   76
Seattle World Trade Organization protest 1999   12–13
Sectarianism   71
Sectarian violence (Northern Ireland)   53, 54, 55, 243–4
Security Service (MI5) (UK)   87, 94, 137, 174, 194, 213, 218–19, 220–3, 317, 319, 349–50
Security Service Act 1989 (UK)   218–19, 221
Security Services Act 1996 (UK)   221
Segregation   43, 45, 62–3, 200–1, 308–9
Self-immolation   291–2
Serious Organised Crime and Police Act 2005 (UK)   263
Shelter   102, 103
Shi'a Muslims   24, 148, 233
Shoot to kill   193–4, 323
Shrewsbury 24 Campaign   69
'Shrewsbury Two'   68–9
Siege of Shoreham   160–2
Signals intelligence (SIGINT)   216, 218
Sinn Féin   91, 244, 248, 249
Sit-ins   34, 77, 101
Situationists   312–13, 344
Smelser, Neil   251–2
Snowden, Edward   16, 224, 351–2
Social media   18, 30, 35, 38, 61, 98, 100, 103–4, 127, 241, 289, 292–5, 307, 355
Society of Graphical and Allied Trades '82 (SOGAT '82)   185–7
Solidarity (*Solidarność*)   130–5
Southall disorders   259, 295–301
Space saturation techniques   45
Special Branch   91, 174, 216–17, 219, 319
Special Category Status   106–7, 191–2
Special Demonstration Squad (SDS)   217–18
Special Patrol Group (SPG)   185, 270, 283, 297–300
Special Weapons and Tactics (SWAT)   285–6

Speciesism 1
State of emergency 45, 167, 169, 232, 301–7, 316
Stevens, Sir John 194–5
Stockholm riots 2013 307–9
Stonehenge 49, 85, 261
Stop and search 31, 88, 198, 202
Stop Huntingdon Animal Cruelty (SHAC) 4, 5
Stop the City demonstrations (1983 and 1984) 9, 11, 274–5
Stop the War Coalition 213
Strategic incapacitation 274
Street parties 335
Street theatre 79
Strikes *see* Workplace protest
Student protests 39, 138
  England 155, 289, 293, 309–11
Student riots (Paris) 312–17
Students for a Democratic Society (SDS) 73, 214
Subversion 137, 216–25, 317–19
Sunni Muslims 24, 151, 226, 233
Supergrasses 193
'Swamp 81' 80
Syndicalism 354
Syrian National Coalition 26, 235
Syrian National Council 24, 234

Tea Party 208, 320–1
Tear gas 12, 14, 18, 25, 34, 42, 229, 230, 327
Tension indicators 83, 269, 289
Terrorism 43, 96–94, 146–53, 180–5, 303, 318, 321–6, 340, 341
Terrorism Act 2000 (UK) 88–9, 93, 263, 321
Terrorism Act 2006 (UK) 88, 89, 321
Terrorism Prevention and Investigation Measures Act 2011 (UK) 88, 90
Terrorist Surveillance Act 2006 (USA) 220
Terrorists 3
Third force 271, 327–8
'Three-day week' 170, 171
Tiananmen Square protests 1976 328–9
  1989 305, 329–30
Toxteth disorders 81, 267
Trade Union Act 1984 (UK) 259, 355
Trade Union and Industrial Relations Act 1974 (UK) 168, 355

Trafalgar Square anti-Poll Tax rally 288, 330–4
Transgressive protests 274–5
Traveller Solidarity Network 97
Travellers 95–7
'Tree sitting' 113
Trespass 77, 101, 120, 136
Trespassory assemblies 260, 261
Troika 33
'Troubles' (Northern Ireland) 32, 52, 71, 244–50, 324
Tupamoros (MLN) 339
Twitter 30, 31
Twyford Down motorway construction protest 104

UK Uncut 39, 293, 335–8
UK Uncut Legal Action 336
Ulster Defence Association (UDA) 184, 194–5
Ulster Defence Regiment 188, 246
Ulster Freedom Fighters 195
Ulster Special Constabulary (B-Specials) 54, 55, 70–1, 188, 189
Ulster Volunteer Force 242–3, 246
Ulsterisation 189–90
Underclass 42, 62, 144, 288
United Nations 25, 26
United Nations Security Council 20, 21
Urban guerrilla groups 338–44

Value-added theory of crowd behaviour 251–2
Vietnam War protests 72–6, 240, 292, 312, 341, 343, 348
Vigils 101, 135–7, 261

Walesa, Lech 130, 132, 133, 134
Walking (with a political purpose) 112, 257, 345–7
Water cannon 14, 18, 32, 56, 71, 139, 229, 327
'Ways and Means Act' 265
'We are the 99 per cent' 205
Weather Underground Organisation (Weathermen) 342–3
Whistleblower Protection Act 1989 (USA) 347
Whistleblowing 17, 78, 140, 222–3, 224, 347–53

Whitelaw, William 247, 299, 318
Widgery, Lord John 56–7
WikiLeaks 18, 141, 350–1
'Wildcat strike' 355
'Winning by appearing to lose' 167, 267
Women's Aid 103
Work-ins 356
Workplace protest 66–9, 129–35, 166–8, 168–72, 185–7, 264, 266–76, 301, 306, 313–16, 353–7
World Bank 6, 8, 12, 13
World Economic Forum 8, 204
World Society for the Protection of Animals (WSPA) 2
World Trade Center attacks (9/11) 151, 324, 325
World Trade Organization (WTO) 6–7, 8, 12
Wright, Peter 349–50

Ya Basta! 14
Yippies 73, 74, 76, 79

Zedong, Mao 329, 339

Printed and bound by CPI Group (UK) Ltd, Croydon, CR0 4YY